CICERO

XVI

LCL 213

CICERO

XVI

DE RE PUBLICA
DE LEGIBUS

WITH AN ENGLISH TRANSLATION BY

CLINTON WALKER KEYES

HARVARD UNIVERSITY PRESS

CAMBRIDGE, MASSACHUSETTS
LONDON, ENGLAND

First published 1928

LOEB CLASSICAL LIBRARY® is a registered trademark
of the President and Fellows of Harvard College

ISBN 978-0-674-99235-1

*Printed on acid-free paper and bound by
The Maple-Vail Book Manufacturing Group*

CONTENTS

LIST OF CICERO'S WORKS
SHOWING ARRANGEMENT
IN THIS EDITION

LIST OF CICERO'S WORKS

LETTERS.   8 VOLUMES

THE REPUBLIC

INTRODUCTION TO THE DE RE PUBLICA

In the year 44 Cicero stated that he had written the *Republic* " when he held the rudder of the State."[1] This was true only in a comparative sense. In later years the period between his return from exile (57) and the outbreak of the Civil War (49) may well have seemed to Cicero one of activity in affairs of State, but it was in fact the transference of the "rudder" to the stronger hands of the First Triumvirate (59) that gave him the leisure to follow in the footsteps of his beloved Plato by composing a second *Republic.*

It was in 54 (probably in May) that the actual writing of the *Republic* was begun.[2] But Cicero found its composition difficult, and the work was also delayed by frequent changes of plan. In October, 54, two books were finished and seven more planned; each book was to contain one day's conversation. The speakers were to be Africanus the Younger, Laelius, and several of their friends. But when Cicero read the two completed books to

---

[1] Sex de re publica, quos tum scripsimus cum gubernacula rei publicae tenebamus. *De Divin.* II, 3.

[2] *Ep. ad Quintum Fr.* II, 12, 1; III, 5, 1–2. It does not seem necessary to suppose, from the words quoted in note 1, that the first draft of the work was made during Cicero's consulship (63) or soon thereafter. That is the theory of J. P Richarz (*De politicorum Ciceronis librorum tempore natali*, Wuerzburg, 1829, p. 9).

his friend Gnaeus Sallustius, he was told that the
work would be much more effective if he presented
his views on the commonwealth in his own person,
instead of putting them into the mouths of statesmen
of an earlier age. This suggestion led Cicero to
adopt the plan of making the work a dialogue
between his brother Quintus and himself. But
later on he completed the work in accordance with
his original plan, except that the length of the
fictive conversation was shortened to three days, and
that of the work to six books, two for each day.[1]
Exactly when the work was completed we do not
know. Atticus appears to have read it for the first
time in 51,[2] and Caelius Rufus wrote of its general
popularity in the same year.[3]

The work is dedicated to the man in whose
youthful company Cicero claims to have heard a
report of the whole conversation from Publius
Rutilius Rufus in Smyrna; the indications seem to
point with some probability to his brother Quintus.[4]

The dialogue is assumed to have taken place
during the Latin holidays of 129 B.C., in the garden
of Publius Cornelius Scipio Africanus the Younger.
Those present were Scipio, Gaius Laelius, Lucius
Furius Philus, Manius Manilius, Quintus Allius
Tubero, Publius Rutilius Rufus, Spurius Mummius,
Gaius Fannius, and Quintus Mucius Scaevola.[5]

[1] De Re Pub. II, 70; VI, 8; De Amicit. 14.
[2] Ep. ad Att. V, 12, 2.
[3] Tui politici libri omnibus vigent. Ep. ad Fam. VIII, 1, 4.
[4] De Re Pub. I, 13. Compare R. Hirzel, Der Dialog,
Leipzig, 1895, I, p. 469, note 2.
[5] De Re Pub. I, 14. For brief identification of these
persons see Index. Cicero's motive for placing the dialogue
in a past age was his fear of causing offence (Ep. ad Quintum
Fr. III, 5, 2).

INTRODUCTION

Prefixed to each day's conversation (*i.e.* at the beginning of Books I, III, and V) is a preface (*prooemium*) by Cicero in his own person.

On account of the fragmentary state of the work, the following general outline of its contents is given.[1]

FIRST DAY.

Book I.

§ § 1–12. Cicero's preface : defence of the life of a statesman.

§ § 13–14. Transition to the dialogue.

§ § 15–34. Preliminary conversation : the " double sun " ; astronomy in general, Archimedes' celestial globe ; eclipses ; comparative importance of heavenly and earthly studies ; transition to the subject of the commonwealth ; Scipio is asked to give his ideas on the best form of government.

§ § 35–71. After some preliminary remarks, Scipio defines the commonwealth (*res publica*), and proceeds to discuss the following subjects : the three simple, good forms of government (kingship, aristocracy, and democracy) ; their tendency to degenerate into the corresponding bad forms ; the arguments in favour of and against each of the three simple forms ; the details of their degeneration ; the balanced form which is a combination of the three simple forms ; its stability ; its ideal character ; the Roman State as a living example of it. He then states his intention of using the Roman Republic as his pattern of the ideal State in the remainder of the discussion.

---

[1] For a more complete outline of the work see T. Petersson, *Cicero: a Biography*, Berkeley, Cal., 1920, pp. 445-51 ; 457-61.

INTRODUCTION

Book II.

§ § 1–63. Carrying out this intention, he traces briefly the history of the Roman State from its origin.

§ § 64–70. After drawing some conclusions from this history in support of the forms of government already discussed, he mentions the ideal statesman, and the necessity for justice in States.

SECOND DAY.

Book III.[1]

§ § 3–7. Cicero's *prooemium*: the nature of man; human reason; its noblest function found in practical statesmanship, which is superior to devotion to political theory alone; the practical-minded Romans therefore to be set above the theorizing Greeks; reason the foundation of justice.

§ § 8–28. The dialogue turns to the controversy between the defenders and opponents of justice in States. Philus, against his convictions, presents the arguments of Carneades in favour of the necessity of injustice in governments.

§ § 32–41. Laelius defends justice and the necessity for it in a commonwealth.

§ § 42–48. Scipio shows by practical examples that any government that is just is therefore a good government, whereas without justice any form of government is necessarily bad; in fact nothing which deserves to be called a commonwealth at all can exist without justice.

[1] Compare St. Augustine's outline of the contents of this book (*De Civ. Dei* II, 21).

5

INTRODUCTION

Book IV.

Only a few fragments remain. The social classification of citizens, the maintenance of high moral
standards, the education of the young, and the
influence of the drama are evidently among the
subjects discussed.

THIRD DAY.

Book V.

This book also is almost entirely lost. It begins
with a *prooemium* in Cicero's own person (§§ 1–2)
on old-fashioned virtue. The dialogue appears to
have treated of law and its enforcement, and of the
ideal statesman (*rector* or *moderator rei publicae*).[1]

Book VI.

The great value and the noble reward of the
statesman's labours are discussed, and the work
closes with *Scipio's Dream*, which extends this theme
beyond the world and the brief span of human life
into the universe and eternity.

SOURCES.

Cicero's indebtedness in the *De Re Publica* to
Plato is, of course, great.[2] The idea of composing
such a treatise evidently originated with the reading

---

[1] In regard to Cicero's ideal statesman, see T. Zielinski,
Cicero im Wandel der Jahrhunderte, third ed., Berlin, 1912,
pp. 5 and 151 ; R. Reitzenstein, *Die Idee des Principats bei
Cicero und Augustus*, Nachrichten der Gött. Ges. der Wiss.,
1917, pp. 399 ff., 436 ff. ; R. Heinze, *Ciceros "Staat" als
politische Tendenzschrift*, Hermes, 59 (1924), pp. 73–94 ;
E. Meyer, *Cäsars Monarchie u. das Prinzipat des Pompeius*,
Stuttgart, 1918, pp. 176 ff.

[2] Compare R. Hirzel, *op. cit.*, I, p. 463 f.

of Plato's *Republic,* and the form and plan of the dialogue owe much to that work. The following are some of the obvious points of imitation : the presence during the dialogue of a fairly large number of persons, while the actual conversation is confined to a few ; the fact that the leisure of a sacred festival gives occasion to the dialogue ; the commencement of the conversation with subjects far removed from the commonwealth ; the introduction of an argument about justice and injustice, and of discussions of the forms of government, the ideal statesman, education, and the influence of the drama ; and, finally, the ending of the dialogue with an account of a mystical experience which carries the reader beyond the boundaries of the present life. The frequent interruption of long disquisitions in order to maintain the character of a dialogue, and the fact that the chief speaker, Scipio, like Socrates, disclaims the rôle of teacher of the other participants in the dialogue,[1] perhaps deserve to be mentioned also.

A reading of Plato's *Phaedo* in the light of the political situation in 54 may also have influenced Cicero to some slight extent. For example, it may have suggested placing the conversation in the last year of the chief speaker's life, and also the concentration of attention upon the life after death in the climax of the dialogue.[2] And Scipio's statement of the superiority of kingship over aristocracy and democracy has a close parallel in Plato's *Politicus.*[3]

---

[1] *De Re Pub.* I, 70.
[2] See R. Hirzel, *op. cit.,* p. 467, note 3.
[3] *De Re Pub.* I, 56–64 ; Plato, *Politicus* 302 E. For other minor borrowings from the works of Plato, Aristotle, and other Greek writers, see the notes.

Cicero himself gives us a hint as to his chief sources for the contents of the dialogue by mentioning the fact that Scipio had frequently conversed on the subject of the State with Panaetius, Polybius also being present.[1]   And in fact it seems most probable that the philosophical and political theories in Books I–III are derived from the eminent Stoic, Panaetius, while in matters of history and practical politics a considerable amount may have been borrowed from Polybius.[2] The general source for the *Dream of Scipio* is a matter of conjecture, none of the theories proposed having found general acceptance.[3]

Cicero found the writing of the *Republic* a slow and difficult task,[4] not a matter of easy transfer of Greek ideas to Latin periods, as in many of his later philosophic works.[5] With the possible exception

---

[1] *De Re Pub.* I, 34.

[2] See Polybius, Book VI. For Panaetius and Polybius as sources, see A. Schmekel, *Die Philosophie der mittleren Stoa*, Berlin, 1892, pp. 47–85 ; R. J. Schubert, *Quos Cicero in libro I et II de re publica auctores secutus esse videatur*, Diss., Wuerzburg, 1883 ; C. Hintze, *Quos scriptores graecos Cicero in libris de re publica componendis adhibuerit*, Diss., Halle, 1900 ; R. Hirzel, *op. cit.*, I, pp. 464 ff. For an exhaustive treatment of the problem of the sources, see Ioh. Galbiatius (= G. Galbiati), *De fontibus M. Tullii Ciceronis librorum qui manserunt de re publica et de legibus quaestiones*, Milan, 1916.

[3] For references in regard to this problem, see M. Schanz, *Geschichte der roemischen Litteratur* (Vol. VIII of Mueller's *Handbuch der Klassischen Altertunswissenschaft*), third ed., Munich, 1909, I, II, p. 345 It seems certain, at any rate, that Cicero made some use of one or more of the "Exhortations to Philosophy" (λόγοι προτρεπτικοί) which Aristotle and other philosophers composed. (Of Cicero's own "Exhortation," the *Hortensius*, only fragments remain.)

[4] *Ep. ad Quintum Fr.* II, 12, 1.

[5] *Ep. ad Att.* XII, 52, 2.

of the *Laws,* it is by far his most original treatise,
and, if it were preserved in full, we should undoubtedly find it the most brilliant and interesting
of them all well worthy of its sublime conclusion.

THE MANUSCRIPTS.

The *De Re Publica,* with the exception of the
Somnium Scipionis and scattered quotations by later
authors, was lost until 1820, when Cardinal Angelo
Mai, then prefect of the Vatican Library, discovered
fragments amounting to perhaps a quarter or a third
of the treatise in a palimpsest containing St. Augustine's commentary on the Psalms. This *Codex
Vaticanus* 5757 ($\dot{V}$) probably dates from the fifth
or sixth century after Christ.[1]

The *Somnium Scipionis* is preserved in manuscripts
of Cicero and of Macrobius, who wrote a commentary
upon it. The manuscripts containing the *Somnium*
which are referred to in the textual notes of this
edition are as follows:[2]

[1] This manuscript has been emended by a second scribe,
and there is great disagreement in regard to the comparative
value of the first and second hands ($\dot{V}^1$ and V^2). For biblio-
graphies of this controversy and of the textual criticism of
the *De Re Publica* in general, see C. Pascal's edition, in the
Corpus Paravianum, Turin, 1916, *Praefatio* by G. Galbiati,
p. viii and note 2; p. ix, note 2; also K. Ziegler's edition,
Teubner, Leipzig, 1915, *Praefatio.*

[2] When a reading is credited to Macrobius in the textual
notes, the reference is to his citation of the passage in his
commentary *(Commentarii in Somnium Scipionis).* The
rhetorician Favonius Eulogius, a pupil of St. Augustine,
also wrote a commentary on the work *(Disputatio de Somnio
Scipionis).*

Monacensis 14619, twelfth century (E).
Monacensis 6362, eleventh century (F).
Mediceus, eleventh century (M).
Parisinus 6371, eleventh century (P).
Monacensis 14436, eleventh century (R).
Monacensis 19471, twelfth century (T).

EDITIONS.

I. Editions of Cicero's Works containing the *De Re Publica* :

J. C. Orelli, Zuerich, 1826–38.
J. C. Orelli, G. Baiter, and C. Halm, Zuerich, 1845–62.
C. F. A. Nobbe, Leipzig, 1827, 1849, 1869.
R. Klotz, Leipzig, 1850–57, 1869–74.
J. G. Baiter and C. L. Kayser, Leipzig, 1860–69.
C. F. W. Mueller, Leipzig (Teubner), 1878.

II. Separate editions of the *De Re Publica* :

A. Mai, Rome and Stuttgart, 1822 ; Rome, 1828, 1846.
A. F. Villemain, Paris, 1823, 1859.
F. Steinacker, Leipzig, 1823.
F. Heinrich, Bonn, 1823, 1828.
G. H. Moser and F. Creuzer, Frankfort, 1826.
C. Zell, Stuttgart, 1827.
F. Osann, Goettingen, 1847.
R. Marchesi, Prato, 1853.
A. C. G. de Mancy, Paris, 1870.
E. Charles (with explanatory notes), Paris, 1874.
K. Ziegler, Leipzig (Teubner), 1915.
C. Pascal, Turin, 1916.

INTRODUCTION

III. Separate editions of the *Somnium Scipionis*:

J. D. Buechling and D. W. Triller, Leipzig, 1800.

C. Meissner, Leipzig, 1869, 1908.

W. D. Pearman, Cambridge, 1883.

S. Hart, Boston, 1887.

A. Pasdera, Turin, 1890, 1915.

H. Anz, Gotha, 1890, 1910.

F. E. Rockwood, Boston and London, 1903.

G. Landgraf, Leipzig, 1908.

J. A. Kleist, New York, 1915.

DE RE PUBLICA

LIBER PRIMUS

[Desiderantur in cod. Vaticano paginae XXXIV.]

1   I. . . . . impetu[1] liberavissent, nec C. Duelius,
A. Atilius, L. Metellus terrore Karthaginis, non duo
Scipiones oriens incendium belli Punici secundi
sanguine suo restinxissent, nec id excitatum maioribus copiis aut Q. Maximus enervavisset aut M. Marcellus contudisset aut a portis huius urbis avolsum
P. Africanus compulisset intra hostium moenia.

   M. vero Catoni, homini ignoto et novo, quo omnes,
qui isdem rebus studemus, quasi exemplari ad
industriam virtutemque ducimur, certe licuit Tusculi
se in otio delectare salubri et propinquo loco. sed
homo demens, ut isti putant, cum cogeret eum

                        [1] . . . *petu* V.

---

[1] Conjectural restorations of the sense in fragmentary
passages are enclosed in brackets.

[2] For these and other persons mentioned in the text,
consult the Index.

[3] Publius Cornelius Scipio (consul 218) and his brother
Gnaeus Cornelius Scipio Calvus (consul 222).

[4] Quintus Fabius Maximus Cunctator.

[5] Publius Cornelius Scipio Africanus Minor.

[6] A *novus homo* is a man who is the first of his family to
hold high office.

THE REPUBLIC

BOOK I

The equivalent of about ten pages in this edition is lost at
the beginning. Our manuscript commences in the midst
of Cicero's preface to the dialogue; at this point he is
evidently combating the Epicurean hostility to patriotism
and the life of a statesman.

I. [WITHOUT active patriotism][1] . . . . could
[never] have delivered [our native land] from attack;
nor could Gaius Duelius, Aulus Atilius, or Lucius
Metellus[2] have freed [Rome] from her fear of
Carthage; nor could the two Scipios[3] have extinguished with their blood the rising flames of the
Second Punic War; nor, when it broke forth again
with greater fury, could Quintus Maximus[4] have
reduced it to impotence or Marcus Marcellus have
crushed it; nor could Publius Africanus[5] have torn
it from the gates of this city and driven it within
the enemy's walls.

Marcus Cato again, unknown and of obscure birth[6]
—by whom, as by a pattern for our emulation, all
of us who are devoted to the same pursuits are
drawn to diligence and valour—might surely have
remained at Tusculum in the enjoyment of the
leisurely life of that healthful spot so near to Rome.
But he, a madman as our friends[7] maintain, preferred, though no necessity constrained him, to be

[7] The Epicureans, whose ideal of a quiet life free from
pain made them discountenance participation in politics.

necessitas nulla, in his undis et tempestatibus ad summam senectutem maluit iactari quam in illa tranquillitate atque otio iucundissime vivere. omitto innumerabilis viros, quorum singuli saluti huic civitati fuerunt, et quia[1] sunt haud[2] procul ab aetatis huius memoria, commemorare eos desino, ne quis se aut suorum aliquem praetermissum queratur. unum hoc definio, tantam esse necessitatem virtutis generi hominum a natura tantumque amorem ad communem salutem defendendam datum, ut ea vis omnia blandimenta voluptatis otiique vicerit.

2   II. Nec vero habere virtutem satis est quasi artem aliquam, nisi utare; etsi ars quidem, cum ea non utare, scientia tamen ipsa teneri potest, virtus in usu sui tota posita est; usus autem eius est maximus civitatis gubernatio et earum ipsarum rerum, quas isti in angulis personant, reapse, non oratione perfectio. nihil enim dicitur a philosophis, quod quidem recte honesteque dicatur, quod non[3] ab his partum confirmatumque sit, a quibus civitatibus iura discripta sunt. unde enim pietas aut a quibus religio? unde ius aut gentium aut hoc ipsum civile quod dicitur? unde iustitia, fides, aequitas? unde pudor, continentia, fuga turpitudinis, adpetentia laudis

---

[1] *quia* Halm ; *qui* V.
[2] *haud* supplied by Mai ; omitted in V.
[3] *non* supplied by Mai ; omitted in V.

---

[1] The *ius gentium* (law of nations) is that common to all peoples ; the *ius civile* is the Roman private law.

tossed by the billows and storms of our public life
even to an extreme old age, rather than to live a life
of complete happiness in the calm and ease of such
retirement. I will not speak of the men, countless
in number, who have each been the salvation of this
republic; and as their lives do not much antedate
the remembrance of the present generation, I will
refrain from mentioning their names, lest someone
complain of the omission of himself or some member
of his family. I will content myself with asserting
that Nature has implanted in the human race so
great a need of virtue and so great a desire to
defend the common safety that the strength thereof
has conquered all the allurements of pleasure and
ease.

II. But it is not enough to possess virtue, as if
it were an art of some sort, unless you make use of
it. Though it is true that an art, even if you never
use it, can still remain in your possession by the
very fact of your knowledge of it, yet the existence
of virtue depends entirely upon its use; and its
noblest use is the government of the State, and the
realization in fact, not in words, of those very things
that the philosophers, in their corners, are continually dinning in our ears. For there is no
principle enunciated by the philosophers—at least
none that is just and honourable—that has not
been discovered and established by those who have
drawn up codes of law for States. For whence
comes our sense of duty? From whom do we
obtain the principles of religion? Whence comes
the law of nations, or even that law of ours which
is called "civil"?[1] Whence justice, honour, fair-
dealing? Whence decency, self-restraint, fear of

15

et honestatis? unde in laboribus et periculis fortitudo?
nempe ab his qui haec disciplinis informata alia
moribus confirmarunt, sanxerunt autem alia legibus.
3 quin etiam Xenocraten ferunt, nobilem in primis
philosophum, cum quaereretur ex eo, quid adseque-
rentur eius discipuli, respondisse, ut id sua sponte
facerent, quod cogerentur facere legibus. ergo ille
civis, qui id cogit omnis imperio legumque poena,
quod vix paucis persuadere oratione philosophi possunt, etiam his, qui illa disputant, ipsis est praeferen-
dus doctoribus. quae est enim istorum oratio tam
exquisita, quae sit anteponenda bene constitutae
civitati publico iure et moribus? equidem quem ad
modum "urbes magnas atque imperiosas," ut
appellat Ennius, viculis et castellis praeferendas puto,
sic eos, qui his urbibus consilio atque auctoritate
praesunt, his, qui omnis negotii publici expertes sint,[1]
longe duco sapientia ipsa esse anteponendos. et
quoniam maxime rapimur ad opes augendas generis
humani studemusque nostris consiliis et laboribus
tutiorem et opulentiorem vitam hominum reddere et
ad hanc voluptatem[2] ipsius naturae stimulis in-
citamur, teneamus eum cursum, qui semper fuit
optimi cuiusque, neque ea signa audiamus, quae
receptui canunt, ut eos etiam revocent, qui iam
processerint.
4   III. His rationibus tam certis tamque inlustribus
opponuntur ab his, qui contra disputant, primum

---

[1] *sint* V; *sunt* Halm.
[2] *voluptatem* V; *voluntatem* Moser.

---

[1] Probably a quotation from the *Annales* of Ennius.

disgrace, eagerness for praise and honour? Whence comes endurance amid toils and dangers? I say, from those men who, when these things had been inculcated by a system of training, either confirmed them by custom or else enforced them by statutes. Indeed Xenocrates, one of the most eminent of philosophers, when asked what his disciples learned, is said to have replied: "To do of their own accord what they are compelled to do by the law." Therefore the citizen who compels all men, by the authority of magistrates and the penalties imposed by law, to follow rules of whose validity philosophers find it hard to convince even a few by their admonitions, must be considered superior even to the teachers who enunciate these principles. For what speech of theirs is excellent enough to be preferred to a State well provided with law and custom? Indeed, just as I think that "cities great and dominant," [1] as Ennius calls them, are to be ranked above small villages and strongholds, so I believe that those who rule such cities by wise counsel and authority are to be deemed far superior, even in wisdom, to those who take no part at all in the business of government. And since we feel a mighty urge to increase the resources of mankind, since we desire to make human life safer and richer by our thought and effort, and are goaded on to the fulfilment of this desire by Nature herself, let us hold to the course which has ever been that of all excellent men, turning deaf ears to those who, in the hope of even recalling those who have already gone ahead, are sounding the retreat.

III. As their first objection to these arguments, so well founded and so obviously sound, those who

labores, qui sint re publica defendenda sustinendi,
leve sane inpedimentum vigilanti et industrio, neque
solum in tantis rebus, sed etiam in mediocribus vel
studiis vel officiis vel vero etiam negotiis contemnendum. adiunguntur pericula vitae, turpisque ab his
formido mortis fortibus viris opponitur, quibus magis
id miserum videri solet, natura se consumi et senectute, quam sibi dari tempus, ut possint eam vitam,
quae tamen esset reddenda naturae, pro patria potissimum reddere. illo vero se loco copiosos et disertos
putant, cum calamitates clarissimorum virorum iniu-
riasque iis ab ingratis inpositas civibus colligunt.
5 hinc enim illa et apud Graecos exempla, Miltiadem,
victorem domitoremque Persarum, nondum sanatis
volneribus iis, quae corpore adverso in clarissima
victoria accepisset, vitam ex hostium telis servatam
in civium vinclis profudisse, et Themistoclem patria,
quam liberavisset, pulsum atque proterritum non in
Graeciae portus per se servatos, sed in barbariae sinus confugisse, quam adflixerat; nec vero levitatis
Atheniensium crudelitatisque in amplissimos civis ex-

attack them plead the severity of the labour that
must be performed in the defence of the State—
surely a trifling obstacle to the watchful and diligent
man, and one that merits only scorn, not merely
with reference to matters of such moment, but even
in the case of things of only moderate importance,
such as a man's studies, or duties, or even his business
affairs.   Then too they allege the danger to which
life is exposed, and confront brave men with a
dishonourable fear of death ; yet such men are wont
to regard it a greater misfortune to be consumed
by the processes of Nature and old age, than to be
granted the opportunity of surrendering for their
country's sake, in preference to all else, that life
which in any event must be surrendered to Nature.
On this point, however, the objectors wax wordy
and, as they imagine, eloquent, going on to cite the
misfortunes of eminent men and the wrongs they
have suffered at the hands of their ungrateful fellow-
citizens.   For at this point they enumerate, first the
famous illustrations taken from Greek history—the
story of Miltiades, vanquisher and conqueror of the
Persians, who, before the wounds had yet healed
which he had received full in the front on the
occasion of his glorious victory, was cast into chains
by his own fellow-countrymen, and at their hands
lost the life which the enemy's weapons had
spared ; and that of Themistocles, who, when driven
in terror from his country, the land which he
had set free, took refuge, not in the harbours of
Greece, saved by his prowess, but in the recesses
of the barbarian land which he had laid prostrate.
Indeed there is no lack of instances of the fickle-
ness and cruelty of Athens toward her most eminent

empla deficiunt ; quae nata et frequentata apud illos
etiam in gravissumam civitatem nostram dicuntur
6 redundasse ; nam vel exilium Camilli vel offensio
commemoratur Ahalae vel invidia Nasicae vel expulsio
Laenatis vel Opimii damnatio vel fuga Metelli vel
acerbissima C. Marii clades principumque[1] caedes
vel eorum multorum pestes, quae paulo post secutae
sunt. nec vero iam meo nomine abstinent et, credo,
quia nostro consilio ac periculo sese in illa vita atque
otio conservatos putant, gravius etiam de nobis que-
runtur et amantius. sed haud facile dixerim, cur,
cum ipsi discendi aut visendi causa maria tramit-
tant . . .

[*Desiderantur paginae duae.*]

7 IV. . . . salvam esse consulatu abiens in contione
populo Romano idem iurante iurassem,[2] facile iniuriarum omnium compensarem curam et molestiam.
quamquam nostri casus plus honoris habuerunt quam
laboris neque tantum molestiae, quantum gloriae,
maioremque laetitiam ex desiderio bonorum percepi-

---

[1] *principumque* Mueller ; *principum* V.
[2] *iurassem* V[1] ; *iuravissem* V[2].

---

[1] For the sufferings of these men, see the Index.   The last
words evidently refer to Sulla's proscriptions in 81.
[2] About fifteen lines are lost at this point ; a conjectural
restoration of the sense is given in brackets.
[3] Compare Cicero, *In Pisonem* III, 6.
[4] Cicero is referring to his exile (March 58—August 57).

citizens; and this vice, originating and spreading there, has, they say, overflowed even into our own powerful republic. For we are reminded of the exile of Camillus, the disgrace suffered by Ahala, the hatred directed against Nasica, the exile of Laenas, the condemnation of Opimius, the flight of Metellus, the bitter disaster to Gaius Marius, and, a little later, the slaughter and ruin of so many eminent men.[1] In fact they now include my name also, and presumably because they think it was through my counsel and at my risk that their own peaceful life has been preserved to them, they complain even more bitterly and with greater kindness of the treatment I have received. But I find it difficult to say why, when these very men cross the seas merely to gain knowledge and to visit other countries,[2] [they should expect us to be deterred by considerations of danger from the much more important task of defending our native land. For if the philosophers are repaid for the dangers of travel by the knowledge they gain thereby, statesmen surely win a much greater reward in the gratitude of their fellow-citizens. IV. Few may have imagined, in view of all I had suffered, that when,] as I retired from the consulship, I took my oath before an assembly of the people, and the Roman people took the same oath, that the republic was safe[3] [as a result of my efforts alone,] I was amply repaid thereby for all the anxiety and vexation that resulted from the injustice done to me. And yet my sufferings brought me more honour than trouble, more glory than vexation, and the joy I found in the affectionate longing felt for me by good citizens[4] was greater than my grief at the exultation of the

mus quam ex laetitia improborum dolorem. sed si
aliter, ut dixi, accidisset, qui possem queri? cum
mihi nihil inproviso nec gravius, quam exspectavis-
sem, pro tantis meis factis evenisset. is enim fueram,
cui cum liceret aut maiores ex otio fructus capere
quam ceteris propter variam suavitatem studiorum,
in quibus a pueritia vixeram, aut si quid accideret
acerbius universis, non praecipuam, sed parem cum
ceteris fortunae condicionem subire, non dubitaverim
me gravissimis tempestatibus ac paene fulminibus
ipsis obvium ferre conservandorum civium causa
meisque propriis periculis parere commune reliquis
8 otium. neque enim hac nos patria lege genuit aut
educavit, ut nulla quasi alimenta exspectaret a nobis
ac tantum modo nostris ipsa commodis serviens tu-
tum perfugium otio nostro suppeditaret et tranquil-
lum ad quietem locum, sed ut plurimas et maximas
nostri animi, ingenii, consilii partis ipsa sibi ad
utilitatem suam pigneraretur tantumque nobis in
nostrum privatum usum, quantum ipsi superesse posset, remitteret.

9 V. Iam illa perfugia, quae sumunt sibi ad excusa-
tionem, quo facilius otio perfruantur, certe minime
sunt audienda, cum ita dicunt, accedere ad rem
publicam plerumque homines nulla re bona dignos,

---

[1] Compare Plato, *Crito* 51 A—C.

wicked. But, as I said before, if it had happened otherwise, how could I complain? For none of the misfortunes that fell to my lot in consequence of my great services was unexpected by me or more serious than I had foreseen. For such was my nature that, although, on account of the manifold pleasures I found in the studies which had engaged me from boyhood, it would have been possible for me, on the one hand, to reap greater profit from a quiet life than other men, or, on the other hand, if any disaster should happen to us all, to suffer no more than my fair share of the common misfortune, yet I could not hesitate to expose myself to the severest storms, and, I might almost say, even to thunderbolts, for the sake of the safety of my fellow-citizens, and to secure, at the cost of my own personal danger, a quiet life for all the rest. For, in truth, our country has not given us birth and education without expecting to receive some sustenance, as it were, from us in return; nor has it been merely to serve our convenience that she has granted to our leisure a safe refuge and for our moments of repose a calm retreat; on the contrary, she has given us these advantages so that she may appropriate to her own use the greater and more important part of our courage, our talents, and our wisdom, leaving to us for our own private uses only so much as may be left after her needs have been satisfied.[1]

V. Moreover we ought certainly not to listen to the other excuses to which these men resort, that they may be more free to enjoy the quiet life. They say, for example, that it is mostly worthless men who take part in politics, men with whom it is

cum quibus comparari sordidum, confligere autem
multitudine praesertim incitata miserum et periculosum sit. quam ob rem neque sapientis esse accipere
habenas, cum insanos atque indomitos impetus volgi
cohibere non possit, neque liberi cum inpuris atque
inmanibus adversariis decertantem vel contumelia-
rum verbera subire vel expectare[1] sapienti non
ferendas iniurias; proinde quasi bonis et fortibus
et magno animo praeditis ulla sit ad rem publicam
adeundi causa iustior, quam ne pareant inprobis
neve ab isdem lacerari rem publicam patiantur, cum
ipsi auxilium ferre, si cupiant, non queant.

10 VI. Illa autem exceptio cui probari tandem
potest, quod negant sapientem suscepturum ullam
rei publicae partem, extra quam si eum tempus et
necessitas coëgerit? quasi vero maior cuiquam necessitas accidere posset,[2] quam accidit nobis; in qua
quid facere potuissem, nisi tum consul fuissem?
consul autem esse qui potui, nisi eum vitae cursum
tenuissem a pueritia, per quem equestri loco natus
pervenirem ad honorem amplissimum? non igitur
potestas est ex tempore, aut cum velis, opitulandi
rei publicae, quamvis ea prematur periculis, nisi eo
11 loco sis, ut tibi id facere liceat. maximeque hoc in
hominum doctorum oratione mihi mirum videri

---

[1] *expectare* V ; *exceptare* Halm.   [2] *posset* V[1] ; *possit* V[2].

degrading to be compared, while to have conflict with them, especially when the mob is aroused, is a wretched and dangerous task. Therefore, they maintain, a wise man should not attempt to take the reins, as he cannot restrain the insane and untamed fury of the common herd; nor is it proper for a freeman, by contending with vile and wicked opponents, to submit to the scourgings of abuse or expose himself to wrongs which are intolerable to the wise —as if, in the view of good, brave, and high-minded men, there could be any nobler motive for entering public life than the resolution not to be ruled by wicked men and not to allow the republic to be destroyed by them, seeing that the philosophers themselves, even if they should desire to help, would be impotent.

VI. And who in the world can approve of the single exception they make, when they say that no wise man will take any part in public affairs unless some emergency compels him to do so? As if any greater emergency could come upon anyone than that with which I was confronted; and what could I have done in that crisis unless I had been consul at the time? And how could I have been consul unless I had held to a manner of life from my boyhood which led me to the highest office of State in spite of my equestrian birth? Hence it is clear that the opportunity of serving the State, however great be the dangers with which it is threatened, does not come suddenly, or when we wish it, unless we are in such a position that it is possible for us to take action. It has always seemed to me that the most amazing of the teachings of learned men is that they deny their own ability to steer when the

solet, quod, qui tranquillo mari gubernare se negent
posse, quod nec didicerint nec umquam scire cura-
verint, iidem ad gubernacula se accessuros profiteantur excitatis maximis fluctibus. isti enim palam
dicere atque in eo multum etiam gloriari solent, se
de rationibus rerum publicarum aut constituendarum
aut tuendarum nihil nec didicisse umquam nec
docere, earumque rerum scientiam non doctis hominibus ac sapientibus, sed in illo genere exercitatis
concedendam putant. quare qui convenit polliceri
operam suam rei publicae tum denique, si necessitate cogantur, cum, quod est multo proclivius, nulla
necessitate premente rem publicam regere nesciant?
equidem, ut verum esset sua voluntate sapientem
descendere ad rationes civitatis non solere, sin autem
temporibus cogeretur, tum id munus denique non
recusare, tamen arbitrarer hanc rerum civilium
minime neglegendam scientiam sapienti, propterea
quod omnia essent ei praeparanda, quibus nesciret
an aliquando uti necesse esset.

12   VII. Haec plurimis[1] a me verbis dicta sunt ob
eam causam, quod his libris erat instituta et suscepta
mihi de re publica disputatio ; quae ne frustra haberetur, dubitationem ad rem publicam adeundi in
primis debui tollere. ac tamen si qui sunt, qui
philosophorum auctoritate moveantur, dent operam
parumper atque audiant eos, quorum summa est
auctoritas apud doctissimos homines et gloria ; quos

---

[1] *plurimis* V ; *vluribus* Moser.

sea is calm, having never learned the art nor cared to
know it, while at the same time they assure us that,
when the waves dash highest, they will take the
helm.   For it is their habit to proclaim openly, and
even to make it their great boast, that they have
neither learned nor do they teach anything about
the principles of the State, either to establish it or to
safeguard it, and that they consider the knowledge
of such things unsuited to learned or wise men, but
better to be left to those who have trained themselves in that business.   How can it be reasonable,
therefore, for them to promise to aid the State in
case they are compelled by an emergency to do so,
when they do not know how to rule the State when
no emergency threatens it, though this is a much
easier task than the other? Indeed, if it be true
that the wise man does not, as a general thing, willingly descend from his lofty heights to statecraft,
but does not decline the duty if conditions force
him to assume it, yet I should think he ought by no
means to neglect this science of politics, because it
is his duty to acquire in advance all the knowledge
that, for aught he knows, it may be necessary for
him to use at some future time.

VII. I have treated these matters at considerable
length because I have planned and undertaken in
this work a discussion of the State ; hence, in order
that this discussion might not be valueless, I had, in
the first place, to remove all grounds for hesitation
about taking part in public affairs.   Yet if there be
any who are influenced by the authority of philosophers, let them for a few moments listen and attend
to those whose authority and reputation stand
highest among learned men ; for even if these have

ego existimo, etiamsi qui ipsi rem publicam non
gesserint, tamen, quoniam de re publica multa quae-
sierint et scripserint, functos esse aliquo rei publicae
munere. eos vero septem, quos Graeci sapientis
nominaverunt, omnis paene video in media re
publica esse versatos. neque enim est ulla res, in
qua propius ad deorum numen virtus accedat
humana, quam civitatis aut condere novas aut
conservare iam conditas.

13   VIII. Quibus de rebus, quoniam nobis contigit, ut
iidem et in gerenda re publica aliquid essemus
memoria dignum consecuti et in explicandis rationibus rerum civilium quandam facultatem non modo
usu, sed etiam studio discendi[1] et docendi essemus
. . .[2] auctores, cum superiores alii fuissent in
disputationibus perpoliti, quorum res gestae nullae
invenirentur, alii in gerendo probabiles, in disserendo rudes. nec vero nostra quaedam est insti-
tuenda nova et a nobis inventa ratio, sed unius
aetatis clarissimorum ac sapientissimorum nostrae
civitatis virorum disputatio repetenda memoria est,
quae mihi tibique quondam adulescentulo est a
P. Rutilio Rufo, Smyrnae cum simul essemus com-
pluris dies, exposita, in qua nihil fere, quod magno

---

[1] *discendi* Mai ; *discedendi* V.
[2] The text is corrupt. I have retained the MS. reading,
conjecturing a gap in the text after *essemus*.

---

[1] The person to whom the work is dedicated; see Introduction, p. 2.

not governed the State themselves, nevertheless, since they have dealt with the State in many investigations and treatises, I consider that they have performed a certain function of their own in the State. And in fact I note that nearly every one of those Seven whom the Greeks called "wise" took an important part in the affairs of government. For there is really no other occupation in which human virtue approaches more closely the august function of the gods than that of founding new States or preserving those already in existence.

VIII. Wherefore, since it is my good fortune to have accomplished, in the actual government of the republic, something worthy to live in men's memories, and also to have acquired some skill in setting forth political principles through practice and also by reason of my enthusiasm for learning and teaching, [I consider myself not unsuited to the task I have now undertaken; for, as a matter of fact, this combination of accomplishments is rare among those who are considered] authorities [on statecraft], since while certain men in former times have shown great skill in theoretical discussion, they are discovered to have accomplished nothing practical, and there have been others who have been efficient in action, but clumsy in exposition. Indeed the principles I am about to state are not at all new or original to myself, but it is my intention to recall a discussion carried on by men who were at a certain period the most eminent and wisest in our republic. This discussion was once reported to you,[1] in your youth, and to me by Publius Rutilius Rufus, when we were spending several days together at Smyrna; in it, I believe, very little is omitted that would

29

opere ad rationes omnium rerum pertineret, praetermissum puto.[1]

14   IX. Nam cum P. Africanus hic, Pauli filius, feriis
Latinis Tuditano cons. et Aquilio constituisset in
hortis esse familiarissimique eius ad eum frequenter
per eos dies ventitaturos se esse dixissent, Latinis
ipsis mane ad eum primus sororis filius venit Q.
Tubero; quem cum comiter Scipio appellavisset
libenterque vidisset, Quid tu, inquit, tam mane,
Tubero? dabant enim hae feriae tibi oportunam
sane facultatem ad explicandas tuas litteras.

Tum ille: Mihi vero omne tempus est ad meos
libros vacuum; numquam enim sunt illi occupati;
te autem permagnum est nancisci otiosum, hoc
praesertim motu rei publicae.

Tum Scipio: Atqui nactus es, sed mehercule
otiosiorem opera quam animo.

Et ille: At tu vero[2] animum quoque relaxes
oportet; sumus enim multi, ut constituimus, parati,
si tuo commodo fieri potest, abuti tecum hoc otio.

SC. Libente me vero, ut aliquid aliquando de
doctrinae studiis admoneamur.

15   X. Tum ille: Visne igitur, quoniam et me quodam
modo invitas et tui spem das, hoc primum, Africane,
videamus, ante quam veniunt alii, quidnam sit, de
isto altero sole quod nuntiatum est in senatu?

---

[1] *praetermissum puto* V [2]; *praetermissum* V [1]; *est praetermissum* Baiter.
[2] *At tu vero* Mai; *atutvero* V [1]; *at vero* V [2].

---

[1] 129 B.C.
[2] Publius Cornelius Scipio Aemilianus Africanus Minor.
[3] These ancient holy days of the Latin cities appear to

contribute greatly to a logical exposition of the whole subject.

IX. In the year when Tuditanus and Aquilius were consuls,[1] Publius Africanus,[2] the son of Paulus, decided to spend the Latin holidays[3] at his country-seat, and a considerable number of his most intimate friends stated their intention of visiting him during that period. Early in the morning of the holiday itself, his nephew, Quintus Tubero, arrived in advance of all the rest. Scipio greeted him cordially, for he was truly glad to see him, and then asked : Why are you here so early, Tubero ? For these holidays would certainly have provided you with an excellent opportunity for pursuing your literary studies.

Tubero. My books are at home to me at any time, for they are never busy, but it is a very great privilege to find you at leisure, especially at this time of political unrest.

Scipio. Yes, you have found me at leisure, but less so in mind than in occupation.

Tubero. Yet it is your duty to relax your mind also. For a large number of us are prepared, as we have decided, to spend this time of leisure with you, if it suits your convenience.

Scipio. I shall be delighted, for at last we shall have an opportunity for the discussion of instructive topics.

X. *Tubero.* Well, then, Africanus, since you give me a sort of invitation, and encourage me in my hope regarding yourself, shall we not first inquire, before the others arrive, what the facts are in regard to that second sun that has been reported to the

have been usually three or four in number ; the time of their celebration was fixed by a proclamation of the consuls.

neque enim pauci neque leves sunt, qui se duo soles vidisse dicant, ut non tam fides non habenda quam ratio quaerenda sit.

Hic Scipio : Quam vellem Panaetium nostrum nobiscum haberemus ! qui cum cetera, tum haec caelestia vel studiosissime solet quaerere. sed ego, Tubero (nam tecum aperte, quod sentio, loquar), non nimis adsentior in omni isto genere nostro illi familiari, qui, quae vix coniectura qualia sint possumus suspicari, sic adfirmat, ut oculis ea cernere videatur aut tractare plane manu. quo etiam sapientiorem Socratem soleo iudicare, qui omnem eius modi curam deposuerit eaque, quae de natura quaererentur, aut maiora, quam hominum ratio consequi posset,[1] aut nihil omnino ad vitam hominum adtinere dixerit.

16   Dein Tubero : Nescio, Africane, cur ita memoriae proditum sit, Socratem omnem istam disputationem reiecisse et tantum de vita et de moribus solitum esse quaerere. quem enim auctorem de illo locupletiorem Platone laudare possumus ? cuius in libris multis locis ita loquitur Socrates, ut etiam, cum de moribus, de virtutibus, denique de re publica disputet, numeros tamen et geometriam et harmoniam studeat Pythagorae more coniungere.

Tum Scipio : Sunt ista, ut dicis ; sed audisse te credo, Tubero, Platonem Socrate mortuo primum in

---

[1] *posset* Lehner ; *possit* V.

[1] See Xenophon, *Memorabilia* I, 1, 11–12 ; I, 1, 16 ; IV, 7, 2–4.

senate? For those who claim to have seen two suns are neither few nor untrustworthy, so that we must rather explain the fact than disbelieve it.

Scipio. How I wish our friend Panaetius were with us! For it is his habit to make careful investigation of such celestial phenomena, as well as of other matters. But, Tubero, to give you my frank opinion, I do not entirely approve of our friend's habit in all matters of this kind: in dealing with things of whose nature we can hardly get an inkling by conjecture, he speaks · with such assurance that one would think that he could see them with his own eyes or actually touch them with his hands. I always consider Socrates to have shown greater wisdom in refusing to take any interest in such matters and maintaining that the problems of natural phenomena were either too difficult for the human understanding to fathom or else were of no importance whatever to human life.[1]

Tubero. I cannot understand, Africanus, why the tradition has been handed down that Socrates refused to indulge in any discussions of that character, and confined himself to the study of human life and human morals. For what more trustworthy authority on Socrates can we cite than Plato? And in many passages of Plato's works Socrates, in the midst of his discussions of morals, of the virtues, and even of the State, makes it clear by what he says that he desires to combine with these subjects the consideration of arithmetic, geometry, and harmony, following the methods of Pythagoras.

Scipio. What you say is quite true, Tubero; but I suppose you have heard that, after Socrates' death, Plato went on journeys, first to Egypt for purposes

Aegyptum discendi causa, post in Italiam et in
Siciliam contendisse, ut Pythagorae inventa per-
disceret, eumque et cum Archyta Tarentino et cum
Timaeo Locro multum fuisse et Philoleo com-
mentarios esse nanctum, cumque eo tempore in his
locis Pythagorae nomen vigeret, illum se et hominibus Pythagoreis et studiis illis dedisse. itaque cum
Socratem unice dilexisset eique omnia tribuere
voluisset, leporem Socraticum subtilitatemque sermonis cum obscuritate Pythagorae et cum illa
plurimarum artium gravitate contexuit.

17   XI. Haec Scipio cum dixisset, L. Furium repente
venientem aspexit, eumque ut salutavit amicissime
adprehendit et in lecto suo conlocavit. et cum simul
P. Rutilius venisset, qui est nobis huius[1] sermonis
auctor, eum quoque ut salutavit, propter Tuberonem
iussit adsidere.

Tum Furius: Quid vos agitis? num sermonem
vestrum aliquem diremit noster interventus?

Minime vero, Africanus; soles enim tu haec
studiose investigare. quae sunt in hoc genere, de quo
instituerat paulo ante Tubero quaerere; Rutilius
quidem noster etiam sub ipsis Numantiae moenibus
solebat mecum interdum eius modi aliquid conquirere.

Quae res tandem inciderat? inquit Philus.

Tum ille: De solibus istis duobus; de quo studeo,
Phile, ex te audire quid sentias.

18   XII. Dixerat hoc ille, cum puer nuntiavit venire
ad eum Laelium domoque iam exisse. tum Scipio

---

[1] *huius* Klotz; *lautus* V; *laudatus* Orelli; *totius* Franke.

---

[1] This passage is our earliest authentic source for Plato's
journeys. His visit to Sicily is now generally accepted as a
fact, but the Egyptian journey is considered very doubtful.

of study, and later to Italy and Sicily [1] in order to become acquainted with the discoveries of Pythagoras; and that he spent a great deal of time in the company of Archytas of Tarentum and Timaeus of Locri, and also got possession of Philolaus' notes. And, as Pythagoras' reputation was then great in that country, he devoted himself entirely to that teacher's disciples and doctrines. And so, as he loved Socrates with singular affection and wished to give him credit for everything, he interwove Socrates' charm and subtlety in argument with the obscurity and ponderous learning of Pythagoras in so many branches of knowledge.

XI. After this speech, Scipio noticed Lucius Furius Philus coming in unannounced, and after greeting him with the greatest cordiality, he took his hand and led him to a place on his own couch. Publius Rutilius, who later reported the conversation to us, came in at the same time, received Scipio's greeting, and was given a place beside Tubero.

Philus. What are you discussing? I hope our arrival has not interrupted your conversation.

Scipio. Certainly not; for the point which Tubero began to inquire into a short time ago belongs to the very class of subjects which you are always interested in investigating. As for our friend Rutilius, he used to discuss such topics with me occasionally, even under the very walls of Numantia.

Philus. What was this particular subject?

Scipio. Those two suns, Philus, and I am anxious to hear your opinion of them.

XII. No sooner had he said this than a servant announced that Laelius was coming, and had already left his house. Whereupon Scipio dressed and put

calceis et vestimentis sumptis e cubiculo est egressus,
et cum paululum inambulavisset in porticu, Laelium
advenientem salutavit et eos, qui una venerant,
Spurium Mummium, quem in primis diligebat, et C.
Fannium et Quintum Scaevolam, generos Laelii,
doctos adulescentes, iam aetate quaestorios ; quos
cum omnis salutavisset, convertit se in porticu et
coniecit in medium Laelium ; fuit enim hoc in
amicitia quasi quoddam ius inter illos, ut militiae
propter eximiam belli gloriam Africanum ut deum
coleret Laelius, domi vicissim Laelium, quod aetate
antecedebat, observaret in parentis loco Scipio. dein
cum essent perpauca inter se uno aut[1] altero spatio
conlocuti Scipionique eorum adventus periucundus
et pergratus fuisset, placitum est, ut in aprico
maxime pratuli loco, quod erat hibernum tempus
anni, considerent ; quod cum facere vellent, inter-
venit vir prudens omnibusque illis et iucundus et
carus, M.' Manilius, qui a Scipione ceterisque amicissime consalutatus adsedit proximus Laelio.

19   XIII. Tum Philus : Non mihi videtur, inquit, quod
hi venerunt, alius nobis sermo esse quaerendus, sed
agendum accuratius et dicendum dignum aliquid
horum auribus.

Hic Laelius : Quid tandem agebatis, aut cui sermoni nos intervenimus ?

PH. Quaesierat ex me Scipio, quidnam sentirem
de hoc, quod duo soles visos esse constaret.

---

[1] *aut* Moser ; *an* V ; *atque* Osann.

---

[1] About thirty years.

on his shoes, and, leaving his bedchamber, walked in the portico for a little while.   On Laelius' arrival, he greeted him and those who had come with him— Spurius Mummius, of whom he was very fond, Gaius Fannius, and Quintus Scaevola, Laelius' sons-in-law, who were young men of excellent education, and had now reached the appropriate age for the quaestorship.[1]   After all these salutations he turned about in the portico, giving Laelius the place in the centre ; for there was a kind of rule in their friendship, according to which Laelius honoured Scipio like a god in the field, on account of his unexcelled glory in war, while at home Scipio in his turn revered Laelius like a father, on account of his greater age. Then after they had conversed for a short time while walking up and down, Scipio, who had been greatly pleased and delighted at their arrival, thought it best that they should seat themselves in the sunniest part of the lawn, as it was winter.   They were quite willing, and just then Manius Manilius came in, a man of good sense, who was agreeable to the whole company and beloved by them.   After receiving a friendly greeting from Scipio and the rest, he sat down beside Laelius.

XIII. *Philus.* I do not see why we should change the subject of our conversation because these friends have come in, but I think we must treat it more carefully, and be sure our remarks are worth their attention.

Laelius. What were you discussing ?   What sort of conversation was it that we have interrupted ?

Philus. Scipio had just asked me what I thought of the generally admitted fact that two suns have been seen.

L. Ain vero, Phile? iam explorata nobis sunt ea, quae ad domos nostras quaeque ad rem publicam pertineant, siquidem, quid agatur in caelo, quaerimus?

Et ille: An tu ad domos nostras non censes pertinere scire, quid agatur et quid fiat domi, quae non ea est, quam parietes nostri cingunt, sed mundus hic totus, quod domicilium quamque patriam di nobis communem secum dederunt, cum praesertim, si haec ignoremus, multa nobis et magna ignoranda sint? ac me quidem, ut hercule etiam te ipsum, Laeli, omnisque avidos sapientiae cognitio ipsa rerum consideratioque delectat.

20   Tum Laelius: Non inpedio, praesertim quoniam feriati sumus; sed possumus audire aliquid an serius venimus?

PH. Nihil est adhuc disputatum, et, quoniam est integrum, libenter tibi, Laeli, ut de eo disseras, equidem concessero.

L. Immo vero te audiamus, nisi forte Manilius interdictum aliquod inter duos soles putat esse componendum, ut ita caelum possideant, ut uterque possederit.

Tum Manilius: Pergisne eam, Laeli, artem inludere, in qua primum excellis [1] ipse, deinde sine qua

---

[1] *excellis* Moser; *excello* V.

---

[1] The profession of counsellor-at-law (*iuris consultus*).

Laelius. Do you really think then, Philus, that we have already acquired a perfect knowledge of those matters that relate to our own homes and to the State, since we are now seeking to learn what is going on in the heavens?

Philus. Do you not think it important for our homes that we should know what is happening and being done in that home which is not shut in by the walls we build, but is the whole universe, a home and a fatherland which the gods have given us the privilege of sharing with them? Surely it is important, especially since, if we are ignorant of these matters, we must remain ignorant of many other important things. Besides, the mere learning about the facts of nature and their investigation gives me at least the greatest pleasure, as it certainly must to you also, Laelius, and to all who are eager for wisdom.

Laelius. I have no objection to the topic, especially as this is a holiday. But are we to hear some discussion of it, or have we come too late?

Philus. There has been no discussion as yet, and, since we have not begun, I should be pleased to yield to you, Laelius, so that you may give us your opinion on the subject.

Laelius. On the contrary, let us hear yours, unless perhaps Manilius thinks that a provisional edict ought to be issued embodying a compromise between the two suns, whereby "they shall have and hold the sky in such manner that they shall both in common have and hold it."

Manilius. Laelius, are you still mocking at that art[1] in which you are so proficient yourself, and without which no one can know what belongs to him

scire nemo potest, quid sit suum, quid alienum? sed
ista mox; nunc audiamus Philum, quem video
maioribus iam de rebus quam me aut quam P.
Mucium consuli.

21   XIV. Tum Philus: Nihil novi vobis adferam,
neque quod a me sit cogitatum aut inventum; nam
memoria teneo C. Sulpicium Gallum, doctissimum,
ut scitis, hominem, cum idem hoc visum diceretur et
esset casu apud M. Marcellum, qui cum eo consul
fuerat, sphaeram, quam M. Marcelli avus captis
Syracusis ex urbe locupletissima atque ornatissima
sustulisset, cum aliud nihil ex tanta praeda domum
suam deportavisset, iussisse proferri; cuius ego
sphaerae cum persaepe propter Archimedi gloriam
nomen audissem, speciem ipsam non sum tanto opere
admiratus; erat enim illa venustior et nobilior in
volgus, quam ab eodem Archimede factam posuerat
in templo Virtutis Marcellus idem. sed posteaquam
22 coepit rationem huius operis scientissime Gallus
exponere, plus in illo Siculo ingenii, quam videretur
natura humana ferre potuisse, iudicavi[1] fuisse.
dicebat enim Gallus sphaerae illius alterius solidae
atque plenae vetus esse inventum, et eam a Thalete
Milesio primum esse tornatam, post autem ab
Eudoxo Cnidio, discipulo, ut ferebat, Platonis, eandem illam astris stellisque, quae caelo inhaererent,[2]

[1] *iudicavi* Krarup; *iudicam* V[1]; *iudicabat* V[2]; *iudicabam*
Mai.
[2] *astris stellisque, quae caelo inhaererent* Baiter; *astellisisq.
caelo inhererent* V; *astris stellisque caelo inhaerentibus* Pascal.

---

[1] 166 B.C.   [2] 212 B.C.
[3] See Cicero, *Tusc. Disp.* I, 63; Ovid, *Fasti* VI, 277.

and what does not? However, we can discuss that later; let us at present listen to Philus, who is already being consulted, I see, about matters of greater import than those on which Publius Mucius or I are asked for our opinions.

XIV. *Philus.* I have nothing new to bring before you, nor anything that I have thought out or discovered by myself. For I remember an incident in the life of Gaius Sulpicius Gallus, a most learned man, as you know: at a time when a similar phenomenon was reported, and he happened to be at the house of Marcus Marcellus, his colleague in the consulship,[1] he ordered the celestial globe to be brought out which the grandfather of Marcellus had carried off from Syracuse, when that very rich and beautiful city was taken,[2] though he took home with him nothing else out of the great store of booty captured. Though I had heard this globe mentioned quite frequently on account of the fame of Archimedes, when I actually saw it I did not particularly admire it; for that other celestial globe, also constructed by Archimedes, which the same Marcellus placed in the temple of Virtue, is more beautiful as well as more widely known among the people.[3] But when Gallus began to give a very learned explanation of the device, I concluded that the famous Sicilian had been endowed with greater genius than one would imagine it possible for a human being to possess. For Gallus told us that the other kind of celestial globe, which was solid and contained no hollow space, was a very early invention, the first one of that kind having been constructed by Thales of Miletus, and later marked by Eudoxus of Cnidus (a disciple of Plato, it was claimed) with the constellations and stars which

41

esse descriptam; cuius omnem ornatum et descrip-
tionem sumptam ab Eudoxo multis annis post non
astrologiae scientia, sed poëtica quadam facultate
versibus Arati extulise. hoc autem sphaerae
genus, in quo solis et lunae motus inessent et earum
quinque stellarum, quae errantes et quasi vagae
nominarentur, in illa sphaera solida non potuisse
finiri, atque in eo admirandum esse inventum Archimedi, quod excogitasset, quem ad modum in dissimil-
limis motibus inaequabiles et varios cursus servaret
una conversio. hanc sphaeram Gallus cum moveret,
fiebat, ut soli luna totidem conversionibus in aere
illo, quot diebus in ipso caelo, succederet, ex quo et
in sphaera[1] solis fieret eadem illa defectio et incideret
luna tum in eam metam, quae esset umbra terrae,
cum sol e regione . . .

[*Octo paginae hic a Maio desiderantur.*]

23 XV. . . . fuit, quod et ipse hominem diligebam
et in primis patri meo Paulo probatum et carum
fuisse cognoveram. memini me admodum adulescentulo, cum pater in Macedonia consul esset et essemus
in castris, perturbari exercitum nostrum religione et
metu, quod serena nocte subito candens et plena
luna defecisset. tum ille, cum legatus noster esset

---

[1] *in* [*caelo*] *sphaera* is the common reading ; *in caelo sphaera*
V ; *in caelo sphaerae* Pascal.

---

[1] The poem referred to is the *Phaenomena*, translated into
Latin by Cicero in his youth.   Fragments of the translation
are extant.
[2] The five planets : Saturn, Jupiter, Mars, Mercury, and
Venus.
[3] 168 B.C.

are fixed in the sky. He also said that many years later Aratus, borrowing this whole arrangement and plan from Eudoxus, had described it in verse, without any knowledge of astronomy, but with considerable poetic talent.[1] But this newer kind of globe, he said, on which were delineated the motions of the sun and moon and of those five stars which are called wanderers, or, as we might say, rovers,[2] contained more than could be shown on the solid globe, and the invention of Archimedes deserved special admiration because he had thought out a way to represent accurately by a single device for turning the globe those various and divergent movements with their different rates of speed. And when Gallus moved the globe, it was actually true that the moon was always as many revolutions behind the sun on the bronze contrivance as would agree with the number of days it was behind it in the sky. Thus the same eclipse of the sun happened on the globe as would actually happen, and the moon came to the point where the shadow of the earth was at the very time when the sun . . . out of the region . . .

About two and one half pages appear to be lost. At the end of the gap, Scipio is speaking of Gaius Sulpicius Gallus.

XV. *Scipio.* . . . for I myself loved the man, and I was aware that he was also greatly esteemed and beloved by my father Paulus. For in my early youth, when my father, then consul, was in Macedonia, and I was in camp with him, I recollect that our army was on one occasion disturbed by superstitious fears because, on a cloudless night, a bright full moon was suddenly darkened. Gallus was at that time[3] our lieutenant (it being then about a year

anno fere ante, quam consul est declaratus, haud
dubitavit postridie palam in castris docere nullum
esse prodigium, idque et tum factum esse et certis
temporibus esse semper futurum, cum sol ita locatus
fuisset, ut lunam suo lumine non posset attingere.

Ain tandem ? inquit Tubero ; docere hoc poterat
ille homines paene agrestes et apud imperitos aude-
bat haec dicere ?

S. Ille vero et magna quidem cum . . .

[*Hic Maio duae minimum paginae videntur deesse.*]

24   . . . neque insolens ostentatio neque oratio ab-
horrens a persona hominis gravissimi ; rem enim
magnam adsecutus, quod hominibus perturbatis
inanem religionem timoremque deiecerat.

25   XVI. Atque eius modi quiddam etiam bello illo
maximo, quod Athenienses et Lacedaemonii summa
inter se contentione gesserunt, Pericles ille, et
auctoritate et eloquentia et consilio princeps civitatis
suae, cum obscurato sole tenebrae factae essent
repente Atheniensiumque animos summus timor
occupavisset, docuisse civis suos dicitur, id quod
ipse ab Anaxagora, cuius auditor fuerat, acceperat,
certo illud tempore fieri et necessario, cum tota se
luna sub orbem solis subiecisset ; itaque, etsi non

---

[1] The Peloponnesian War (431–404 B.C.).

[2] The eclipse referred to is that of Aug. 3, 431 (Thucyd. II,
28). The story of Pericles' explanation of it is told in
slightly different form by Plutarch, *Pericles* 35.

[3] *i.e.*, when the moon comes between the earth and the
sun.

before his election to the consulship), and on the next day he unhesitatingly made a public statement in the camp that this was no miracle, but that it had happened at that time, and would always happen at fixed times in the future, when the sun was in such a position that its light could not reach the moon.

Tubero. Do you really mean to say that he could convince men who were little more than simple peasants of such a thing, or that he dared even to state it before the ignorant?

Scipio. He certainly did, and with great . . .

About fifteen lines appear to be lost. There is no change of subject.

. . . for his speech showed no conceited desire to display his knowledge, nor was it unsuitable to the character of a man of the greatest dignity; in fact, he accomplished a very important result in relieving the troubled minds of the soldiers from foolish superstitious fear.

XVI. And a similar story is told of an event in that great war in which the Athenians and Lacedaemonians contended so fiercely.[1] For when the sun was suddenly obscured and darkness reigned,[2] and the Athenians were overwhelmed with the greatest terror, Pericles, who was then supreme among his countrymen in influence, eloquence, and wisdom, is said to have communicated to his fellow-citizens the information he had received from Anaxagoras, whose pupil he had been—that this phenomenon occurs at fixed periods and by inevitable law, whenever the moon passes entirely beneath the orb of the sun,[3] and that therefore, though it does

45

omni intermenstruo, tamen id fieri non posse nisi
certo intermenstruo tempore. quod cum disputando
rationibusque docuisset, populum liberavit metu ;
erat enim tum haec nova et ignota ratio, solem
lunae oppositu[1] solere deficere, quod Thaletem
Milesium primum vidisse dicunt. id autem postea
ne nostrum quidem Ennium fugit ; qui ut scribit,
anno trecentesimo quinquagesimo fere post Romam
conditam

Nonis Iunis soli luna obstitit et nox.

Atque hac in re tanta inest ratio atque sollertia,
ut ex hoc die, quem apud Ennium et in maximis
annalibus consignatum videmus, superiores solis
defectiones reputatae sint usque ad illam, quae
Nonis Quinctilibus fuit regnante Romulo ; quibus
quidem Romulum tenebris etiamsi natura ad humanum exitum abripuit, virtus tamen in caelum
dicitur sustulisse.

26   XVII. Tum Tubero : Videsne, Africane, quod
paulo ante secus tibi videbatur, doc . . .

[*Desiderantur paginae duae.*]

. . . lis, quae videant ceteri. quid porro aut
praeclarum putet in rebus humanis, qui haec deorum

[1] *oppositu* V[2]; *oppositum* V[1].

---

[1] *i.e.*, about 401 B.C., if Cicero is consistent in his
chronology (see Book II, 18 and note) ; perhaps the eclipse
of June 21, 400 B.C., is referred to.

[2] Probably from Book IV of the *Annales* of Ennius.

[3] The *Annales Maximi*, kept by the chief pontiffs, contained
the names of the consuls and other important officials of the
year, and other very important events, including those
believed to be prodigies.

not happen at every new moon, it cannot happen except at certain periods of the new moon. When he had discussed the subject and given the explanation of the phenomenon, the people were freed of their fears. For at that time it was a strange and unfamiliar idea that the sun was regularly eclipsed by the interposition of the moon—a fact which Thales of Miletus is said to have been the first to observe. But later even our own Ennius was not ignorant of it, for he wrote that, in about the three hundred and fiftieth year[1] after Rome was founded :

In the month of June—the day was then the fifth—
The moon and night obscured the shining sun.[2]

And now so much exact knowledge in regard to this matter has been gained that, by the use of the date recorded by Ennius and in the Great Annals,[3] the dates of previous eclipses of the sun have been reckoned, all the way back to that which occured on July fifth in the reign of Romulus. For even though, during the darkness of that eclipse, Nature carried Romulus away to man's inevitable end, yet the story is that it was his merit that caused his translation to heaven.[4]

XVII. *Tubero.* Do you see, Africanus, that what you had a different opinion of a short time ago . . .

About fifteen lines are lost.

Scipio. . . . things which others may see. Furthermore how can any man regard anything in human affairs either as exalted, if he has examined

---

[4] In 714 B.C., according to Cicero's chronology ; this is fiction, of course. Livy's version of the story (I, 16) mentions a storm but no eclipse (compare *De Re Pub.* II, 17).

regna perspexerit, aut diuturnum, qui cognoverit
quid sit aeternum, aut gloriosum, qui viderit quam
parva sit terra, primum universa, deinde ea pars
eius, quam homines incolant, quamque nos in exigua
eius parte adfixi plurimis ignotissimi gentibus speremus
tamen nostrum nomen volitare et vagari
27 latissime? agros vero et aedificia et pecudes et
inmensum argenti pondus atque auri qui bona nec
putare nec appellare soleat, quod earum rerum
videatur ei levis fructus, exiguus usus, incertus
dominatus, saepe etiam deterrimorum hominum
inmensa possessio, quam est hic fortunatus putandus,
cui soli vere liceat omnia non Quiritium, sed sapientium
iure pro suis vindicare, nec civili nexo, sed
communi lege naturae, quae vetat ullam rem esse
cuiusquam nisi eius, qui tractare et uti sciat; qui
inperia consulatusque nostros in necessariis, non in
expetendis rebus, muneris fungendi gratia subeundos,
non praemiorum aut gloriae causa adpetendos putet;
qui denique, ut Africanum avum meum scribit Cato
solitum esse dicere, possit idem de se praedicare,
numquam se plus agere, quam nihil cum ageret,
numquam minus solum esse, quam cum solus esset.
28 quis enim putare vere potest plus egisse Dionysium
tum, cum omnia moliendo eripuerit civibus suis

---

[1] Compare Plato, *Republic* I, 347 B: "good men will not
consent to hold office for the sake either of money or of
honour."

[2] The same saying is quoted in somewhat different terms
in Cicero's *De Officiis* III, 1. We do not know whether it
comes from the *Origines* or some other work of Cato.

into yonder realms of the gods, or as of long duration, if he has realized the meaning of eternity, or as glorious, if he has perceived how small is the earth—not only the earth as a whole, but especially that part of it which is inhabited by man—and has noticed how we Romans, though confined to a scanty portion of it and entirely unknown to many races of men, hope nevertheless that our name will be borne abroad on wings and will spread to the ends of the earth? But as far as our lands, houses, herds, and immense stores of silver and gold are concerned, the man who never thinks of these things or speaks of them as "goods," because he sees that the enjoyment of them is slight, their usefulness scanty, their ownership uncertain, and has noticed that the vilest of men often possess them in unmeasured abundance—how fortunate is he to be esteemed! For only such a man can really claim all things as his own, by virtue of the decision, not of the Roman People, but of the wise, not by any obligation of the civil law, but by the common law of Nature, which forbids that anything shall belong to any man save to him that knows how to employ and to use it; only such a man will consider that our military commands and consulships are to be classed among things necessary rather than things desirable, and that they are to be undertaken from a sense of duty and not sought for profit or glory; [1] only such a man, finally, can say of himself what my grandfather Africanus used to say, according to Cato's account [2]—that he was never doing more than when he was doing nothing, and never less alone than when alone. For who can really believe that Dionysius, when by the greatest exertions he deprived his fellow-citizens

49

libertatem, quam eius civem Archimedem, cum istam ipsam sphaeram, nihil cum agere videretur, effecerit?[1] quis autem non magis solos esse, qui in foro turbaque, quicum conloqui libeat, non habeant, quam qui nullo arbitro vel secum ipsi loquantur vel quasi doctissimorum hominum in concilio adsint, cum eorum inventis scriptisque se oblectent? quis vero divitiorem quemquam putet quam eum, cui nihil desit, quod quidem natura desideret, aut potentiorem quam illum, qui omnia, quae expetat, consequatur, aut beatiorem, quam qui sit omni perturbatione animi liberatus, aut firmiore fortuna, quam qui ea possideat, quae secum, ut aiunt, vel e naufragio possit ecferre? quod autem imperium, qui magistratus, quod regnum potest esse praestantius quam despicientem omnia humana et inferiora sapientia ducentem nihil umquam nisi sempiternum et divinum animo volutare? cui persuasum sit appellari ceteros homines, esse solos eos, qui essent politi propriis humanitatis artibus; ut mihi Platonis illud,
29 seu quis dixit alius, perelegans esse videatur; quem cum ex alto ignotas ad terras tempestas et in desertum litus detulisset, timentibus ceteris propter ignorationem locorum animadvertisse dicunt in arena geometricas formas quasdam esse descriptas; quas ut vidisset, exclamavisse, ut bono essent animo; videre enim se hominum vestigia; quae videlicet ille non ex agri consitura, quam cernebat, sed ex

---

[1] *videretur,* [*de qua modo dicebatur*] *effecerit* is the common reading; *videretur de qua modo dicebatur effecerit* V.

---

[1] This saying is credited by Vitruvius (VI, 1) to Aristippus.

of their liberty, was doing more than Archimedes, one of those citizens, when he made that very globe of which we have spoken, in making which he appeared to be doing nothing? And who does not believe that those are more alone who, though in the crowded forum, have no one with whom they care to talk, than those who, when no one else is present, either commune with themselves or, as we may say, participate in a gathering of most learned men, finding delight in their discoveries and writings? Who in truth would consider anyone richer than the man who lacks nothing that his nature requires, or more powerful than one who gains all he strives for, or happier than one who is set free from all perturbation of mind, or more secure in his wealth than one who possesses only what, as the saying goes, he can carry away with him out of a shipwreck? What power, moreover, what office, what kingdom can be preferable to the state of one who despises all human possessions, considers them inferior to wisdom, and never meditates on any subject that is not eternal and divine; who believes that, though others may be called men, only those are men who are perfected in the arts appropriate to humanity? In this connection the remark made by Plato, or perhaps someone else,[1] seems to me particularly apt. For when a storm at sea had driven him to an unknown land and stranded him on a deserted shore, and his companions were frightened on account of their ignorance of the country, he, according to the story, noticed certain geometrical figures traced in the sand, and immediately cried out, "Be of good courage; I see the tracks of men." He drew his inference, evidently, not from the cultivation of the soil, which

51

doctrinae indiciis interpretabatur. quam ob rem, Tubero, semper mihi et doctrina et eruditi homines et tua ista studia placuerunt.

30 XVIII. Tum Laelius: Non audeo quidem, inquit, ad ista, Scipio, dicere, neque tam te aut Philum aut Manilium. . .

[*Desiderantur paginae duae.*]

. . . in ipsius paterno genere fuit noster ille amicus, dignus huic ad imitandum,

egregie cordatus homo, catus Aelius Sextus,

qui "egregie cordatus" et "catus" fuit et ab Ennio dictus est, non quod ea quaerebat, quae numquam inveniret, sed quod ea respondebat, quae eos, qui quaesissent, et cura et negotio solverent, cuique contra Galli studia disputanti in ore semper erat ille de Iphigenia Achilles:[1]

Ástrologorum sígna in caelo quíd sit[2] observat, Iovis[3]
cúm capra aut nepa aút exoritur nómen aliquod béluarum !
quód est ante pedes némo spectat, caéli scrutantúr plagas.

Atque idem (multum enim illum audiebam et libenter) Zethum illum Pacuvii nimis inimicum

---

[1] *erat ille de Iphigenia Achilles* Osann ; *erat illa de Ifigenia Achillis* V ; *erant illa de Iphigenia Achillis* Mai.
[2] *quid sit* V ; *quaesit* Leopardi.
[3] *observat, Iovis* Mai ; *observationis* V.

---

[1] Probably from Ennius, *Annales* X. This line is also quoted by Cicero in *De Oratore* I, 198 and *Tusc. Disp.* I, 18.
[2] Usually taken as part of a speech of Achilles in the

he also observed, but from the indications of learning.
For these reasons, Tubero, I have always delighted
in learning, in men of erudition, and in such studies
as those which you pursue.

XVIII. *Laelius.* In regard to these arguments,
Scipio, I dare not say that either you or Philus or
Manilius . . . to such an extent . . .

About fifteen lines are lost, in which Laelius evidently
says that, while he has no desire to disparage abstract
learning, it ought not to interfere with the practical duties
of a public man.

Laelius. . . . that friend of ours belonged to his
father's family, and was worthy of his emulation,

> Sagacious Aelius Sextus, a man most wise,[1]

who was really most wise and sagacious, and was
called so by Ennius, not because he sought what he
could never find, but because he gave counsel which
freed his clients from trouble and anxiety. And
when he was arguing against the favourite studies
of Gallus, he always had on his lips those famous
words of Achilles in the *Iphigenia,*[2]

> The astral signs that are observed above,
> When goat or scorpion of Jove arise,
> Or other beasts; all gaze intent thereon,
> Nor ever see what lies before their feet!

Yet this same man used to say (for I have often
listened to him, and with pleasure) that the Zethus
of Pacuvius[3] was too hostile to culture; the

Iphigenia of Ennius, but the text is doubtful. Compare
Plato, *Theaetetus* 174 A.

[3] Probably a reference to a speech in the *Antiopa* of
Pacuvius. Compare Cicero, *De Oratore* II, 155; *Rhet. ad
Herenn.* II, 43.

doctrinae esse dicebat; magis eum delectabat Neoptolemus Ennii, qui se ait "philosophari velle, sed paucis; nam omnino haud placere." quodsi studia Graecorum vos tanto opere delectant, sunt alia liberiora et transfusa[1] latius, quae vel ad usum vitae vel etiam ad ipsam rem publicam conferre possumus. istae quidem artes, si modo aliquid, valent[2] ut paulum acuant et tamquam inritent ingenia puerorum, quo facilius possint maiora discere.

31 XIX. Tum Tubero: Non dissentio a te, Laeli, sed quaero, quae tu esse maiora intellegas.

L. Dicam mehercule et contemnar a te fortasse, cum tu ista caelestia de Scipione quaesieris, ego autem haec, quae videntur ante oculos esse, magis putem quaerenda. quid enim mihi L. Pauli nepos, hoc avunculo, nobilissima in familia atque in hac tam clara re publica natus, quaerit, quo modo duo soles visi sint, non quaerit, cur in una re publica duo senatus et duo paene iam populi sint? nam, ut videtis, mors Tiberii Gracchi et iam ante tota illius ratio tribunatus divisit populum unum in duas partis; obtrectatores autem et invidi Scipionis initiis factis a P. Crasso et Appio Claudio tenent nihilo minus illis mortuis senatus alteram partem dissi-

---

[1] *transfusa* V ; *fusa* Madvig (cf. I, 60 *translata*).
[2] *aliquid, valens ut* V, Pascal ; *aliquid valent, id valent, ut* Mueller.

---

[1] Probably from a play entitled either *Neoptolemus* or *Philoctetes.* We find the same quotation in *Tusc. Disp* II, 1 and *De Oratore* II, 156 ; it is also cited by Aulus Gellius (V, 15, 9) and by Apuleius (*Apologia* 13). A very similar sentiment is expressed by Plato (*Gorgias* 484 C).
[2] Tubero ; see sections 14–15.

Neoptolemus of Ennius was more to his taste in saying that he desired "to study philosophy, but in moderation; for he did not approve of doing so entirely." [1] But if the studies which occupied the Greeks attract you so powerfully, there are others, of a more free character and of wider range, which we can employ either for the conduct of our own lives or even for the service of the State. As for those arts of yours, if for anything at all, they are valuable only to sharpen somewhat and, we may say, stir up the faculties of the young, so that they find it easier to learn things of greater importance.

XIX. *Tubero.* I do not disagree with you, Laelius, but I should like to know what those things are which you consider of greater importance.

Laelius. I will tell you, to be sure, and perchance you may scorn my opinion, since it was you who inquired of Scipio about those celestial matters. Nevertheless, I should consider those things which are directly before our own eyes more worthy of investigation. For why is it that the grandson [2] of Lucius Paulus, the nephew of our friend here, a scion of a most worthy family and of this most glorious republic, is asking how two suns could have been seen, instead of asking why, in one State, we have almost reached the point where there are two senates and two separate peoples? For, as you observe, the death of Tiberius Gracchus, and, even before his death, the whole character of his tribunate, divided one people into two factions. And in fact Scipio's slanderers and enemies, at first led by Publius Crassus and Appius Claudius, even now that those men are dead keep a part of the senate in opposition to you under the leadership

dentem a vobis auctore Metello et P. Mucio neque
hunc, qui unus potest, concitatis sociis et nomine
Latino, foederibus violatis, triumviris seditiosissimis
aliquid cotidie novi molientibus,[1] bonis viris[2] perturbatis his tam periculosis rebus subvenire patiuntur.

32 quam ob rem, si me audietis, adulescentes, solem
alterum ne metueritis; aut enim nullus esse potest,
aut sit sane, ut visus est, modo ne sit molestus, aut
scire istarum rerum nihil aut, etiamsi maxime scie-
mus, nec meliores ob eam scientiam nec beatiores
esse possumus; senatum vero et populum ut unum
habeamus, et fieri potest, et permolestum est, nisi
fit, et secus esse scimus et videmus, si id effectum
sit, et melius nos esse victuros et beatius.

33 XX. Tum Mucius : Quid esse igitur censes, Laeli,
discendum nobis, ut istud efficere possimus ipsum,
quod postulas?

L. Eas artis, quae efficiant ut usui civitati simus ;
id enim esse praeclarissimum sapientiae munus
maximumque virtutis vel documentum vel officium
puto. quam ob rem, ut hae feriae nobis ad utilis-
simos rei publicae sermones potissimum conferantur,
Scipionem rogemus, ut explicet, quem existimet esse
optimum statum civitatis. deinde alia quaeremus ;
quibus cognitis spero nos ad haec ipsa via perven-

---

[1] *molientibus* Moser ; *moventibus* V.
[2] *viris [locupletibus] perturbatis* Mueller ; *viris locupletibus
perturbatis* V.

---

[1] The troubles following the enactment of Tiberius
Gracchus' agrarian measures in 133 B.C. are referred to here.
(It should be remembered that the imaginary date of the
dialogue is 129 B.C.)

of Metellus and Publius Mucius; and these men will not allow our friend here, who is the only man able to do so, to help us in our present dangerous emergency, though our allies and the Latins are roused against us, treaties have been broken, seditious triumvirs are plotting some new villainy daily, and our good citizens are in despair.[1] For these reasons, young gentlemen, if you will listen to me, you will not be alarmed by the second sun (for either no such thing can really exist, or else let it exist, since it has been seen, provided it does us no harm; and we are either unable to learn anything at all about such matters, or else, even if we do learn all there is to know, we can never become better or happier through such knowledge); but as to our having a united senate and people, it is possible, and unless it is brought about, we shall have serious trouble; we know and observe that the situation is far from being as it should be, and that, if this can be brought about, our lives will be better and happier.

XX. *Mucius.* What knowledge then, Laelius, do you think we ought to acquire, in order to be able to accomplish the result you demand of us?

Laelius. The knowledge of those arts which can make us useful to the State; for I consider this the noblest function of wisdom, and the highest duty of virtue as well as the best proof of its possession. Therefore, in order that these holidays may be devoted to discussions which, beyond any other object, are highly useful to the State, let us ask Scipio to tell us which form of government he considers the best. After that we will investigate other subjects, the knowledge of which will, I hope,

turos earumque rerum rationem, quae nunc instant, explicaturos.

34   XXI. Cum id et Philus et Manilius et Mummius admodum adprobavissent . . .

[*Desiderantur paginae duae.*]

. . . quare, si placet, deduc orationem tuam de caelo ad haec citeriora . . . (*Nonius* p. 85. 19 *et* 289. 8.)

. . . non solum ob eam causam fieri volui, quod erat aequum de re publica potissimum principem rei publicae dicere, sed etiam quod memineram persaepe te cum Panaetio disserere solitum coram Polybio, duobus Graecis vel peritissimis rerum civilium, multaque colligere ac docere, optimum longe statum civitatis esse eum, quem maiores nostri nobis reliquissent. qua in disputatione quoniam tu paratior es, feceris, ut etiam pro his dicam, si, de re publica quid sentias, explicaris, nobis gratum omnibus.

35   XXII. Tum ille: Non possum equidem dicere me ulla in cogitatione acrius aut diligentius solere versari quam in ista ipsa, quae mihi, Laeli, a te proponitur. etenim cum in suo quemque opere artificem, qui quidem excellat, nihil aliud cogitare, meditari, curare videam, nisi quo sit in illo genere melior, ego, cum mihi sit unum opus hoc a parentibus maioribusque meis relictum, procuratio atque

lead us at the same time to the consideration of the
present situation and to an understanding of what
now lies before us.

XXI. When Philus, Manilius, and Mummius had
expressed their enthusiastic approval of this suggestion . . .

About fifteen lines are lost. The following fragment is
probably a part of the missing passage.

. . . therefore, if you please, bring your conversation down from the heavens to these things which
lie nearer to us. . .

Laelius. . . . I desired this, not only because it
was proper that an eminent statesman rather than
anyone else should discuss the State, but also because
I recollected that you used to converse very frequently with Panaetius on this subject in company
with Polybius—two Greeks who were perhaps the
best versed of them all in politics—and that you
assembled many arguments to prove that the form
of government handed down to us by our ancestors
is by far the best of all. Now since you are better
prepared than the rest of us to undertake this discussion, you will do us all a favour, if I may speak for
the company, by presenting your ideas on the State.

XXII. *Scipio.* I cannot, indeed, assert that any
other subject claims more of my interest and careful
thought, Laelius, than the one which you now
assign to me. Furthermore, since I have noticed
that the thoughts and efforts of every craftsman, if
he is proficient, are directed to no other end than
the improvement of his skill in his own craft, should
not I, seeing that the guardianship and administration of the State have been handed down to me by

59

administratio rei publicae, non me inertiorem esse
confitear quam opificem quemquam, si minus in
maxima arte, quam illi in minimis, operae consump-
36 serim? sed neque his contentus sum, quae de ista
consultatione scripta nobis summi ex Graecia sapien-
tissimique homines reliquerunt, neque ea, quae mihi
videntur, anteferre illis audeo. quam ob rem peto
a vobis, ut me sic audiatis, neque ut omnino expertem
Graecarum rerum neque ut eas nostris in hoc praesertim genere anteponentem, sed ut unum e togatis
patris diligentia non inliberaliter institutum studioque discendi a pueritia incensum, usu tamen et
domesticis praeceptis multo magis eruditum quam
litteris.

37 XXIII. Hic Philus : Non hercule, inquit, Scipio,
dubito, quin tibi ingenio praestiterit nemo, usu
quidem in re publica rerum maximarum facile omnis
viceris ; quibus autem studiis semper fueris, tenemus. quam ob rem, si, ut dicis, animum quoque
contulisti in istam rationem et quasi artem, habeo
maximam gratiam Laelio ; spero enim multo uberiora
fore, quae a te dicentur, quam illa, quae a Graecis
hominibus[1] scripta sunt, omnia.

Tum ille : Permagnam tu quidem expectationem,
quod onus est ei, qui magnis de rebus dicturus est,
gravissimum, inponis orationi meae.

Et Philus : Quamvis sit magna, tamen eam vinces,
ut soles ; neque enim est periculum, ne te de re
publica disserentem deficiat oratio.

----

[1] *hominibus* Orelli ; *nobis* V ; *nobilissimis* Creuzer.

----

[1] He is evidently thinking primarily of Plato's *Republic*,
though the reference undoubtedly includes many other
treatises (see *De Legg.* III, 13–14 and notes).

my parents and ancestors as my sole task, have to confess that I am more slothful than any craftsman, if I have devoted less labour to the supreme craft than they to their humble tasks ? But I am not satisfied with the works dealing with this subject which the greatest and wisest men of Greece have left us;[1] nor on the other hand am I bold enough to rate my opinion above theirs. Therefore I ask you to listen to me as to one who is neither entirely ignorant of the Greek authorities, nor, on the other hand, prefers their views, particularly on this subject, to our own, but rather as to a Roman who, though provided by a father's care with a liberal education and eager for knowledge from boyhood, yet has been trained by experience and the maxims learned at home much more than by books.

XXIII. *Philus.* By Hercules, I am confident, Scipio, that no one is your superior in innate ability, and that your experience in the highest spheres of government is absolutely unsurpassed ; we are also aware to what studies you have always devoted yourself. Wherefore if, as you say, you have also devoted your attention to this science, or craft, as it may be called, I am very grateful to Laelius ; for I hope that what you tell us will be far more profitable than anything contained in the treatises of the Greeks.

Scipio. You are setting very great expectations on what I shall say—a heavy burden to one who is about to discuss matters of such importance.

Philus. However great our expectations may be, you will still surpass them as usual ; for there is no danger that you will lack eloquence in discussing such a topic as the State.

38 XXIV. Hic Scipio : Faciam, quod vultis, ut potero,
et iam[1] ingrediar in disputationem ea lege, qua
credo omnibus in rebus disserendis utendum esse,
si errorem velis tollere, ut eius rei, de qua quae-
retur, si nomen quod sit conveniat, explicetur, quid
declaretur eo nomine ; quod si convenerit, tum
demum decebit ingredi in sermonem ; numquam
enim, quale sit illud, de quo disputabitur, intellegi
poterit, nisi, quid sit, fuerit intellectum prius.
quare, quoniam de re publica quaerimus, hoc primum
videamus, quid sit id ipsum, quod quaerimus.

Cum adprobavisset Laelius, Nec vero, inquit
Africanus, ita disseram de re tam inlustri tamque
nota, ut ad illa elementa revolvar, quibus uti docti
homines his in rebus solent, ut a prima congressione
maris et feminae, deinde a progenie et cognatione
ordiar verbisque, quid sit et quot modis[2] quidque
dicatur, definiam saepius ; apud prudentes enim
homines et in maxima re publica summa cum gloria
belli domique versatos cum loquar, non committam,
ut sit[3] inlustrior illa ipsa res, de qua disputem,
quam oratio mea ; nec enim hoc suscepi, ut tamquam magister persequerer omnia, neque hoc pol-
liceor me effecturum, ut ne qua particula in hoc
sermone praetermissa sit.

Tum Laelius : Ego vero istud ipsum genus
orationis, quod polliceris, expecto.

---

[1] *et iam* Halm ; *etiam* V ; *iam* is commonly omitted.
[2] *quo modis* Mai ; *commodis* V.
[3] *ut sit* V ; *ut non sit* Mueller.

---

[1] This seems to mean : "As the nature of a commonwealth
is practically quite clear to my present audience. I shall not
becloud the subject with abstruse and obscure definitions."

XXIV. *Scipio.* I will do as you wish, as well as I can, and shall at once begin my discussion, following the rule which, I think, ought always to be observed in the exposition of a subject if one wishes to avoid confusion ; that is, that if the name of a subject is agreed upon, the meaning of this name should first be explained. Not until this meaning is agreed upon should the actual discussion be begun ; for the qualities of the thing to be discussed can never be understood unless one understands first exactly what the thing itself is. Therefore, since the commonwealth is the subject of our investigation, let us first consider exactly what it is that we are investigating.

As Laelius approved of this, Africanus continued as follows : But naturally, in taking up a topic so familiar and well known, I shall not go all the way back to its original elements, as learned men usually do in treating this subject, and begin with the first union of male and female, the birth of offspring, and the origin of kinship; nor shall I give repeated definitions of exactly what the subject of discussion is, how many forms of it exist, or what different names are given to it. For, as I am speaking to intelligent men who have taken a glorious part, both in the field and at home, in the administration of the greatest of all States, I will not allow the subject of my discussion to be clearer than my discussion itself.[1]   For I have not undertaken the task of making an absolutely complete examination of the topic, as a schoolmaster might, nor do I promise that no single point will be omitted in my discussion of it.

Laelius. For my part, I am looking forward to exactly the kind of discussion you promise.

63

39   XXV. Est igitur, inquit Africanus, res publica res populi, populus autem non omnis hominum coetus quoquo modo congregatus, sed coetus multitudinis iuris consensu et utilitatis communione sociatus. eius autem prima causa coëundi est non tam inbecillitas quam naturalis quaedam hominum quasi congregatio ; non est enim singulare nec solivagum genus hoc, sed ita generatum, ut ne in omnium quidem rerum adfluentibus copiis . . .[1]

[Desiderantur paginae duae.]

40   . . . Brevi multitudo dispersa atque vaga concordia civitas facta erat . . . (*Augustinus ep.* 138. 10 *T.* 11 *p.* 414 *Ben.*)

41   XXVI. . . . quaedam[2] quasi semina, neque reliquarum virtutum nec ipsius rei publicae reperiatur ulla institutio. hi coetus igitur hac, de qua exposui, causa instituti sedem primum certo loco domiciliorum causa constituerunt ; quam cum locis manuque saepsissent, eius modi coniunctionem tectorum oppidum vel urbem appellaverunt delubris distinctam spatiisque communibus. omnis ergo populus, qui est talis coetus multitudinis, qualem exposui, omnis civitas, quae est constitutio populi, omnis res publica, quae, ut dixi, populi res est, consilio quodam regenda est,

---

[1] *adfluentibus copiis* . . . Klotz ; *affluen* . . . V.
[2] . . . *dam* V.

---

[1] *i.e.*, *res publica* (public thing or property) is the same as *res populi* (thing or property of a people).
[2] Compare Aristotle, *Politics* I, 1253 A : " Man is by nature a political animal."

XXV. *Scipio.* Well, then, a commonwealth is the property of a people.[1] But a people is not any collection of human beings brought together in any sort of way, but an assemblage of people in large numbers associated in an agreement with respect to justice and a partnership for the common good. The first cause of such an association is not so much the weakness of the individual as a certain social spirit which nature has implanted in man.[2] For man is not a solitary or unsocial creature, but born with such a nature that not even under conditions of great prosperity of every sort [is he willing to be isolated from his fellow men.] . . .

About fifteen lines are lost. The following fragment may be part of the missing passage.

. . . In a short time a scattered and wandering multitude had become a body of citizens by mutual agreement. . . .

XXVI. . . . certain seeds, as we may call them, for [otherwise] no source for the other virtues nor for the State itself could be discovered. Such an assemblage of men, therefore, originating for the reason I have mentioned, established itself in a definite place, at first in order to provide dwellings; and this place being fortified by its natural situation and by their labours, they called such a collection of dwellings a town or city, and provided it with shrines and gathering places which were common property. Therefore every people, which is such a gathering of large numbers as I have described, every city, which is an orderly settlement of a people, every commonwealth, which, as I said, is "the property of a people," must be governed by

ut diuturna sit. id autem consilium primum semper
ad eam causam referendum est, quae causa genuit
42 civitatem. deinde aut uni tribuendum est aut
delectis [1] quibusdam aut suscipiendum est multi-
tudini atque omnibus. quare [2] cum penes unum
est omnium summa rerum, regem illum unum vocamus et regnum eius rei publicae statum. cum autem
est penes delectos, tum illa civitas optimatium
arbitrio regi dicitur. illa autem est civitas popularis
(sic enim appellant), in qua in populo sunt omnia.
atque horum trium generum quodvis, si teneat illud
vinclum, quod primum homines inter se rei publicae
societate devinxit, non perfectum illud quidem
neque mea sententia optimum, sed tolerabile tamen,
ut aliud alio [3] possit esse praestantius. nam vel rex
aequus ac sapiens vel delecti ac principes cives vel
ipse populus, quamquam id est minime probandum,
tamen nullis interiectis iniquitatibus aut cupiditatibus posse videtur aliquo esse non incerto statu.

43   XXVII. Sed et in regnis nimis expertes sunt
ceteri communis iuris et consilii, et in optimatium
dominatu vix particeps libertatis potest esse multitudo, cum omni consilio communi ac potestate
careat, et cum omnia per populum geruntur quamvis
iustum atque moderatum, tamen ipsa aequabilitas
est iniqua, cum habet nullos gradus diguitatis.

[1] *aut delectis* V²; *adlectis* V¹.
[2] *quare* V²; omitted V¹.
[3] *ut aliud alio* Orelli; *et aliut alio* V.

some deliberative body if it is to be permanent. And this deliberative body must, in the first place, always owe its beginning to the same cause as that which produced the State itself. In the second place, this function must either be granted to one man, or to certain selected citizens, or must be assumed by the whole body of citizens. And so when the supreme authority is in the hands of one man, we call him a king, and the form of this State a kingship. When selected citizens hold this power, we say that the State is ruled by an aristocracy. But a popular government (for so it is called) exists when all the power is in the hands of the people. And any one of these three forms of government (if only the bond which originally joined the citizens together in the partnership of the State holds fast), though not perfect or in my opinion the best, is tolerable, though one of them may be superior to another. For either a just and wise king, or a select number of leading citizens, or even the people itself, though this is the least commendable type, can nevertheless, as it seems, form a government that is not unstable, provided that no elements of injustice or greed are mingled with it.

XXVII. But in kingships the subjects have too small a share in the administration of justice and in deliberation; and in aristocracies the masses can hardly have their share of liberty, since they are entirely excluded from deliberation for the common weal and from power; and when all the power is in the people's hands, even though they exercise it with justice and moderation, yet the resulting equality itself is inequitable, since it allows no distinctions in rank. Therefore, even though the

67

itaque si Cyrus ille Perses iustissimus fuit sapientissimusque rex, tamen mihi populi res (ea enim est, ut dixi antea, publica) non maxime expetenda fuisse illa videtur, cum regeretur unius nutu ac modo.[1] si Massilienses, nostri clientes, per delectos et principes cives summa iustitia reguntur, inest tamen in ea condicione populi similitudo quaedam servitutis. si Athenienses quibusdam temporibus sublato Areopago nihil nisi populi scitis ac decretis agebant, quoniam distinctos dignitatis gradus non habebant, non tenebat ornatum suum civitas.

44 XXVIII. Atque hoc loquor de tribus his generibus rerum publicarum non turbatis atque permixtis, sed suum statum tenentibus. quae genera primum sunt in iis singula vitiis, quae ante dixi, deinde habent perniciosa alia vitia; nullum est enim genus illarum rerum publicarum, quod non habeat iter ad finitimum quoddam malum praeceps ac lubricum. nam illi regi, ut eum potissimum nominem, tolerabili aut, si voltis, etiam amabili, Cyro, subest ad inmutandi animi licentiam crudelissimus ille Phalaris, cuius in similıtudinem dominatus unius proclivi cursu et facile delabitur. illi autem Massiliensium paucorum et principum administrationi civitatis finitimus est, qui fuit quodam tempore apud Athenienses triginta virorum[2] consensus et factio.

---

[1] *nutu ac modo.* *si* Orelli; *nutu. ac modo si* is the common punctuation. Mueller suggests *motu* or *voltu* to replace *modo*.

[2] *virorum* supplied by Mai; omitted in V.

---

[1] The so-called "Thirty Tyrants" (404—403 B.C.).

Persian Cyrus was the most just and wisest of kings, that form of government does not seem to me the most desirable, since "the property of the people" (for that is what a commonwealth is, as I have said) is administered at the nod and caprice of one man; even though the Massilians, now under our protection, are ruled with the greatest justice by a select number of their leading citizens, such a situation is nevertheless to some extent like slavery for a people; and even though the Athenians at certain periods, after they had deprived the Areopagus of its power, succeeded in carrying on all their public business by the resolutions and decrees of the people, their State, because it had no definite distinctions in rank, could not maintain its fair renown.

XXVIII. I am now speaking of these three forms of government, not when they are confused and mingled with one another, but when they retain their appropriate character. All of them are, in the first place, subject each to the faults I have mentioned, and they suffer from other dangerous faults in addition: for before every one of them lies a slippery and precipitous path leading to a certain depraved form that is a close neighbour to it. For underneath the tolerable, or, if you like, the lovable King Cyrus (to cite him as a pre-eminent example) lies the utterly cruel Phalaris, impelling him to an arbitrary change of character; for the absolute rule of one man will easily and quickly degenerate into a tyranny like his. And a close neighbour to the excellent Massilian government, conducted by a few leading citizens, is such a partisan combination of thirty men as once ruled Athens.[1] And as for the

iam Atheniensium populi potestatem omnium rerum
ipsi, ne alios requiramus, ad furorem multitudinis
licentiamque conversam pesti . . .

[Desiderantur paginae duae.]

45 XXIX. . . . deterrimus et ex hac vel optimatium vel factiosa tyrannica illa vel regia vel
etiam persaepe popularis, itemque ex ea genus
aliquod ecflorescere ex illis, quae ante dixi, solet,
mirique sunt orbes et quasi circumitus in rebus
publicis commutationum et vicissitudinum: quos
cum cognosse sapientis est, tum vero prospicere
inpendentis in gubernanda re publica moderantem
cursum atque in sua potestate retinentem magni
cuiusdam civis et divini paene est viri. itaque
quartum quoddam genus rei publicae maxime probandum esse sentio, quod est ex his, quae prima
dixi, moderatum et permixtum tribus.

46 XXX. Hic Laelius: Scio tibi ita placere, Africane;
saepe enim ex te audivi; sed tamen, nisi molestum
est, ex tribus istis modis rerum publicarum velim
scire quod optimum iudices. nam vel profuerit
aliquod ad cog. . .

[Desiderantur paginae duae.]

47 XXXI. . . . et talis est quaeque res publica,
qualis eius aut natura aut voluntas, qui illam regit

---

[1] Compare Aristotle, *Politics* III, 1279 A–B.

absolute power of the Athenian people—not to seek
other examples of popular government—when it
changed into the fury and licence of a mob . . .

About fifteen lines are lost. The first two lines of what
follows (to *itemque*) appear to be corrupt, and cannot be
translated.

XXIX. . . . and likewise some other form usually
arises from those I have mentioned, and remarkable
indeed are the periodical revolutions and circular
courses followed by the constant changes and
sequences in governmental forms.[1] A wise man
should be acquainted with these changes, but it calls
for great citizens and for a man of almost divine
powers to foresee them when they threaten, and,
while holding the reins of government, to direct
their courses and keep them under his control.
Therefore I consider a fourth form of government
the most commendable—that form which is a well-
regulated mixture of the three which I mentioned
at first.

XXX. *Laelius.* I know that is your opinion, Africanus, for I have often heard you say so. Nevertheless,
if it will not give you too much trouble, I should like
to know which you consider the best of the three
forms of government of which you have been
speaking For it might help us somewhat to understand . . .

About fifteen lines are lost. In what follows Scipio is
evidently stating the common opinion that liberty is impossible in a monarchy or an aristocracy.

XXXI. *Scipio.* . . . and every State is such as its
ruler's character and will make it. Hence liberty
has no dwelling-place in any State except that in

71

itaque nulla alia in civitate, nisi in qua populi
potestas summa est, ullum domicilium libertas
habet; qua quidem certe nihil potest esse dulcius,
et quae, si aequa non est, ne libertas quidem est.
qui autem aequa potest esse, omitto dicere in
regno, ubi ne obscura quidem est aut dubia servitus,
sed in istis civitatibus, in quibus verbo sunt liberi
omnes? ferunt enim suffragia, mandant inperia,
magistratus, ambiuntur, rogantur, sed ea dant,[1]
quae, etiamsi nolint, danda sint, et quae ipsi non
habent, unde alii petunt; sunt enim expertes
imperii, consilii publici, iudicii delectorum iudicum,
quae familiarum vetustatibus aut pecuniis ponde-
rantur. in libero autem populo, ut Rhodii sunt,
ut Athenienses,[2] nemo est civium, qui. . .

[*Desiderantur paginae duae.*]

48   XXXII. . . . populo aliquis unus pluresve di-
vitiores opulentioresque extitissent, tum ex eorum
fastidio et superbia nata esse commemorant ceden-
tibus ignavis et inbecillis et adrogantiae divitum
succumbentibus. si vero ius suum populi teneant,
negant quicquam esse praestantius, liberius, beatius,
quippe qui domini sint legum, iudiciorum, belli,

---

[1] *dant, quae* Mueller; *dant magis quae* V.
[2] *ut Rhodii sunt, ut Athenienses* Pascal; *ut Rhodii ut Rhodii
Athenienses* V[1]; *ut Rhodi, ut Athenis* V[2].

which the people's power is the greatest, and surely nothing can be sweeter than liberty; but if it is not the same for all, it does not deserve the name of liberty. And how can it be the same for all, I will not say in a kingdom, where there is no obscurity or doubt about the slavery of the subject, but even in States where everyone is ostensibly free? I mean States in which the people vote, elect commanders and officials, are canvassed for their votes, and have bills proposed to them, but really grant only what they would have to grant even if they were unwilling to do so, and are asked to give to others what they do not possess themselves. For they have no share in the governing power, in the deliberative function, or in the courts, over which selected judges preside, for those privileges are granted on the basis of birth or wealth. But in a free nation, such as the Rhodians or the Athenians, there is not one of the citizens who [may not hold the offices of State and take an active part in the government.] . . .

About fifteen lines are lost. In what follows Scipio evidently continues his summing up of the common arguments in favour of democratic government.

XXXII. . . . [Our authorities] say [that] when one person or a few stand out from the crowd as richer and more prosperous, then, as a result of the haughty and arrogant behaviour of these, there arises [a government of one or a few], the cowardly and weak giving way and bowing down to the pride of wealth. But if the people would maintain their rights, they say that no form of government would be superior, either in liberty or happiness, for they themselves would be masters of the laws and the courts, of war

pacis, foederum, capitis unius cuiusque, pecuniae.
hanc unam rite rem publicam, id est rem populi,
appellari putant. itaque et a regum et a patrum
dominatione solere in libertatem rem populi vin-
dicari, non ex liberis populis reges requiri aut
49 potestatem atque opes optimatium. et vero negant
oportere indomiti populi vitio genus hoc totum
liberi populi repudiari, concordi populo et omnia
referente ad incolumitatem et ad libertatem suam
nihil esse inmutabilius, nihil firmius; facillimam
autem in ea re publica esse concordiam, in qua
idem conducat omnibus; ex utilitatis varietatibus,
cum aliis aliud expediat, nasci discordias; itaque,
cum patres rerum potirentur, numquam constitisse
civitatis statum; multo iam id in regnis minus,
quorum, ut ait Ennius, "nulla[1] sancta societas nec
fides est." quare cum lex sit civilis societatis vinculum, ius autem legis aequale, quo iure societas
civium teneri potest, cum par non sit condicio
civium? si enim pecunias aequari non placet, si
ingenia omnium paria esse non possunt, iura certe
paria debent esse eorum inter se, qui sunt cives in

---

[1] *nulla [regni] sancta* is commonly read ; *nulla regni sancta*
V ; Pascal suggests *quoniam, ut ait Ennius, nulla regni
sancta.*

---

[1] Probably from one of Ennius' dramas.

and peace, of international agreements, and of every citizen's life and property; this government alone, they believe, can rightly be called a commonwealth, that is, "the property of the people." And it is for that reason, they say, that "the property of the people" is often liberated from the domination of kings or senators, while free peoples do not seek kings or the power and wealth of aristocracies. And indeed they claim that this free popular government ought not to be entirely rejected on account of the excesses of an unbridled mob, for, according to them, when a sovereign people is pervaded by a spirit of harmony and tests every measure by the standard of their own safety and liberty, no form of government is less subject to change or more stable. And they insist that harmony is very easily obtainable in a State where the interests of all are the same, for discord arises from conflicting interests, where different measures are advantageous to different citizens. Therefore they maintain that when a senate has been supreme, the State has never had a stable government, and that such stability is less attainable by far in kingdoms, in which, as Ennius says,

No sacred partnership or honour is.[1]

Therefore, since law is the bond which unites the civic association, and the justice enforced by law is the same for all, by what justice can an association of citizens be held together when there is no equality among the citizens? For if we cannot agree to equalize men's wealth, and equality of innate ability is impossible, the legal rights at least of those who are citizens of the same commonwealth ought to

75

eadem re publica. quid est enim civitas nisi iuris
societas? . . .

[*Desiderantur paginae duae.*]

50 XXXIII. . . . Ceteras vero res publicas ne appel-
landas quidem putant iis nominibus, quibus illae
sese appellari velint. cur enim regem appellem Iovis
optimi nomine hominem dominandi cupidum aut
imperii singularis, populo oppresso dominantem, non
tyrannum potius? tam enim esse clemens tyrannus
quam[1] inportunus potest; ut hoc populorum intersit,
utrum comi domino an aspero serviant; quin serviant quidem, fieri non potest. quo autem modo
adsequi poterat Lacedaemo illa tum, cum praestare
putabatur disciplina rei publicae, ut bonis uteretur
iustisque regibus, cum esset habendus rex, quicumque genere regio natus esset? nam optimatis
quidem quis ferat, qui non populi concessu, sed suis
comitiis hoc sibi nomen adrogaverunt? qui enim
iudicatur iste optimus? doctrina, artibus, studiis. . .

[*Desiderantur paginae quattuor.*]

51 XXXIV. . . . si fortuito id faciet, tam cito
evertetur quam navis, si e vectoribus sorte ductus

---

[1] *quam [rex] importunus* Madvig; *quam rex importunus* V.

---

[1] *i.e.*, chooses its rulers by lot, as had been done in Athens.

be equal.   For what is a State except an association or partnership in justice ? . . .

About fifteen lines are lost.   There is no change of topic.

XXXIII. . . . Indeed they think that States of the other kinds have no right at all to the names which they arrogate to themselves.   For why should I give the name of king, the title of Jupiter the Best, to a man who is greedy for personal power and absolute authority, a man who lords it over an oppressed people?   Should I not rather call him tyrant?   For tyrants may be merciful as well as oppressive ; so that the only difference between the nations governed by these rulers is that between the slaves of a kind and those of a cruel master; for in any case the subjects must be slaves.   And how could Sparta, at the time when the mode of life inculcated by her constitution was considered so excellent, be assured of always having good and just kings, when a person of any sort, if he was born of the royal family, had to be accepted as king?   As to aristocrats, who could tolerate men that have claimed the title without the people's acquiescence, but merely by their own will?   For how is a man adjudged to be "the best"?   On the basis of knowledge, skill, learning, [and similar qualities surely, not because of his own desire to possess the title !] . . .

About thirty lines are lost.   At the end of the gap, Scipio is criticizing the arguments for democracy, and stating those for aristocracy.

XXXIV. . . . If [the State] leaves [the selection of its rulers] to chance,[1] it will be as quickly over-turned as a ship whose pilot should be chosen by

ad gubernacula accesserit. quodsi liber populus deliget, quibus se committat, deligetque, si modo salvus esse vult, optimum quemque, certe in optimorum consiliis posita est civitatium salus, praesertim cum hoc natura tulerit, non solum ut summi virtute et animo praeessent inbecillioribus, sed ut hi etiam parere summis vellent.[1]

Verum hunc optimum statum pravis hominum opinionibus eversum esse dicunt, qui ignoratione virtutis, quae cum in paucis est, tum a paucis iudicatur et cernitur, opulentos homines et copiosos, tum genere nobili natos esse optimos putant. hoc errore vulgi cum rem publicam opes paucorum, non virtutes tenere coeperunt, nomen illi principes optimatium mordicus tenent, re autem car nt.[2] nam divitiae, nomen, opes vacuae consilio et vivendi atque aliis imperandi modo dedecoris plenae sunt et insolentis superbiae, nec ulla deformior species est civitatis quam illa, in qua opulentissimi optimi

52 putantur. virtute vero gubernante rem publicam quid potest esse praeclarius, cum is, qui inperat aliis, servit ipse nulli cupiditati, cum, quas ad res civis instituit et vocat, eas omnis complexus est ipse nec leges inponit populo, quibus ipse non pareat, sed suam vitam ut legem praefert suis civibus ?

---

[1] *vellent* Creuzer ; *velint* V, Mueller.
[2] *carent [eo nomine].* nam Madvig ; *carent eo nomine nam* V.

lot from among the passengers.   But if a free
people chooses the men to whom it is to entrust its
fortunes, and, since it desires its own safety, chooses
the best men, then certainly the safety of the State
depends upon the wisdom of its best men, especially
since Nature has provided not only that those men
who are superior in virtue and in spirit should rule
the weaker, but also that the weaker should be
willing to obey the stronger.

But they claim that this ideal form of State has
been rejected on account of the false notions of men,
who, through their ignorance of virtue—for just as
virtue is possessed by only a few, so it can be
distinguished and perceived by only a few—think
that the best men are those who are rich, prosperous,
or born of famous families.   For when, on account
of this mistaken notion of the common people, the
State begins to be ruled by the riches, instead of
the virtue, of a few men, these rulers tenaciously
retain the title, though they do not possess the
character, of the "best."   For riches, names, and
power, when they lack wisdom and the knowledge
of how to live and to rule over others, are full of
dishonour and insolent pride, nor is there any more
depraved type of State than that in which the
richest are accounted the best.   But what can be
nobler than the government of the State by virtue?
For then the man who rules others is not himself a
slave to any passion, but has already acquired for
himself all those qualities to which he is training and
summoning his fellows.   Such a man imposes no laws
upon the people that he does not obey himself, but
puts his own life before his fellow-citizens as their
law.   If a single individual of this character could

qui si unus satis omnia consequi posset, nihil opus
esset pluribus; si universi videre optimum et in
eo consentire possent, nemo delectos principes
quaereret. difficultas ineundi consilii rem a rege
ad plures, error et temeritas populorum a multitudine ad paucos transtulit. sic inter infirmitatem
unius temeritatemque multorum medium optimates
possederunt locum, quo nihil potest esse moderatius;
quibus rem publicam tuentibus beatissimos esse
populos necesse est vacuos omni cura et cogitatione
aliis permisso otio suo, quibus id tuendum est neque
committendum, ut sua commoda populus neglegi
53 a principibus putet. nam aequabilitas quidem iuris,
quam amplexantur liberi populi, neque servari potest
(ipsi enim populi, quamvis soluti ecfrenatique sint,
praecipue multis multa tribuunt, et est in ipsis
magnus dilectus hominum et dignitatum), eaque,
quae appellatur aequabilitas, iniquissima est. cum
enim par habetur honos summis et infimis, qui sint
in omni populo necesse est, ipsa aequitas iniquissima est; quod in iis civitatibus, quae ab optimis
reguntur, accidere non potest. haec fere, Laeli, et
quaedam eiusdem generis ab iis, qui eam formam
rei publicae maxime laudant, disputari solent.

54 XXXV. Tum Laelius: Quid tu, inquit, Scipio? e
tribus istis quod maxime probas?

order all things properly in a State, there would be
no need of more than one ruler; or if the citizens as
a body could see what was best and agree upon it,
no one would desire a selected group of rulers. It
has been the difficulty of formulating policies that
has transferred the power from a king to a larger
number; and the perversity and rashness of popular
assemblies that have transferred it from the many to
the few. Thus, between the weakness of a single
ruler and the rashness of the many, aristocracies have
occupied that intermediate position which represents
the utmost moderation; and in a State ruled by
its best men, the citizens must necessarily enjoy the
greatest happiness, being freed from all cares and
worries, when once they have entrusted the preservation of their tranquillity to others, whose duty it
is to guard it vigilantly and never to allow the people
to think that their interests are being neglected by
their rulers. For that equality of legal rights of
which free peoples are so fond cannot be maintained
(for the people themselves, though free and un-
restrained, give very many special powers to many
individuals, and create great distinctions among men
and the honours granted to them), and what is called
equality is really most inequitable. For when equal
honour is given to the highest and the lowest—for
men of both types must exist in every nation—then
this very "fairness" is most unfair; but this cannot
happen in States ruled by their best citizens. These
arguments and others like them, Laelius, are approximately those which are advanced by men who consider
this form of government the best.

XXXV. *Laelius.* But what about yourself, Scipio?
Which of these three forms do you consider the best?

S. Recte quaeris, quod maxime e tribus, quoniam eorum nullum ipsum per se separatim probo anteponoque singulis illud, quod conflatum fuerit ex omnibus. Sed si unum ac simplex probandum sit, regium probem . . . . pri . . . . in . . . .[1] hoc loco appellatur, occurrit nomen quasi patrium regis, ut ex se natis, ita consulentis suis civibus et eos conservantis studiosius quam . . . . . entis . . . . tem . . . . is . . . . tibus . . . .

55 uos[2] sustentari unius optimi et summi viri diligentia. adsunt optimates, qui se melius hoc idem facere profiteantur plusque fore dicant in pluribus consilii quam in uno et eandem tamen aequitatem et fidem. ecce autem maxima voce clamat populus neque se uni neque paucis velle parere; libertate ne feris quidem quicquam esse dulcius; hac omnes carere, sive regi sive optimatibus serviant. ita caritate nos capiunt reges, consilio optimates, libertate populi, ut in comparando difficile ad eligendum sit, quid maxime velis.

L. Credo, inquit, sed expediri, quae restant, vix poterunt, si hoc incohatum reliqueris.

56 XXXVI. *S.* Imitemur[3] ergo Aratum, qui magnis de rebus dicere exordiens a Iove incipiendum putat.

---

[1] *Sed si unum ac simplex . . . bandum . . . regium . . . bem . . . pri . . . in* V; the additions are due to Mai.

[2] *et eos con-ervantis stu . . . ius quam . . . . entis . . . tem . . . is . . . tibus . . . vos* V; the additions are due to Mai.

[3] *imitemur* V[2]; *imitabor* V[1], Halm, etc.

---

[1] The text of this passage is fragmentary and obscure, but it evidently contains a brief statement of the advantages of the kingship.

Scipio. You are right to ask which I consider the best of the three, for I do not approve of any of them when employed by itself, and consider the form which is a combination of all them superior to any single one of them. But if I were compelled to approve one single unmixed form, [I might choose] the kingship . . . the name of king seems like that of father to us, since the king provides for the citizens as if they were his own children, and is more eager to protect them than [1] . . . to be sustained by the care of one man who is the most virtuous and most eminent. But here are the aristocrats, with the claim that they can do this more effectively, and that there will be more wisdom in the counsels of several than in those of one man, and an equal amount of fairness and scrupulousness. And here also are the people, shouting with a loud voice that they are willing to obey neither one nor a few, that nothing is sweeter than liberty even to wild beasts, and that all who are slaves, whether to a king or to an aristocracy, are deprived of liberty. Thus kings attract us by our affection for them, aristocracies by their wisdom, and popular governments by their freedom, so that in comparing them it is difficult to say which one prefers.

Laelius. No doubt; but it will be almost impossible to solve the problems that follow, if you abandon this one before reaching a solution.

XXXVI. *Scipio.* Then let us imitate Aratus,[2] who, in beginning the treatment of lofty subjects, thought he must commence with Jupiter.

---

[2] See section 22. The first words of the poem are: Ἐκ Διὸς ἀρχώμεσθα.

L. Quo Iove? aut quid habet illius carminis simile haec oratio?

S. Tantum, inquit, ut rite ab eo dicendi principia capiamus, quem unum omnium deorum et hominum regem esse omnes docti indoctique pariter[1] consentiunt.

Quid? inquit Laelius.

Et ille: Quid censes, nisi quod est ante oculos? sive haec ad utilitatem vitae constituta sunt a principibus rerum publicarum, ut rex putaretur unus esse in caelo, qui nutu, ut ait Homerus, totum Olympum converteret idemque et rex et pater haberetur omnium, magna auctoritas est multique testes, siquidem omnis multos appellari placet, ita consensisse gentes decretis videlicet principum, nihil esse rege melius, quoniam deos omnis censent unius regi numine; sive haec in errore inperitorum posita esse et fabularum similia didicimus, audiamus communis quasi doctores eruditorum hominum, qui tamquam oculis illa viderunt, quae nos vix audiendo cognoscimus.

Quinam, inquit Laelius, isti sunt?

Et ille: Qui natura omnium rerum pervestiganda senserunt omnem hunc mundum mente . . .

[*Desiderantur paginae quattuor.*]

---

[1] *indoctique pariter consentiunt* Orelli; *indoctique expoliri consentiunt* V; *indoctique consentiunt* Osann.

---

[1] *e.g.*, Iliad I, 527–530:

ἦ καὶ κυανέῃσιν ἐπ' ὀφρύσι νεῦσε Κρονίων·
ἀμβρόσιαι δ' ἄρα χαῖται ἐπερρώσαντο ἄνακτος
κρατὸς ἀπ' ἀθανάτοιο, μέγαν δ' ἐλέλιξεν Ὄλυμπον.

Laelius. With Jupiter? And what similarity has Aratus' poem with our present discussion?

Scipio. Only this, that it is proper for us to begin our discussion with that god who alone is admitted by everyone, learned and unlearned alike, to be king of all gods and men.

Laelius. Why?

Scipio. Why do you imagine, except for the reason that lies before your eyes? It may be that the rulers of States have introduced, for its usefulness in practical life, the belief that there is one king in heaven, who moves all Olympus with a nod, as Homer says,[1] and is both king and father of all; in that case we have an excellent precedent and the testimony of many witnesses—if all can be called "many"—to the fact that the nations have agreed (to wit, by the decisions of their rulers) that nothing is better than a king, since, as they believe, all the gods are ruled by the authority of one.[2] But if, on the other hand, we have become convinced that these beliefs have their origin in the false ideas of the ignorant and are to be classed as fables, then let us listen to those who may be called the teachers of educated men, to those who, as we may say, have seen with their own eyes things of which we hardly get an inkling through our ears.

Laelius. What men are these?

Scipio. Those who by searching out the nature of all things have come to realize that the whole universe [is ruled] by [a single] mind . . .

About thirty lines are lost. At the end of the gap, Scipio is still presenting the arguments in favour of monarchy.

---

[2] Compare the argument in Isocrates, *Nicocles* 26.

58   XXXVII. . . . Sed, si vis, Laeli, dabo tibi testes[1] nec nimis antiquos nec ullo modo barbaros.

L. Istos, inquit, volo.

S. Videsne igitur minus quadringentorum annorum esse hanc urbem, ut sine regibus sit?

L. Vero minus.

S. Quid ergo? haec quadringentorum annorum aetas ut urbis et civitatis num valde longa est?

L. Ista vero, inquit, adulta vix.

S. Ergo his annis quadringentis Romae rex erat?

L. Et superbus quidem.

S. Quid supra?

L. Iustissimus, et deinceps retro usque ad Romulum, qui ab hoc tempore anno sescentesimo rex erat.

S. Ergo ne iste quidem pervetus?

L. Minime ac prope senescente iam Graecia.

S. Cedo, num, Scipio, barbarorum Romulus rex fuit?

L. Si, ut Graeci dicunt omnis aut Graios esse aut barbaros, vereor, ne barbarorum rex fuerit; sin id nomen moribus dandum est, non linguis, non Graecos minus barbaros quam Romanos puto.

Et Scipio: Atqui ad hoc, de quo agitur, non quaerimus gentem, ingenia quaerimus. si enim et prudentes homines et non veteres reges habere voluerunt, utor neque perantiquis neque inhumanis ac feris testibus.

---

    [1] Tarquinius Superbus.   [2] Servius Tullius.

XXXVII. *Scipio.* . . . But, if you like, Laelius, I will bring before you witnesses who are neither so very ancient nor by any means barbarians.

Laelius. It is such witnesses that I desire.

Scipio. Are you aware that it is less than four hundred years since this city was ruled by kings?

Laelius. It is certainly less than that.

Scipio. Well, four hundred years is not very long, is it, in the life of a city or State?

Laelius. Hardly enough to bring it to maturity.

Scipio. Then there was a king at Rome less than four hundred years ago?

Laelius. Yes, and a proud one.[1]

Scipio. And who preceded him?

Laelius. A very just king,[2] and the line reaches all the way back to Romulus, who reigned six hundred years ago.

Scipio. Then even he is not very remote from us?

Laelius. Not at all; for Greece was already approaching old age in his time.

Scipio. Now tell me: was Romulus a king of barbarians?

Laelius. If, as the Greeks say, all men are either Greeks or barbarians, I am afraid he was; but if that name ought to be applied on the basis of men's manners rather than their language, I do not consider the Greeks less barbarous than the Romans.

Scipio. Yet for the purposes of our present subject we consider only character, not race. For if they were sensible men and lived at a period not very remote, who desired to be ruled by kings, then the witnesses I am bringing forward are neither of very ancient date nor uncivilized savages.

59   XXXVIII. Tum Laelius: Video te, Scipio, testi-
moniis satis instructum, sed apud me, ut apud bonum
iudicem, argumenta plus quam testes valent.

Tum Scipio: Utere igitur argumento, Laeli, tute
ipse sensus tui.

Cuius, inquit ille, sensus?

S. Si quando, si forte,[1] tibi visus es irasci alicui.

L. Ego vero saepius, quam vellem.

S. Quid? tum, cum tu es iratus, permittis illi
iracundiae dominatum animi tui?

L. Non mehercule, inquit, sed imitor Archytam
illum Tarentinum, qui cum ad villam venisset et
omnia aliter offendisset ac iusserat, "A te infelicem,"
inquit vilico, "quem necassem iam verberibus, nisi
iratus essem."

60   Optime, inquit Scipio. ergo Archytas iracundiam
videlicet dissidentem a ratione seditionem quandam
animi vere ducebat, atque eam consilio sedari volebat;
adde avaritiam, adde imperii, adde gloriae cupiditatem, adde libidines; et illud vides, si in animis
hominum regale imperium sit, unius fore dominatum,
consilii scilicet (ea est enim animi pars optima),
consilio autem dominante nullum esse libidinibus,
nullum irae, nullum temeritati locum.

L. Sic, inquit, est.

S. Probas igitur animum ita adfectum?

---

[1] *si forte* deleted by Steinacher et al.

XXXVIII. *Laelius.* I see that you are plentifully supplied with witnesses, Scipio, but to me, as to any good judge, demonstrations are more convincing than the testimony of witnesses.

Scipio. Then, Laelius, make use of an argument from your own feelings.

Laelius. What feelings are those?

Scipio. Those which you have experienced in case, by any chance, you have ever been conscious of being angry with anyone.

Laelius. I have been in that state, and oftener than I could wish.

Scipio. Well, when you are angry, do you allow your anger to rule your mind?

Laelius. Certainly not, but I imitate the famous Archytas of Tarentum, who, when he found, upon arriving at his country place, that all his orders had been disobeyed, said to his superintendent: "You are at fault, wretched man, and I should have had you flogged to death ere this were I not angry!"

Scipio. Excellent! Then Archytas clearly regarded anger, when it disagreed with calm judgment, as a sort of rebellion within the mind, which he desired should be put down by reason. Take as further examples avarice, greed for power and glory, and the passions; you see, if there is any kingly power in the minds of men, it must be the domination of a single element, and this is reason (for that is the best part of the mind), and, if reason holds dominion, there is no room for the passions, for anger, for rash action.

Laelius. That is true.

Scipio. Well then, does a mind so governed meet with your approval?

microcosm vs. macrocosm
mind vs. state
but also
state vs. divine mind

L. Nihil vero, inquit, magis.

S. Ergo non probares, si consilio pulso libidines, quae sunt innumerabiles, iracundiaeve tenerent omnia?

L. Ego vero nihil isto animo, nihil ita animato homine miserius ducerem.

S. Sub regno igitur tibi esse placet omnis animi partes, et eas regi consilio?

L. Mihi vero sic placet.

S. Cur igitur dubitas, quid de re publica sentias? in qua, si in plures translata res sit, intellegi iam licet nullum fore, quod praesit, inperium, quod quidem, nisi unum sit, esse nullum potest.

61 XXXIX. Tum Laelius: Quid, quaeso, interest inter unum et plures, si iustitia est in pluribus?

Et Scipio: Quoniam testibus meis intellexi, Laeli, te non valde moveri, non desinam te uti teste, ut hoc, quod dico, probem.

Me, inquit ille, quonam modo?

S. Quia animum adverti nuper, cum essemus in Formiano, te familiae valde interdicere, ut uni dicto audiens esset.

L. Quippe vilico.

S. Quid? domi pluresne praesunt negotiis tuis?

L. Immo vero unus, inquit.

S. Quid? totam domum num quis alter praeter te regit?

Laelius. Nothing could be better.

Scipio. In that case you would not approve if reason should be dethroned, and our innumerable passions, or our anger, should obtain complete domination?

Laelius. I can think of nothing more wretched than such a mind, or than the man that possesses it.

Scipio. Then you think that the mind should be a kingdom, all of whose parts are to be ruled by reason?

Laelius I certainly do.

Scipio. How then can you be doubtful as to your conclusion about the State? For if the management of a State is committed to more than one, you can see that there will be no authority at all to take command, for unless such authority is a unit, it can amount to nothing.

XXXIX. *Laelius.* But let me ask what difference there is between one and many, if the many possess justice.

Scipio. As I realize that no great impression has been made upon you by my witnesses, I shall continue using you as my witness in order to prove what I say.

Laelius. Me? In what way?

Scipio. A short time ago, when we were at your place at Formiae, I noticed that you gave your people emphatic orders to obey the directions of one person only.

Laelius. Certainly; my superintendent, of course.

Scipio. How about your residence in the city? Are several persons in charge there?

Laelius. Of course not; only one.

Scipio. And no one else but yourself rules your whole household?

L. Minime vero.

S. Quin tu igitur concedis idem in re publica, singulorum dominatus, si modo iusti sint, esse optimos?

L. Adducor, inquit, ut prope modum adsentiar.

62 XL. Et Scipio: Tum magis adsentiare, Laeli, si, ut omittam similitudines, uni gubernatori, uni medico, si digni modo sint iis artibus, rectius esse alteri navem committere, aegrum alteri quam multis, ad maiora pervenero.

L. Quaenam ista sunt?

S. Quid? tu non vides unius inportunitate et superbia Tarquinii nomen huic populo in odium venisse regium?

L. Video vero, inquit.

S. Ergo etiam illud vides, de quo progrediente oratione plura me dicturum puto, Tarquinio exacto mira quadam exultasse populum insolentia libertatis; tum exacti in exilium innocentes, tum bona direpta multorum, tum annui consules, tum demissi populo fasces, tum provocationes omnium rerum, tum secessiones plebei, tum prorsus ita acta pleraque, ut in populo essent omnia.

63 *L.* Est, inquit, ut dicis.

Est vero, inquit Scipio, in pace et otio; licet enim lascivire, dum nihil metuas, ut in navi ac saepe

---

[1] Such comparisons are very common in Plato; for one similar to this, developed in detail, see *Politicus* 298–299.

[2] The bundle of rods (*fasces*) with the axe was a symbol of the highest governmental authority. These rods were carried by attendants (lictors), who lowered them in the presence of an assembly of the people. The axe was not carried within the city.

[3] These events are related in Livy, Book II.

Laelius. Certainly not.

Scipio. Why then will you not admit that in the State likewise, the rule of one man is best, if he be just?

Laelius. I am almost forced to agree with you.

XL. *Scipio.* You will be all the more inclined to agree, Laelius, if, omitting the analogies of the ship and the sick man, more advantageously entrusted to a single pilot and a single physician, if only they are proficient in their professions,[1] I go on to examples of greater importance.

Laelius. What examples are these?

Scipio. Are you not aware that it was the insolence and pride of one man, Tarquinius, that made the title of king odious to our people?

Laelius. Certainly I am aware of it.

Scipio. Then you are also aware of a fact about which I expect to have more to say in the course of my discussion—that when Tarquinius was driven out, the people showed a strange way of rejoicing in their unwonted liberty; then it was that innocent men were driven into exile, then that the property of many citizens was pillaged, that the annual consulship was introduced, that the rods were lowered before the people,[2] that appeals were allowed in cases of every sort, that secessions of the plebeians took place, and that, in a word, almost everything was done to give the people full power in all things.[3]

Laelius. What you say is quite true.

Scipio. Yes, and it is generally true in times of peace and security, for licence is possible as long as one has nothing to fear; as, for example, on board a ship, or frequently in the case of an illness that is

etiam in morbo levi. sed ut ille, qui navigat, cum
subito mare coepit horrescere, et ille aeger ingrave-
scente morbo unius opem inplorat, sic noster populus
in pace et domi imperat et ipsis magistratibus mina-
tur, recusat, appellat, provocat, in bello sic paret ut
regi; valet enim salus plus quam libido. graviori-
bus vero bellis etiam sine collega omne imperium
nostri penes singulos esse voluerunt, quorum ipsum
nomen vim suae [1] potestatis indicat. nam dictator
quidem ab eo appellatur, quia dicitur, sed in nostris
libris vides eum, Laeli, magistrum populi appellari.

L. Video, inquit.

Et Scipio : Sapienter igitur illi veteres. . .

[*Desiderantur paginae duae.*]

64 XLI. . . . iusto quidem rege cum est populus
orbatus, "pectora diu tenet desiderium," sicut ait
Ennius, "post optimi regis obitum";

simul inter

sese sic memorant : " o Romule, Romule die,
qualem te patriae custodem di genuerunt !
o pater, o genitor, o sanguen dis oriundum ! "

non eros nec dominos appellabant eos, quibus iuste
paruerunt, denique ne reges quidem, sed patriae cus-

---

[1] *suae* V ; *summae* Bake.

---

[1] Cicero derives the title *dictator* from *dico*, "to name" or
"to appoint."
[2] The records of the augurs (*libri augurum*). Compare
Seneca, *Epist. Mor.* 108, 31.

trivial. But just as the sailor, when the sea suddenly
grows rough, and the invalid when his illness becomes
severe, both implore the assistance of one man,
so our people, that in times of peace and while
engaged at home wield authority, threaten even
their magistrates, refuse to obey them, and appeal
from one to another or to the people, yet in time of
war yield obedience to their rulers as to a king; for
safety prevails over caprice. Indeed, in wars of more
serious import our people have preferred that all the
power should be granted to one man without a
colleague. And this man's title shows the character
of his power; for though he is commonly called
" dictator " from the fact that he is " named," [1] yet you
know, Laelius, that in our books [2] he is called
" master of the people."

Laelius. I do.

Scipio. Therefore the men of old time [acted]
wisely . . .

About fifteen lines are lost.

XLI. . . . indeed when a people is orphaned by
the loss of a just king, as Ennius says,

> For many a day doth sorrow fill their breasts,
> Whene'er a goodly king hath met his end ;
> In grief one to another thus they speak :
> O Romulus, O Romulus divine,
> A mighty bulwark of our native land
> Wast thou,—sent down from heaven to our need ;
> O sire, O father, blood from gods derived !

Neither " masters " nor " lords " did they call those
men whom they lawfully obeyed, nay, not " kings "
either, but " guardians of the fatherland," " fathers,"

todes, sed patres, sed deos; nec sine causa; quid enim adiungunt?

Tu produxisti nos intra luminis oras.

vitam, honorem, decus sibi datum esse iustitia regis existimabant.[1] mansisset eadem voluntas in eorum posteris, si regum similitudo permansisset, sed vides unius iniustitia concidisse genus illud totum rei publicae.

L. Video vero, inquit, et studeo cursus istos mutationum non magis in nostra quam in omni re publica noscere.

65 XLII. Et Scipio: Est omnino, cum de illo genere rei publicae, quod maxime probo, quae sentio, dixero accuratius mihi dicendum de commutationibus rerum publicarum, etsi minime facile eas in ea re publica futuras puto. sed huius regiae prima et certissima est illa mutatio: cum rex iniustus esse coepit, perit illud ilico genus, et est idem ille tyrannus, deterrimum genus et finitimum optimo; quem si optimates oppresserunt, quod ferme evenit, habet statum res publica de tribus secundarium; est enim quasi regium, id est patrium consilium populo bene consulentium principum. sin per se populus interfecit aut eiecit tyrannum, est moderatior, quoad sentit et sapit, et sua re gesta laetatur tuerique vult per se constitutam rem publicam. si quando aut regi iusto

---

[1] *existimabant* V²; *existimant* V¹, Halm, et al.

---

[1] Both these quotations are probably from Book I of the *Annales* of Ennius.

" gods " ; and not without reason, for what is the next line?

To realms of light thy people hast thou led.[1]

They thought that life, honour, and glory had been granted to them through the justice of their king. And the same good-will toward kings would have abided in their descendants had the true image of kingship abided; but, as you know, it was through the injustice of one man alone that this whole form of government was overthrown.

Laelius. I know it, and am eager to learn the course taken by such changes of government, not merely in our own State, but in all others as well.

XLII. *Scipio.* When I have set forth my ideas in regard to the form of State which I consider the best, I shall have to take up in greater detail those changes to which States are liable, though I think it will not be at all easy for any such changes to take place in the State which I have in mind. But the first and most certain of these changes is the one that takes place in kingships : when the king begins to be unjust, that form of government is immediately at an end, and the king has become a tyrant. This is the worst sort of government, though closely related to the best. If the best men overthrow it, as usually happens, then the State is in the second of its three stages; for this form is similar to a kingship, being one in which a paternal council of leading men makes good provision for the people's welfare. But if the people themselves have killed or driven out the tyrant, they govern rather moderately, as long as they are wise and prudent, and, delighting in their exploit, they endeavour to maintain the government they have themselves set up. But if

vim populus attulit regnove eum spoliavit aut etiam,
id quod evenit saepius, optimatium sanguinem
gustavit ac totam rem publicam substravit libidini
suae (cave putes autem mare ullum aut flammam
esse tantam, quam non facilius sit sedare quam
effrenatam insolentia multitudinem), tum fit illud,
quod apud Platonem est luculente dictum, si modo
id exprimere Latine potuero; difficile factu est, sed
66 conabor tamen. XLIII. "Cum" enim inquit "inexplebiles populi fauces exaruerunt libertatis siti malisque usus ille ministris non modice temperatam, sed
nimis meracam libertatem sitiens hausit, tum
magistratus et principes, nisi valde lenes et remissi
sint et large sibi libertatem ministrent, insequitur,
insimulat, arguit, praepotentes, reges, tyrannos
vocat." puto enim tibi haec esse nota.

    L. Vero mihi, inquit ille, notissima.

67   *S.* Ergo illa sequuntur : " eos, qui pareant principibus, agitari ab eo populo et servos voluntarios
appellari ; eos autem, qui in magistratu privatorum
similes esse velint, eosque privatos, qui efficiant, ne
quid inter privatum et magistratum differat, ferunt
laudibus et mactant honoribus, ut necesse sit in eius
modi re publica plena libertatis esse omnia, ut et
privata domus omnis vacet dominatione et hoc
malum usque ad bestias perveniat, denique ut pater

---

    [1] Plato, *Republic* VIII, 562 C–563 E. What follows is an
abbreviated paraphrase, not a translation.

the people ever rebel against a just king and
deprive him of his kingdom, or, as happens more
frequently, taste the blood of the aristocracy and
subject the whole State to their own caprices (and do
not dream, Laelius, that any sea or any conflagration
is so powerful that it cannot be more easily subdued
than an unbridled multitude enjoying unwonted
power), then we have a condition which is splendidly
described by Plato,[1] if only I can reproduce his
description in Latin; it is difficult, but I will
attempt it. XLIII. He says: "When the insatiable
throats of the people have become dry with the
thirst for liberty, and, served by evil ministers, they
have drained in their thirst a draught of liberty
which, instead of being moderately tempered, is too
strong for them, then, unless the magistrates and
men of high rank are very mild and indulgent, serving
them with liberty in generous quantities, the people
persecute them, charge them with crime and impeach
them, calling them despots, kings, and tyrants." I
think you are acquainted with this passage.

Laelius. It is very familiar to me.

Scipio. He continues thus: "Those who follow
the lead of prominent citizens are persecuted
by such a people and called willing slaves; but
those who, though in office, try to act like private
citizens, and those private citizens who try to
destroy all distinction between a private citizen and
a magistrate are praised to the skies and loaded with
honours. It necessarily follows in such a State that
liberty prevails everywhere, to such an extent that
not only are homes one and all without a master,
but the vice of anarchy extends even to the domestic
animals, until finally the father fears his son, the

filium metuat, filius patrem neglegat, absit omnis pudor, ut plane liberi sint, nihil intersit, civis sit an peregrinus, magister ut discipulos metuat et iis blandiatur spernantque discipuli magistros, adulescentes ut senum sibi pondus adsumant, senes autem ad ludum adulescentium descendant, ne sint iis odiosi et graves; ex quo fit, ut etiam servi se liberius gerant, uxores eodem iure sint, quo viri, inque tanta libertate canes etiam et equi, aselli denique liberi sic incurrant, ut iis de via decedendum sit. Ergo ex hac infinita," inquit, "licentia haec summa cogitur, ut ita fastidiosae mollesque mentes evadant civium, ut, si minima vis adhibeatur imperii, irascantur et perferre nequeant; ex quo leges quoque incipiunt neglegere, ut plane sine ullo domino sint."

68 XLIV. Tum Laelius: Prorsus, inquit, expressa sunt a te, quae dicta sunt ab illo.

S. Atque, ut iam ad sermonis mei morem [1] revertar, ex hac nimia licentia, quam illi solam libertatem putant, ait ille ut ex stirpe quadam existere et quasi nasci tyrannum. nam ut ex nimia potentia principum oritur interitus principum, sic hunc nimis liberum populum libertas ipsa servitute adficit. sic omnia nimia, cum vel in tempestate vel in agris vel in corporibus laetiora fuerunt, in contraria fere convertun-

---

[1] *morem*, V; *auctorem* Zell; *tenorem* Heinrich. See *De Legibus* II, 4, 9

son flouts his father, all sense of shame disappears, and all is so absolutely free that there is no distinction between citizen and alien; the schoolmaster fears and flatters his pupils, and pupils despise their masters; youths take on the gravity of age, and old men stoop to the games of youth, for fear they may be disliked by their juniors and seem to them too serious. Under such conditions even the slaves come to behave with unseemly freedom, wives have the same rights as their husbands, and in the abundance of liberty even the dogs, the horses, and the asses are so free in their running about that men must make way for them in the streets. Therefore," he concludes, "the final result of this boundless licence is that the minds of the citizens become so squeamish and sensitive that, if the authority of government is exercised in the smallest degree, they become angry and cannot bear it. On this account they begin to neglect the laws as well, and so finally are utterly without a master of any kind."

XLIV. *Laelius.* You have given us his description with great exactness.

Scipio. Well, to return now to my own style of discourse, he also says that from this exaggerated licence, which is the only thing such people call liberty, tyrants spring up as from a root, and are, as it were, engendered. For just as an excess of power in the hands of the aristocrats results in the overthrow of an aristocracy, so liberty itself reduces a people who possess it in too great degree to servitude. Thus everything which is in excess—when, for instance, either in the weather, or in the fields, or in men's bodies, conditions have been too favourable—is

tur, maximeque id [1] in rebus publicis evenit, nimiaque
illa libertas et populis et privatis in nimiam servitu-
tem cadit.[2] itaque ex hac maxima libertate tyrannus gignitur et illa iniustissima et durissima servitus.
ex hoc enim populo indomito vel potius immani
deligitur aliqui plerumque dux contra illos principes
adflictos iam et depulsos loco audax, inpurus, con-
sectans proterve bene saepe de re publica meritos,
populo gratificans et aliena et sua ; cui quia privato
sunt oppositi timores, dantur imperia et ea continu
antur, praesidiis etiam, ut Athenis Pisistratus, sae-
piuntur, postremo, a quibus producti sunt, existunt
eorum ipsorum tyranni ; quos si boni oppresserunt,
ut saepe fit, recreatur civitas ; sin audaces, fit illa
factio, genus aliud tyrannorum, eademque oritur
etiam ex illo saepe optimatium praeclaro statu, cum
ipsos principes aliqua pravitas de via deflexit. sic
tamquam pilam rapiunt inter se rei publicae statum
tyranni ab regibus, ab iis autem principes aut populi,
a quibus aut factiones aut tyranni, nec diutius umquam tenetur idem rei publicae modus.

69   XLV. Quod ita cum sit, ex [3] tribus primis generi-

---

[1] *id* supplied by Moser : omitted in V.
[2] *cadit* V ; *cedit* Mai ; *evadit* Seyffert.
[3] *ex* supplied by Heinrich ; omitted in V.

usually changed into its opposite; and this is especially true in States, where such excess of liberty either in nations or in individuals turns into an excess of servitude. This extreme liberty gives birth to a tyrant and the utterly unjust and cruel servitude of the tyranny. For out of such an ungoverned, or rather, untamed, populace someone is usually chosen as leader against those leading citizens who have already been subjected to persecution and cast down from their leadership—some bold and depraved man, who shamelessly harasses oftentimes even those who have deserved well of the State, and curries favour with the people by bestowing upon them the property of others as well as his own. To such a man, because he has much reason to be afraid if he remains a private citizen, official power is given and continually renewed; he is also surrounded by armed guards, as was Pisistratus at Athens; and finally he emerges as a tyrant over the very people who have raised him to power. If the better citizens overthrow such a tyrant, as often happens, then the State is re-established; but if it is the bolder sort who do so, then we have that oligarchy which is only a tyranny of another kind. This same form of government also arises from the excellent rule of an aristocracy, when some bad influence turns the leading citizens themselves from the right path. Thus the ruling power of the State, like a ball, is snatched from kings by tyrants, from tyrants by aristocrats or the people, and from them again by an oligarchical faction or a tyrant, so that no single form of government ever maintains itself very long.

XLV. Since this is true, the kingship, in my

bus longe praestat mea sententia regium, regio
autem ipsi praestabit id, quod erit aequatum et
temperatum ex tribus optimis rerum publicarum
modis. placet enim esse quiddam in re publica
praestans et regale, esse aliud auctoritati principum
inpartitum ac tributum, esse quasdam res servatas
iudicio voluntatique multitudinis. haec constitutio
primum habet aequabilitatem quandam magnam,
qua carere diutius vix possunt liberi, deinde firmitu-
dinem, quod et illa prima facile in contraria vitia
convertuntur, ut existat ex rege dominus, ex optimatibus factio, ex populo turba et confusio, quodque
ipsa genera generibus saepe conmutantur novis, hoc
in hac iuncta moderateque permixta conformatione
rei publicae non ferme sine magnis principum vitiis
evenit. non est enim causa conversionis, ubi in suo
quisque est gradu firmiter collocatus et non subest,
quo praecipitet ac decidat.

70   XLVI. Sed vereor, Laeli vosque homines amicissimi ac prudentissimi, ne, si diutius in hoc genere
verser, quasi praecipientis cuiusdam et docentis et
non vobiscum simul considerantis esse videatur
oratio mea. quam ob rem ingrediar in ea, quae nota
sunt omnibus, quaesita autem a nobis iam diu. sic
enim decerno, sic sentio, sic adfirmo, nullam omnium
rerum publicarum aut constitutione aut discriptione

opinion, is by far the best of the three primary forms, but a moderate and balanced form of government which is a combination of the three good simple forms is preferable even to the kingship. For there should be a supreme and royal element in the State, some power also ought to be granted to the leading citizens, and certain matters should be left to the judgment and desires of the masses. Such a constitution, in the first place, offers in a high degree a sort of equality, which is a thing free men can hardly do without for any considerable length of time, and, secondly, it has stability. For the primary forms already mentioned degenerate easily into the corresponding perverted forms, the king being replaced by a despot, the aristocracy by an oligarchical faction, and the people by a mob and anarchy; but whereas these forms are frequently changed into new ones, this does not usually happen in the case of the mixed and evenly balanced constitution, except through great faults in the governing class. For there is no reason for a change when every citizen is firmly established in his own station, and there underlies it no perverted form into which it can plunge and sink.

XLVI. But I am afraid that you, Laelius, and you, my very dear and learned friends, may think, if I spend more time upon this aspect of the subject, that my discourse is rather that of a master or teacher than of one who is merely considering these matters in company with yourselves. Therefore I will pass to a topic which is familiar to everyone, and which we ourselves discussed some time ago. For I am convinced, I believe, and I declare that no other form of government is comparable, either in

aut disciplina conferendam esse cum ea, quam patres
nostri nobis acceptam iam inde a maioribus reliquerunt. quam, si placet, quoniam ea, quae tenebatis
ipsi, etiam ex me audire voluistis, simul et qualis sit
et optimam esse ostendam expositaque ad exemplum
nostra re publica accommodabo ad eam, si potero,
omnem illam orationem, quae est mihi habenda de
optimo civitatis statu. quod si tenere et consequi
potuero, cumulate munus hoc, cui me Laelius prae-
posuit, ut opinio mea fert, effecero.

71   XLVII. Tum Laelius : Tuum vero, inquit, Scipio,
ac tuum quidem unius.[1]   quis enim te potius aut de
maiorum dixerit institutis, cum sis clarissimis ipse
maioribus ? aut de optimo statu civitatis ? quem si
habemus, etsi ne nunc quidem, tum vero quis te
possit esse florentior ? aut de consiliis in posterum
providendis, cum tu duobus huius urbis terroribus
depulsis in omne tempus prospexeris ?

---

[1] *unius* Moser ; *munus* V.

---

[1] *i.e.*, its two rivals, Carthage and Numantia, both taken
by Scipio.

its general character, in its distribution of powers, or in the training it gives, with that which our ancestors received from their own forefathers, and have handed down to us. Therefore, if you have no objection—since you have desired to hear me discourse upon matters with which you are already familiar—I will explain the character of this constitution and show why it is the best; and, using our own government as my pattern, I will fit to it, if I can, all I have to say about the ideal State. If I can keep to this intention and carry it through, the task that Laelius has imposed upon me will, in my opinion, have been abundantly accomplished.

XLVII. *Laelius.* The task is yours indeed, Scipio, and yours alone; for who is better qualified than yourself to speak of the institutions of our ancestors, since you yourself are descended from most famous forefathers? Or who is better able to speak of the ideal State? For if we are to have such a constitution (surely at present that is not the case), who would be more prominent in its administration than yourself? Or who is better qualified to speak of provisions for the future, when you have provided for all future time by freeing our city from the two dangers that threatened it?[1]

FRAGMENTA LIBRI I

1. . . . nec doctíssimis.
Manium Persium haec légere nolo, Iúnium
Congúm volo.[1] (*Plin. Nat. Hist. Praef.* 7.)

2. Sic, quoniam plura beneficia continet patria et
est antiquior parens quam is, qui creavit, maior ei
profecto quam parenti debetur gratia. (*Nonius,* p.
426. 9.)

3. Nec tantum Karthago habuisset opum sescentos
fere annos sine consiliis et disciplina. (*Nonius,* p.
526. 5.)

4. Cognoscere mehercule, inquit, consuetudinem
istam et studium sermonis. (*Nonius,* p. 276. 5.)

5. Profecto omnis istorum disputatio, quamquam
uberrimos fontes virtutis et scientiae continet, tamen
collata cum eorum actis perfectisque rebus vereor ne
non tantum videatur attulisse negotii hominibus,
quantam oblectationem. (*Lactantius, Inst. Div. III.*
16. 5.)

6. A qua isti avocabant. (*Arusianus Messius,*
Exempl. Elocut., p. 216 *Lindem.*)

[1] The text of this quotation is evidently corrupt. Cf. *De Oratore* II, 6, 25.

FRAGMENTS OF BOOK I

1. . . . nor for very learned men.
   That Manius Persius read these words I care
   No whit; let Junius Congus read them all.[1]

2. Therefore, as our fatherland is the author of
more benefits, and is an earlier parent than the
father who begot us, surely greater gratitude is due
to it than to a father.

3. Nor could Carthage have prospered so greatly
for about six hundred years without good counsel
and strict training.

4. . . . that I certainly am acquainted, he said,
with this habit of yours, and with your eagerness
for discussion . . .

5. Surely all the discussions of the men you
mention, though they contain abundant springs of
virtue and knowledge, nevertheless, if compared
with what the others have actually performed and
accomplished, would appear, I am afraid, to have
provided men with more entertainment than stimu-
lus to practical work.

6. . . . from which these friends of yours were
summoning away . . .

[1] Quoted from Lucilius; probably from Book **XXVI** of the
Saturae; compare Cicero, *De Oratore* II, 25; *De Fin.* I, 7.
The idea seems to be that the work is not intended for very
learned men, but for the student or "general reader."

DE RE PUBLICA

LIBER SECUNDUS

1   I. Cum omnes flagrarent cupiditate audiendi,[1]
ingressus est sic loqui Scipio :

Catonis hoc senis est, quem, ut scitis, unice dilexi
maximeque sum admiratus cuique vel patris utriusque
iudicio vel etiam meo studio me totum ab adule-
scentia dedidi ; cuius me numquam satiare potuit
oratio ; tantus erat in homine usus rei publicae, quam
et domi et militiae cum optime, tum etiam diutissime
gesserat, et modus in dicendo et gravitate mixtus
lepos et summum vel discendi[2] studium vel docendi
et orationi vita admodum congruens.

2   Is dicere solebat ob hanc causam praestare nostrae
civitatis statum ceteris civitatibus, quod in illis singuli
fuissent fere, qui suam quisque rem publicam con-
stituissent legibus atque institutis suis, ut Cretum
Minos, Lacedaemoniorum Lycurgus, Atheniensium,
quae persaepe commutata esset, tum Theseus, tum
Draco, tum Solo, tum Clisthenes, tum multi alii,
postremo exsanguem iam et iacentem doctus vir
Phalereus sustentasset Demetrius, nostra autem res

---

[1] *cum omnes flagrarent cupiditate* Heinrich ; . . . *ditate* V.
[2] *discendi* Mai ; *dicendi* V.

---

[1] *i.e.*, his father, Lucius Aemilius Paulus, and his adoptive
father, Publius Cornelius Scipio, son of Scipio Africanus
Maior.

THE REPUBLIC

BOOK II

I. All being on fire with eagerness to hear him,
Scipio began as follows:

What I am about to say is derived from the aged
Cato, for whom, as you know, I cherished a singular
affection and had the highest admiration. Indeed, I
spent all my time with him from my youth up,
following my own inclination as well as the advice of
both my fathers;[1] and I never could get enough of
his conversation, so remarkable was his experience
of public affairs, with which he had dealt both in
peace and war with the greatest success and for a
very long period, his observance of due measure in
speaking, his union of charm with dignity, his zeal
for either learning or teaching, and the complete
harmony between his life and his words.

Cato used to say that our constitution was superior
to those of other States on account of the fact that
almost every one of these other commonwealths had
been established by one man, the author of their
laws and institutions; for example, Minos in Crete,
Lycurgus in Sparta, and in Athens, whose form of
government had frequently changed, first Theseus,
and later Draco, Solon, Clisthenes, and many others;
and last of all, when the State lay bloodless and
prostrate, that learned man of Phalerum, Demetrius,
revived it again. On the other hand our own

publica non unius esset ingenio, sed multorum, nec una hominis vita, sed aliquot constituta saeculis et aetatibus. nam neque ullum ingenium tantum extitisse dicebat, ut, quem res nulla fugeret, quisquam aliquando fuisset, neque cuncta ingenia conlata in unum tantum posse uno tempore providere, ut omnia complecterentur sine rerum usu ac vetustate.

3 Quam ob rem, ut ille solebat, ita nunc mea repetet oratio populi Romani originem; libenter enim etiam verbo utor Catonis. facilius autem, quod est propositum, consequar, si nostram rem publicam vobis et nascentem et crescentem et adultam et iam firmam atque robustam ostendero, quam si mihi aliquam, ut apud Platonem Socrates, ipse finxero.

4 II. Hoc cum omnes adprobavissent, Quod habemus, inquit,[1] institutae rei publicae tam clarum ac tam omnibus notum exordium quam huius urbis condendae principium profectum a Romulo? qui patre Marte natus (concedamus enim famae hominum, praesertim non inveteratae solum, sed etiam sapienter a maioribus proditae, bene meriti de rebus communibus ut genere etiam putarentur, non solum esse ingenio divino)—is igitur, ut natus sit, cum Remo fratre dicitur ab Amulio, rege Albano, ob labefactandi regni timorem ad Tiberim exponi iussus esse; quo in loco cum esset silvestris beluae sustentatus uberibus pastoresque eum sustulissent et in agresti

---

[1] *inquit* Halm; *igitur* V; *igitur inquit* Moser.

[1] A reference to Cato's historical work, the *Origines*.
[2] The *Republic*.

commonwealth was based upon the genius, not of one man, but of many; it was founded, not in one generation, but in a long period of several centuries and many ages of men. For, said he, there never has lived a man possessed of so great genius that nothing could escape him, nor could the combined powers of all the men living at one time possibly make all necessary provisions for the future without the aid of actual experience and the test of time.

Therefore, following Cato's precedent, my discourse will now go back to "the origin of the Roman People,"[1] for I like to make use of his very words. I shall, however, find my task easier if I place before you a description of our Roman State at its birth, during its growth, at its maturity, and finally in its strong and healthy state, than if I should follow the example of Socrates in Plato's work [2] and myself invent an ideal State of my own.

II. When all had signified their approval, he continued : What State's origin is so famous or so well known to all men as the foundation of this city by Romulus? He was the son of Mars (for we may grant that much to the popular tradition, especially as it is not only very ancient, but has been wisely handed down by our ancestors, who desired that those who have deserved well of the commonwealth should be deemed actual descendants of the gods, as well as endowed with godlike qualities), and after his birth they say that Amulius, the Alban king, fearing the overthrow of his own royal power, ordered him, with his brother Remus, to be exposed on the banks of the Tiber. There he was suckled by a wild beast from the forest, and was rescued by shepherds, who brought him up to the life and labours of the

cultu laboreque aluissent, perhibetur, ut adoleverit,
et corporis viribus et animi ferocitate tantum ceteris
praestitisse, ut omnes, qui tum eos agros, ubi hodie
est haec urbs incolebant, aequo animo illi libenterque
parerent quorum copiis cum se ducem praebuisset,
ut iam a fabulis ad facta veniamus, oppressisse Lon-
gam Albam, validam urbem et potentem temporibus
illis, Amuliumque regem interemisse fertur.

5 III. Qua gloria parta urbem auspicato condere et
firmare dicitur primum cogitavisse rem publicam
urbi autem locum quod est ei, qui diuturnam rem
publicam serere conatur diligentissime providendum,
incredibili oportunitate delegit. neque enim ad
mare admovit, quod ei fuit illa manu copiisque
facillim im. ut in agrum Rutulorum Aboriginumque
procederet, aut in ostio Tiberino quem in locum
multis post annis rex Ancus coloniam deduxit. urbem
ipse conderet, sed hoc vir excellenti providentia
sensit ac vidit, non esse oportunissimos situs mariti-
mos urbibus eis, quae ad spem diuturnitatis conde-
rentur atque imperii, primum quod essent urbes mari-
timae non solum multis periculis oppositae, sed etiam
6 caecis. nam terra continens adventus hostium non
modo expectatos, sed etiam repentinos multis indiciis
et quasi fragore quodam et sonitu ipso ante denun-
tiat; neque vero quisquam potest hostis advolare
terra, quin eum non modo esse, sed etiam quis et

---

[1] *urbem et potentem* Baiter; *urbem vel potentem* V; *urbem
[vel potentem]* Creuzer.

---

[1] Compare Livy I, 4–6.
[2] *i.e.*, he might have chosen a site on the coast (1) directly
south of Rome. near Laurentum or Ardea, or (2) on the spot
where Ostia was placed later.

countryside.   And when he grew up, we are told, he
was so far superior to his companions in bodily strength
and boldness of spirit that all who then lived in the
rural district where our city now stands were willing
and glad to be ruled by him.   After becoming the
leader of such forces as these (to turn now from fable
to fact), we are informed that with their assistance he
overthrew Alba Longa, a strong and powerful city
for those times, and put King Amulius to death.[1]

III. After doing this glorious deed he conceived
the plan, it is said, of founding a new city, if favourable auspices were obtained, and of establishing a
commonwealth.   As regards the site of his city—a
matter which calls for the most careful foresight on
the part of one who hopes to plant a commonwealth
that will endure—he made an incredibly wise choice.
For he did not build it down by the sea, though it
would have been very easy for him, with the men
and resources at his command, to invade the
territory of the Rutuli and the Aborigines, or he
might have founded his city on the mouth of the
Tiber, where King Ancus planted a colony many years
later.[2]   But with remarkable foresight our founder
perceived that a site on the sea-coast is not the most
desirable for cities founded in the hope of long life
and extended dominion, primarily because maritime
cities are exposed to dangers which are both manifold
and impossible to foresee.   For the mainland gives
warning of the coming of the foeman, whether this
be unexpected or expected, by means of many signs,
and by what I may call a sort of rumbling din, the
bare sound of moving men ; nor can any enemy come
upon us by land so swiftly that we are not able to
learn not only that he is present, but also who he is

unde sit, scire possimus. maritimus vero ille et
navalis hostis ante adesse potest, quam quisquam
venturum esse suspicari queat, nec vero, cum venit,
prae se fert, aut qui sit aut unde veniat aut etiam quid
velit, denique ne nota quidem ulla, pacatus an hostis
sit, discerni ac iudicari potest.

7   IV. Est autem maritimis urbibus etiam quaedam
corruptela ac demutatio morum; admiscentur enim
novis sermonibus ac disciplinis et inportantur non
merces solum adventiciae, sed etiam mores, ut nihil
possit in patriis institutis manere integrum. iam
qui incolunt eas urbes, non haerent in suis sedibus,
sed volucri semper spe et cogitatione rapiuntur a
domo longius, atque etiam cum manent corpore,
animo tamen exulant et vagantur. nec vero ulla res
magis labefactatam diu et Carthaginem et Corinthum
pervertit aliquando quam hic error ac dissipatio
civium, quod mercandi cupiditate et navigandi et
8 agrorum et armorum cultum reliquerant. multa
etiam ad luxuriam invitamenta perniciosa civitatibus
subpeditantur mari, quae vel capiuntur vel inportantur; atque habet etiam amoenitas ipsa vel
sumptuosas vel desidiosas inlecebras multas cupidi-
tatum. et, quod de Corintho dixi, id haud scio an
liceat de cuncta Graecia verissime dicere; nam et
ipsa Peloponnesus fere tota in mari est, nec praeter
Phliasios [1] ulli sunt, quorum agri non contingant

---

[1] Cicero wrote *Phliuntios* originally, but corrected it to
Phliasios in *Ep. ad Att. VI*, 2, 3 ; *Phliuntios* V.

---

[1] Both these cities were taken by Rome in 146 B.C.

and whence he comes. But a seafaring, ship-borne enemy can arrive before anyone is able to suspect that he is coming, and when he arrives he does not disclose who he is or whence he comes or even what his intentions are—in short, not even a single mark, showing whether he be friend or foe, can be made out and passed judgment upon.

IV. Maritime cities also suffer a certain corruption and degeneration of morals; for they receive a mixture of strange languages and customs, and import foreign ways as well as foreign merchandise, so that none of their ancestral institutions can possibly remain unchanged. Even their inhabitants do not cling to their dwelling places, but are constantly being tempted far from home by soaring hopes and dreams; and even when their bodies stay at home, their thoughts nevertheless fare abroad and go wandering. In fact, no other influence did more to bring about the final overthrow of Carthage and Corinth,[1] though they had long been tottering, than this scattering and dispersion of their citizens, due to the fact that the lust for trafficking and sailing the seas had caused them to abandon agriculture and the pursuit of arms. Many things too that cause ruin to states as being incitements to luxury are supplied by the sea, entering either by capture or import; and even the mere delightfulness of such a site brings in its train many an allurement to pleasure through either extravagance or indolence. And what I said of Corinth may perhaps be said with truth of the whole of Greece; for even the Peloponnesus is almost in its entire extent close to the sea, and there is no people in it except the Phliasians whose territory does not touch the sea; and out-

mare, et extra Peloponnesum Aenianes et Doris et
Dolopes soli absunt a mari. quid dicam insulas
Graeciae, quae fluctibus cinctae natant paene ipsae
9 simul cum civitatum institutis et moribus? atque haec
quidem, ut supra dixi, veteris sunt Graeciae; coloni-
arum vero quae est deducta a Graiis in Asiam,
Thracam, Italiam, Siciliam, Africam praeter unam
Magnesiam, quam unda non adluat? ita barbarorum
agris quasi adtexta quaedam videtur ora esse Graeciae; nam e barbaris quidem ipsis nulli erant antea
maritumi praeter Etruscos et Poenos, alteri mercandi
causa, latrocinandi alteri. quae causa perspicua est
malorum commutationumque Graeciae propter ea
vitia maritimarum urbium, quae ante paulo perbre-
viter adtigi. sed tamen in his vitiis inest illa magna
commoditas, et, quod ubique genitum[1] est, ut ad eam
urbem, quam incolas, possit adnare, et rursus ut id,
quod agri efferant sui, quascumque velint in terras,
portare possint ac mittere.

10   V. Qui potuit igitur divinius et utilitates conplecti
maritimas Romulus et vitia vitare, quam quod urbem
perennis amnis et aequabilis et in mare late influen-
tis posuit in ripa? quo posset urbs et accipere a
mari, quo egeret, et reddere, quo redundaret, eo-

---

[1] *genitum* V[2]; *gentium* V[1].

side the Peloponnesus the Aenianes, the inhabitants of Doris, and the Dolopes are the only peoples who lie at a distance from the sea. Why should I speak of the islands of Greece? For surrounded as they are by the billows, not only they themselves but also the customs and institutions of their cities can be said to be afloat. The situation of the Greek homeland is what I have described; of all the colonies, on the other hand, which have been sent out by the Greeks to Asia, Thrace, Italy, Sicily, and Africa, which, except Magnesia alone, is not washed by the waves? Indeed it seems as if the lands of the barbarians had been bordered round with a Greek sea-coast; for none of the barbarians themselves were originally seafaring peoples except the Etruscans and the Phoenicians, the latter for purposes of trade and the former as pirates. Clearly the cause of the evils and the revolutions to which Greece has been subject is to be traced to those disadvantages which I have just mentioned briefly as peculiar to maritime cities. But nevertheless with all these disadvantages they possess one great advantage—all the products of the world can be brought by water to the city in which you live, and your people in turn can convey or send whatever their own fields produce to any country they like.

V. How, then, could Romulus have acted with a wisdom more divine, both availing himself of all the advantages of the sea and avoiding its disadvantages, than by placing his city on the bank of a never-failing river whose broad stream flows with unvarying current into the sea? Such a river enables the city to use the sea both for importing what it lacks and for exporting what it produces in superfluity;

demque ut flumine res ad victum cultumque maxime
necessarias non solum mari asportaret,[1] sed etiam
invectas acciperet ex terra, ut mihi iam tum divinasse
ille videatur hanc urbem sedem aliquando et domum
summo esse imperio praebituram ; nam hanc rerum
tantam potentiam non ferme facilius ulla in parte
Italiae posita urbs tenere potuisset.

11   VI. Urbis autem ipsius nativa praesidia quis est
tam neglegens qui non habeat animo notata planeque
cognita ? cuius is est tractus ductusque muri cum
Romuli, tum etiam reliquorum regum sapientia defini-
tus ex omni parte arduis praeruptisque montibus, ut
unus aditus, qui esset inter Esquilinum Quirinalem-
que montem, maximo aggere obiecto fossa cingeretur
vastissima, atque ut ita munita arx circumiectu arduo
et quasi circumciso saxo niteretur, ut etiam in illa
tempestate horribili Gallici adventus incolumis atque
intacta permanserit. locumque delegit et fontibus
abundantem et in regione pestilenti salubrem ; colles
enim sunt, qui cum perflantur ipsi, tum adferunt
umbram vallibus.

12   VII. Atque haec quidem perceleriter confecit ;
nam et urbem constituit, quam e suo nomine Romam
iussit nominari, et ad firmandam novam civitatem
novum quoddam et subagreste consilium, sed ad

---

[1] *asportaret* Maehly ; *absorberet* **V** ; *subreheret* Niebuhr.

---

[1] The text of this sentence is uncertain, but the general
meaning is clear.

[2] 390 B.C. is the date according to the usual Roman tradition ; the Greek writers put it three or four years later.

and by means of it likewise the city can not only bring in by sea but also obtain from the land, carried on its waters, whatever is most essential for its life and civilization.[1] Consequently it seems to me that Romulus must at the very beginning have had a divine intimation that the city would one day be the seat and hearthstone of a mighty empire; for scarcely could a city placed upon any other site in Italy have more easily maintained our present widespread dominion.

VI. As to the natural defences of the city itself, who is so unobserving as not to have a clear outline of them imprinted upon his mind? The line and course of its walls were wisely planned by Romulus and the kings who succeeded him, being so placed on the everywhere steep and precipitous hillsides that the single approach which lies between the Esquiline and the Quirinal hills was girt about by a huge rampart facing the foe and by a mighty trench; and our citadel was so well fortified by the sheer precipices which encompass it and the rock which appears to be cut away on every side that it remained safe and impregnable even at the terrible time of the advent of the Gauls.[2] In addition, the site which he chose abounds in springs and is healthful, though in the midst of a pestilential region; for there are hills, which not only enjoy the breezes but at the same time give shade to the valleys below.

VII. And Romulus accomplished all this very quickly; for after founding the city, which by his command was called Rome after his own name, in order to strengthen the new commonwealth he adopted a plan which, though original and somewhat savage in character, yet for securing the prosperity

muniendas opes regni ac populi sui magni hominis
et iam tum longe providentis secutus est, cum
Sabinas honesto ortas loco virgines, quae Romam
ludorum gratia venissent, quos tum primum anni-
versarios in circo facere instituisset, Consualibus[1]
rapi iussit easque in familiarum amplissimarum matri-
13 moniis collocavit. qua ex causa cum bellum Romanis
Sabini intulissent proeliique certamen varium atque
anceps fuisset, cum T. Tatio, rege Sabinorum, foedus
icit matronis ipsis, quae raptae erant, orantibus ; quo
foedere et Sabinos in civitatem adscivit sacris con-
municatis et regnum suum cum illorum rege sociavit.
14   VIII. Post interitum autem Tatii cum ad eum
potentatus[2] omnis reccidisset, quamquam cum Tatio
in regium consilium delegerat principes (qui appel-
lati sunt propter caritatem patres) populumque et
suo et Tatii nomine et Lucumonis, qui Romuli socius
in Sabino proelio occiderat, in tribus tris curiasque
triginta discripserat (quas curias earum nominibus
nuncupavit, quae ex Sabinis virgines raptae postea
fuerant oratrices pacis et foederis)—sed quamquam
ea Tatio sic erant discripta vivo, tamen eo interfecto
multo etiam magis Romulus patrum auctoritate con-
silioque regnavit.

[1] *Consualibus* Mai ; *consulibus* V.
[2] *potentatus* V[1] ; *dominatus* V[2].

---

[1] A festival to the harvest god Consus, who seems later to
have been confused with Neptune.
[2] Compare Livy I, 9 and 13.
[3] The three tribes were called *Ramnes* (*Ramnenses,*
Ramnetes), *Tities* (*Titienses*), and *Luceres* (*Lucerenses*). The

of his kingdom and people revealed a great man who even then saw far into the future. For when Sabine maidens of honourable lineage had come to Rome on the occasion of the Consualia,[1] to witness the games whose annual celebration in the circus he had just instituted, he ordered their seizure and married them to young men of the most prominent families. When the Sabines, thus provoked, made war on the Romans, and the fortunes of the conflict were various and its issue doubtful, Romulus made a treaty with Titus Tatius, the Sabine king, the stolen women themselves petitioning that this be done. By this treaty he not only added the Sabines to the body of Roman citizens, giving them participation in the religious rites of the State, but also made their king a partner in his royal power.[2]

VIII. But after the death of Tatius, when all the powers of government reverted to Romulus, although Tatius had been associated with him when he chose a royal council consisting of the most eminent men (who were called "Fathers" on account of the affection felt for them), and when he divided the people into three tribes (named after himself, after Tatius, and after his ally Lucumo,[3] who had been killed in the Sabine War), and also into thirty curiae (which he named after the stolen Sabine maidens who had pleaded for a treaty of peace)—although these arrangements had been made during the lifetime of Tatius, yet after this king's death Romulus had paid even greater deference in his conduct of the government to the influence and advice of the Fathers.

actual origin of the names is uncertain. Compare Livy I, 13.

15 IX. Quo facto primum vidit iudicavitque idem,
quod Spartae Lycurgus paulo ante viderat, singulari
imperio et potestate regia tum melius gubernari et
regi civitates, si esset optimi cuiusque ad illam vim
dominationis adiuncta auctoritas. itaque hoc consilio
et quasi senatu fultus et munitus et bella cum
finitimis felicissime multa gessit et, cum ipse nihil
ex praeda domum suam reportaret, locupletare civis
16 non destitit. tum,[1] id quod retinemus hodie magna
cum salute rei publicae, auspiciis plurimum obsecutus
est Romulus. nam et ipse, quod principium rei
publicae fuit, urbem condidit auspicato et omnibus
publicis rebus instituendis, qui sibi essent in
auspiciis, ex singulis tribubus singulos cooptavit
augures. et habuit plebem in clientelas principum
discriptam (quod quantae fuerit utilitati, post videro)
multaeque dictione ovium et bovum (quod tum erat
res in pecore et locorum possessionibus, ex quo
pecuniosi et locupletes vocabantur), non vi et sup-
pliciis coërcebat.

17 X. Ac Romulus cum septem et triginta regnavisset annos et haec egregia duo firmamenta rei publicae peperisset, auspicia et senatum, tantum est

[1] *tum* Steinacker ; *tunc* V.

---

[1] *Senatus* is derived from *senex*, "old man."
[2] Compare Livy I, 6-7.

IX. It was after he had adopted this policy that Romulus first discovered and approved the principle which Lycurgus had discovered at Sparta a short time before—that a State can be better governed and guided by the authority of one man, that is by the power of a king, if the influence of the State's most eminent men is joined to the ruler's absolute power. Accordingly, supported and guarded by such a body of advisers, to which we may give the name of "Senate," [1] he waged many wars against his neighbours with the greatest good fortune, and, though he brought none of the booty to his own home, he never ceased enriching his people. He also gave complete obedience to the auspices, a custom which we still observe to the great security of the State. For he not only took the auspices himself when he founded the city—an act that was the beginning of our commonwealth [2]—but also, before the performance of any public act, he chose augurs, one from each tribe, to act with him in taking the auspices. He also divided the plebeians up among the prominent citizens, who were to be their patrons (the usefulness of which arrangement I shall consider later), and punished the guilty, not by doing violence to their persons, but by the infliction of fines consisting of sheep and cattle; for wealth at that time consisted of domestic animals (*pecus*) and the ownership of places (*loci*) and from these two kinds of property we get our words "wealthy" (*pecuniosus*) and "rich" (*locuples*).

X. And after Romulus had reigned thirty-seven years, and established those two excellent foundations of our commonwealth, the auspices and the senate, his great achievements led to the belief that,

consecutus, ut, cum subito sole obscurato non conpa-
ruisset, deorum in numero conlocatus putaretur;
quam opinionem nemo umquam mortalis adsequi
18 potuit sine eximia virtutis gloria. atque hoc eo magis
est in Romulo admirandum, quod ceteri, qui dii ex
hominibus facti esse dicuntur, minus eruditis hominum saeculis fuerunt, ut fingendi proclivis esset
ratio, cum imperiti facile ad credendum inpellerentur,
Romuli autem aetatem minus his sescentis annis iam
inveteratis litteris atque doctrinis omnique illo
antiquo ex inculta hominum vita errore sublato
fuisse cernimus. nam si, id quod Graecorum investi-
gatur annalibus, Roma condita est secundo anno
Olympiadis septumae, in id saeculum Romuli cecidit
aetas, cum iam plena Graecia poëtarum et musicorum
esset minorque fabulis nisi de veteribus rebus
haberetur fides. nam centum et octo annis postquam
Lycurgus leges scribere instituit, prima posita est
Olympias, quam quidam nominis errore ab eodem
Lycurgo constitutam putant; Homerum autem, qui
minimum dicunt, Lycurgi aetati triginta annis ante-
19 ponunt fere. ex quo intellegi potest permultis annis
ante Homerum fuisse quam Romulum, ut iam doctis
hominibus ac temporibus ipsis eruditis ad fingendum
vix quicquam esset loci. antiquitas enim recepit

---

[1] See Book I, 25.
[2] *i.e.*, 751 B.C. The traditional dates for the founding of
Rome differed greatly.

when he disappeared during a sudden darkening of
the sun,[1] he had been added to the number of the
gods; indeed such an opinion could never have
gotten abroad about any human being save a man
pre-eminently renowned for virtue. And the case of
Romulus is all the more remarkable because all other
men who are said to have become gods lived in ruder
ages when there was a great inclination to the
invention of fabulous tales, and ignorant men were
easily induced to believe them; but we know that
Romulus lived less than six hundred years ago, at a
period when writing and education had long been in
existence, and all those mistaken primitive ideas
which grew up under uncivilized conditions had been
done away with. For if, as we learn from the annals
of the Greeks, Rome was founded in the second year
of the seventh Olympiad,[2] the life of Romulus fell in
a period when Greece already abounded in poets
and musicians, and when small credence was given
to fables, except in regard to events of a much earlier
time. For the first Olympiad [3] is placed one hundred
and eight years after Lycurgus began to write his
laws, though some, deceived by a name, think that the
Olympiads were instituted by this same Lycurgus.
But Homer, according to the least estimate, lived
about thirty years before Lycurgus.[4] Hence it is
clear that Homer lived a great many years before
Romulus, so that in the lifetime of the latter, when
learned men already existed and the age itself was
one of culture, there was very little opportunity for
the invention of fables. For whereas antiquity

[3] In 776 B.C.
[4] Cicero here dates Lycurgus in 884 B.C. and Homer in
914 B.C. or earlier.

fabulas fictas etiam non numquam[1] incondite, haec aetas autem iam exculta praesertim eludens omne, quod fieri non potest, respuit.

20   . . . us nepos eius, ut dixerunt quidam, ex filia. quo autem ille mortuus, eodem est anno natus Simonides Olympiade sexta et quinquagesima, ut facilius intellegi possit tum de Romuli[2] inmortalitate creditum, cum iam inveterata vita hominum ac tractata esset et cognita. sed profecto tanta fuit in eo vis ingenii atque virtutis, ut id de Romulo Proculo Iulio, homini agresti, crederetur, quod multis iam ante saeculis nullo alio de mortali homines credidissent; qui inpulsu patrum, quo illi a se invidiam interitus Romuli pellerent, in contione dixisse fertur a se visum esse in eo colle Romulum, qui nunc Quirinalis vocatur; eum sibi mandasse, ut populum rogaret, ut sibi eo in colle delubrum fieret; se deum esse et Quirinum vocari.

21   XI. Videtisne igitur unius viri consilio non solum ortum novum populum neque ut in cunabulis vagientem relictum, sed adultum iam et paene puberem?

---

[1] *numqu* . . . V ; the rest of the sentence is supplied from St. Augustine, *De Civ. Dei* XXII, 6.

[2] . . . *us ne* . . . *us ut di* . . . *nt quidam- x filia quo* . . . *ille mor* . . . *odem* . . . *no na* . . . *moxi* . . . *ympia* . . . *xta et quin* . . . *gesimu* . . . *acilius* . . . *legi pos* . . . *m de Ro* . . . *li* V.

---

[1] The 56th Olympiad = 556–553 B.C. The traditional date of the birth of Simonides of Ceos is 556 B.C., and, as it was believed that Simonides' birth and the death of Stesichorus fell in the same year, these are probably the persons referred to.

would accept fabulous tales, sometimes even when they were crudely fabricated, the age of Romulus, which was already one of culture, was quick to mock at and reject with scorn that which could not possibly have happened.

A few lines are lost. The following passage is fragmentary and its restoration is uncertain. It seems probable, however, that Scipio mentioned several Greek poets who lived in the period under consideration, ending the list with Simonides.

. . . . his grandson through his daughter, as some said. In the very year of his death, in the fifty-sixth Olympiad,[1] Simonides was born, so that it is easy to see that the period in which the story of Romulus' immortality gained credence was one in which human life had become a matter of old experience, and men had already reflected upon it and ascertained its nature. And yet certainly there was in Romulus such conspicuous ability that men believed about him, on the authority of that untutored peasant Proculus Julius, that which for many ages before they had not believed about any human being. For we are told that this Proculus, at the instigation of the senators, who wanted to free themselves from all suspicion in regard to Romulus' death, stated before a public assembly that he had seen Romulus on the hill now called Quirinal; and that Romulus had charged him to ask the people to build him a shrine on that hill, as he was now a god and was called Quirinus.

XI. Do you not perceive, then, that by the wisdom of a single man a new people was not simply brought into being and then left like an infant crying in its cradle, but was left already full-grown and almost in the maturity of manhood?

MARCUS TULLIUS CICERO

Tum Laelius: Nos vero videmus, et te quidem ingressum ratione ad disputandum nova, quae nusquam est in Graecorum libris. nam princeps ille, quo nemo in scribendo praestantior fuit, aream sibi sumsit, in qua civitatem extrueret arbitratu suo, praeclaram ille quidem fortasse, sed a vita hominum abhor-
22 rentem et moribus,[1] reliqui disseruerunt sine ullo certo exemplari formaque rei publicae de generibus et de rationibus civitatum ; tu mihi videris utrumque facturus ; es enim ita ingressus, ut, quae ipse reperias, tribuere aliis malis quam, ut facit apud Platonem Socrates, ipse fingere et illa de urbis situ revoces ad rationem, quae a Romulo casu aut necessitate facta sunt, et disputes non vaganti oratione, sed defixa in una re publica. quare perge, ut instituisti ; prospicere enim iam videor te reliquos reges persequente quasi perfectam rem publicam.

23   XII. Ergo, inquit Scipio, cum ille Romuli senatus, qui constabat ex optimatibus, quibus ipse rex tantum tribuisset, ut eos patres vellet nominari patriciosque eorum liberos, temptaret post Romuli excessum, ut ipse regeret[2] sine rege rem publicam, populus id non tulit desiderioque Romuli postea regem flagitare non destitit ; cum prudenter illi

----

[1] *et moribus* V²; *et a maioribus* V¹.
[2] *regeret* V²; *gereret* V¹.

----

[1] Plato ; the reference in what follows is to the *Republic*.
[2] Aristotle, Theophrastus, etc. (Compare Cicero, *De Divin.* II, 3 ; *De Leg.* III, 13-14.)
[3] Cicero derives *patricii* (patricians) from *patres* (fathers).

Laelius. We do indeed perceive this, and also that you on your part have entered upon a new style of discussion, one that is nowhere employed in the writings of the Greeks. For that eminent Greek,[1] whose works have never been surpassed, began with the assumption of an unoccupied tract of land, so that he might build a State upon it to suit himself. His State may perhaps be an excellent one, but it is quite unsuited to men's actual lives and habits. His successors[2] have discussed the different types of State and their basic principles without presenting any definite example or model. But you, I infer, mean to combine these two methods; for you have approached your subject as if you preferred to give the credit for your own discoveries to others rather than, following the example of Socrates in Plato's work, to invent a new State yourself; and in what you have said about the site of your State you are referring to a definite principle the things done by Romulus either by chance or necessity; and, in the third place your discussion does not wander about, but confines itself to a single State. Therefore continue as you have begun, for I think I can foresee, as you follow the reigns of the succeeding kings, the State's progress toward perfection.

XII. *Scipio.* Well, then, when the senate of Romulus, which consisted of the most eminent men, and had been so much favoured by the king that he desired its members to be called "Fathers" and their children "patricians"[3]—when this senate attempted, after the death of Romulus, to rule the State by itself, dispensing with a king, the people would not tolerate it, but, in their affectionate longing for Romulus, continually thereafter demanded a king.

principes novam et inauditam ceteris gentibus in-
terregni ineundi rationem excogitaverunt, ut, quoad
certus rex declaratus esset, nec sine rege civitas nec
diuturno rege esset uno nec committeretur, ut
quisquam inveterata potestate aut ad deponendum
imperium tardior esset aut ad optinendum munitior.

24 quo quidem tempore novus ille populus vidit tamen
id, quod fugit Lacedaemonium Lycurgum, qui regem
non deligendum duxit, si modo hoc in Lycurgi
potestate potuit esse, sed habendum, qualiscumque
is foret, qui modo esset Herculis stirpe generatus ;
nostri illi etiam tum agrestes viderunt virtutem et
sapientiam regalem, non progeniem quaeri oportere.

25 XIII. Quibus cum esse praestantem Numam
Pompilium fama ferret, praetermissis suis civibus
regem alienigenam patribus auctoribus sibi ipse
populus adscivit eumque ad regnandum Sabinum
hominem Romam Curibus accivit. qui ut huc venit,
quamquam populus curiatis eum comitiis regem esse
iusserat, tamen ipse de suo imperio curiatam legem
tulit, hominesque Romanos instituto Romuli bellicis
studiis ut vidit incensos, existimavit eos paulum ab
illa consuetudine esse revocandos.

---

[1] See Livy I, 17.

Then that body of leading men with great wisdom devised a plan which was entirely new and had never been heard of in any other State—the interregnum.[1] Their purpose was that, until a permanent king was chosen, the State should neither be without a king nor yet subject to any one king who should hold office for a long time; and that the State should not be put into such a position that any man, growing accustomed to power, might become either too reluctant to lay aside the royal prerogative or too well intrenched for holding it. For even at that period the new nation perceived a fact that had escaped the Spartan Lycurgus; for it was his thought that the king should be, not one freely chosen (assuming that the power of Lycurgus could have extended as far as that), but one retained in power, whatever sort of man he might chance to be, if he were but the offspring of the stock of Hercules. Yet our ancestors, rustics though they even then were, saw that kingly virtue and wisdom, not royal ancestry, were the qualities to be sought.

XIII. And since Numa Pompilius had the reputation of being pre-eminent in these qualities, the people themselves, by the advice of the Fathers, passed over their own citizens and chose a foreigner as their king, inviting this man, a Sabine of Cures, to come to Rome and rule over them. When he arrived, although the people had already chosen him king in the assembly of the curiae, he nevertheless of his own accord caused another curiate law to be passed confirming him in his royal authority. And seeing that, as a result of their mode of life under Romulus, the Romans were filled with ardour for the pursuit of war, he thought it best to discourage that propensity to some slight extent.

26 XIV. Ac primum agros, quos bello Romulus ceperat, divisit viritim civibus docuitque sine depopulatione atque praeda posse eos colendis agris abundare commodis omnibus amoremque eis otii et pacis iniecit, quibus facillime iustitia et fides convalescit, et quorum patrocinio maxime cultus agrorum perceptioque frugum defenditur. idemque Pompilius et auspiciis maioribus inventis ad pristinum numerum duo augures addidit et sacris e principum numero pontifices quinque praefecit et animos propositis legibus his,[1] quas in monumentis habemus, ardentis consuetudine et cupiditate bellandi religionum caerimoniis mitigavit adiunxitque praeterea flamines, Salios virginesque Vestales omnisque partis religionis statuit sanctissime.

27 sacrorum autem ipsorum diligentiam difficilem, apparatum perfacilem esse voluit; nam quae perdiscenda quaeque observanda essent, multa constituit, sed ea sine inpensa. sic religionibus colendis operam addidit, sumtum removit, idemque mercatus, ludos omnesque conveniundi causas et celebritates invenit. quibus rebus institutis ad humanitatem atque mansuetudinem revocavit animos hominum studiis bellandi iam immanis ac feros. sic ille cum undequadraginta annos summa in pace concordiaque

---

[1] *his* V²; omitted V¹.

---

[1] For the institution of these priestly offices, compare Livy I, 20.

[2] Compare *De Leg.* II, 19 and 25.

[3] Livy (I, 21) gives the length of his reign as 43 years.

XIV. And first of all he divided up among the citizens the land which Romulus had won by conquest, giving each man a share, and showed them that by the cultivation of their farms they could have an abundance of all manner of possessions without resort to pillage or plunder. Thus he implanted in them a love for peace and tranquillity, which enable justice and good faith to flourish most easily, and under whose protection the cultivation of the land and the enjoyment of its products are most secure. Pompilius also instituted the "greater auspices," added two augurs to the original number, and put five pontiffs, selected from the most eminent citizens, in charge of the religious rites; and by the introduction of religious ceremonial, through laws which still remain on our records, he quenched the people's ardour for the warlike life to which they had been accustomed. He also appointed flamens, Salii, and Vestal Virgins,[1] and established all the branches of our religion with the most devout solicitude. He desired that the proper performance of the rites themselves should be difficult, but that the equipment necessary therefor should be easily obtainable, for he provided that much should be learned by heart and scrupulously observed, but made the expenditure of money unnecessary.[2] Thus he made the performance of religious duties laborious but not costly. He also established markets, games, and all sorts of other occasions for the gathering of large numbers. By the institution of such customs as these he turned toward benevolence and kindliness the thoughts of men who had become savage and brutish through their passion for war. Thus, when he had reigned for thirty-nine years[3] in complete

regnavisset (sequamur enim potissimum Polybium
nostrum, quo nemo fuit in exquirendis temporibus
diligentior), excessit e vita duabus praeclarissimis
ad diuturnitatem rei publicae rebus confirmatis,
religione atque clementia.

28   XV. Quae cum Scipio dixisset, Verene, inquit
Manilius, hoc memoriae proditum est, Africane,
regem istum Numam Pythagorae ipsius discipulum
aut certe Pythagoreum fuisse? saepe enim hoc de
maioribus natu audivimus et ita intellegimus vulgo
existimari; neque vero satis id annalium publicorum
auctoritate declaratum videmus.

Tum Scipio: Falsum est enim, Manili, inquit,
id totum, neque solum fictum, sed etiam imperite
absurdeque fictum; ea sunt enim demum non
ferenda in mendacio, quae non solum ficta esse,
sed ne fieri quidem potuisse cernimus. nam quartum
iam annum regnante Lucio Tarquinio Superbo
Sybarim et Crotonem et in eas Italiae partis Pythagoras venisse reperitur; Olympias enim secunda et
sexagesima eadem Superbi regni initium et Pytha-
29   gorae declarat adventum. ex quo intellegi regiis
annis dinumeratis potest anno fere centesimo et
quadragesimo post mortem Numae primum Italiam
Pythagoram attigisse; neque hoc inter eos, qui
diligentissime persecuti sunt temporum annales, ulla
est umquam in dubitatione versatum.

Di inmortales, inquit Manilius, quantus iste est
hominum et quam inveteratus error! ac tamen
facile patior non esse nos transmarinis nec inportatis

---

[1] Olympiad 62 = 532–529 B.C.
[2] Numa's death is thus placed about 672 B.C.; from the
length of his reign and that of Romulus given above it would
fall about 675 B.C.

peace and harmony (to follow as our chief authority our friend Polybius, who is unsurpassed in chronological accuracy), he died, after having established the two elements which most conspicuously contribute to the stability of a State—religion and the spirit of tranquillity.

XV. At this point in Scipio's discourse Manilius said: Is there really a tradition, Africanus, that this King Numa was a pupil, or at least a follower, of Pythagoras? For we have often heard this statement made by our elders and are aware that it is commonly believed; and yet we are quite certain that it cannot be definitely proved by reference to our official records.

Scipio. This story is entirely false, Manilius, and not merely an invention, but an ignorant and absurd one as well. For falsehoods are indeed intolerable which are not merely obvious inventions, but even relate what we know could not possibly have happened. For it has been ascertained that, in the fourth year of the reign of Lucius Tarquinius Superbus, Pythagoras visited Sybaris and Croton and the neighbouring parts of Italy; for the accession of Superbus and the arrival of Pythagoras are both recorded to have fallen in the same Olympiad, the sixty-second.[1] From this fact, by adding up the reigns of all the kings, we can see that Pythagoras came to Italy for the first time about one hundred and forty years after Numa's death;[2] and there never has been any doubt about this in the minds of those who have made a careful study of the chronological records.

Manilius. Ye immortal gods! What a blunder to pass current so long! Yet I am not sorry that we Romans got our culture, not from arts imported from

artibus eruditos, sed genuinis domesticisque virtutibus.

30   XVI. Atqui multo id facilius cognosces, inquit
Africanus, si progredientem rem publicam atque in
optimum statum naturali quodam itinere et cursu
venientem videris ; quin hoc ipso sapientiam maiorum statues esse laudandam, quod multa intelleges
etiam aliunde sumta meliora apud nos multo [1] esse
facta, quam ibi fuissent, unde huc translata essent
atque ubi primum extitissent, intellegesque non
fortuito populum Romanum, sed consilio et disciplina
confirmatum esse nec tamen adversante fortuna.

31   XVII. Mortuo rege Pompilio Tullum Hostilium
populus regem interrege rogante comitiis curiatis
creavit, isque de imperio suo exemplo Pompilii
populum consuluit curiatim. cuius excellens in re
militari gloria magnaeque extiterunt res bellicae,
fecitque idem et saepsit de manubiis [2] comitium et
curiam constituitque ius, quo bella indicerentur,
quod per se iustissime inventum sanxit fetiali
religione, ut omne bellum, quod denuntiatum
indictumque non esset, id iniustum esse atque in-
pium iudicaretur. et ut advertatis animum, quam
sapienter iam reges hoc nostri viderint, tribuenda
quaedam esse populo (multa enim nobis de eo

----

[1] *multo* V[2] ; omitted V[1].
[2] *manubiis* Mueller ; *manubis* V[2]; *manibus* V[1] ; *manibiis*
Halm.

----

[1] Literally, "curia by curia."
[2] The *fetiales* were a college of priests with ritual duties
connected with international relationships, particularly
declarations of war and treaties of peace.

overseas, but from the native excellence of our own
people.

XVI. *Scipio.* Yet you will be able to realize this
more easily if you watch our commonwealth as it
advances, and, by a route which we may call
Nature's road, finally reaches the ideal condition.
Nay more, you will deem our ancestors' wisdom
worthy of praise for the very reason that, as you
will learn, even of those institutions that have been
borrowed from abroad, many have been improved
by us until they are much better than they were in
the countries from which we obtained them and
where they had their origin. And you will learn
that the Roman People has grown great, not by
chance, but by good counsel and discipline, though
to be sure fortune has favoured us also.

XVII. After the death of King Pompilius the
people, in their curiate assembly presided over by
an interrex, chose Tullius Hostilius as their king,
and he followed the example of Pompilius by con-
sulting the people, in the same curiate assembly,[1]
in regard to his possession of the royal power. This
king excelled in military skill and mighty deeds of
war; he built and walled in, from the proceeds of
the sale of his spoils, a meeting-place for the popular
assemblies and one for the senate; and he formulated rules for the declaration of war. He consecrated this eminently just code, which he himself
had originated, by means of the fetial rites.[2] so that
any war which had not been declared and announced
should be considered unjust and impious. And that
you may take note how wisely even our early kings
perceived that certain rights should be granted to
the people (a subject on which I shall have a great

genere dicenda sunt), ne insignibus quidem regiis
Tullus nisi iussu populi est ausus uti. nam ut
sibi duodecim lictores cum fascibus anteire liceret . . .

[*Desiderantur paginae duae.*]

33　XVIII. . . . neque [1] enim serpit, sed volat
in optimum statum instituto tuo sermone res
publica.

S. Post eum Numae Pompilii nepos ex filia rex
a populo est Ancus Marcius constitutus, itemque
de imperio suo legem curiatam tulit. qui cum
Latinos bello devicisset, adscivit eos in civitatem,
atque idem Aventinum et Caelium montem adiunxit
urbi, quosque agros ceperat, divisit et silvas maritimas omnis publicavit, quas ceperat, et ad ostium
Tiberis urbem condidit colonisque firmavit. atque
ita cum tres et viginti regnavisset annos, est
mortuus.

Tum [2] Laelius: laudandus etiam iste rex; sed
obscura est historia Romana, siquidem istius regis
matrem habemus, ignoramus patrem.

S. Ita est, inquit; sed temporum illorum tantum
fere regum inlustrata sunt nomina.

---

[1] *neque* is commonly supplied; . . . *enim* V.
[2] *tum* V[2]; *et* V[1].

---

[1] Compare Livy's account of the reign of Tullius Hostilius
(I, 22—31 ; see 31 for his death).
[2] *i e.*, Tullius Hostilius.
[3] Ostia ("Rivermouth"), the seaport of Rome.
[4] Compare Livy I, 32—33.

deal to say later), observe that Tullius did not venture to assume even the insignia of royalty without the permission of the people. For, that he might be allowed to be preceded by twelve lictors carrying the rods . . . .

About fifteen lines are lost. According to St. Augustine (*De Civ. Dei* III, 15) the lost passage included the statement that, though Tullius Hostilius was killed by a stroke of lightning, it was not rumoured, as in the case of Romulus, that he had been taken up into heaven, perhaps because the Romans were unwilling that their first king should share this honour with another.[1]

XVIII. . . . for the commonwealth, according to the account you have begun to give of it, is not creeping but flying toward the ideal condition.

Scipio. To succeed him [2] Ancus Martius, grandson of Numa Pompilius through his daughter, was chosen king by the people, and he too caused a curiate law to be passed comfirming his royal authority. After conquering the Latins in war he incorporated them in the Roman State; he also added the Aventine and Caelian Hills to the city, divided among the citizens the territory he had conquered, made all the forests along the sea-coast, which he had obtained by conquest, public property, built a city at the mouth of the Tiber,[3] and settled it with colonists. And so, after a reign of twenty-three years,[4] he died.

Laelius. Truly a praiseworthy king! But the history of Rome is indeed obscure if we know who this king's mother was, but are ignorant of his father's name!

Scipio. That is true; but of that period very little more than the names of the kings has been handed down to us with any definiteness.

MARCUS TULLIUS CICERO

34   XIX. Sed hoc loco primum videtur insitiva
quadam disciplina doctior facta esse civitas. influxit
enim non tenuis quidam e Graecia rivulus in hanc
urbem, sed abundantissimus amnis illarum discipli-
narum et artium. fuisse enim quendam ferunt
Demaratum Corinthium et honore et auctoritate et
fortunis facile civitatis suae principem; qui cum
Corinthiorum tyrannum Cypselum ferre non potuisset, fugisse cum magna pecunia dicitur ac se
contulisse Tarquinios, in urbem Etruriae florentissi-
mam. cumque audiret dominationem Cypseli confirmari, defugit[1] patriam vir liber ac fortis et
adscitus est civis a Tarquiniensibus atque in ea
civitate domicilium et sedes collocavit. ubi cum de
matre familias Tarquiniensi duo filios procreavisset,
omnibus eos artibus ad Graecorum disciplinam
erudiit. . . . .[2]

[Desiderantur paginae duae.]

35   XX. . . . facile in civitatem receptus esset,
propter humanitatem atque doctrinam Anco regi
familiaris est factus usque eo, ut consiliorum omnium
particeps et socius paene regni putaretur. erat in
eo praeterea summa comitas, summa in omnis civis
opis, auxilii, defensionis, largiendi etiam benignitas.
itaque mortuo Marcio cunctis populi suffragiis rex
est creatus L. Tarquinius; sic enim suum nomen
ex Graeco nomine inflexerat, ut in omni genere
huius populi consuetudinem videretur imitatus. isque
ut de suo imperio legem tulit, principio duplicavit

---

[1] *confirmari, defugit* V[2]; *confirmatam, fugit* V[1].
[2] *erudiit* is commonly read; *eru* . . . V.

XIX. Still it was at this time that the common-wealth appears first to have become familiar with an alien system of education. For it was indeed no little rivulet that flowed from Greece into our city, but a mighty river of culture and learning. For we are told that a certain Demaratus of Corinth, easily pre-eminent in his own city in rank, influence, and wealth, fled with his great riches, not being able to endure the tyranny of Cypselus at Corinth, and came to Tarquinii, the most prosperous city of Etruria. And when he heard that the despotism of Cypselus was firmly established, this bold lover of liberty became a permanent exile from his country, and, being received as a citizen at Tarquinii, made his home there. When his Tarquinian wife had borne him two sons, he educated them in all the arts in accordance with the Greek system . . .

About ten lines are lost. In what follows Lucius Tarquinius, the son of Demaratus, is referred to.

XX. . . . having easily obtained citizenship, [Lucius] became the friend of King Ancus on account of his geniality and great learning; and they were so intimate that he was believed to share all the king's counsels and to be almost a sharer in the throne. In addition, he possessed great personal charm, and he showed the greatest kindness in granting help and assistance, protection, and even pecuniary aid, to all the citizens. Therefore, when Marcius died, the people by a unanimous vote elected Lucius Tarquinius king (for he had in this manner modified his Greek name, that he might appear to be adopt-ing the customs of his new country in every respect). After having caused a law to be passed confirming his royal authority, he first of all doubled the

illum pristinum patrum numerum et antiquos patres
maiorum gentium appellavit, quos priores sententiam
36 rogabat, a se adscitos minorum. deinde equitatum
ad hunc morem constituit, qui usque adhuc est
retentus, nec potuit Titiensium et Rhamnensium et
Lucerum mutare, cum cuperet, nomina, quod auctor
ei summa augur gloria Attus Navius non erat.
atque etiam Corinthios video publicis equis adsig-
nandis et alendis orborum et viduarum tributis fuisse
quondam diligentis. sed tamen prioribus equitum
partibus secundis additis mille et octingentos fecit
equites numerumque duplicavit. postea[1] bello
subegit Aequorum magnam gentem et ferocem et
rebus populi Romani imminentem, idemque Sabinos
cum a moenibus urbis reppulisset, equitatu fudit
belloque devicit. atque eundem primum ludos
maximos, qui Romani dicti sunt, fecisse accepimus
aedemque in Capitolio Iovi optimo maximo bello
Sabino in ipsa pugna vovisse faciendam mortuumque
esse, cum duodequadraginta regnavisset annos.
37   XXI. Tum Laelius : Nunc fit illud Catonis certius,
nec temporis unius nec hominis esse constitutionem
rei publicae ; perspicuum est enim, quanta in
singulos reges rerum bonarum et utilium fiat ac-

---

[1] *postea* Vaucher ; *postquam* V ; *post* Madvig.

---

[1] See section 14.   [2] Compare Livy I, 43, 9.
[3] See Livy I, 35.

original number of senators, and gave to those who had previously been called "Fathers" the title of "senators of the greater families" (these were always asked for their opinion first), and those whom he himself had added he designated "senators of the lesser families." Then he established that organization of the knights which we still retain; but though he desired to change the names of the Ramnes, Tities, and Luceres,[1] he was unable to do so, because the celebrated augur Attus Navius would not consent to it. I understand that the Corinthians also were given to the practice of supplying their knights with horses owned by the State, and feeding them, from contributions exacted from widows and orphans.[2] At any rate Lucius added new cavalry organizations to the old ones, making a total of 1800 horse, thus doubling the original number. Later he conquered the Aequi, a powerful and warlike nation which threatened the welfare of the Roman people, and also drove the Sabines from the walls of the city, routed them with his cavalry, and finally conquered them completely. Tradition also informs us that he instituted those great games called "Roman";[3] that, in the war with the Sabines, he made a vow during a battle to build a temple to Jupiter the Greatest and Best on the Capitoline Hill; and that he died after a reign of thirty-eight years.[4]

XXI. *Laelius.* Now we have further proof of the accuracy of Cato's statement that the foundation of our State was the work neither of one period nor of one man; for it is quite clear that every king contributed many good and useful institutions. But

[4] Compare Livy I, 34—38.

cessio. sed sequitur is, qui mihi videtur ex omnibus
in re publica vidisse plurimum.

Ita est, inquit Scipio. nam post eum Servius
Tullius primus iniussu populi regnavisse traditur,
quem ferunt ex serva Tarquiniense natum, cum
esset ex quodam regis cliente conceptus. qui cum
famulorum in[1] numero educatus ad epulas regis
adsisteret, non latuit scintilla ingenii, quae iam tum
elucebat in puero; sic erat in omni vel officio vel
sermone sollers. itaque Tarquinius, qui admodum
parvos tum haberet liberos, sic Servium diligebat,
ut is eius vulgo haberetur filius, atque eum summo
studio omnibus iis artibus, quas ipse didicerat, ad
exquisitissimam consuetudinem Graecorum erudiit.

38   Sed cum Tarquinius insidiis Anci filiorum interisset
Serviusque, ut ante dixi, regnare coepisset non iussu,
sed voluntate atque concessu civium, quod, cum
Tarquinius ex vulnere aeger fuisse et vivere falso
diceretur, ille regio ornatu ius dixisset obaeratosque
pecunia sua liberavisset multaque comitate usus
iussu Tarquinii se ius dicere probavisset, non com-
misit se patribus, sed Tarquinio sepulto populum
de se ipse consuluit iussusque regnare legem de

---

[1] *in* supplied by Moser; omitted in V.

the one who comes next, in my opinion, had a better understanding of the government of a State than any of the rest.

Scipio. Quite true; for Servius Tullius followed Tarquinius; he, according to tradition, was the first to hold the royal power without being chosen by the people. They say that his mother was a slave in the household of Tarquinius, and his father one of the king's dependents. Though he was brought up as a slave, and served the king's table, yet the spark of genius, which shone even then in the boy, did not remain unnoticed, so capable was he in every duty and in every word he spoke. On this account Tarquinius, whose children were still very young, became so fond of Servius that the latter was popularly regarded as his son; and the king took the greatest care to have him educated in all the branches which he himself had studied, in accordance with the most careful practice of the Greeks.

But when Tarquinius was killed by a plot formed by the sons of Ancus, Servius began to rule, as I have said, without being formally chosen by the people, but with their good-will and consent. For the false report was given out that Tarquinius, though ill from his wound, was still alive; and Servius, assuming the royal garb, pronounced judgments, freed debtors at his own expense, and acting with great affability, convinced the people that he was administering justice by the orders of Tarquinius. He did not put himself in the senate's power, but, after the burial of Tarquinius, consulted the people himself in regard to his own power, and, when they had bidden him to be king, caused a curiate law to

imperio suo curiatam tulit. et primum Etruscorum
iniurias bello est ultus; ex quo cum ma. . .

[*Desiderantur paginae duae.*]

39   XXII. . . . duodeviginti censu maximo. deinde
equitum magno numero ex omni populi summa
separato relicuum populum distribuit in quinque
classis senioresque a iunioribus divisit easque[1] ita
disparavit, ut suffragia non in multitudinis, sed in
locupletium potestate essent, curavitque, quod semper
in re publica tenendum est, ne plurimum valeant
plurimi. quae discriptio si esset ignota vobis, expli-
caretur a me; nunc rationem videtis esse talem, ut
equitum centuriae cum sex[2] suffragiis et prima
classis addita centuria, quae ad summum usum urbis
fabris tignariis est data, octoginta novem[3] centurias
habeat; quibus ex centum quattuor centuriis (tot
enim reliquae sunt) octo solae si accesserunt, confecta est vis populi universa, relicuaque multo maior
multitudo sex et nonaginta centuriarum neque ex-
cluderetur suffragiis, ne superbum esset, nec valeret
40 nimis, ne esset periculosum. in quo etiam verbis
ac nominibus ipsis fuit diligens; qui cum locupletis

---

  [1] *easque* Francke; *eosque* V.
  [2] *centuriae cum sex* V[2]; *certamine cum et* V[1]. The text is
corrupt.
  [3] LXXXVIII *centurias habeat, quibus e centum quattor
centuriis tot* V[2]; VIIII *centurias tot* V[1].

---

  [1] The text on which the remainder of this sentence, and
the one which follows, depend is uncertain. Therefore the
details are in doubt, but the general principle is clear;
namely, that this assembly was to be so constituted that the
upper classes, though in the minority, controlled a majority
of the centuries.

be passed confirming his royal authority. At the very beginning of his reign he made war on the Etruscans and avenged the wrongs of which they were guilty. From this [war] . . .

About fifteen lines are lost. After the gap we find Scipio describing the reforms of King Servius, particularly the institution of the centuriate assembly.

XXII. . . . eighteen of the greatest wealth. Then after choosing a large number of knights out of the whole people, Servius divided the rest of the citizens into five classes, and separated the older from the younger. He made this division in such a way that the greatest number of votes belonged, not to the common people, but to the rich, and put into effect the principle which ought always to be adhered to in the commonwealth, that the greatest number should not have the greatest power. If his system were not well known to you, I should describe it, but you are already aware that the arrangement is such that[1] the centuries of knights with their six votes, and the first class, with the addition of the century composed of the carpenters on account of their great usefulness to the city, make up a total of 89 centuries. Now if, out of a total of 104 centuries—for that is the number left—only eight centuries should adhere to the 89, the whole power of the people would be exerted. And the remaining 96 centuries, which contain a large majority of the citizens, would neither be deprived of the suffrage, for that would be tyrannical, nor be given too much power, for that would be dangerous. In this arrangement Servius was careful even in his use of titles and names, for he called the rich "money-

assiduos appellasset ab asse dando, eos, qui aut non
plus mille quingentos aeris aut omnino nihil in suum
censum praeter caput attulissent, proletarios nomin
avit, ut ex iis quasi proles, id est quasi progenie
civitatis, expectari videretur. illarum autem sex e
nonaginta centuriarum in una centuria tum quidem
plures censebantur quam paene in prima classe tota
ita nec prohibebatur quisquam iure suffragii, et i
valebat in suffragio plurimum, cuius plurimum in
tererat esse in optimo statu civitatem. quin etiam
accensis velatis, liticinibus, cornicinibus, proletarii
. . .

[Desiderantur paginae quattuor.]

41   XXIII. . . . statu esse optimo constitutam rem
publicam, quae ex tribus generibus illis, regali e
optumati et populari, confusa modice nec puniend
inritet animum inmanem ac ferum . . . (*Nonius*, p
342. 28.)

42   . . . . quinque et sexaginta[1] annis antiquior, quo
erat trigesimo nono ante primam Olympiadem con
dita. et antiquissimus ille Lycurgus eadem vidi
fere. itaque ista aequabilitas atque hoc triple
rerum publicarum genus videtur mihi commun
nobis cum illis populis fuisse. sed, quod proprium
sit in nostra re publica, quo nihil possit esse prae
clarius, id persequar, si potero, subtilius; quod eri

---

[1] *quinque et sexaginta* is commonly read ; . . . *sexaginta* V

[1] Cicero derives *assiduus* from *as*, a coin, and *do*, give
Cmopare Aulus Gellius XVI, 10, 15.

givers," [1] because they paid the expenses of the
State, and named those who had less than 1500
denarii or nothing at all except their own persons,
"child-givers," [2] to give the impression that offspring, that is to say, the progeny of the State, were
to be expected from them. A number of individuals
which was almost larger than that contained in the
whole first class was placed in every one of the 96
centuries of this proletarian class. Thus, while no
one was deprived of the suffrage, the majority of
votes was in the hands of those to whom the highest
welfare of the State was the most important. And
indeed the official messengers, the auxiliary troops,
the trumpeters and buglers, the proletarians . . .

About thirty lines are lost, of which the following fragment may be a part. At the end of the gap Carthage is
referred to.

XXIII. . . . [I consider] the best constitution for
a State to be that which is a balanced combination
of the three forms mentioned, kingship, aristocracy,
and democracy, and does not irritate by punishment
a rude and savage heart . . .

. . . sixty-five years older, for it was founded in
the thirty-ninth year before the first Olympiad.[3]
And Lycurgus, who lived in very ancient times, had
almost the same idea. This equalized system, this
combination of three constitutions, is in my opinion
common to those nations and to ours. But the
unique characteristic of our own commonwealth—
the most splendid conceivable—I shall describe more
completely and accurately, if I can, because nothing

[2] Cicero derives *proletarius* from *proles*, offspring.
[3] *i.e.*, Carthage was founded 815 B.C., being about 65 years
older than Rome.

eius modi, nihil ut tale ulla in re publica reperiatur.
haec enim, quae adhuc exposui, ita mixta fuerunt
et in hac civitate et in Lacedaemoniorum et in
Karthaginiensium, ut temperata nullo fuerint modo.
43 nam in qua re publica est unus aliquis perpetua
potestate, praesertim regia, quamvis in ea sit et
senatus, ut tum fuit Romae, cum erant reges, ut
Spartae Lycurgi legibus, et ut sit aliquod etiam
populi ius, ut fuit apud nostros reges, tamen illud
excellit regium nomen, neque potest eius modi res
publica non regnum et esse et vocari. ea autem
forma civitatis mutabilis maxime est hanc ob causam,
quod unius vitio praecipitata in perniciosissimam
partem facillime decidit. nam ipsum regale genus
civitatis non modo non est reprehendendum, sed
haud scio an reliquis simplicibus longe anteponendum,
si ullum probarem simplex rei publicae genus, sed
ita, quoad statum suum retinet. is est autem status,
ut unius perpetua potestate et iustitia omnique
sapientia regatur salus et aequabilitas et otium
civium. Desunt omnino ei populo multa, qui sub
rege est, in primisque libertas, quae non in eo est,
ut iusto utamur domino, sed ut nullo[1] . . .

[*Desiderantur paginae duae.*]

44 XXIV. . . . ferebant. etenim illi iniusto domino
atque acerbo aliquam diu in rebus gerundis prospera[2]

---

[1] *nullo* is commonly read ; *nul* . . . V.
[2] *prospera* Moser ; *prospere* V.

---

[1] *i.e.*, in the time of the kingship. The elements referred
to are the royal, aristocratic, and democratic.

like it is to be found in any other State. For those
elements which I have mentioned were combined in
our State as it was then,[1] and in those of the Spartans
and Carthaginians, in such a way that there was no
balance among them whatever. For in a State where
there is one official who holds office for life, particularly
if he be a king, even if there is a senate, such as
existed at Rome under the monarchy and at Sparta
under the code of Lycurgus, and even if the people
possess some power, as they did under our kings – in
spite of these facts the royal power is bound to be
supreme, and such a government is inevitably a
monarchy and will inevitably be so called. And this
form of government is the most liable of all to change,
because one man's vices can overthrow it and turn it
easily toward utter destruction. For not only is the
kingship in itself not at all reprehensible, but I am
inclined to consider it by far the best of the simple
forms of government—if I could approve any of the
simple forms—but only so long as it retains its true
character. But it does that only when the safety,
equal rights, and tranquillity of the citizens are
guarded by the life-long authority, the justice, and
the perfect wisdom of a single ruler. To be sure a
nation ruled by a king is deprived of many things,
and particularly of liberty, which does not consist in
serving a just master, but in [serving] no [master at
all] . . .

About fifteen lines are lost. At the end of the gap the
reign of Tarquinius Superbus is being cited as an example of
the degeneration of monarchy.

XXIV. . . . They bore [the tyranny of Tarquinius nevertheless;] for even that unjust and cruel
master occasionally enjoyed good fortune in his

fortuna comitata est. nam et omne Latium bello
devicit et Suessam Pometiam, urbem opulentam re-
fertamque, cepit et maxima auri argentique praeda
locupletatus votum patris Capitolii aedificatione per-
solvit et colonias deduxit et institutis eorum, a quibus
ortus erat, dona magnifica quasi libamenta praedarum
Delphos ad Apollinem misit.

45   XXV. Hic ille iam vertetur orbis, cuius naturalem
motum atque circuitum a primo discite adgnoscere.[1]
id enim est caput civilis prudentiae, in qua omnis
haec nostra versatur oratio, videre itinera flexusque
rerum publicarum, ut, cum sciatis quo quaeque res
inclinet, retinere aut ante possitis occurrere.

Nam rex ille, de quo loquor, primum optimi regis
caede maculatus integra mente non erat, et cum
metueret ipse poenam sceleris sui summam, metui
se volebat; deinde victoriis divitiisque subnixus
exultabat insolentia neque suos mores regere poterat
46 neque suorum libidines. itaque cum maior eius
filius Lucretiae, Tricipitini filiae, Conlatini uxori,
vim attulisset mulierque pudens et nobilis ob illam
iniuriam sese ipsa morte multavisset, tum vir ingenio
et virtute praestans, L. Brutus, depulit a civibus
suis iniustum illud durae servitutis iugum. qui cum

---

[1] *discite adgnoscere* V[2]; *discite adque cognoscere* V[1]; *discite
atque cognoscite* Mai.

---

[1] See Livy I, 55.   [2] Tarquinius Superbus.
                    [3] Servius Tullius.

undertakings. Indeed, he conquered the whole of Latium and took the prosperous city of Suessa Pometia with its vast wealth, winning thereby an enormous store of gold and silver, with which he paid his father's vow by building the Capitol;[1] he also planted colonies, and, following the example of his ancestors, sent magnificent gifts—an offering of the first-fruits, as it were, of his booty—to Apollo at Delphi.

XXV. At this point begins that orbit of development with whose natural motion and circular course you must become acquainted from its beginning. For the foundation of that political wisdom which is the aim of our whole discourse is an understanding of the regular curving path through which governments travel, in order that, when you know what direction any commonwealth tends to take, you may be able to hold it back or take measures to meet the change.

Now this king[2] of whom I am speaking, his hands being stained with the blood of a most excellent king,[3] did not begin his reign with a clear conscience, and as he was himself in fear of suffering the extreme penalty for his crime, he wished to make himself feared by others. Later, relying upon his victories and his wealth, he became swollen with pride and was unable to control either his own conduct or the lustful desires of his family. Wherefore, when his elder son violated Lucretia, the daughter of Tricipitinus and wife of Collatinus, and this noble and virtuous woman inflicted the death penalty upon herself as a result of the outrage, Lucius Brutus, a man pre-eminent for wisdom and bravery, freed his fellow-citizens from the unjust yoke of cruel servitude.

privatus esset, totam rem publicam sustinuit pri-
musque in hac civitate docuit in conservanda civium
libertate esse privatum neminem, quo auctore et
principe concitata civitas et hac recenti querella
Lucretiae patris ac propinquorum et recordatione
superbiae Tarquinii multarumque iniuriarum et
ipsius et filiorum exulem et regem ipsum et liberos
eius et gentem Tarquiniorum esse iussit.

47 XXVI. Videtisne igitur, ut de rege dominus extiterit uniusque vitio genus rei publicae ex bono in
deterrumum conversum sit? hic est enim dominus
populi, quem Graeci tyrannum vocant; nam regem
illum volunt esse, qui consulit ut parens populo
conservatque eos, quibus est praepositus, quam
optima in condicione vivendi, sane bonum, ut dixi,
rei publicae genus, sed tamen inclinatum et quasi
48 pronum ad perniciosissimum statum. simul atque
enim se inflexit hic rex in dominatum iniustiorem,
fit continuo tyrannus, quo neque taetrius neque
foedius nec dis hominibusque invisius animal ullum
cogitari potest; qui quamquam figura est hominis,
morum tamen inmanitate vastissimas vincit beluas.
quis enim hunc hominem rite dixerit, qui sibi cum
suis civibus, qui denique cum omni hominum genere

---

[1] For the story of the rape of Lucretia and the deposition
of Tarquinius, see Livy I, 57–60.

And though Brutus was only a private citizen, he sustained the whole burden of the government, and was the first in our State to demonstrate that no one is a mere private citizen when the liberty of his fellows needs protection. On his initiative and under his leadership the people, aroused not only by the bitter complaints, still fresh in their memories, of Lucretia's father and kinsmen, but also by their own recollection of the pride of Tarquinius and the many acts of injustice committed by him and his sons, banished the king himself, his children, and the whole race of the Tarquinii.[1]

XXVI. Do you not see, therefore, how a king was transformed into a despot, and how a good form of government was changed into the worst possible form through the fault of one man? For here we have a master over the people, whom the Greeks call a tyrant; for they maintain that the title of king should be given only to a ruler who is as solicitous for the welfare of his people as is a father for his children, and maintains in the best possible conditions of life those over whom he is set. Such a government is truly a good one, as I have said, but nevertheless it inclines, and, I may almost say, naturally tends, toward the condition which is the most depraved of all. For as soon as this king turned to a mastery less just than before, he instantly became a tyrant; and no creature more vile or horrible than a tyrant, or more hateful to gods and men, can be imagined; for, though he bears a human form, yet he surpasses the most monstrous of the wild beasts in the cruelty of his nature. For how could the name of human being rightly be given to a creature who desires no community of justice, no

nullam iuris communionem, nullam humanitatis
societatem velit? sed erit hoc de genere nobis
alius aptior dicendi locus, cum res ipsa admonuerit,
ut in eos dicamus, qui etiam liberata iam civitate
dominationes adpetiverunt.

49 XXVII. Habetis igitur primum ortum tyranni;
nam hoc nomen Graeci regis iniusti esse voluerunt;
nostri quidem omnes reges vocitaverunt, qui soli in
populos perpetuam potestatem haberent. itaque et
Spurius Cassius et M. Manlius et Spurius Maelius
regnum occupare voluisse dicti sunt, et modo Tib.
Gracchus [1] . . .

[Desiderantur paginae duae.]

50 XXVIII. . . . Lycurgus γέροντας Lacedaemone [2]
appellavit, nimis is quidem paucos, octo et viginti,
quos penes summam consilii voluit esse, cum imperii summam rex teneret; ex quo nostri idem
illud secuti atque interpretati, quos senes ille appellavit, nominaverunt senatum, ut etiam [3] Romulum
patribus lectis fecisse diximus; tamen excellit atque
eminet vis, potestas nomenque regium. inperti
etiam populo potestatis aliquid, ut et Lycurgus et
Romulus; non satiaris eum libertate, sed incenderis
cupiditate libertatis, cum tantum modo potestatem
gustandi feceris; ille quidem semper inpendebit

---

[1] *Tib. Gracchus* is commonly supplied; lacking in **V**.
[2] *Lycurgus γέροντας La*—commonly supplied; lacking in **V**.
[3] *ut etiam* **V**; *ut iam* Heinrich; *utei iam* Haupt.

---

[1] *i.e.*, old men   [2] See section 15.

partnership in human life with his fellow-citizens—
aye, even with any part of the human race? But
we shall find a more suitable point in our discourse
for the consideration of this subject, when the very
course of events constrains us to condemn those who,
even after the liberation of the State, have sought
despotic power.

XXVII. Here, then, you have the origin of the
tyrant; for that is the title given by the Greeks to
an unjust king, while we Romans have always given
the name of king to all who exercise for life sole
authority over a nation. Thus, for example, it has
been said that Spurius Cassius, Marcus Manlius, and
Spurius Maelius attempted to win the kingship, and
recently [Tiberius Gracchus] . . .

About fifteen lines are lost. Lycurgus is evidently the
subject of the sentence which follows.

XXVIII. [Lycurgus] called [this body *gerontes*[1]]
at Sparta; but it was a very small number of men,
twenty-eight in fact, who according to his plan were
to have the supreme authority in counsel, while the
king held the supreme executive power. And our
ancestors, imitating his example and translating the
title he used, gave the name of "senate"[2] to the
body which he had called "old men"; this was
done by Romulus himself, as we have said, after he
had chosen the Fathers. Yet the power, authority,
and very title of the king stand out supreme in such
a State. Grant some power to the people also, as
did both Lycurgus and Romulus; you will not give
them their fill of liberty, but merely excite their
appetite for it, when you permit them to do no
more than taste its flavour. And all the while

159

timor, ne rex, quod plerumque evenit, exsistat
iniustus. est igitur fragilis ea fortuna populi, quae
posita est in unius, ut dixi antea, voluntate vel
moribus.

51 XXIX. Quare prima sit haec forma et species et
origo tyranni inventa nobis in ea re publica, quam
auspicato Romulus condiderit, non in illa, quam, ut
perscripsit Plato, sibi ipse Socrates peripatetico[1]
illo in sermone depinxerit, ut, quem ad modum
Tarquinius, non novam potestatem nactus, sed, quam
habebat, usus iniuste totum genus hoc regiae civitatis everterit; sit huic oppositus alter, bonus et
sapiens et peritus utilitatis dignitatisque civilis
quasi tutor et procurator rei publicae; sic enim
appelletur, quicumque erit rector et gubernator
civitatis. quem virum facite ut agnoscatis; iste est
enim, qui consilio et opera civitatem tueri potest.
quod quoniam nomen minus est adhuc tritum
sermone nostro saepiusque genus eius hominis erit
in reliqua nobis oratione tractandum[2] . . .

[Desiderantur paginae duodecim.]

52 XXX. . . . sas requisivit civitatemque optandam
magis quam sperandam, quam minimam potuit, non

[1] *peripatetico* is commonly read; *peripeatelo* V; *tripertito*
Bernays; περὶ πολιτείας Ziegler.
[2] *tractandum* is commonly read; *trac* . . . V.

---

[1] Plato's *Republic.* For the tyrant, see VIII, 565—IX,
580.

there weighs heavily upon their hearts the fear that
an unjust king may arise, as indeed often happens.
The fortune of any people is therefore a fragile thing,
as I have explained already, when it depends on the
will or the character of one man.

XXIX. Therefore we may consider that the first
form and variety of tyranny, and its way of coming
into being, have come to light in this State of ours
which Romulus founded after taking the auspices,
and not in the commonwealth described by Socrates,
as Plato tells us in his famous peripatetic discourse.[1]
For, just as happened in the case of Tarquinius, the
tyrant overthrows the whole monarchical constitution,
not by seizing any new powers, but by his misuse of
the powers he already possesses. With him we may
place in contrast that other type of ruler, the good,
wise, and skilful guardian and protector, as one may
say, of the practical interests and of the self-respect
of the citizens of the State; for these are titles
which will be granted to one who is truly the guide
and pilot of a nation. See to it that you are able to
recognize such a man, for he is one who can maintain the safety of the State both by counsel and by
action. As, however, this subject has not been very
fully treated so far in our conversation, and as this
type of man will have to be considered rather often
later in our discourse, [we shall say no more of him
at the present time.]

About four pages are lost. Plato is the subject of the
sentence which follows.

XXX. . . . has sought for . . . and has created
a State of a kind that is to be desired rather than
hoped for—one of the smallest size, not such as to

quae posset esse, sed in qua ratio rerum civı̄lium
perspici posset, effecit. ego autem, si modo [1] consequi potuero, rationibus eisdem, quas ille vidit, non
in umbra et imagine civitatis, sed in amplissima
re publica enitar, ut cuiusque et boni publici et
mali causam tamquam virgula videar attingere.

Iis enim regiis quadraginta annis et ducentis
paulo cum interregnis fere amplius praeteritis ex-
pulsoque Tarquinio tantum odium populum Romanum regalis nominis tenuit, quantum tenuerat
post obitum vel potius excessum Romuli desiderium.
itaque ut tum carere rege, sic pulso Tarquinio
nomen regis audire non poterat. Hic facultatem
cum . . .

[Desiderantur paginae sedecim.]

53   XXXI. . . . Itaque illa praeclara constitutio
Romuli cum ducentos annos et viginti fere firma
mansisset . . . (*Nonius*, p. 526. 7.)

. . . lex illa tota sublata est. hac mente tum
nostri maiores et Conlatinum innocentem suspicione
cognationis expulerunt et reliquos Tarquinios offen-

----

[1] *si modo* V²; *si quo modo* V¹.

----

[1] *i.e.*, 751–509.
[2] *i.e.*, the relationship of Lucius Tarquinius Collatinus to
the expelled king. Compare Livy II, 2.

be actually possible, but in which it might be possible to see the workings of his theory of the State. As for me, however, I shall endeavour, if I am able to accomplish my purpose, employing the same principles which Plato discerned, yet taking no shadowy commonwealth of the imagination, but a real and very powerful State, to seem to you to be pointing out, as with a demonstrating rod, the causes of every political good and ill.

Now after these two hundred and forty years of monarchy [1] (or a little longer, if one included the periods of interregnum), when Tarquinius had been banished, the title of king came to be as bitterly hated by the Romans as it had been longingly desired after the death, or rather the departure, of Romulus. Hence, just as then they could not bear to be without a king, so now, after the banishment of Tarquinius, they could not bear even to hear the title of king mentioned . . .

About five pages are lost, of which the following fragment may be a part; a further clue to the contents of the lost passage may possibly be found in St. Augustine, *De Civ. Dei* V, 12. According to this passage Cicero perhaps went on to say that the Romans substituted two supreme magistrates with annual tenure of office, and with an inoffensive title (*consul*, here derived from *consulere*, to consult) for the king (*rex*, here connected with *regno*, to reign).

XXXI. . . . Thus that excellent constitution of Romulus, after maintaining itself firmly for about two hundred and twenty years . . .

. . . that law was entirely abolished. It was on account of this feeling that our ancestors banished the unoffending Collatinus at that time, on account of the suspicion caused by his relationship,[2] and all the other Tarquinii, on account of the hatred felt

sione nominis; eademque mente P. Valerius et
fasces primus demitti iussit, cum dicere in contione
coepisset, et aedis suas detulit sub Veliam, posteaquam, quod in excelsiore loco Veliae coepisset
aedificare eo ipso, ubi rex Tullus habitaverat,
suspicionem populi sensit moveri; idemque, in quo
fuit Publicola maxime, legem ad populum tulit
eam, quae centuriatis comitiis prima lata est, ne
quis magistratus civem Romanum adversus provo-
54 cationem necaret neve verberaret.   Provocationem
autem etiam a regibus fuisse declarant pontificii
libri, significant nostri etiam augurales, itemque ab
omni iudicio poenaque provocari licere indicant
duodecim tabulae conpluribus legibus; et[1] quod
proditum memoriae est decemviros, qui leges scripserint, sine provocatione creatos, satis ostendit[2]
reliquos sine provocatione magistratus non fuisse;
Luciique Valerii Potiti et M. Horatii Barbati, hominum concordiae causa sapienter popularium, con-
sularis lex sanxit, ne qui magistratus sine provocatione crearetur; neque vero leges Porciae, quae
tres sunt trium Porciorum, ut scitis, quicquam
praeter sanctionem attulerunt novi.
55   Itaque Publicola lege illa de provocatione perlata

---

[1] *et* Madvig; *ut* V.   [2] *ostendit* V[2]; *ostenderit* V[1].

---

[1] Compare Book I, section 62. Traditional date, 509 B.C.

[2] His cognomen *Publicola* or *Poplicola* is here given its
lietral meaning (*populus*, people, and *colo*, to cultivate,
favour).

[3] According to tradition the code composed by the
decemvirs; see section 61.

[4] Traditional date 449 B.C.; compare Livy III, 55.

[5] Compare Livy X. 9; Cicero, *Pro Rabirio* 12. The first
of these Porcian Laws is perhaps to be dated in 199 or
195 B.C.

for the name. Another manifestation of the same spirit was the institution by Publius Valerius of the custom of ordering the rods [1] to be lowered when he began to speak before the people ; also the fact that he moved the site of his house to the foot of the Velian Hill when he noticed that popular suspicion was aroused because he had begun to build on the very spot on the top of that hill where King Tullius had resided. It was the same man who, by an act whereby he shows himself in the highest sense " the people's friend," [2] proposed to the citizens that first law passed by the centuriate assembly, which forbade any magistrate to execute or scourge a Roman citizen in the face of an appeal. The records of the pontiffs, however, state that the right of appeal, even against a king's sentence, had been previously recognized, and our augural books confirm the statement. Besides, many laws of the Twelve Tables [3] show that an appeal from any judgment or sentence was allowed ; and the tradition that the decemvirs who wrote the laws were elected with the provision that there should be no appeal from their decision shows clearly enough that other officials were subject to this right of appeal. And a law proposed by the consuls Lucius Valerius Potitus and Marcus Horatius Barbatus,[4] men who wisely favoured popular measures to preserve peace, provides that no magistrate not subject to appeal shall be elected. Nor indeed did the Porcian laws,[5] which, as you know, are three in number and were proposed by three different members of the Porcian family, add anything new to previous statutes except the provision of a penalty for violations.

Thus Publicola, as soon as that law of his in regard

statim securis de fascibus demi iussit postridieque
sibi collegam Sp. Lucretium subrogavit suosque ad
eum, quod erat maior natu, lictores transire iussit
instituitque primus, ut singulis consulibus alternis
mensibus lictores praeirent, ne plura insignia essent
inperii in libero populo quam in regno fuissent.
haud mediocris hic, ut ego quidem intellego, vir
fuit, qui modica libertate populo data facilius tenuit
auctoritatem principum.

Neque ego haec nunc sine causa tam vetera vobis
et tam obsoleta decanto, sed inlustribus in personis
temporibusque exempla hominum rerumque definio,
ad quae reliqua oratio dirigatur mea.

56   XXXII. Tenuit igitur hoc in statu senatus rem
publicam temporibus illis, ut in populo libero pauca
per populum, pleraque senatus auctoritate et instituto ac more gererentur, atque uti consules potestatem haberent tempore dumtaxat annuam, genere
ipso ac iure regiam.   quodque erat ad optinendam[1]
potentiam nobilium vel maximum, vehementer id
retinebatur, populi comitia ne essent rata, nisi ea
patrum adprobavisset auctoritas. atque his ipsis
temporibus dictator etiam est institutus decem fere

---

[1] *optinendam* V[2]; omitted V[1].

---

[1] *i.e.*, the patrician senators.

to the right of appeal was passed, ordered the axes
to be removed from the bundle of rods; and the
next day he caused Spurius Lucretius to be elected
as his colleague and ordered his own lictors to be
transferred to Spurius as his senior in age. Publicola also introduced the rule that the lictors should
precede each consul alternately for one month, so
that the insignia of executive power might not
be more numerous in the free State than they had
been under the monarchy. In my opinion, it was a
man of no ordinary talents who, by granting the
people a moderate amount of liberty, the more easily
maintained the power of the leaders of the State.

Now it is not without a definite purpose that I am
reviewing events so ancient and remote, but I am
taking my standards of character and action, to
which the rest of my discourse must conform, from
distinguished men and famous periods of our own
history.

XXXII. Well then, at the period of which I have
been speaking, the government was so administered
by the senate that, though the people were free, few
political acts were performed by them, practically
everything being done by the authority of the
senate and in accordance with its established
customs, and that the consuls held a power which,
though only of one year's duration, was truly regal
in general character and in legal sanction. Another
principle that was most important to the retention
of the power by the aristocracy was also strictly
maintained, namely, that no act of a popular
assembly should be valid unless ratified by the
Fathers.[1] It was in the same period that the
dictatorship was also instituted, Titus Larcius, the

annis post primos consules, T. Larcius, novumque id genus imperii visum est et proximum similitudini regiae. sed tamen omnia summa cum auctoritate a principibus cedente populo tenebantur, magnaeque res temporibus illis a fortissimis viris summo imperio praeditis, dictatoribus atque consulibus, belli gerebantur.

57   XXXIII. Sed id, quod fieri natura rerum ipsa cogebat, ut plusculum sibi iuris populus adscisceret liberatus a regibus, non longo intervallo, sexto decimo fere anno, Postumo Cominio Sp. Cassio consulibus consecutum[1] est; in quo defuit fortasse ratio, sed tamen vincit ipsa rerum publicarum natura saepe rationem. id enim tenetote, quod initio dixi, nisi aequabilis haec in civitate conpensatio sit et iuris et officii et muneris, ut et potestatis satis in magistratibus et auctoritatis in principum consilio et libertatis in populo sit, non posse hunc incommutabilem rei

58 publicae conservari statum. nam cum esset ex aere alieno commota civitas, plebs montem sacrum prius, deinde Aventinum occupavit. ac ne Lycurgi quidem disciplina tenuit illos in hominibus Graecis frenos; nam etiam Spartae regnante Theopompo sunt item quinque, quos illi ephoros appellant, in Creta autem decem, qui cosmoe vocantur, ut contra consulare imperium tribuni plebis, sic illi contra vim regiam constituti.

---

[1] *consecutum* Leopardi; *secututusegutus* V[1]; *consegutus* V[2]; *consecutus* is the common reading; *secutum* Halm.

---

[1] Compare Livy II, 18   Traditional date, 498 B.C.
[2] Traditional date, 494 B.C.

first dictator, being appointed about ten years after
the election of the first consuls.[1] This office was
looked upon as embodying an entirely new sort of
executive power which was very close to that of a
king. Yet the whole government was kept, with
the people's consent, in the strong hands of the
aristocracy, and in those times mighty deeds of war
were done by the brave men who held the supreme
power either as dictators or as consuls.

XXXIII. But after a short period, in about the
sixteenth year of the republic, in the consulship of
Postumus Cominius and Spurius Cassius, an event
occurred which in the nature of things was bound to
happen : the people, freed from the domination of
kings, claimed a somewhat greater measure of
rights. Such a claim may have been unreasonable,
but the essential nature of the commonwealth often
defeats reason. For you must keep in mind a fact
which I mentioned at the beginning : unless there is
in the State an even balance of rights, duties, and
functions, so that the magistrates have enough
power, the counsels of the eminent citizens enough
influence, and the people enough liberty, this kind
of government cannot be safe from revolution. For
at a time when the State was troubled by debt, the
plebeians seized first the Sacred Mount, and then the
Aventine Hill. And indeed not even the disciplinary
system of Lycurgus was able to hold his subjects,
though they were Greeks, under bridle and bit ; for,
in Sparta also, in the reign of Theopompus, the five
officials called ephors, and in Crete the ten so-called
cosmoi, were set up in opposition to the royal authority,
just as at Rome the plebeian tribunes were chosen to
counterbalance the power of the consuls.[2]

59   XXXIV. Fuerat fortasse aliqua ratio maioribus
nostris in illo aere alieno medendi,[1] quae neque
Solonem Atheniensem non longis temporibus ante
fugerat neque post aliquanto nostrum senatum, cum
sunt propter unius libidinem omnia nexa civium
liberata nectierque postea desitum ; semperque huic
generi,[2] cum plebes publica calamitate inpendiis
debilitata deficeret, salutis omnium causa aliqua
sublevatio et medicina quaesita est. quo tum consilio
praetermisso causa populo nata est, duobus tribunis
plebis per seditionem creatis ut potentia senatus
atque auctoritas minueretur ; quae tamen gravis et
magna remanebat sapientissimis et fortissimis et
armis et consilio civitatem tuentibus, quorum auctoritas maxime florebat, quod, cum honore longe ante-
cellerent ceteris, voluptatibus erant inferiores nec
pecuniis ferme superiores ; eoque erat cuiusque
gratior in re publica virtus, quod in rebus privatis
diligentissime singulos cives opera, consilio, re tue-
bantur.

60   XXXV. Quo in statu rei publicae Sp. Cassium de
occupando regno molientem, summa apud populum
gratia florentem, quaestor accusavit, eumque, ut

---

[1] The text of this clause is corrupt ; the reading of V is
given here. *Defuerat* or *Defugerat* Maehly.
[2] *generi* V ; *oneri* Moser.

---

[1] The text is corrupt and the meaning uncertain.
[2] Lucius Papirius is referred to. See Livy VIII, 28.
[3] According to tradition, about 485 B.C.

XXXIV. Perhaps our ancestors, to relieve the pressure of debt, might have used some such method as that[1] which Solon the Athenian, who lived only a short time before, had not failed to discover, and which came to our own senate's notice some time later; for then, on account of one man's lust,[2] all those citizens who had been enslaved for debt were released, and such enslavement was no longer permitted; and always, when the plebeians have been so weakened by the expenditures brought on by a public calamity that they give way under their burden, some relief or remedy has been sought for the difficulties of this class, for the sake of the safety of the whole body of citizens. But at the time of which I have been speaking such measures had not been taken, and thus the people were given an occasion, through the creation of two plebeian tribunes by means of an insurrection, for curtailing the power and influence of the senate. This power, however, remained great and respected, because the wisest and bravest still guarded the State by arms and counsel, and their influence continued to be supreme because, while they surpassed the masses in preferment, they had a smaller share of the pleasures of life, and in property were not, as a rule, better off than their fellows. And the public services of every patrician were the more highly esteemed because they scrupulously made it their practice to aid individual citizens most liberally in their private difficulties by action, advice, and financial support.

XXXV. When the State was in this situation, Spurius Cassius,[3] who enjoyed the greatest popularity, plotted to make himself king. The quaestor accused him of the crime (you have heard the story), and,

audistis, cum pater in ea culpa esse conperisse se
dixisset, cedente populo morte mactavit. gratamque
etiam illam legem [1] quarto circiter et quinquagesimo
anno post primos consules de multa et sacramento
Sp. Tarpeius et A. Aternius consules comitiis centuriatis tulerunt. Annis postea viginti ex eo, quod L.
Papirius P. Pinarius censores multis dicendis vim
armentorum a privatis in publicum averterant, levis
aestumatio pecudum in multa lege C. Iulii P. Papirii
consulum constituta est.

61   XXXVI. Sed aliquot ante annis, cum summa esset
auctoritas in senatu populo patiente atque parente,
inita ratio est, ut et consules et tribuni plebis magistratu se abdicarent, atque ut decemviri maxima
potestate sine provocatione crearentur, qui et summum imperium haberent et leges scriberent. qui
cum decem tabulas summa legum [2] aequitate pru-
dentiaque conscripsissent, in annum posterum decemviros alios subrogaverunt, quorum non similiter fides
nec iustitia laudata. quo tamen e collegio laus est
illa eximia C. Iulii, qui hominem nobilem, L. Sestium,
cuius in cubiculo ecfossum esse se praesente mortuum
diceret, cum ipse potestatem summam haberet, quod
decemvirum unus sine provocatione esset, vades

---

[1] *legem* Mai ; *rem* V.
[2] *legum* bracketed by Halm.

---

[1] Traditional date, 454 B.C. See Dionys. Halic., *Antiq.
Rom.* X. 50. The origin of this use of the word *sacramentum*
is doubtful ; see Harper's *Latin Dictionary* and Daremberg et
Saglio, *Dictionnaire des Antiquités* IV, 952—955.
[2] Traditional date, 430 B.C. ; compare Livy IV, 30.
[3] See Livy III, 35—37. The traditional date usually given
is 451 B.C.

when the father of Spurius testified that he knew him to be guilty, put him to death with the approval of the people. Later, about the fifty-fourth year after the election of the first consuls, the centuriate assembly passed that popular law regulating fines and amounts deposited in court, this law having been proposed by the consuls Spurius Tarpeius and Aulus Aternius.[1] Twenty years later, because the censors Lucius Papirius and Publius Pinarius had transferred, by the imposition of fines, a large number of cattle from private to public ownership, a method of appraising cattle that lightened the fines was introduced, in a law proposed by the consuls Gaius Julius and Publius Papirius.[2]

XXXVI. But several years before this, when the senate held supreme authority with the compliance and consent of the people, a plan was adopted whereby both the consuls and the plebeian tribunes should resign their offices, and a board of ten, possessing very great powers and not subject to the right of appeal, should be elected; and they were not only to exercise the supreme executive power but also to draw up a code of law.[3] When these men had composed, with the greatest justice and wisdom, ten tables of the law, they caused another board of ten to be elected in their stead for the following year; but the honour and justice of these latter have not been praised so highly. One member of this college, however, Gaius Julius, deserves the highest praise; for, after stating that he himself had seen a corpse dug up in the chamber of Lucius Sestius, a man of high rank, although Julius himself held the supreme power, because no appeal was permitted from the sentence of any decemvir, he

tamen poposcit, quod se legem illam praeclaram
neglecturum negaret, quae de capite civis Romani
nisi comitiis centuriatis statui vetaret.

62   XXXVII. Tertius est annus decemviralis consecutus, cum iidem essent nec alios subrogare voluissent.
in hoc statu rei publicae, quem dixi iam saepe non
posse esse diuturnum, quod non esset in omnis
ordines civitatis aequabilis, erat penes principes tota
res publica praepositis decemviris nobilissimis, non
oppositis tribunis plebis, nullis aliis adiunctis magistratibus, non provocatione ad populum contra necem
63 et verbera relicta.   ergo horum ex iniustitia subito
exorta est maxima perturbatio et totius commutatio
rei publicae ; qui duabus tabulis iniquarum legum
additis, quibus, etiam quae diiunctis populis tribui
solent conubia, haec illi ut ne plebei cum patribus [1]
essent, inhumanissima lege sanxerunt, quae postea
plebei scito Canuleio abrogata est, libidinoseque
omni imperio et acerbe et avare populo praefuerunt.
nota scilicet illa res et celebrata monumentis plurimis
litterarum, cum Decimus quidam Verginius virginem
filiam propter unius ex illis decemviris intemperiem
in foro sua manu interemisset ac maerens ad exercitum, qui tum erat in Algido, confugisset, milites

---

[1] *plebei cum patribus* V[2] ; *plebi et patribus* V[1].

---

[1] Traditional date, 445 B.C.

merely demanded that Lucius give bail for his appearance, explaining that he would not violate that excellent law which forbade a Roman citizen to be tried for his life except before the centuriate assembly.

XXXVII. A third year of the decemvirate followed, the same decemvirs continuing in office, and being unwilling to have others elected in their stead. While the government was in this situation (which, as I have stated repeatedly, can never last long, because it is not fair to all classes in the State), the whole commonwealth was in the hands of the leading citizens, there being ten eminent men in command, with no plebeian tribunes to oppose them, no other magistrates whatever in office, and not even any right of appeal to the people against execution or scourging. Consequently, as a result of the injustice of these rulers, there was a great insurrection, followed by a complete change in the government. For the decemvirs had added two tables of unjust laws, among which was one that most cruelly prohibited intermarriage between plebeians and patricians, though this privilege is usually permitted even between citizens of different States; this was later repealed by the Canuleian Law,[1] a decree of the plebeian assembly. These decemvirs also indulged in licence in all their governmental acts, and in cruelty and greed toward the people. The story of Decimus Verginius is of course well known, being recorded in many of the greatest works of our literature: how, after killing his virgin daughter with his own hand in the Forum on account of the mad lust of one of these decemvirs, he fled weeping to the army, then encamped on Mount Algidus;

bellum illud, quod erat in manibus, reliquisse et
primum montem sacrum, sicut erat in simili causa
antea factum, deinde Aventinum armatos insedisse . . .[1]

[*Desiderantur paginae octo.*]

. . . dictatore L. Quinctio dicto . . . (*Philargyrius
ad Vergil. Georg. III.* 125.)

. . . maiores[2] nostros et probavisse maxime et
retinuisse sapientissime iudico.

64   XXXVIII. Cum ea Scipio dixisset silentioque
omnium reliqua eius expectaretur oratio, tum
Tubero : Quoniam nihil ex te, Africane, hi maiores
natu requirunt, ex me audias, quid in oratione tua
desiderem.

Sane, inquit Scipio, et libenter quidem.

Tum ille : Laudavisse mihi videris nostram rem
publicam, cum ex te non de nostra, sed de omni re
publica quaesisset Laelius. nec tamen didici ex
oratione tua, istam ipsam rem publicam, quam laudas,
qua disciplina, quibus moribus aut legibus constituere
vel conservare possimus.

65   XXXIX. Hic Africanus : Puto nobis mox de
instituendis et conservandis civitatibus aptiorem,
Tubero, fore disserundi locum ; de optimo autem
statu equidem arbitrabar me satis respondisse ad id,
quod quaesierat Laelius. Primum enim numero
definieram genera civitatum tria probabilia, perniciosa
autem tribus illis totidem contraria, nullumque ex
eis unum esse optimum, sed id praestare singulis,

---

[1] *armatos insedisse* is commonly read ; *ar* . . . **V.**
[2] *maiores* is commonly read ; . . . *res* **V.**

---

[1] Traditional date, 449 B.C.

whereupon the soldiers abandoned the war in which they were engaged and [occupied under arms] at first the Sacred Mount, as they had done before for a similar reason, and later the Aventine Hill[1] . . .

About three pages are lost, of which the following short fragment may be a part.

. . . Lucius Quinctius being appointed dictator[2] . . .

. . . [which,] in my opinion, [our ancestors] approved most fully and retained most wisely.

XXXVIII. After Scipio had spoken thus, everyone was silent in expectation that he would continue. Finally Tubero said: Since my elders here make no further demands on you, Africanus, I will tell you what I should like you to add to your discourse.

Scipio. Certainly; I shall be glad to hear.

Tubero. It seems to me that you have praised our own commonwealth, though Laelius asked you to discuss, not our own State, but the State in general. And yet I have not learned from your discourse by what training, customs, or laws we shall be able to establish or to preserve the kind of commonwealth you yourself recommend.

XXXIX. *Scipio.* I think, Tubero, we shall soon find a more suitable point in our conversation at which to consider the formation and preservation of States; but as far as the ideal State is concerned, I thought I had given an adequate response to the inquiry of Laelius. For in the first place I defined the three commendable types of States and the three bad types which are their opposites. Next I demonstrated that no single one of these types is the ideal, but that a form of government which is an equal

[2] Traditional date, 458 B.C.

quod e tribus primis esset modice temperatum
66 quod autem exemplo nostrae civitatis usus sum, non
ad definiendum optimum statum valuit (nam id fieri
potuit sine exemplo), sed ut civitate maxima reapse
cerneretur quale esset id, quod ratio oratioque descri-
beret. sin autem sine ullius populi exemplo genus
ipsum exquiris optimi status, naturae imagine utendum est nobis, quoniam tu hanc imaginem urbis et
populi ni . . .

[*Multa desiderantur.*]

67 XL. . . . quem[1] iam dudum quaero et ad quem
cupio pervenire.

L. Prudentem fortasse quaeris?

Tum ille : Istum ipsum.

L. Est tibi ex eis ipsis, qui adsunt, bella copia,
vel ut a te ipso ordiare.

Tum Scipio : Atque utinam ex omni senatu pro
rata parte esset! sed tamen est ille prudens, qui,
ut saepe in Africa vidimus, immani et vastae insidens
beluae coërcet et regit beluam quocumque vult,
et levi admonitu aut tactu inflectit illam feram.

L. Novi et, tibi cum essem legatus, saepe vidi.

S. Ergo ille Indus aut Poenus unam coërcet

---

[1] *quem* commonly supplied ; lacking in V.

---

[1] The elephant.

mixture of the three good forms is superior to any of them by itself. As for my using our own State as a pattern, I did so, not to help me to define the ideal constitution (for that could be done without using any pattern at all), but in order to show, by illustrations from the actual history of the greatest State of all, what it was that reason and speech were striving to make clear. But if you inquire as to the nature of the ideal State in itself, without reference to a pattern furnished by any people, we must make use of a model supplied by nature, since you [are not satisfied with] our present model for a city and a people . . .

A passage of considerable but uncertain length is lost. After the gap Scipio appears to be discussing the ideal statesman.

XL. *Scipio.* . . . whom I have long been seeking and am anxious to discover.

Laelius. Perhaps it is a man of good sense that you seek?

Scipio. Exactly.

Laelius. You have a goodly supply of such among those now present; you might begin with yourself, for example.

Scipio. And indeed I only wish there were as high an average of good sense in the senate as a whole! However, that is also a man of good sense who rides upon a huge and monstrous beast[1] (a sight we have often met with in Africa) and guides this animal in whatever direction he wishes by gentle word or touch.

Laelius. I remember seeing this frequently when I was an officer under your command.

Scipio. Well, that Indian or Carthaginian governs

beluam, et eam docilem et humanis moribus adsue-
tam; at vero ea, quae latet in animis hominum
quaeque pars animi mens vocatur, non unam aut
facilem ad subigendum frenat et domat, si quando
id efficit, quod perraro potest. namque et illa
tenenda est ferox . . .

[*Desiderantur quattuor minimum paginae.*]

68   XLI. . . . quae sanguine alitur, quae in omni
crudelitate sic exultat, ut vix hominum acerbis
funeribus satietur . . . (*Nonius*, p. 300. 24.)

. . . cupido autem et expetenti et lubidinoso
et volutabundo in voluptatibus . . . (*Nonius*, p.
491. 16.)

. . . quartaque anxitudo prona ad luctum et
maerens semperque ipsa se sollicitans . . . (*Nonius*,
p. 72. 30.)

. . . esse autem angore, esse miseria adflictas aut
abiectas timiditate et ignavia . . . (*Nonius*, p. 228.
19.)

. . . ut auriga indoctus e curru trahitur, opteritur,
laniatur, eliditur . . . (*Nonius*, p. 292. 32 *Merc.*,
292. 3 *Quich.*)

69   XLII. . . . dici possit.

Tum Laelius : Video iam, illum, quem expectabam,
virum cui praeficias officio et muneri.

Huic scilicet, Africanus, uni paene (nam in hoc
fere uno sunt cetera), ut numquam a se ipso instituendo [1] contemplandoque discedat, ut ad imitationem
sui vocet alios, ut sese splendore animi et vitae suae
sicut speculum praebeat civibus.   ut enim in fidibus
aut tibiis atque ut in cantu ipso ac vocibus concentus

---

[1] *instituendo* V ; *intuendo* Maehly.

180

a single animal which is gentle and accustomed to the ways of man; but that power which is hidden in men's minds and forms a part of them, and is called reason, controls and subdues not merely one animal, or one which is easily mastered—that is, if it ever does accomplish that which is rarely possible; for that fierce [beast] also must be held in check . . .

A page or more is lost, from which the short fragments in XLI may be quoted. Scipio continues his description of the ideal statesman in XLII.

XLI. . . . [a beast] which feeds on blood; which takes such delight in every sort of cruelty that it can hardly be sated even by the merciless slaughter of men . . .

. . . but to one who is greedy and acquisitive and lustful, and who wallows in sensual pleasure . . .

. . . and, in the fourth place, anxiety, prone to sorrow, ever grieving and torturing itself . . .

. . . to have been afflicted by anguish and suffering, or degraded by fear and cowardice . . .

. . . as an untrained charioteer is dragged from his chariot, trampled, lacerated, crushed . . .

XLII. *Scipio.* . . . might be said.

Laelius. I now understand what duty and function [1] you would entrust to the sort of man I was seeking.

Scipio. Of course he should be given almost no other duties than this one (for it comprises most of the others)—of improving and examining himself continually, urging others to imitate him, and furnishing in himself, as it were, a mirror to his fellow-citizens by reason of the supreme excellence of his life and character. For just as in the music of harps and flutes or in the voices of singers a

---

[1] *i.e.*, the work of the ideal statesman.

est quidam tenendus ex distinctis sonis, quem inmu-
tatum aut discrepantem aures eruditae ferre non
possunt, isque concentus ex dissimillimarum vocum
moderatione concors tamen efficitur et congruens,
sic ex summis et infimis et mediis interiectis ordinibus ut sonis moderata ratione civitas consensu[1]
dissimillimorum concinit; et quae harmonia a musicis
dicitur in cantu, ea est in civitate concordia, artissi-
mum atque optimum omni in re publica vinculum
incolumitatis, eaque sine iustitia nullo pacto esse
potest.

70   XLIV. . . . plenam esse iustitiae.

Tum Scipio: Adsentior vero renuntioque vobis
nihil esse, quod adhuc de re publica dictum putemus
aut quo possimus longius progredi, nisi erit confirmatum non modo falsum illud esse, sine iniuria
non posse, sed hoc verissimum esse, sine summa
iustitia rem publicam geri nullo modo posse.   sed,
si placet, in hunc diem hactenus; reliqua (satis enim
multa restant) differamus in crastinum.

Cum ita placuisset, finis disputandi in eum diem
factus est.

---

[1] The rest of the sentence is supplied from August. *de Civ.
Dei* II, 21 ; *civitas con* . . . V.

certain harmony of the different tones must be preserved, the interruption or violation of which is intolerable to trained ears, and as this perfect agreement and harmony is produced by the proportionate blending of unlike tones, so also is a State made harmonious by agreement among dissimilar elements, brought about by a fair and reasonable blending together of the upper, middle, and lower classes, just as if they were musical tones. What the musicians call harmony in song is concord in a State, the strongest and best bond of permanent union in any commonwealth ; and such concord can never be brought about without the aid of justice.

A passage of uncertain length is lost. In it, according to St. Augustine (*De Civ. Dei* II, 21), when Scipio had spoken further of the importance of justice in a State and the unfortunate results of its absence, Philus asked that this question be considered more fully, and that justice be taken up at greater length, because it was a common opinion that the government of a State cannot be carried on without injustice.

XLIV. . . . to be full of justice.

Scipio. I agree with you, and wish to assure you that we must consider all the statements we have made so far about the commonwealth as amounting to nothing, and must admit that we have no basis whatever for further progress, unless we can not merely disprove the contention that a government cannot be carried on without injustice, but are also able to prove positively that it cannot be carried on without the strictest justice. However, with your permission, we shall go no further to-day, but shall put off what remains (for that is a considerable amount) until to-morrow.

This proposal being agreed to, they made an end of the conversation for that day.

DE RE PUBLICA
LIBER TERTIUS

[Desiderantur hic paginae minimum quattuor.]

3   II. . . . et vehiculis tarditati, eademque cum accepisset homines inconditis vocibus inchoatum quiddam et confusum sonantes, incidit has et distinxit in partis et ut signa quaedam sic verba rebus inpressit hominesque antea dissociatos iucundissimo inter se sermonis vinclo conligavit. a simili etiam mente vocis, qui videbantur infiniti, soni paucis notis inventis sunt omnes signati et expressi, quibus et conloquia cum absentibus et indicia voluntatum et monumenta rerum praeteritarum tenerentur. accessit eo numerus, res cum ad vitam necessaria, tum una

---

[1] Compare the discussion of justice and injustice in Plato, *Republic* I, II, and IV.

THE REPUBLIC

BOOK III

Cicero prefaces the second day's discussion with an introduction of considerable length, of which sections 3–7 form a part. St. Augustine (*De Civ. Dei* II, 21) has given us a brief outline of the discussion itself. Philus is prevailed upon to undertake the defence of the thesis that the government cannot be carried on without injustice (sections 8–28). Laelius then takes up the defence of justice, maintaining that nothing is so harmful to a State as injustice, and that a State cannot be preserved without justice (sections 32–41). Scipio then resumes his discourse, and argues that his commonwealth as previously defined cannot be said to exist at all except where the government is just (sections 42–48).[1]

A page or more is lost at the beginning of the book. According to St. Augustine (*Contra Iulianum Pelag.* IV, 12, 60), the book begins with some reflections on man's weakness at birth, and how it is overcome by the divine spirit planted within him.

II. . . . and by vehicles [to remedy] his slowness of motion . . . and [reason] likewise, when it found men uttering unformed and confused sounds with unpractised voices, separated these sounds into distinct classes, imprinting names upon things just as distinguishing marks are sometimes placed upon them, thus uniting the race of men, solitary before, by the pleasant bond of communication by speech. Reason also marked and represented all the sounds of the voice, which seemed innumerable, by a few characters which it invented, so that conversation could be carried on with persons at a distance, and indications of our desires and records of past events could be set down. To this art was added that of numbers, which is not only necessary for human life

185

inmutabilis et aeterna; quae prima inpulit etiam,
ut suspiceremus in caelum nec frustra siderum
motus intueremur dinumerationibusque noctium ac
dierum[1] . . .

[Desiderantur fere octo paginae.]

4   III. . . . quorum animi altius se extulerunt et
aliquid dignum dono, ut ante dixi, deorum aut
efficere aut excogitare potuerunt. quare sint nobis
isti, qui de ratione vivendi disserunt, magni homines,
ut sunt, sint eruditi, sint veritatis et virtutis magistri,
dum modo sit haec quaedam, sive a viris in rerum
publicarum varietate versatis inventa sive etiam in
istorum otio ac litteris tractata res, sicut est, minime
quidem contemnenda, ratio civilis et disciplina populorum, quae perficit in bonis ingeniis, id quod iam
persaepe perfecit, ut incredibilis quaedam et divina
5 virtus exsisteret. quodsi quis ad ea instrumenta
animi, quae natura quaeque civilibus institutis habuit,
adiungendam sibi etiam doctrinam et uberiorem
rerum cognitionem putavit, ut ii ipsi, qui in horum
librorum disputatione versantur, nemo est, quin eos
anteferre omnibus debeat. quid enim potest esse
praeclarius, quam cum rerum magnarum tractatio
atque usus cum illarum artium studiis et cognitione

---

[1] *dierum* is commonly read; *die* . . . V.

[1] Compare Lucretius' account of the rise of civilization (*De
Rerum Natura* V; in regard to the invention of speech, see
especially lines 1028 ff.).

but also unique in being unchangeable and eternal
in itself. And acquaintance with this art first encouraged men to look up at the sky and to gaze, no
longer idly, upon the motions of the stars, and by
the numbering of nights and days . . .[1]

About three pages are lost. The account of the development
of civilization is concluded in what follows, with the rise of
philosophy and the art of statesmanship as its climax.

III. . . . whose thoughts rose to an even higher
plane, and they were able to achieve, by action or
reflection, things worthy of the gift they had received, as I have said, from the gods. Wherefore
let us admit that those who discuss the principles of
living are great men, which is indeed the truth; let
us recognize them as learned, and as teachers of
truth and virtue, if only we do not forget that
another science is by no means to be scorned,
whether it was discovered by men who had had
actual experience with various kinds of States, or
was developed through the quiet study of these
same learned men—I mean the art of government
and the training of peoples, which, in men of ability
and good character, calls into being, as it has
very often done in the past, an almost incredible
and divine virtue. But if anyone has believed, as
these men do who are carrying on the discussion
recorded in the present treatise, that learning and a
richer knowledge should be added to those faculties
which the mind possesses by nature and has acquired
by experience in public affairs, then everyone ought
to consider a man who combines these attainments
superior to all others. For what can be more admirable than the union of experience in the management of great affairs with the study and mastery of

coniungitur? aut quid P. Scipione, quid C. Laelio,
quid L. Philo perfectius cogitari potest, qui, ne
quid praetermitterent, quod ad summam laudem
clarorum virorum pertineret, ad domesticum [1] maiorumque morem etiam hanc a Socrate adventiciam
6 doctrinam adhibuerunt? quare qui utrumque voluit
et potuit, id est ut cum maiorum institutis, tum
doctrina se instrueret, ad laudem hunc omnia consecutum puto. sin altera est utra via prudentiae
deligenda, tamen, etiamsi cui videbitur illa in
optimis studiis et artibus quieta vitae ratio beatior,
haec civilis laudabilior est certe et inlustrior, ex qua
vita sic summi viri ornantur, ut vel M'. Curius,

quem nemo ferro potuit superare nec auro,

vel . . .

[*Desiderari videntur paginae sex.*]

7 IV. . . . fuisse sapientiam, tamen hoc in ratione
utriusque generis interfuit, quod illi verbis et artibus
aluerunt naturae principia, hi autem institutis et
legibus. pluris vero haec tulit una civitas, si minus
sapientis, quoniam id nomen illi tam restricte tenent,
at certe summa laude dignos, quoniam sapientium
praecepta et inventa coluerunt. atque etiam, quot

---

[1] *domesticum* Heinrich; *domesticorum* V.

---

[1] Probably from Ennius, *Annales* XII.
[2] *i.e.,* by and to the philosophers.

those other arts? Or who can be considered closer
to the ideal than Publius Scipio, Gaius Laelius, and
Lucius Philus, who, for fear of omitting something
that might be necessary to the complete excellence
of eminent men, added the foreign learning which
originated with Socrates to the traditional customs
of their own country and their ancestors? Therefore
those who have had the desire and ability to attain
both these objects—who, that is, have perfected
themselves by acquiring learning as well as by the
observance of their ancestral customs, deserve from
every point of view, in my opinion, the highest
honour. But if only one of these two paths to
wisdom can be chosen, even though a quiet life
devoted to the study of the noblest arts will seem
happier to some, surely the life of a statesman is
more deserving of praise and more conducive to
fame; by such a life the greatest men win honour;
as for example, Manius Curius,

Whom none could overcome with sword or gold,[1]

or . . .

About two pages appear to be lost.

IV. [We must admit that both these types of
learning] deserved the name of wisdom, yet the
difference between these two classes of men has
consisted in the fact that one nourished Nature's
first gifts to man by admonition and instruction,
while the other did so by institutions and laws.
Indeed, our own country alone has produced many
men, who, if they have not been " wise," since that
name is so carefully restricted,[2] have surely deserved
the highest praise, since they have fostered the
precepts and the discoveries of the wise. And if

et sunt laudandae civitates et fuerunt, quoniam id
est in rerum natura longe maximi consilii, constituere eam rem publicam, quae possit esse diuturna,
si singulos numeremus in singulas, quanta iam reperiatur virorum excellentium multitudo! quodsi aut
Italiae Latium aut eiusdem Sabinam aut Volscam
gentem, si Samnium, si Etruriam, si magnam illam
Graeciam conlustrare animo voluerimus, si deinde
Assyrios, si Persas, si Poenos, si haec. . .

[Desiderantur paginae duodecim.]

8   V. . . . cati.

Et Philus : Praeclaram vero causam ad me defertis,
cum me improbitatis patrocinium suscipere voltis.

Atqui id tibi, inquit Laelius, verendum est,[1] si ea
dixeris, quae contra iustitiam dici solent, ne sic
etiam sentire videare, cum et ipse sis quasi unicum
exemplum antiquae probitatis et fidei neque sit
ignota consuetudo tua contrarias in partis disserendi,
quod ita facillume verum inveniri putes.

Et Philus : Heia vero, inquit, geram morem vobis
et me oblinam sciens ; quod quoniam, qui aurum
quaerunt, non putant sibi recusandum, nos, cum
iustitiam quaeramus, rem multo omni auro cariorem,
nullam profecto molestiam fugere debemus. atque
utinam, quem ad modum oratione sum usurus aliena,

---

[1] *verendum est* V ; *verendum non est* Leopardi, Halm.

---

[1] *Magna Graecia* ; *i.e.*, the Greek cities of Southern Italy
(sometimes including those of Sicily).

we consider how many praiseworthy commonwealths exist now and have existed in the past, and remember that the establishment of a State which is stable enough to endure for ages requires by far the highest intellectual powers that nature can produce, what a multitude of great geniuses there must have been, even if we suppose that every such State possessed only one! But if we survey the nations of Italy; the Latins, Sabines, Volscians, Samnites, or Etruscans; if we examine Great Greece;[1] and then if [we consider] the Assyrians, the Persians, the Punic peoples, if . . . these . . .

About four pages are lost. At the end of the gap we find that the dialogue has been resumed, and that Philus has evidently just been asked to defend the cause of injustice.

V. *Philus.* It is indeed an excellent cause that you are handing over to me, when you request me to undertake the defence of wickedness!

Laelius. I suppose you have great reason to fear that, if you repeat the usual arguments against justice, you may be thought also to approve them, when you are yourself an almost incomparable example of our old-fashioned probity and honour, and when we are quite familiar with your habit of arguing on the other side, because you think that it is the easiest means of reaching the truth!

Philus. Very well, then, I will humour you and cover myself with mud with a full realization of what I am doing. For just as those who seek gold do not hesitate to do this, so we who seek Justice, which is much more valuable than all the gold in the world, surely ought not to shrink from any hardship. And I wish, just as I am going to present another's argument, that I could also make use of

sic mihi ore uti liceret alieno! nunc ea dicenda
sunt L. Furio Philo, quae Carneades, Graecus homo
et consuetus, quod commodum esset, verbis . . .

[*Desiderari videntur paginae quattuor.*]

9 . . . ut Carneadi respondeatis, qui saepe optimas
causas ingenii calumnia ludificari solet . . . (*Nonius,*
p. 263. 14.)

11 VII. . . . iustitia foras spectat et proiecta tota
est atque eminet . . . (*Nonius,* p. 373. 25.)

. . . quae virtus praeter ceteras totam se ad
alienas porrigit utilitatis atque explicat . . . (*Nonius,*
p. 299. 30.)

12 VIII. . . . et reperiret et tueretur, alter autem
de ipsa iustitia quattuor implevit sane grandis libros.
nam ab Chrysippo nihil magnum nec magnificum
desideravi, qui suo quodam more loquitur, ut omnia
verborum momentis, non rerum ponderibus examinet.
illorum fuit heroum eam virtutem, quae est una, si
modo est, maxime munifica et liberalis, et quae
omnis magis quam sepse diligit, aliis nata potius
quam sibi, excitare iacentem et in illo divino solio

13 non longe a sapientia conlocare. nec vero illis aut
voluntas defuit (quae enim iis scribendi alia causa
aut quod omnino consilium fuit?) aut ingenium,
quo omnibus praestiterunt; sed eorum et volun-

---

[1] Plato and Aristotle are evidently referred to. Aristotle's
lost work on Justice, in four books, is mentioned by Diogenes
Laertius (V, 1, 9, 22).

another's tongue! For Lucius Furius Philus must now report what the Greek Carneades, who was accustomed . . . whatever suited him . . . in words . . .

About thirty lines appear to be lost, of which the three short fragments which follow are perhaps part. Lactantius (*Inst. Div.* V, 14, 3–5 ; *Epitom.* 55, 5–8) tells us that the disputation of Carneades, as quoted by Philus, began with a review of the arguments of Plato and Aristotle in favour of justice and then turned to a refutation of them.

. . . [do not] reply [to me but] to Carneades, whose way it is frequently to make the best causes appear ridiculous by his talent for sophistry . . .

VII. . . . justice looks out of doors and is completely prominent and conspicuous . . .

. . . a virtue which, beyond all others, is entirely devoted and applied to the advantage of others . . .

VIII. *Philus.* . . . should both discover and preserve . . . but the other[1] filled four very large volumes with a treatise on justice itself. For I expected nothing great or remarkable from Chrysippus, who has his own peculiar method of discussion, examining everything on the basis of the meaning of words rather than by the weighing of facts. It was appropriate for those heroes to raise up this fallen virtue (which, where it really exists, is the most generous and liberal of them all, loving as it does all others more than itself, and existing for others' advantage rather than its own), and to seat it upon that divine throne not far from Wisdom herself. Nor indeed did they lack the desire to exalt it (for what other reason had they for writing? What was their purpose if not this?), nor the ability, in which they surpassed all others; but the weak-

tatem et copiam causa vicit. ius enim, de quo
quaerimus, civile est aliquod, naturale nullum; nam
si esset, ut[1] calida et frigida, ut amara et dulcia,
sic essent iusta et iniusta eadem omnibus.

14   IX. Nunc autem, si quis illo Pacuviano "inve-
hens alitum anguium curru" multas et varias gentis
et urbes despicere et oculis conlustrare possit, videat
primum in illa incorrupta maxime gente Aegypti-
orum, quae plurimorum saeculorum et eventorum
memoriam litteris continet, bovem quendam putari
deum, quem Apim Aegyptii nominant, multaque
alia portenta apud eosdem et cuiusque generis
beluas numero consecratas deorum; deinde Graeciae,
sicut apud nos, delubra magnifica humanis consecrata simulacris, quae Persae nefaria putaverunt;
eamque unam ob causam Xerses[2] inflammari
Atheniensium fana iussisse dicitur, quod deos,
quorum domus esset omnis hic mundus, inclusos
15 parietibus contineri nefas esse duceret.   post autem
cum Persis et Philippus, qui cogitavit, et Alexander,
qui gessit, hanc bellandi causam inferebat, quod
vellet Graeciae fana poenire; quae ne reficienda
quidem Graii putaverunt, ut esset posteris ante os
documentum Persarum sceleris sempiternum.   quam

---

    [1] *ut* Zell ; *et* **V**.   [2] *Xerses* **V** ; *Xerxes* Orelli.

---

    [1] The play from which these words are quoted is unknown,
Compare Cicero, *De Invent.* I, 27.

ness of their case defeated both their enthusiasm
and their eloquence. For the justice which we are
investigating is a product of government, not of
nature at all; for if it were natural, then, like heat
and cold, or bitter and sweet, justice and injustice
would be the same thing to all men.

IX. But in actual fact, if one could visit many
diverse nations and cities and examine them, travel-
ling about in Pacuvius' famous "chariot of winged
snakes," [1] he would see first of all that in Egypt,
famed as ever changeless, which preserves written
records of the events of countless ages, a bull, which
the Egyptians call Apis, is deemed a god, and many
other monsters and animals of every sort are held
sacred as divine. Then, too, he would see in Greece,
just as with us Romans, magnificent shrines, adorned
with sacred statues in human form; a custom which
the Persians considered wicked. And in fact Xerxes
is said to have ordered the Athenian temples to be
burned for the sole reason that he thought it sacrilege to keep the gods whose home is the whole
universe shut up within walls. [2] But later Philip, who
planned an attack on the Persians, and Alexander,
who actually made one, gave as their excuse for war
the desire to avenge the temples of Greece, which
the Greeks had thought it proper never to rebuild,
so that posterity might have ever before its eyes a
monument of Persian impiety. [3] How many peoples,

[2] Compare Cicero, *De Leg.* II, 26; *De Nat. Deor.* I, 115.
See also Herodotus I, 131 and VIII, 109.
[3] Compare Pausanias X, 35, 2. But such an intention is
probably a later invention; otherwise it would be difficult
to explain Pericles' resolution that all these temples be
restored (Plutarch, *Pericles* 17).

multi, ut Tauri in Axino, ut rex Aegypti Busiris,
ut Galli, ut Poeni, homines immolare et pium et
dis immortalibus gratissumum esse duxerunt! vitae
vero instituta sic distant, ut Cretes et Aetoli latrocinari honestum putent, Lacedaemonii suos omnes
agros esse dictitarint, quos spiculo possent attingere.
Athenienses iurare etiam publice solebant omnem
suam esse terram, quae oleam frugesve ferret; Galli
turpe esse ducunt frumentum manu quaerere,
16 itaque armati alienos agros demetunt; nos vero
iustissimi homines, qui Transalpinas gentis oleam
et vitem serere non sinimus, quo pluris sint nostra
oliveta nostraeque vineae; quod cum faciamus,
prudenter facere dicimur, iuste non dicimur, ut
intellegatis discrepare ab aequitate sapientiam.
Lycurgus autem, ille legum optumarum et aequis-
sumi iuris inventor, agros locupletium plebi ut
servitio colendos dedit.

17 X. Genera vero si velim iuris, institutorum,
morum consuetudinumque describere, non modo in
tot gentibus varia, sed in una urbe, vel in hac
ipsa, milliens mutata demonstrem, ut hic iuris noster
interpres alia nunc Manilius iura dicat esse de

---

[1] Compare Euripides, *Iphigenia in Tauris*, and Herodotus
IV, 103.

[2] Son of Poseidon ; killed by Hercules.

[3] See Caesar, *Gallic War* VI, 16.

[4] See, for example, Diodor. Sicul. V, 31–32 ; XIX, 14.

[5] In regard to the Aetolians compare Thucyd. I, 5. The
Cretans allied themselves with the Cilician pirates against
the Romans.

[6] This saying is credited to Antalcidas (Plutarch, *Apoph.
Lac.* VI, p. 819 ; *Quaest. Rom.* VII, p. 83).

[7] Part of the oath of the *Ephebi* (Plutarch, *Alcibiades* 15, 8 :
Ὀμνύουσι γὰρ ὅροις χρήσασθαι τῆς Ἀττικῆς πυροῖς κριθαῖς

such as the Taurians[1] on the shores of the Euxine, the Egyptian king Busiris,[2] the Gauls,[3] and the Carthaginians,[4] have believed human sacrifice both pious and most pleasing to the immortal gods! Indeed, men's principles of life are so different that the Cretans and Aetolians[5] consider piracy and brigandage honourable, and the Spartans used to claim as their own all the territory they could touch with their spears.[6] The Athenians also used actually to take public oaths[7] that all lands which produced olives or grain were their own. The Gauls[8] think it disgraceful to grow grain by manual labour; and consequently they go forth armed and reap other men's fields. We ourselves, indeed, the most just of men, who forbid the races beyond the Alps to plant the olive or the vine, so that our own olive groves and vineyards may be the more valuable, are said to act with prudence in doing so, but not with justice; so that you can easily understand that wisdom and equity do not agree. Indeed, Lycurgus, famed as the author of excellent laws and a most equitable system of justice, provided that the lands of the rich should be cultivated by the poor as if the latter were slaves.

X. But if I wished to describe the conceptions of justice, and the principles, customs, and habits which have existed, I could show you, not merely differences in all the different nations, but that there have been a thousand changes in a single city, even in our own, in regard to these things. For example, our friend Manilius here, being an interpreter of the law, would

ἀμπέλοις σύκαις ἐλίαις, οἰκείαν ποιεῖσθαι διδασκόμενοι τὴν ἥμερον καὶ καρποφόρον).

[8] Compare Diodor. Sicul. V, 32, 4.

mulierum legatis et hereditatibus, alia solitus sit
adulescens dicere nondum Voconia lege lata; quae
quidem ipsa lex utilitatis virorum gratia rogata in
mulieres plena est iniuriae. cur enim pecuniam
non habeat mulier? cur virgini Vestali sit heres,
non sit matri suae? cur autem, si pecuniae modus
statuendus fuit feminis, P. Crassi filia posset habere,
si unica patri esset, acris milliens salva lege, mea
triciens non posset . . .

[*Desiderari videntur paginae duae.*]

18 XI. . . . sanxisset iura nobis, et omnes isdem et
iidem non alias aliis uterentur. quaero autem, si
iusti hominis et si boni est viri parere legibus,
quibus? an quaecumque erunt? at nec incon-
stantiam virtus recipit, nec varietatem natura pati-
tur, legesque poena, non iustitia nostra compro-
bantur; nihil habet igitur naturale ius; ex quo
illud efficitur, ne iustos quidem esse natura. an
vero in legibus varietatem esse dicunt, natura autem
viros bonos eam iustitiam sequi, quae sit, non eam,
quae putetur? esse enim hoc boni viri et iusti,
19 tribuere id cuique, quod sit quoque dignum. ecquid
ergo primum mutis tribuemus beluis? non enim

---

[1] Women's rights of inheritance were limited by the
Voconian Law in 169 B.C. (or 174).

[2] A million sesterces is approximately £10,000.

[3] An allusion to the well-known controversy as to whether
Justice is founded on Nature (φύσις) or Law (νόμος).

[4] For this definition of Justice, see Plato, *Republic* I, 331 ff.

give you different advice about the rights of women in regard to legacies and inheritances from that which he used to give in his youth, before the passage of the Voconian law.[1] In fact that law, passed for men's advantage, is full of injustice to women. For why should a woman not have money of her own? Why may a Vestal Virgin have an heir, while her mother may not? Why, on the other hand, if it was necessary to limit the amount of property a woman could own, should the daughter of Publius Crassus, if she were her father's only child, be permitted by law to have a hundred million sesterces,[2] while mine is not even allowed three million? . . .

About fifteen lines appear to be lost.

XI. . . . . [if the supreme God] had provided laws for us, then all men would obey the same laws, and the same men would not have different laws at different times. But, I ask, if it is the duty of a just and good man to obey the laws, what laws is he to obey? All the different laws that exist? But virtue does not allow inconsistency, nor does nature permit variation; and laws are imposed upon us by fear of punishment, not by our sense of justice. Therefore there is no such thing as natural justice, and from this it follows that neither are men just by nature.[3] Or will they tell us that, though laws vary, good men naturally follow what is truly just, not what is thought to be so? For, they say, it is the duty of a good and just man to give everyone that which is his due.[4] Well then, first of all, what is it, if anything, that we are to grant to dumb animals as their due? For it is not men of mediocre talents,

mediocres viri, sed maxumi et docti, Pythagoras et Empedocles, unam omnium animantium condicionem iuris esse denuntiant ' clamantque inexpiabilis poenas impendere iis, a quibus violatum sit animal. scelus est igitur nocere bestiae, quod scelus qui velit . . .

[*Multa desiderantur.*]

23 XIII. . . . sunt enim omnes, qui in populum vitae necisque potestatem habent, tyranni, sed se Iovis optimi nomine malunt reges vocari. cum autem certi propter divitias aut genus aut aliquas opes rem publicam tenent, est factio, sed vocantur illi optimates. si vero populus plurimum potest omniaque eius arbitrio reguntur, dicitur illa libertas,

but those who are eminent and learned, such as Pythagoras and Empedocles, who declare that the same principles of justice apply to all living creatures, and insist that inevitable penalties threaten those who injure an animal. It is a crime, therefore, to harm a brute beast, and this crime . . . who wishes . . .

A passage of considerable, but uncertain, length is lost. Some information as to its contents is supplied by Lactantius (*Inst. Div.* V, 16, 2–4; VI, 9, 2–4; and VI. 6 19 and 23) and Tertullian (*Apolog.* 25, p. 164 Oehl.). The outlines of the argument appear to have been as follows :

The variety of laws in different States proves that these codes must be based on utility, which differs in different places, not on justice. Changes in the laws of a single State prove the same thing. There is no natural justice or law, but men as well as all other living creatures are governed naturally by utility. There is therefore no such thing as justice, or, if it exists, it is the height of folly, inasmuch as it leads us to injure ourselves to the advantage of others. The best proof of this is found in history, particularly in that of Rome. She has won her empire by injustice both to gods and men ; a policy of justice would make her again what she was originally, a miserable poverty-stricken village. What is commonly called justice in States is nothing but an agreement for mutual self-restraint, which is a result of weakness, and is based on nothing whatever but utility. Rulers of all sorts rule for their own advantage solely, not in the interest of the governed.

XIII. *Philus.* . . . for all who have the power of life and death over a people are tyrants, but they prefer to be called kings, the title given to Jupiter the Best. But when a certain number of men, by means of riches or noble birth or some other advantage, hold a commonwealth in their power, that is a ruling faction, but the rulers are called aristocrats. But if the people hold the supreme power and everything is administered according to their

est vero licentia. sed cum alius alium timet, et
homo hominem et ordo ordinem, tum quia sibi
nemo confidit, quasi pactio fit inter populum et
potentis; ex quo existit id, quod Scipio laudabat,
coniunctum civitatis genus; etenim iustitiae non
natura nec voluntas, sed inbecillitas mater est.
nam cum de tribus unum est optandum, aut facere
iniuriam nec accipere aut et facere et accipere aut
neutrum, optimum est facere, impune si possis,
secundum nec facere nec pati, miserrimum digla-
diari semper tum faciendis, tum accipiendis iniuriis.
ita qui primum illud adsequi . . .

[Aliquot paginae desunt.]

24   XIV. . . . nam cum quaereretur ex eo, quo scelere
inpulsus mare haberet infestum uno myoparone,
"Eodem," inquit, "quo tu orbem terrae." [2] . . .
(*Nonius*, p. 125. 12, p. 318. 16, p. 535. 16.)

XV. . . . omni . . . tote. sapientia iubet
augere opes, amplificare divitias, proferre finis (unde
enim esset illa laus in summorum imperatorum
incisa monimentis: [1] " Finis imperii propagavit," nisi
aliquid de alieno accessisset?), imperare quam
plurimis, frui voluptatibus, pollere, regnare, domi-
nari; iustitia autem praecipit parcere omnibus, consulere generi hominum, suum cuique reddere, sacra,

---

[1] The common reading is printed here; *sapientia iubet
aug-r- opes, amplificare divitias, proferre finis unde enim esset
illa la . . in summo . . . m imperatoru . . inci . . . m- n . .
finis,* etc. V.

---

[1] The reference is to Alexander the Great. St. Augustine
(*De Civ. Dei* IV, 4, 25) tells this story of Alexander and the
pirate, which he probably took from Cicero.

[2] Compare Nepos, *Hamilcar* 2, 5; Livy XXXVI, 1, 3.

desires, that is called liberty, but is really licence. But when there is mutual fear, man fearing man and class fearing class, then, because no one is confident in his own strength, a sort of bargain is made between the common people and the powerful; this results in that mixed form of government which Scipio has been recommending; and thus, not nature or desire, but weakness, is the mother of justice. For we must choose one of three things—to do injustice and not to suffer it, or both to do it and to suffer it, or else neither to do it nor to suffer it. The happiest choice is to do it with impunity, if you can; the second best is neither to do it nor to suffer it; and the worst fate of all is to engage in the everlasting struggle of doing and suffering injustice. Thus he who first . . . . to accomplish that . . . .

A passage of considerable length is lost, of which the following fragment may be a part.

XIV. . . . for when he was asked what wickedness drove him to harass the sea with his one pirate galley, he replied: "The same wickedness that drives you to harass the whole world."[1] . . .

XV. *Philus.* . . . Wisdom urges us to increase our resources, to multiply our wealth, to extend our boundaries; for what is the meaning of those words of praise inscribed on the monuments of our greatest generals, "He extended the boundaries of the empire,"[2] except that an addition was made out of the territory of others? Wisdom urges us also to rule over as many subjects as possible, to enjoy pleasures, to become rich, to be rulers and masters; justice, on the other hand, instructs us to spare all men, to consider the interests of the whole human race, to give everyone his due, and not to touch

publica, aliena non tangere.[1] quid igitur efficitur,
si sapientiae pareas? divitiae, potestates, opes,
honores, imperia, regna vel privatis vel populis.
sed quoniam de re publica loquimur, sunt inlustriora,
quae publice fiunt, quoniamque eadem est ratio
iuris in utroque, de populi sapientia dicendum puto.
ut[2] iam omittam alios, noster hic populus, quem
Africanus hesterno sermone a stirpe repetivit, cuius
imperio iam orbis terrae tenetur, iustitia an sapientia
est e minimo omnium maximus factus?[3] . . .

[*Desiderantur minimum quattuor paginae.*]

25   . . . praeter Arcadas et Atheniensis, qui, credo, ti-
mentes hoc interdictum iustitiae ne quando existeret,
commenti sunt se de terra tamquam hos ex arvis
musculos extitisse.

26   XVI. Ad haec illa dici solent primum ab iis,
qui minime sunt in disserendo mali, qui in ea causa
eo plus auctoritatis habent, quia, cum de viro bono
quaeritur, quem apertum et simplicem volumus
esse, non sunt in disputando vafri,[4] non veteratores,
non malitiosi ; negant enim sapientem idcirco
virum bonum esse, quod eum sua sponte ac per se
bonitas et iustitia delectet, sed quod vacua metu,

---

[1] The common reading is printed here : *reddere, s . . ra,
publica alie . .*, etc. V.

[2] *ut* Heinrich ; *et* V.

[3] *maximus factus* added by Mai ; lacking in V.

[4] *vafri* V[2], Nonius p. 19 ; *veri* V[1].

---

[1] See Pausanias II, 14, 4 ; V, 1, 1. These two peoples
alone, if their claim to be autochthonous was recognized,
could retain with a show of justice the territory they
occupied.

sacred or public property, or that which belongs to others. What, then, is the result if you obey wisdom? Wealth, power, riches, public office, military commands, and royal authority, whether we are speaking of individuals or of nations. But, as we are discussing the State at present, what is done by a State is more important for our purpose, and, since the same facts in reference to justice are applicable in both cases, I think it better to discuss the wisdom of a people. Not to mention others, did our own people, whose record Africanus traced from the beginning in yesterday's discussion, and whose empire now embraces the whole world, [grow] from the smallest [to the greatest] through justice or through wisdom? . . .

Thirty lines or more are lost.

Philus. . . . . except the Arcadians and Athenians, who, I suppose, feared that this provision dictated by justice might at some time be put into effect, and therefore invented the story that they had sprung from the earth, as field-mice come out of ploughed ground.[1]

XVI. To such arguments as these the following are usually the replies first given by those who are not unskilful in disputation, and whose discussions of this subject have all the greater weight because, in the search for the good man, whom we require to be open and frank, they do not themselves use crafty and rascally tricks of argument—these men[2] say first of all that a wise man is not good because goodness and justice of or in themselves give him pleasure, but because the life of a good man is free from fear,

[2] The Epicureans, who advocated justice as an aid to happiness.

cura, sollicitudine, periculo vita bonorum virorum
sit, contra autem improbis semper aliqui scrupus
in animis haereat, semper iis ante oculos iudicia et
supplicia versentur ; nullum autem emolumentum
esse, nullum iniustitia partum praemium tantum,
semper ut timeas, semper ut adesse, semper ut
impendere aliquam poenam putes, damna....

[*Desiderantur in cod. Vat. quattuor minimum paginae,
sed una fere pagina loco ab Lactantio adlato suppletur.*]

27 XVII. Quaero, si duo sint, quorum alter optimus
vir, aequissimus, summa iustitia, singulari fide, alter
insigni scelere et audacia, et si in eo sit errore
civitas, ut bonum illum virum sceleratum, facinoro-
sum, nefarium putet, contra autem, qui sit impro-
bissimus, existimet esse summa probitate ac fide,
proque hac opinione omnium civium bonus ille vir
vexetur, rapiatur, manus ei denique adferantur,
effodiantur oculi, damnetur, vinciatur, uratur,
exterminetur,[1] egeat, postremo iure etiam optimo
omnibus miserrimus esse videatur, contra autem
ille improbus laudetur, colatur, ab omnibus diligatur,
omnes ad eum honores, omnia imperia, omnes
opes, omnes undique copiae conferantur, vir denique
optimus omnium existimatione et dignissimus omni
fortuna optima iudicetur, quis tandem erit tam
demens, qui dubitet, utrum se esse malit?

28 XVIII. Quod in singulis, idem est in populis :
nulla est tam stulta civitas, quae non iniuste in-
perare malit quam servire iuste. nec vero longius

---

[1] All of this sentence up to this point is supplied from
Lactant. *Inst. Div.* V, 12, 5–6 ; ...*netur, egeat,* etc., V.

---

[1] Compare Plato, *Republic* II, 361–362.

anxiety, worry, and danger, while on the other hand the minds of the wicked are always troubled by one thing or another, and trial and punishment always stand before their eyes. They add, on the other hand, that no advantage or reward won by injustice is great enough to offset constant fear, or the ever-present thought that some punishment is near, or is threatening, ... losses . . . .

About one page appears to be lost.

XVII. *Philus* . . . . Suppose there are two men, one a pattern of virtue, fairness, justice, and honour, and the other an example of extreme wickedness and audacity; and suppose a nation is so mistaken as to believe the good man a wicked, treacherous criminal, and the wicked man on the other hand a model of probity and honour. Then let us imagine that, in accordance with this opinion, held by all his fellow-citizens, the good man is harassed, attacked, and arrested; blinded, sentenced, bound, branded, banished, and reduced to beggary, and finally is also most justly deemed by all men to be most miserable. Then let the wicked man, on the contrary, be praised, courted, and universally loved; let him receive all sorts of public offices, military commands, wealth and riches from every source; and finally, let him have the universal reputation of being the best man in the world and most worthy of all the favours of fortune. Now I ask you, who could be so insane as to doubt which of the two he would prefer to be?[1]

XVIII. The same thing is true of States as of persons; no people would be so foolish as not to prefer to be unjust masters rather than just slaves. I do

abibo. consul ego quaesivi, cum vos mihi essetis
in consilio, de Numantino foedere. quis ignorabat
Q. Pompeium fecisse foedus, eadem in causa esse
Mancinum? alter, vir optimus, etiam suasit rogationem me ex senatus consulto ferente, alter
acerrime se defendit. si pudor quaeritur, si pro-
bitas, si fides, Mancinus haec attulit, si ratio,
consilium, prudentia, Pompeius antistat. utrum....

[*Aliquot desunt paginae.*]

32 XXI. . . . Non gravarer, Laeli, nisi et hos velle
putarem et ipse cuperem te quoque aliquam partem
huius nostri sermonis attingere, praesertim cum
heri ipse dixeris te nobis etiam superfuturum.
verum id quidem fieri non potest; ne desis, omnes
te rogamus. . . . (*Gellius I,* 22. 8.)

---

not need to go far for an example : during my consulship, with you as my advisers, I had under consideration the treaty with Numantia. Who was not aware that Quintus Pompeius had made a treaty and that Mancinus was in the same situation ? But the latter, an excellent man, went so far as to favour the bill which I proposed in accordance with a resolution of the senate, while the former defended himself with energy. If we are seeking modesty, probity, and honour, these qualities belong to Mancinus ; but if we look for reason, wisdom, and prudence, then Pompeius is superior.[1]

The rest of Philus' report of the defence of injustice made by Carneades is lost, but we are given some idea of its contents by Lactantius (*Inst. Div.* V, 16, 5–13). Toward the end he seems to have turned to men's personal relations for further proofs that justice is equivalent to folly, and to have given, among others, the following illustrations :

If a man knows of serious faults in something he has for sale and reveals them to a prospective purchaser, he is a just man but a fool ; if he conceals them, he is unjust, but wise ! Similarly if there is a shipwreck, and two men are clutching a plank which can support only one, what is the stronger of the two to do ? If he lets go, he will be a just man and he will drown ! If he is wise, he will be unjust and send the other man to his death.

Only the following fragments (sections 32–41) of the reply of Laelius remain, but some further information about its contents can be obtained from Cicero's own references to it in other works. See *De Fin.* 18, 59 ; *Ep. ad. Att.* X, 4, 4 ; VII, 2, 4.

XXI. . . . I should not hesitate, Laelius, if I did not think that our friends here desired exactly what I am eager for myself, namely, that you should take some part in our discussion, especially since you told us yesterday that you would talk at even too great length. But that indeed is impossible ; we all beg you not to fail us. . . .

. . sed iuventuti nostrae minime audiendus ; quippe, si ita sensit, ut loquitur, est homo impurus ; sin aliter, quod malo, oratio est tamen immanis. . . . (*Nonius*, p. 323. 17 *et* 324. 15.)

33   XXII. . . . Est quidem vera lex recta ratio naturae congruens, diffusa in omnes, constans, sempiterna, quae vocet ad officium iubendo, vetando a fraude deterreat ; quae tamen neque probos frustra iubet aut vetat nec improbos iubendo aut vetando movet. huic legi nec obrogari fas est neque derogari ex hac aliquid licet neque tota abrogari potest, nec vero aut per senatum aut per populum solvi hac lege possumus, neque est quaerendus explanator aut interpres eius alius, nec erit alia lex Romae, alia Athenis, alia nunc, alia posthac, sed et omnes gentes et omni tempore una lex et sempiterna et immutabilis continebit, unusque erit communis quasi magister et imperator omnium deus, ille legis huius inventor, disceptator, lator ; cui qui non parebit, ipse se fugiet ac naturam hominis aspernatus hoc ipso luet maximas poenas, etiamsi cetera supplicia, quae putantur, effugerit. . . . (*Lactantius Inst. Div. VI*, 8. 6–9.)

34   XXIII. . . . nullum bellum suscipi a civitate optima nisi aut pro fide aut pro salute. . . . (*Augustinus de Civ. Dei XXII*, 6.)

. . . Sed his poenis quas etiam stultissimi sentiunt, egestate, exilio, vinculis, verberibus, elabuntur saepe privati oblata mortis celeritate, civitatibus autem

---

[1] Probably the reference is to Carneades.

Laelius. . . . But he[1] certainly ought not to have our young men as his audience. For if he really believes what he says, he is a villain; but if not, as I prefer to think, what he says is at any rate pernicious. . . .

XXII. . . . True law is right reason in agreement with nature; it is of universal application, unchanging and everlasting; it summons to duty by its commands, and averts from wrongdoing by its prohibitions. And it does not lay its commands or prohibitions upon good men in vain, though neither have any effect on the wicked. It is a sin to try to to alter this law, nor is it allowable to attempt to repeal any part of it, and it is impossible to abolish it entirely. We cannot be freed from its obligations by senate or people, and we need not look outside ourselves for an expounder or interpreter of it. And there will not be different laws at Rome and at Athens, or different laws now and in the future, but one eternal and unchangeable law will be valid for all nations and all times, and there will be one master and ruler, that is, God, over us all, for he is the author of this law, its promulgator, and its enforcing judge. Whoever is disobedient is fleeing from himself and denying his human nature, and by reason of this very fact he will suffer the worst penalties, even if he escapes what is commonly considered punishment. . . .

XXIII. . . . a war is never undertaken by the ideal State, except in defence of its honour or its safety. . . .

. . . But private citizens often escape those punishments which even the most stupid can feel—poverty, exile, imprisonment and stripes—by taking refuge in a swift death. But in the case of a State, death

mors ipsa poena est, quae videtur a poena singulos
vindicare ; debet enim constituta sic esse civitas,
ut aeterna sit.   itaque nullus interitus est rei
publicae naturalis ut hominis, in quo mors non
modo necessaria est, verum etiam optanda persaepe.
civitas autem cum tollitur, deletur, extinguitur,
simile est quodam modo, ut parva magnis conferamus,
ac si omnis hic mundus intereat et concidat. . .
(*Augustinus de Civ. Dei XXII*, 6.)

35   . . . Illa iniusta bella sunt, quae sunt sine causa
suscepta. nam extra ulciscendi aut propulsandorum
hostium causam bellum geri iustum nullum potest
. . (*Isidorus Orig. XVIII*, 1.)

. . Nullum bellum iustum habetur nisi denuntiatum, nisi indictum, nisi repetitis rebus. . . . (*Isidorus
Orig. XVIII*, 1.)

. . . Noster autem populus sociis defendendis
terrarum iam omnium potitus est. . . . (*Nonius*,
p. 498. 13.)

37   XXV. . . . An non cernimus optimo cuique dominatum ab ipsa natura cum summa utilitate infirmorum
datum ? cur igitur deus homini, animus imperat
corpori, ratio libidini iracundiaeque et ceteris vitiosis
eiusdem animi partibus ? . . . (*Augustinus contra
Iulianum Pelag. IV*, 12. 61 *T. X* p. 613 *Ben.*)

. . . Sed et imperandi et serviendi sunt dissimilitu-
dines cognoscendae. nam ut animus corpori dicitur
imperare, dicitur etiam libidini, sed corpori ut rex
civibus suis aut parens liberis, libidini autem ut servis

---

[1] Compare Aristotle, *Politics* I, 1254 A–B.

itself is a punishment, though it seems to offer individuals an escape from punishment; for a State ought to be so firmly founded that it will live for ever. Hence death is not natural for a State as it is for a human being, for whom death is not only necessary, but frequently even desirable. On the other hand, there is some similarity, if we may compare small things with great, between the overthrow, destruction, and extinction of a State, and the decay and dissolution of the whole universe. . . .

. . . Those wars are unjust which are undertaken without provocation. For only a war waged for revenge or defence can actually be just. . . .

. . . No war is considered just unless it has been proclaimed and declared, or unless reparation has first been demanded. . . .

. . . But our people by defending their allies have gained dominion over the whole world. . . .

The following fragments, as St. Augustine explains (*De Civ. Dei* XIX, 21), are part of the argument for the justice of slavery and imperialism, in which it is maintained that certain nations and individuals are naturally fitted for and benefited by subjection to others.[1]

XXV. . . . Do we not observe that dominion has been granted by Nature to everything that is best, to the great advantage of what is weak? For why else does God rule over man, the mind over the body, and reason over lust and anger and the other evil elements of the mind? . . .

. . . But we must distinguish different kinds of domination and subjection. For the mind is said to rule over the body, and also over lust; but it rules over the body as a king governs his subjects, or a father his children, whereas it rules over lust as a master

dominus, quod eam coërcet et frangit, sic regum, sic
imperatorum, sic magistratuum, sic patrum, sic populorum imperia civibus sociisque praesunt ut corporibus
animus, domini autem servos ita fatigant, ut optima
pars animi, id est sapientia, eiusdem animi vitiosas
imbecillasque partes, ut libidines, ut iracundias,
ut perturbationes ceteras. . . . (*Augustinus contra
Iulianum Pelag. IV*, 12. 61 *T. X* p. 613 *Ben.*)

. . . ut filiis imperari corporis membris propter
oboediendi facilitatem, vitiosas vero animi partes ut
servos asperiore imperio coërceri . . . (*Augustinus de
Civ. Dei XIV*, 23.)

. . . Est enim genus iniustae servitutis, cum ii sunt
alterius, qui sui possunt esse; cum autem ii famul-
antur . . . (*Nonius*, p. 109. 1.)

39 XXVII. . . . in quibus adsentior sollicitam et
periculosam iustitiam non esse sapientis. . . .
(*Priscianus VIII*, 6. 32 p. 399. 13 *Hertz.*)

40 XXVIII. . . . Vult plane virtus honorem, nec est
virtutis ulla alia merces . . . quam tamen illa
accipit facile, exigit non acerbe . . . huic tu viro
quas divitias obicies? quae imperia? quae regna?
qui ista putat humana, sua bona divina iudicat . . .
sed si aut ingrati universi aut invidi multi aut inimici
potentes suis virtutem praemiis spoliant, ne illa se
multis solaciis oblectat maximeque suo decore se ipsa
sustentat. . . . (*Lactant. Inst. Div. V*, 18. 4—8.)

. . . Quorum non corpora sunt in caelum elata;
neque enim natura pateretur, ut id, quod esset e
terra, nisi in terra maneret. . . . (*Augustinus de
Civ. Dei XXII*, 4.)

rules his slaves, restraining it and breaking its power. So kings, commanders, magistrates, senators, and popular assemblies govern citizens as the mind governs the body; but the master's restraint of his slaves is like the restraint exercised by the best part of the mind, the reason, over its own evil and weak elements, such as the lustful desires, anger, and the other disquieting emotions. . . .

. . . . the parts of the body are ruled like sons on account of their ready obedience, but the evil parts of the mind are restrained with a stricter curb, like slaves . . . .

. . . For there is a kind of unjust slavery, when those who are capable of governing themselves are under the domination of another; but when such men are slaves. . . .

XXVII. . . . . In which I agree that an anxious and hazardous justice is not appropriate to a wise man. . . .

XXVIII. . . . Virtue clearly desires honour, and has no other reward . . . . yet though she receives it gladly, she does not exact it rigorously. . . . . What riches, what power, what kingdoms can you offer such a man? For he thinks these things are human, but deems his own possessions divine. . . . . But if universal ingratitude, or the envy of many, or the hostility of the powerful, deprive virtue of its proper rewards, yet it is soothed by many consolations, and firmly upheld by its own excellence. . . .

. . . Their bodies were not taken up to heaven, for Nature would not allow that which comes from the earth to be removed from earth.[1] . . .

[1] Cicero is referring to the deification of Hercules and Romulus (St. Augustine, *De Civ. Dei XXII*, 4).

MARCUS TULLIUS CICERO

. . . numquam viri fortissimi fortitudinis, inpigritatis, patientiae . . . (*Nonius*, p. 125. 20.)

. . . Pyrrhi videlicet largitas Fabricio[1] aut Samnitium copiae Curio defuerunt. . . . (*Nonius*, p. 132. 17.)

. . . cuius etiam focum Cato ille noster, cum venerat ad se in Sabinos, ut ex ipso audiebamus, visere solebat, apud quem sedens ille Samnitium, quondam hostium, tum iam clientium suorum, dona repudiaverat. (*Nonius*, p. 522. 28 *et* p. 68. 17.)

41 XXIX. . . . Asia Ti. Gracchus, perseveravit in civibus, sociorum nominisque Latini iura neglexit ac foedera. quae si consuetudo ac licentia manare coeperit latius imperiumque nostrum ad vim a iure traduxerit, ut, qui adhuc voluntate nobis oboediunt, terrore teneantur, etsi nobis, qui id aetatis sumus, evigilatum fere est, tamen de posteris nostris et de illa immortalitate rei publicae sollicitor, quae poterat esse perpetua, si patriis viveretur institutis et moribus.

42 XXX. Quae cum dixisset Laelius, etsi omnes, qui aderant, significabant ab eo se esse admodum delectatos, tamen praeter ceteros Scipio quasi quodam gaudio elatus:

Multas tu quidem, inquit, Laeli, saepe causas ita defendisti, ut ego non modo tecum Servium Galbam, collegam nostrum, quem tu, quoad vixit, omnibus

---

[1] *Fabricio* Mercer ; *acos* MSS. ; *consuli* Pascal ; *consulibus* Lambinus.

. . . The bravest men never . . . of bravery, energy, endurance. . . .

. . . Fabricius, I suppose, felt the lack of the wealth of Pyrrhus, and Curius of the riches of the Samnites![1] . . .

. . . Our glorious Cato, when he went out to his farm in the Sabine country, as we have heard him say, often visited the hearth of this man, sitting in whose home he had declined the gifts of the Samnites, once his enemies, but then under his protection. . . .

XXIX. . . . . . Asia . . . . Tiberius Gracchus . . . . he kept faith with his fellow-citizens, but violated the treaty rights of our allies and the Latins. If this habit of lawlessness begins to spread and changes our rule from one of justice to one of force, so that those who up to the present have obeyed us willingly are held faithful by fear alone, then, though our own generation has perhaps been vigilant enough to be safe, yet I am anxious for our descendants, and for the permanent stability of our commonwealth, which might live on for ever if the principles and customs of our ancestors were maintained.

XXX. After these words from Laelius, all expressed their great pleasure in his remarks; but Scipio, whose delight went beyond that of the rest, was almost carried away with enthusiasm.

Scipio. Laelius, you have often defended cases so eloquently that I believed that neither our colleague Servius Galba, whom you, during his lifetime,

---

[1] The incorruptibility of Roman magistrates of the past is here alluded to (for the persons, see Index).

anteponebas, verum ne Atticorum quidem oratorum
quemquam aut suavitate.[1] . . . .

[*Desiderantur paginae duodecim.*]

. . . duas sibi res, quo minus in vulgus et in foro
diceret, confidentiam et vocem, defuisse . . .
(*Nonius*, p. 262. 22.)

. . . inclusorum hominum gemitu mugiebat taurus
. . . (*Schol. Iuvenal. ad Sat. VI*, 480.)

43 XXXI. . . . . reportare. ergo illam rem populi,
id est rem publicam, quis diceret tum, cum crudelitate unius oppressi essent universi, neque esset
unum vinculum iuris nec consensus ac societas
coetus, quod est populus ? atque hoc idem Syracusis.
urbs illa praeclara, quam ait Timaeus Graecarum
maxumam, omnium autem esse pulcherrimam, arx
visenda, portus usque in sinus oppidi[2] et ad urbis
crepidines infusi, viae latae, porticus, templa, muri
nihilo magis efficiebant, Dionysio tenente, ut esset
illa res publica; nihil enim populi et unius erat
populus ipse. ergo ubi tyrannus est, ibi non vitiosam,
ut heri dicebam, sed, ut nunc ratio cogit, dicendum
est plane nullam esse rem publicam.

44 XXXII. Praeclare quidem dicis, Laelius; etenim
video iam, quo pergat oratio.

[1] *suavitate* is commonly read; *sua* . . . V.
[2] *oppidi* Leopardi ; *oppidis* V.

---

[1] Isocrates, or possibly Laelius. See Cicero, *De Oratore* II,
10 ; III, 28.

always considered unrivalled, nor even any of the Attic orators [could equal] you either in charm . . .

About four pages are lost; the two following fragments may perhaps be from this passage.

. . . . that his lack of two qualities, self-confidence and vocal powers, prevented him from speaking to the people or in the forum . . . .[1]

. . . . the bull roared with the groans of imprisoned men. . . .[2]

XXXI. *Scipio.* . . . . to bring back. . . . . Therefore how could that be called "the property of the people," which is what "commonwealth" means? For all were oppressed by the cruelty of one, and there was no bond of justice whatever, nor any agreement of partnership amongst those gathered together, though that is part of the definition of a people. And the same was true of Syracuse: that famous city, which Timaeus calls both the largest of the Greek towns and the most beautiful city in the world, with its admirable citadel, its harbours, whose waters penetrated to the very heart of the town and to the foundations of its buildings, its broad streets, its porticoes, temples, and walls, could not be a commonwealth in spite of all these things while Dionysius was its ruler, for nothing belonged to the people, and the people itself was the property of one man. Therefore, wherever a tyrant rules, we ought not to say that we have a bad form of commonwealth, as I said yesterday, but, as logic now demonstrates, that we really have no commonwealth at all.

XXXII. *Laelius.* Excellently said; and now I understand the purport of your remarks.

[2] The reference is to the famous bull of Phalaris, tyrant of Acragas, Sicily, in the early sixth century.

S. Vides igitur ne illam quidem, quae tota sit in factionis potestate, posse vere dici rem publicam.

L. Sic plane iudico.

S. Et rectissime quidem iudicas; quae enim fuit tum Atheniensium res, cum post magnum illud Peloponnesiacum bellum triginta viri illi urbi iniustissime praefuerunt ? num aut vetus gloria civitatis aut species praeclara oppidi aut theatrum, gymnasia, porticus aut propylaea nobilia aut arx [1] aut admiranda opera Phidiae aut Piraeus ille magnificus rem publicam efficiebat ?

Minime vero, Laelius, quoniam quidem populi res non erat.

S. Quid ? cum decemviri Romae sine provocatione fuerunt tertio illo anno, cum vindicias amisisset ipsa libertas ?

L. Populi nulla res erat, immo vero id populus egit, ut rem suam recuperaret.

45   XXXIII. *S.* Venio nunc ad tertium genus illud, in quo esse videbuntur fortasse angustiae. cum per populum agi dicuntur et esse in populi potestate omnia, cum, de quocumque volt, supplicium sumit multitudo, cum agunt, rapiunt, tenent, dissipant, quae volunt, potesne tum, Laeli, negare rem esse illam publicam, cum populi sint omnia, quoniam quidem populi esse rem volumus rem publicam ?

Tum Laelius: Ac nullam quidem citius negaverim

------

[1] *arx* Mai ; *ara* V.

------

[1] See Book I, 44.

Scipio. You understand, then, that not even a State which is entirely in the control of a faction can truly be called a commonwealth?

Laelius. That is indeed my opinion.

Scipio. And you are absolutely right; for where was there any "property of the Athenian people," when, after the great Peloponnesian War, the notorious Thirty most unjustly governed their city?[1] Did the ancient glory of that State, the transcendent beauty of its buildings, its theatre, its gymnasiums, its porticoes, its famous Propylaea, its citadel, the exquisite works of Phidias, or the splendid Piraeus, make it a commonwealth?

Laelius. By no means, since nothing was the "property of the people."

Scipio. What of the period when the decemvirs[2] ruled Rome without being subject to appeal, in that third year of their power, when liberty had lost all her legal bulwarks?

Laelius. There was no "property of the people"; indeed the people rose in revolt to recover their property.

XXXIII. *Scipio.* I come now to the third form of government, in regard to which we may appear to be in difficulty. For when everything is said to be administered by the people, and to be in the people's power; when the multitude inflicts punishment on whomsoever it will, when it seizes, plunders, retains, and wastes whatever it will, can you deny, Laelius, that we have a commonwealth then, when everything belongs to the people, and we have defined a commonwealth as the "property of a people"?

Laelius. There is no government to which I should

<hr>

[2] See Book II, 61.

esse rem publicam, quam istam, quae tota plane
sit in multitudinis potestate. nam si nobis non
placebat Syracusis fuisse rem publicam neque Agri-
genti neque Athenis, cum essent tyranni, nec hic,
cum decemviri, non video, qui magis in multitudinis dominatu rei publicae nomen appareat, quia
primum mihi populus non est, ut tu optime definisti,
Scipio, nisi qui consensu iuris continetur, sed est
tam tyrannus iste conventus, quam si esset unus,
hoc etiam taetrior, quia nihil ista, quae populi
speciem et nomen imitatur, immanius belua est.
nec vero convenit, cum furiosorum bona legibus in
adgnatorum potestate sint, quod eorum iam. . . . .

[Desiderantur paginae octo.]

46   XXXIV. . . . . dici possint, cur illa sit res
publica resque populi, quae sunt dicta de regno.

Et multo etiam magis, inquit Mummius ; nam in
regem potius cadit domini similitudo, quod est unus ;
plures vero boni in qua re publica rerum potientur,
nihil poterit esse illa beatius. sed tamen vel regnum
malo quam liberum populum ; id enim tibi restat
genus vitiosissumae rei publicae tertium.

more quickly deny the title of commonwealth than
one in which everything is subject to the power
of the multitude. For as we have decided that there
was no commonwealth at Syracuse or at Agrigentum
or at Athens when those cities were ruled by tyrants,
or here at Rome when the decemvirs were in power,
I cannot see how the name of commonwealth would
be any more applicable to the despotism of the
multitude. For in the first place a people exists
only when the individuals who form it are held
together by a partnership in justice, according to
your excellent definition, Scipio. But such a gathering as you have mentioned is just as surely a tyrant
as if it were a single person, and an even more cruel
tyrant, because there can be nothing more horrible
than that monster which falsely assumes the name
and appearance of a people. Nor indeed is it right,
when the property of the insane is entrusted by law
to their relatives in the male line, because [they are
unable to manage it properly themselves, that an
insane multitude should be left in uncontrolled
possession of the " property of the people."] . . .

About three pages are lost.

XXXIV. . . . [And indeed many of the arguments]
cited to prove that a kingdom is a commonwealth,
"the property of a people," could be applied [with
equal justice to an aristocratic government.]

Mummius. And with even greater justice, for a
king is more like a master, because he is a single
individual, while nothing could be more advantageous
for a State than to be ruled by a select number of
good men. Nevertheless I prefer even a kingship
to a free popular government, for that third possibility
is the worst of all governments.

47   XXXV. Hic Scipio: Adgnosco, inquit, tuum
morem istum, Spuri, aversum a ratione populari; et
quamquam potest id lenius ferri, quam tu soles
ferre, tamen adsentior nullum esse de tribus his
generibus, quod sit probandum minus. illud tamen
non adsentior tibi, praestare regi optimates; si enim
sapientia est, quae gubernet rem publicam, quid
tandem interest, haec in unone sit an in pluribus?
sed errore quodam fallimur ita disputando; cum
enim optumates appellantur, nihil potest videri
praestabilius; quid enim optumo melius cogitari
potest? cum autem regis est facta mentio, occurrit
animis rex etiam iniustus. nos autem de iniusto rege
nihil loquimur nunc, cum de ipsa regali re publica
quaerimus.   quare cogitato Romulum aut Pompilium
aut Tullum regem: fortasse non tam illius te rei
publicae paenitebit.

48   *M.* Quam igitur relinquis populari rei publicae
laudem?

S. Tum ille: Quid? tibi tandem, Spuri, Rhodi-
orum, apud quos nuper fuimus una, nullane videtur
esse res publica?

M. Mihi vero videtur, et minime quidem vitu-
peranda.

S. Recte dicis; sed, si meministi, omnes erant
iidem tum de plebe, tum senatores vicissitudinesque
habebant, quibus mensibus populari munere fun-
gerentur, quibus senatorio; utrobique autem con-

---

¹ The Romans had a traditional hatred of the title king
(*rex*), somewhat as Americans have.

224

XXXV. *Scipio.* I am aware, Spurius, that you are always opposed to the power of the people ; and, though that power might be borne with less resentment than you are accustomed to show, I agree with you that none of these three constitutions deserves less approbation.   But I cannot assent to your statement that aristocratic government is superior to kingship ; for if wisdom rules the State, what difference does it make whether that wisdom is the possession of one person or of several ?   But we are being misled in our present argument by certain deceptive terms ; for when we speak of " the best men," nothing can possibly seem preferable ; for what can be deemed better than the best ?   But when we mention a king we immediately think of an unjust king ; [1] yet at present we are not referring to unjust kings at all in our consideration of the kingship itself.   Therefore, if you will only imagine that the king we are referring to is Romulus or Pompilius or Tullus, perhaps you will not think so unfavourably of that form of government.

Mummius. What praise do you reserve, then, for popular government ?

Scipio. What of Rhodes, Spurius, which we visited together ?   Does that seem to you no commonwealth at all ?

Mummius. I certainly consider it a commonwealth, and one by no means deserving of our scorn.

Scipio. You are quite right.   But, you may remember, all the people were senators and common citizens alternately, and they had a regular system of rotation in accordance with which they acted as senators for certain months of the year, and as private citizens during certain other months.   They received

venticium accipiebant, et in theatro et in curia res
capitalis et reliquas omnis iudicabant iidem ; tantum
poterat tantique erat, quanti multitudo, senatus[1]

. . .

[*Multa desiderantur.*]

[1] *senatus* added by Halm ; lacking in *V*.

payment for attending meetings in both capacities, and, both in the theatre and the senate-house, the same men decided capital cases and those of every other sort. The senate possessed as much power and influence as the multitude. . . .

The rest of the book is lost. The length of the missing passage is unknown.

FRAGMENTA LIBRI III

1. Est igitur quiddam turbulentum in hominibus singulis, quod vel exultat voluptate vel molestia frangitur. (*Nonius,* p. 301. 6.)

2. Sed ut ipsi seu animum periclitentur sum vident, quid se putent esse facturos.[1] (*Nonius,* p. 364. 8.)

3. Poeni primi mercaturis et mercibus suis avaritiam et magnificentiam et inexplebiles cupiditates omnium rerum importaverunt in Graeciam. (*Nonius,* p. 431. 15.)

4. Sardanapallus ille vitiis multo quam nomine ipso deformior. (*Schol. Iuv. ad Sat. X.* 362.)

5. Nisi si quis Athonem pro monumento vult funditus efficere. quis enim est Athos aut Olympus tantus? (*Priscianus VI.* 13. 70, p. 255. 9 *Hertz.*)

[1] The text is corrupt.

FRAGMENTS OF BOOK III

1. There is therefore a certain restless element in individuals which is exalted by pleasure and broken by tribulation.

2. . . . . they see what they think they will do.[1]

3. The Phoenicians with their traffic in merchandise were the first to introduce into Greece greed, luxurious living, and insatiable desires of all sorts.

4. . .   the notorious Sardanapalus, far more ugly in his vices than in his name. . . .

5. . .   . . unless someone wished to use the whole of Mount Athos as a monument.   For what Athos or Olympus is so great . . .?

---

[1] The first part of this fragment is meaningless in its present form.

DE RE PUBLICA

LIBER QUARTUS

1   I. . . . atque ipsa mens ea, quae futura videt, praeterita meminit. . . . (*Non.* p. 500. 9.)

. . . Etenim, si nemo est quin emori malit quam converti in aliquam figuram bestiae, quamvis hominis mentem sit habiturus, quanto est miserius in hominis figura animo esse efferato ! mihi quidem tanto videtur, quanto praestabilior est animus corpore. . . . (*Lactantius Inst. Div. V*, 11. 2.)

. . . se non putare idem esse arietis et P. Africani bonum. . . . (*Augustinus contra Iulian. Pelag. IV.* 12. 59 *T. X.* p. 612 *Ben.*)

. . . eademque obiectu suo umbram noctemque efficiat cum ad numerum dierum aptam, tum ad laborum quietem. . . . (*Nonius* p. 234. 12.)

. . . Cumque autumno terra se ad concipiendas fruges patefecerit, hieme ad concipiendas [1] relaxarit, aestiva maturitate alia mitigaverit, alia torruerit. . . . (*Nonius* p. 343. 18.)

---

[1] The text is corrupt. *concipiendas* V ; *conficiendas* is commonly read.

THE REPUBLIC

BOOK IV

The Vatican manuscript contains only two short passages
from this book, sections 2–3 and section 4. The order of the
other fragments printed here is of course uncertain.

The social classification of citizens, the maintenance of high
moral standards in the State, the physical and mental training of the young, and the influence of drama, lyric poetry,
and music, are evidently among the subjects discussed.

I. . . . . and the same mind that foresees the
future also remembers the past. . . .

. . . . And indeed, if there is no one who would
not prefer death to transformation into an animal of
any sort, even if he could retain the mind of a man,
how much more wretched is it to have the mind of a
beast while retaining human form! As much more
so, in my opinion, as the mind is superior to the
body. . . .

. . . . he does not think the good of a ram and
the good of Publius Africanus are the same. . . .

. . . . and the same body, by its interposition,
makes darkness and night, useful both for the
reckoning of the days and for rest from labour. . . .

. . . . and when in the autumn the earth has
opened to receive the seed of her produce, in winter
has rested so that she may [transform] this seed,
and in the maturity of summer has softened some
and parched others . . . .

. . . cum adhibent in pecuda pastores. . . .
(*Nonius* p. 159. 13.)

2   II. . . . gratiam. quam commode ordines dis-
cripti, aetates, classes, equitatus, in quo suffragia sunt
etiam senatus, nimis multis iam stulte hanc utilitatem tolli cupientibus, qui novam largitionem quaerunt aliquo plebei scito reddendorum equorum.

3   III. Considerate nunc, cetera quam sint provisa
sapienter ad illam civium beate et honeste vivendi
societatem; ea est enim prima causa coëundi, et id
hominibus effici ex re publica debet partim institutis,
alia legibus. principio disciplinam puerilem inge-
nuis, de qua Graeci multum frustra laborarunt, et in
qua una Polybius noster hospes nostrorum institutorum neglegentiam accusat, nullam certam aut
destinatam legibus aut publice expositam aut unam
omnium esse voluerunt. nam . . .

[*Desiderantur paginae minimum quattuor.*]

. . . ad militiam euntibus dari solitos esse custodes,
a quibus primo anno regantur. . . . (*Servius ad Verg.
Aen. V.* 546.)

. . . non modo ut Spartae, rapere ubi pueri et
clepere discunt. . . . (*Nonius* p. 20. 4.)

. . . opprobrio fuisse adulescentibus, si amatores
non haberent. . . . (*Servius ad Verg. Aen. X.* 325.)

---

[1] Evidently a reference to the Servian reforms; see Book
II, 39–40.

[2] Compare Aristotle, *Politics* I, 1252 B—1253 A.

[3] See Plutarch, *Lycurgus* 17–18; [Xenophon,] *Laced. Polit.*
II, 6-9.

. . . . when they employ shepherds for the flocks . . . .

II. . . . How conveniently the orders are arranged, the ages, the classes, the knights, among whom the votes of the senators also are included ![1] Too many foolishly desire to abolish this useful system in their search for a new distribution of money through some resolution of the plebs providing for the return of the horses.

III. Now consider the other wise provisions for that association of the citizens in a happy and honourable life; for that is the original purpose of men's coming together,[2] and it should be accomplished for them in their commonwealth partly by established customs and partly by laws. Now in the first place our people have never wished to have any system of education for the free-born youth which is either definitely fixed by law, or officially established, or uniform in all cases, though the Greeks have expended much vain labour on this problem, and it is the only point which our guest Polybius finds neglected in our institutions. For . . . .

At least thirty lines are lost between this passage and section 4. The following three fragments may be quoted from the lost passage.

. . . . it is the custom to assign guardians to those who are entering upon military service, in order to direct them during their first year . . .

. . . . not only as at Sparta, where the boys learn to steal and thieve [3] . . . .

. . . . it was [considered] a disgrace to youths if they did not have lovers [4] . . . .

[4] A probable reference to Spartan custom; see the following fragment.

IV. . . . nudari puberem. ita sunt alte repetita
quasi fundamenta quaedam verecundiae. iuventutis
vero exercitatio quam absurda in gymnasiis! quam
levis epheborum illa militia! quam contrectationes
et amores soluti et liberi! mitto apud Eleos et
Thebanos, apud quos in amore ingenuorum libido
etiam permissam habet et solutam licentiam; Lacedaemonii ipsi, cum omnia concedunt in amore
iuvenum praeter stuprum, tenui sane muro dissae-
piunt id quod excipiunt; conplexus enim concubit-
usque permittunt palliis interiectis.

Hic Laelius: Praeclare intellego, Scipio, te in iis
Graeciae disciplinis, quas reprendis, cum populis
nobilissimis malle quam cum tuo Platone luctari,
quem ne attingis quidem, praesertim cum . . . .

5 V. . . . et noster Plato magis etiam quam
Lycurgus, omnia qui prorsus iubet esse communia,
ne quis civis propriam aut suam rem ullam queat
dicere. . . . (*Nonius* p. 362. 9 *Merc.*, 361. 27 *Quich.*)

. . . Ego vero eodem, quo ille Homerum redimitum
coronis et delibutum unguentis emittit ex ea urbe,
quam sibi ipse fingit. . . . (*Nonius* p. 308 *sq.*)

6 VI. . . . Censoris iudicium nihil fere damnato

---

[1] Evidently a reference to Athenian institutions. The
young men were *ephebi*, or cadets, for two years, from eighteen to twenty. The first year was spent in preliminary
physical and military training; the second in the ordinary
duties of a soldier.

[2] See Plato, *Republic* III, 416–417, where the Guardians, as
distinguished from the rest of the citizens, are forbidden to
possess private property. For the community of wives, see

IV. *Scipio.* . . . . that a young man should go naked. From such ancient sources are derived what we may call the foundation-stones of modesty! And how absurd their system of exercise for young men in gymnasiums! How far from rigorous is their system of military training for the ephebi![1] How free and easy are their contacts and love relations! To say nothing of the Eleans and Thebans, among whom lust is actually given free rein in the relations of free men, the Spartans themselves, who give every freedom to love relations with young men except that of actual defilement, protect only by a very thin wall this one exception; for, providing only that cloaks be interposed, they allow embraces and the sharing of the bed.

Laelius. I see clearly, Scipio, that in regard to the Greek systems of training which you criticize, you prefer to attack the most famous States rather than your beloved Plato, whom you do not even mention, especially as . . . .

V. . . . And our beloved Plato went even further than Lycurgus, for he actually provided that all property should be owned in common, so that no citizen might be able to say of anything that it was his very own.[2] . . .

. . . But I . . . in the same way as [Plato] sends Homer out of the city which he invented, buying him off with wreaths and anointing him with perfumes.[3] . . .

VI. . . . The censor's judgment imposes almost

V, 47. For "communism" in the constitution of Lycurgus, see Plutarch, *Lycurgus* 8–10; 15; [Xenophon,] *Laced. Polit.* I, 7–9; VI; VII; Polybius VI, 45, 3; 48, 3.

[3] Plato, *Republic* III, 397 E–398 A.

nisi ruborem offert.[1] itaque, ut omnis ea iudicatio
versatur tantum modo in nomine, animadversio illa
ignominia dicta est. . . . (*Nonius* p. 24 *in.*)

. . . horum in severitatem dicitur inhorruisse
primum civitas.[2] . . . (*Nonius* p. 423. 4.)

. . . nec vero mulieribus praefectus praeponatur,
qui apud Graecos creari solet, sed sit censor, qui
viros doceat moderari uxoribus. . . . (*Nonius* p.
499. 13.)

. . . Ita magnam habet vim disciplina verecundiae ;
carent temeto omnes mulieres. . . . (*Nonius* p. 5. 14.)

. . . Atque etiam si qua erat famosa, ei cognati
osculum non ferebant. . . . (*Nonius* p. 306. 3.)

. . . itaque a petendo petulantia, a procando, id
est poscendo, procacitas nominata est. . . . (*Nonius*
p. 23 *v.* 18 *et v.* 24.)

7 VII. . . . Nolo enim eundem populum imperatorem
et portitorem esse terrarum. optimum autem et in
privatis familiis et in re publica vectigal duco esse
parsimoniam. . . . (*Nonius* p. 24. 21.)

. . . Fides enim nomen ipsum mihi videtur habere,
cum fit, quod dicitur. . . . (*Nonius* p. 24. 18.)

. . . In cive excelso atque homine nobili blandi-
tiam, adsentationem, ambitionem meam esse levitatis.[3]
. . . (*Nonius* p. 194. 27.)

8 VIII. . . . Admiror, nec rerum solum, sed verborum
etiam elegantiam. si iurgant, inquit. benivolorum

---

[1] *offert* Mueller ; *offerent* or *offerrent* MSS. : *adfert* is
commonly read.

[2] The text is corrupt.

[3] The text is corrupt ; *notam* to replace *meam* (the MS.
reading) suggested by Orelli.

---

[1] *Ignominia*, derived from *in* and *nomen*, means a depriva-
tion of one's good name.

no penalty except a blush upon the man he condemns. Therefore, as his decision affects nothing
but the reputation, his condemnation is called
"ignominy."[1] . . .

. . . The State is said at first to have been terrified
by their severity. . . .

. . . Nor indeed should there be a governor placed
over women, as is usually done among the Greeks,[2]
but there should be a censor to teach men to rule
their wives. . . .

. . . Thus training in modesty has great effect; all
women abstain from intoxicating drinks. . . .

. . . And besides, if any woman had a bad reputation, her relatives refused to kiss her. . . .

. . . Thus impudence is derived from seeking, and
shamelessness from demanding. . . .[3]

VII. . . . For I do not approve of the same nation
being the ruler of the world and also its tax-gatherer;
on the other hand, I consider frugality the best
revenue both for private families and for States. . . .

. . . Credit seems to me to get its very name from
the fact that what is promised is performed.[4] . . .

. . . In a citizen of high rank or a man of high
reputation, [I judge] flattery, ingratiation, and can-
vassing to be [indications] of shallowness. . . .

VIII. . . . I admire the excellence, not only of
the subject matter, but also of the style. "If they
disagree,"[5] it says. A contest between friends, not

---

[2] Compare Aristotle, *Politics* VI, 1322 B.
[3] Cicero derives *petulantia* (impudence) from *peto* (seek),
and *procacitas* (shamelessness), from *proco = posco* (demand).
[4] Cicero derives *fides* (faith, credit) from *fio* (to be done).
[5] Probably a quotation from the Twelve Tables (see Book II,
54–56).

concertatio, non lis inimicorum, iurgium dicitur . . .
iurgare igitur lex putat inter se vicinos, non litigare
. . . (*Nonius* p. 430 *sq.*)

. . . eosdem terminos hominum curae atque vitae,
sic pontificio iure sanctitudo sepulturae . . . (*Nonius*
p. 174. 5.)

. . . quod insepultos reliquissent eos, quos e mari
propter vim tempestatis excipere non potuissent,
innocentes necaverint . . . (*Nonius* p. 293. 24
Merc., 293. 43 *Quich.*)

. . . nec in hac dissensione suscepi populi causam,
sed bonorum . . . (*Nonius* p. 519. 14.)

. . . Non enim facile valenti populo resistitur, si
aut nihil iuris impertias aut parum . . . (*Priscianus
XV* 4. 20. p. 76. 14 *Hertz.*)

. . . cui quidem utinam vere fideliter abundiente
auguraverim.[1] . . . (*Nonius* p. 469. 14.)

9 · IX. . . . Ad quos cum accessit clamor et adpro-
batio populi quasi magni cuiusdam et sapientis
magistri, quas illi obducunt tenebras, quos invehunt
metus, quas inflammant cupiditates! . . . (*Augustinus
de Civ. Dei II*, 14 *ext.*)

10 X. . . . Cum artem ludicram scaenamque totam
in probro ducerent, genus id hominum non modo
honore civium reliquorum carere, sed etiam tribu
moveri notatione censoria voluerunt. . . . (*Augustinus
de Civ. Dei II*, 13.)

11 S. . . . Numquam comoediae, nisi consuetudo vitae

[1] The text is corrupt; *quidem certe* suggested by Madvig to
replace *abundiente* (the MS. reading).

a quarrel between enemies, is called a disagreement.
. . . Therefore the law considers that neighbours
disagree rather than quarrel. . . .

. . . . the boundaries of men's care and men's
life [to be] the same; thus by the pontifical law the
sanctity of burial . . .

. . . . because they had left unburied those whom
they could not rescue from the sea on account of the
severity of the storm, they put innocent men to
death[1] . . .

. . . . and in this controversy I sided not with
the people but with the good . . .

. . . It is not easy to resist the people in their
might if you give them no legal rights or only a
few . . .

. . . Would that I might prophesy honestly to
him. . . .

IX. . . . When the applause and approval of the
people, as of some great and wise master, have
been granted to them, what darkness they produce! What fears they cause! What desires they
inflame![2] . . .

X. . . . Since they considered the dramatic art
and the theatre in general disgraceful, they desired[3]
that all persons connected with such things should
not only be deprived of the privileges of other
citizens, but should even be removed from their
tribes by sentence of the censors. . . .

Scipio. . . . Nor would comedy, unless the customs

---

[1] *i.e.*, the Athenian commanders at the Battle of Arginusae
in 406 B.C. (Xenophon, *Hellenica* I, 7).

[2] Cicero is speaking of the poets, probably of the writers of
comedy.

[3] *i.e.*, the Romans. Compare Livy VII, 2, 12.

pateretur, probare sua theatris flagitia potuissent.
. . . quem illa non adtigit vel potius quem non
vexavit? cui pepercit? esto, populares homines
inprobos, in re publica seditiosos, Cleonem, Cleo-
phontem, Hyperbolum laesit. patiamur, etsi eius
modi cives a censore melius est quam a poëta notari;
sed Periclen, cum iam suae civitati maxima auctoritate plurimos annos domi et belli praefuisset, violari
versibus, et eos agi [1] in scaena non plus decuit, quam
si Plautus noster voluisset aut Naevius Publio et
Gnaeo Scipioni [2] aut Caecilius Marco Catoni male

12 dicere . . . nostrae contra duodecim tabulae cum
perpaucas res capite sanxissent, in his hanc quoque
sanciendam putaverunt, si quis occentavisset sive
carmen condidisset, quod infamiam faceret flagi-
tiumve alteri. praeclare; iudiciis enim magistratuum, disceptationibus legitimis propositam vitam,
non poëtarum ingeniis, habere debemus nec probrum audire nisi ea lege, ut respondere liceat et
iudicio defendere . . . veteribus displicuisse Romanis vel laudari quemquam in scaena vivum hominem vel vituperari. . . . (*Augustinus de Civ. Dei
II*, 9.)

13   XI. . . . Aeschines Atheniensis, vir eloquentissimus,

[1] *et eos agi* MSS.; *et agi* Cobet; *et exagitari* Halm.
[2] *Scipioni* MSS.; *Scipionibus* Halm.

of daily life had so permitted, ever have been able to make its disgraceful exhibitions acceptable to the spectators . . . . Whom has [comedy] not attacked, or rather persecuted? Whom has it spared? It is true that it has wounded wicked demagogues and men who stirred up sedition in the State, like Cleon, Cleophon, and Hyperbolus.[1] This we might allow, though it is preferable for such citizens to suffer disgrace from a censor rather than from a poet. But it was no more proper that Pericles, who by reason of his commanding influence had already governed his commonwealth for many years, both in peace and war, should be insulted in verse, and that such verses should be recited on the stage, than it would have been for our own Plautus or Naevius to have selected Publius and Gnaeus Scipio for abuse, or for Caecilius to have vilified Marcus Cato. . . . On the other hand, our Twelve Tables,[2] though they provided the death penalty for only a few crimes, did provide it for any person who sang or composed a song which contained a slander or insult to anyone else. This was an excellent rule; for our mode of life ought to be liable to judgment by the magistrates and the courts of law, but not by clever poets; nor ought we to be subject to disgrace unless we have an opportunity to answer and defend ourselves in a court of law. . . . The early Romans did not desire that any living man should either be praised or blamed on the stage. . . .

XI. . . . Aeschines of Athens, a most eloquent

---

[1] Aristophanes and other writers of the Old Comedy ridiculed these Athenian demagogues.

[2] See Book II, 61.

cum adulescens tragoedias actitavisset, rem publicam capessivit, et Aristodemum, tragicum item actorem, maximis de rebus pacis et belli legatum ad Philippum Athenienses saepe miserunt. . . . (*Augustinus de Civ. Dei II,* 11.)

orator, took part in affairs of State though he had been a tragic actor in his youth, and the Athenians frequently sent Aristodemus,[1] also a tragic actor, as ambassador to Philip in regard to the most important questions of peace and war. . . .

[1] In regard to Aristodemus, see J. B. O'Connor, *Chapters in the History of Actors and Acting in Ancient Greece*, Diss., Princeton, 1908, pp. 82–84.

DE RE PUBLICA

LIBER QUINTUS

1   I.   Moribus antiquis res stat Romana virisque,

quem quidem ille versum vel brevitate vel veritate
tamquam ex oraculo mihi quodam esse effatus videtur.   nam neque viri, nisi ita morata civitas fuisset,
neque mores, nisi hi viri praefuissent, aut fundare
aut tam diu tenere potuissent tantam et tam fuse [1]
lateque imperantem rem publicam.   itaque ante
nostram memoriam et mos ipse patrius praestantes
viros adhibebat, et veterem morem ac maiorum in-
2 stituta retinebant excellentes viri.   nostra vero aetas
cum rem publicam sicut picturam accepisset egre-
giam, sed iam evanescentem vetustate, non modo
eam coloribus eisdem, quibus fuerat, renovare neglexit, sed ne id quidem curavit, ut formam saltem
eius et extrema tamquam liniamenta servaret.   quid

---

[1] *fuse* Halm ; *iuste* or *iustae* MSS. (cf. *Tusc. Disp.* IV, 57 ;
Orat. 113).

---

[1] A verse from Ennius' *Annales.*

244

THE REPUBLIC

BOOK V

The Vatican manuscript contains only three short passages from this book : sections 3, 5, and 6–7. The order of the other fragments given is uncertain. St. Augustine (*De Civ. Dei II*, 21) states that section 1 is quoted from Cicero's preface to the book, and not from the dialogue.

The qualifications and functions of the ideal statesman are evidently the main subject of the book.

I. THE commonwealth of Rome is founded firm
    On ancient customs and on men of might.[1]

Our poet seems to have obtained these words, so brief and true, from an oracle. For neither men alone, unless a State is supplied with customs too, nor customs alone, unless there have also been men to defend them, could ever have been sufficient to found or to preserve so long a commonwealth whose dominion extends so far and wide. Thus, before our own time, the customs of our ancestors produced excellent men, and eminent men preserved our ancient customs and the institutions of their forefathers. But though the republic, when it came to us, was like a beautiful painting, whose colours, however, were already fading with age, our own time not only has neglected to freshen it by renewing the original colours, but has not even taken the trouble to preserve its configuration and, so to speak, its general outlines. For what is now left

245

enim manet ex antiquis moribus, quibus ille dixit
rem stare Romanam ? quos ita oblivione obsoletos
videmus, ut non modo non colantur, sed iam igno-
rentur.   nam de viris quid dicam ?   mores enim ipsi
interierunt virorum penuria, cuius tanti mali non
modo reddenda ratio nobis, sed etiam tamquam reis
capitis quodam modo dicenda causa est.   nostris
enim vitiis, non casu aliquo, rem publicam verbo
retinemus, re ipsa vero iam pridem amisimus. . . .
(*Augustinus de Civ. Dei II*, 21, *Nonius* 417. 7.)

3   II. . . . nihil esse tam [1] regale quam explanationem
aequitatis, in qua iuris erat interpretatio, quod ius
privati petere solebant a regibus, ob easque causas
agri arvi et arbusti et pascui lati atque uberes de-
finiebantur, qui essent regii [2] colerenturque [3] sine
regum opera et labore, ut eos nulla privati negotii
cura a populorum rebus abduceret.   nec vero quisquam privatus erat disceptator aut arbiter litis, sed
omnia conficiebantur iudiciis regiis.   et mihi quidem
videtur Numa noster maxime tenuisse hunc morem
veterem Graeciae regum.   nam ceteri, etsi hoc
quoque munere fungebantur, magnam tamen partem
bella gesserunt et eorum iura coluerunt ; illa autem
diuturna pax Numae mater huic urbi iuris et religionis fuit, qui legum etiam scriptor fuisset, quas scitis

---

[1] *nihil esse tam* supplied by Mai , lacking in V.
[2] *regii* Orelli ; *regi* V.
[3] [*qui*] *colerenturque* is commonly read ; *qui colerenturque* V.

of the "ancient customs" on which he said "the commonwealth of Rome" was "founded firm"? They have been, as we see, so completely buried in oblivion that they are not only no longer practised, but are already unknown. And what shall I say of the men? For the loss of our customs is due to our lack of men, and for this great evil we must not only give an account, but must even defend ourselves in every way possible, as if we were accused of capital crime. For it is through our own faults, not by any accident, that we retain only the form of the commonwealth, but have long since lost its substance. . . .

II. . . . [that nothing was so] kingly as the administration of justice, which included the interpretation of the law, for subjects used to seek legal decisions from their kings. And for these reasons, broad and rich lands and fields, suitable both for cultivation and pasturage, were set aside as the property of the king, and were cultivated for him without any labour or attention on his part, so that he might not be distracted from the people's business by any need of attention to his own private affairs. Nor did any private citizen act as judge or arbitrator in any suit, but every suit was decided by the king himself. And in my opinion our own King Numa followed most closely this ancient custom of the Greek kings. For our other kings, though they performed this duty also, spent a great deal of their time in waging war, and therefore paid attention to the laws of war, while the long period of peace under Numa was the mother of justice and religion in our city. This king even composed laws which are still in force, as you know. Such indeed

MARCUS TULLIUS CICERO

extare, quod quidem huius civis proprium, de quo agimus. . . .

4 III. . . . sed tamen ut bono patri familias colendi, aedificandi, ratiocinandi quidam usus opus est. . . . (*Nonius,* p. 497. 19.)

5 . . . . radicum[1] seminumque cognoscere num te offendet?

M. Nihil, si modo opus extabit.

S. Num id studium censes esse vilici?

M. Minime; quippe cum agri culturam saepissime opera deficiat.

S. Ergo, ut vilicus naturam agri novit, dispensator litteras scit, uterque autem se a scientiae delectatione ad efficiendi utilitatem refert, sic noster hic rector studuerit sane iuri et legibus cognoscendis, fontis quidem earum utique perspexerit, sed se responsitando et lectitando et scriptitando ne impediat, ut quasi dispensare rem publicam et in ea quodam modo vilicare possit, summi iuris peritissimus, sine quo iustus esse nemo potest, civilis non inperitus, sed ita, ut astrorum gubernator, physicorum medicus; uterque enim illis ad artem suam

---

[1] *radicum* is commonly read; . . . *dicum* V.

248

are the proper concerns of this citizen of whom we
are speaking. . . .

III. . . . but nevertheless, as in the case of an
efficient head of a family, some experience in the
cultivation of the land, the construction of buildings,
and the keeping of accounts is necessary. . . .

Scipio. . . . it would not displease you to know
. . . of roots and seeds, would it?

Mummius. Not at all, if any necessity for it should
arise.

Scipio. Then you do not think that such knowledge is suitable only for the superintendent of a
farm?

Mummius. By no means; since lack of careful
attention is the most frequent fault in farming.

Scipio. The field-superintendent, then, knows the
nature of the land, the household-superintendent
knows how to read and write, and both are interested
in the practical utility of their knowledge rather
than in the pleasure they take in its possession. In
the same way, then, this governing statesman of
ours should surely have taken the pains to become
familiar with justice and law, and should have
examined their origins. But he should not allow
his time constantly to be taken up with consultations
or by reading and writing on these subjects, for
he must be able, as we may say, to act as both
field-superintendent and household-superintendent
of the commonwealth; he must be fully conversant
with justice in its highest aspects, for without that
no one can be just; and he must not be ignorant of
the civil law, but his knowledge of it should be like
the pilot's knowledge of the stars, or a physician's
knowledge of physics; for each uses his knowledge

utitur, sed se a suo munere non inpedit. illud
autem videbit hic vir . . . .

6   IV. . . . civitatibus[1] in quibus expetunt laudem
optumi et decus, ignominiam fugiunt ac dedecus.
nec vero tam metu poenaque terrentur, quae est
constituta legibus, quam verecundia, quam natura
homini dedit quasi quendam vituperationis non
iniustae timorem.   hanc ille rector rerum publicarum
auxit opinionibus perfecitque institutis et disciplinis,
ut pudor civis non minus a delictis arceret quam
metus.   Atque haec quidem ad laudem pertinent,
quae dici latius uberiusque potuerunt.

7   V. Ad vitam autem usumque vivendi ea discripta
ratio est iustis nuptiis, legitimis liberis, sanctis pena-
tium deorum Larumque familiarium sedibus, ut
omnes et communibus commodis et suis uterentur.
nec bene vivi sine bona re publica posset nec esse
quicquam civitate bene constituta beatius.   quocirca
permirum mihi videri solet, quae sit[2] tanta doc . . . .

8   VI. . . . Ut enim gubernatori cursus secundus,
medico salus, imperatori victoria, sic huic moderatori
rei publicae beata civium vita proposita est, ut opibus
firma, copiis locuples, gloria ampla, virtute honesta
sit ; huius enim operis maximi inter homines atque
optimi illum esse perfectorem volo. . . . (*Cicero
ad Att. VIII*, 11. 1.)

[1] *civitatibus* is commonly read ; . . . *tatibus* V.
[2] *sit* Mai ; *si* V.

in his own art, but does not allow it to keep him from his own special duties. But this man will see to it . . . .

IV. . . . . states in which the best men seek praise and glory, and avoid disgrace and dishonour. Nor indeed are they deterred from crime so much by the fear of the penalties ordained by law as by the sense of shame which Nature has given to man in the form of a certain fear of justified censure. The governing statesman strengthens this feeling in commonwealths by the force of public opinion and perfects it by the inculcation of principles and by systematic training, so that shame deters the citizens from crime no less effectively than fear. And these remarks have to do with praise, and might have been stated more broadly and developed more fully.

V. But, as regards the practical conduct of life, this system provides for legal marriage, legitimate children, and the consecration of homes to the Lares and Penates of families, so that all may make use of the common property and of their own personal possessions. It is impossible to live well except in a good commonwealth, and nothing can produce greater happiness than a well-constituted State. Therefore it always seems very remarkable to me, [that] what is so important . . . .

VI. *Scipio.* . . . For just as the aim of the pilot is a successful voyage, of the physician, health, and of the general, victory, so this director of the commonwealth has as his aim for his fellow-citizens a happy life, fortified by wealth, rich in material resources, great in glory and honoured for virtue. I want him to bring to perfection this achievement, which is the greatest and best possible among men. . . .

. . . Et ubi est, quod et vestrae litterae illum laudant patriae rectorem, qui populi utilitati magis consulat quam voluntati? . . . (*Augustinus ep.* 104. 7 *ext. T. II.* p. 292, *Ben.*)

9   VII. . . . maiores suos multa mira atque praeclara gloriae cupiditate fecisse . . . (*Augustinus de Civ. Dei V,* 13.)

. . . principem civitatis gloria esse alendum, et tam diu stare rem publicam, quam diu ab omnibus honor principi exhiberetur. . . . (*Petrus Pictaviensis ad calumn. Bibl. PP. Ludg. Tom. XXII,* p. 824.)

. . . tum virtute, labore, industria tueretur[1] summi viri indolem, nisi nimis animose ferox natura illum nescio quo . . . (*Nonius,* p. 233. 25.)

. . . quae virtus fortitudo vocatur, in qua est magnitudo animi, mortis dolorisque magna contemptio . . . (*Nonius* p. 201. 29.)

10   VIII. . . . Marcellus ut acer et pugnax, Maximus ut consideratus et lentus . . . (*Nonius,* p. 337. 30.)

. . . orbi terrarum comprehensos . . . (*Charisius I.* p. 139. 17 *Keil.*)

. . . quod molestiis[2] senectutis suae vestras familias[3] impertire posset . . . (*Nonius,* p. 37. 25.)

11   IX. . . . ut Menelao Laconi quaedam fuit suaviloquens iucunditas . . . . breviloquentiam in dicendo colat . . . (*Gellius XII,* 2. 6 *sq.*)

. . . Cumque nihil tam incorruptum esse debeat in re publica quam suffragium, quam sententia, non intellego cur, qui ea pecunia corruperit, poena dignus sit, qui eloquentia, laudem etiam ferat. mihi quidem hoc plus mali facere videtur, qui oratione, quam qui

---

[1] *tueretur* Mercer ; *quaereretur* MSS.

[2] *molestiis* Mueller ; *molestis* MSS. ; *molestias* is commonly read.

. . . And where does your literature as well praise that ruler of his native land who considers the good of his people rather than their desires ? . . .

VII. . . . . [our] ancestors were inspired to many wonderful and admirable deeds by their eagerness for glory . . .

. . . . the leading man of a State must be fed on glory, and the State can stand firm only so long as honour is given by all to their leader. . . .

. . . . then by virtue, labour, and industry . . . . should preserve the native talents of the most eminent man, unless a fierce spirit in a too headstrong manner . . . . him . . . . in some [way] . . . .

. . . . this virtue is called bravery, which is made up of nobility of spirit and an entire contempt for pain and death . . . .

VIII. . . . . As Marcellus was spirited and pugnacious, and Maximus thoughtful and cautious . . . .

. . . . included in the world . . . .

. . . . because he could make your families share some of the annoyances of his old age . . . .

IX. . . . . as Menelaus of Sparta possessed a certain pleasing and charming eloquence [1] . . . . let him cultivate brevity in speech. . . .

. . . and since nothing ought to be so free from corruption in a State as the vote and the expression of opinion, I cannot understand why the man who corrupts them by the use of money deserves punishment, if the one who does so by eloquence is praised for it. In fact, it seems to me that the man who corrupts a judge by a speech commits a worse crime

---

[1] See *Iliad* III, 212 ff.

---

[1] *familias* MSS. ; *familiis* is commonly read.

pretio iudicem corrumpit, quod pecunia corrumpere pudentem nemo potest, dicendo potest. . . . (*Ammianus Marcellinus XXX*, 4. 10.)

. . . Quae cum Scipio dixisset, admodum probans Mummius (erat enim odio quodam rhetorum inbutus) . . . (*Nonius*, p. 521. 12.)

. . . tum in optimam segetem praeclara essent sparsa semina. . . . (*Comment. anon. ad Verg. Georg. I in. apud Bandin. Catal. Lat. Bibl. Laur. II* p. 348.)

than the one who does so by a bribe, for even a virtuous man can be corrupted by oratory, though not by a bribe. . . .

. . . After Scipio had spoken thus, Mummius gave his full approval, for he was filled with a kind of hatred for the rhetoricians. . . .

. . . . then excellent seeds would have been sown in a most fertile field. . . .

DE RE PUBLICA

LIBER SEXTUS

1 I. . . . Totam igitur expectas prudentiam huius
rectoris, quae ipsum nomen hoc nacta est ex providendo . . . (*Nonius, p.* 42. 3.)

. . . Quam ob rem se comparet hic civis ita necesse
est, ut sit contra haec, quae statum civitatis per-
movent, semper armatus. . . . (*Nonius* p. 256. 23.)

. . . eaque dissensio civium, quod seorsum eunt
alii ad alios, seditio dicitur . . . (*Nonius* p. 25. 3 *et
Servius ad Verg. Aen. I.* 149.)

. . . Et vero in dissensione civili, cum boni plus
quam multi valent, expendendos civis, non numer-
andos puto . . . (*Nonius* p. 519. 14.)

. . . Graves enim dominae cogitationum lubidines
infinita quaedam cogunt atque imperant, quae quia
nec expleri nec satiari ullo modo possunt, ad omne
facinus inpellunt eos, quos inlecebris suis incen-
derunt. . . . (*Nonius* p. 424. 28.)

. . . qui contuderit[1] eius vim et ecfrenatam illam
ferociam. . . . (*Nonius* p. 492. 1.)

---

[1] *contuderit* Roth ; *contuperit* or *comperit* MSS. ; *compescit*
Halm.

---

[1] *Prudentia* (prudence) is derived from *provideo* (foresee).
[2] *Seditio* is derived from the prefix *se* (apart) and *itio*
(going).

THE REPUBLIC

BOOK VI

The Vatican manuscript has preserved no part of this book. But in addition to the scattered fragments printed below, the famous *Dream of Scipio* has been handed down to us by Macrobius, in connection with his commentary upon it.

The lost portion of the book was evidently devoted to further discussion of the qualities and duties of the statesman, and of the value and reward of his labours.

I. . . . WHAT you look for, then, is an account of this ruling statesman's prudence in its entirety, a quality which derives its name from foreseeing . . .[1]

. . . Wherefore this citizen must see to it that he is always armed against those influences which disturb the stability of the State. . . .

. . . and such a dissension among the citizens, in which one party separates from the rest, is called sedition . . [2]

. . . And indeed in civil strife, when virtue is of greater importance than numbers, I think the citizens ought to be weighed rather than counted . . .

. . . For our desires are hard masters over our thoughts, compelling and commanding us to do an infinite number of things; and as these desires can never be appeased or satisfied in any way, they urge to every sort of crime those whom they have inflamed by their allurements.

. . . who has restrained its power and that unbridled ferocity. . . .

257

2   II. . . . Quod quidem eo fuit maius, quia, cum
causa pari collegae essent, non modo invidia pari
non erant, sed etiam Claudii invidiam Gracchi caritas
deprecabatur . . . (*Gellius VII* 16. 11, *Nonius* p.
290. 15.)

. . . qui numero[1] optumatum et principum optulit
is vocibus et gravitatis suae liquit illum tristem et
plenum dignitatis sonum . . . (*Nonius* p. 409. 26.)

. . . ut, quem ad modum scribit ille, cotidiano in
forum mille hominum cum palliis conchylio tinctis
descenderent . . . (*Nonius* p. 501. 27.)

. . . in his, ut meministis, concursu levissimae
multitudinis et aere congesto funus desubito esset
ornatum . . . (*Nonius* p. 517. 32.)

. . . Firmiter enim maiores nostri stabilita matri-
monia esse voluerunt . . . (*Nonius* p. 512. 24 *et
Priscian. XV*, 3. 13 p. 70. 11 *Hertz.*)

. . . oratio Laelii, quam omnes habemus in manibus, quam simpuvia[2] pontificum dis immortalibus
grata sint Samiaeque, ut is[3] scribit, capudines . .
(*Nonius* p. 398. 26.)

3   III. . . . qui rogo impositus revixisset multaque de
inferis secreta narrasset . . . haec, quae de animae
immortalitate dicerentur caeloque, non[4] somni-
antium philosophorum esse commenta nec fabulas
incredibiles, quas Epicurei derident, sed prudentium
coniecturas . . . (*Favonius Eulogius comm. ad Somn.
Scip.* p. 401 *Or.*)

[1] The text is corrupt, *numeros . . . optudit* is conjectured
by Halm.
[2] *simpuvia* is commonly read; *simpuia* MSS.; *simpula*
Halm.
[3] *is* Mueller; *hi* MSS.
[4] *non* commonly supplied; omitted in MSS.

II. . . This indeed was so much the greater because, though the colleagues were in agreement, they were not only not equally hated, but the affection felt for Gracchus even lessened the unpopularity of Claudius . . .[1]

. . . who continually attacked the forces of the aristocrats and the eminent men in these words, and left behind him that sad, resounding echo of his dignity . . .

. . . so that, according to this author, every day a thousand men came down into the forum in robes dyed with purple . . .

. . . in those cases, as you remember, the funeral was unexpectedly honoured by the gathering of the fickle crowd and the heaping up of bronze . . .

. . . for our ancestors desired that marriages should be stable and permanent . . .

. . . the speech of Laelius, which we all have in our hands, tells us how pleasing to the gods are the pontiffs' ladles, and, to quote his words, the Samian bowls . . .

III. . . . [Er the Pamphylian],[2] who, after being laid on the pyre, came to life again and told many secrets of the world below. . . . The things that are told of the immortality of the soul and of the heavens [are not] the fictions of dreaming philosophers, or such incredible tales as the Epicureans mock at, but the conjectures of sensible men . . .

---

[1] Gaius Claudius Pulcher and Tiberius Sempronius Gracchus were censors in 169 B.C.

[2] See Plato, *Republic* X, 614–621. The story of Er is evidently referred to in the remarks which introduce the *Dream of Scipio.* The fragments which follow are also from this introductory conversation.

4   IV. . . . ut eum lusisse potius quam quod id verum
    esse adfirmet [1] dicere voluisse . . . (*Augustinus de
    Civ. Dei XXII* 28.)

8   VIII. . . . Sed quamquam sapientibus conscientia
    ipsa factorum egregiorum amplissimum virtutis est
    praemium, tamen illa divina virtus non statuas plumbo
    inhaerentes nec triumphos arescentibus laureis, sed
    stabiliora quaedam et viridiora praemiorum genera
    desiderat.

    Quae tandem ista sunt? inquit Laelius.

    Tum Scipio: Patimini me, quoniam tertium diem
    iam feriati sumus . . . (*Macrob. I* 4. 2 *sq.*)

SOMNIUM SCIPIONIS

9   IX. *S.* Cum in Africam venissem M'. Manilio
    consuli ad quartam legionem tribunus, ut scitis,
    militum, nihil mihi fuit potius, quam ut Masinissam
    convenirem regem, familiae nostrae iustis de causis
    amicissimum.   ad quem ut veni, conplexus me senex
    conlacrimavit aliquantoque post suspexit ad caelum
    et: Grates, inquit, tibi ago, summe Sol, vobisque,
    reliqui caelites, quod, ante quam ex hac vita migro,
    conspicio in meo regno et his tectis P. Cornelium
    Scipionem, cuius ego nomine ipso recreor; itaque
    numquam ex animo meo discedit illius optimi atque
    invictissimi viri memoria.   deinde ego illum de suo
    regno, ille me de nostra re publica percontatus est,
    multisque verbis ultro citroque habitis ille nobis
    consumptus est dies.

---

[1] The text is corrupt; *quod* [*id*] *verum esset, adfirmet*
Halm.

---

[1] In 149 B.C., at the beginning of the Third Punic War.

IV. . . . [that Plato] was rather jesting than intending to claim that this was true . . .

VIII. *Scipio.* . . . But though the consciousness of the worth of his deeds is the noblest reward of virtue for a wise man, yet that godlike virtue longs, not indeed for statues fixed in lead, or triumphs with their fading laurels, but for rewards of a more stable and lasting nature.

Laelius. What are they, then?

Scipio. Allow me, since this is the third day of our holiday celebration . . .

SCIPIO'S DREAM

IX. *Scipio.* I was military tribune in the Fourth Legion in Africa under the consul Manius Manilius,[1] as you know. When I arrived in that country my greatest desire was to meet King Masinissa, who for excellent reasons[2] was a very close friend of my family. When I came into his presence the aged man embraced me and wept copiously; after a short interval, turning his eyes up to heaven, he uttered these words: "I thank thee, O supreme Sun, and ye other heavenly beings, that, before I depart this life, I see within my kingdom and under my roof Publius Cornelius Scipio, by the mere sound of whose name I am refreshed; so little has the memory of that noble and invincible hero[3] faded from my memory!" Then I questioned him about his kingdom, while he inquired of me about our commonwealth, and we spent the whole day in an extended discussion of both.

[2] Scipio the Elder had restored Masinissa's hereditary domains, and added other territory to his kingdom.
[3] Publius Cornelius Scipio Africanus the Elder.

10   X. Post autem apparatu regio accepti sermonem
in multam noctem produximus, cum senex nihil
nisi de Africano loqueretur omniaque eius non facta
solum, sed etiam dicta meminisset.   deinde, ut
cubitum discessimus, me et de via fessum, et qui
ad multam noctem vigilassem, artior quam solebat
somnus complexus est.   hic mihi (credo equidem
ex hoc, quod eramus locuti; fit enim fere, ut
cogitationes sermonesque nostri pariant aliquid in
somno tale, quale de Homero scribit Ennius, de
quo videlicet saepissime vigilans solebat cogitare et
loqui) Africanus se ostendit ea forma, quae mihi ex
imagine eius quam ex ipso erat notior; quem ubi[1]
agnovi, equidem cohorrui, sed ille:

Ades, inquit, animo et omitte timorem, Scipio,
et, quae dicam, trade memoriae.

11   XI. Videsne illam urbem, quae parere populo
Romano coacta per me renovat pristina bella nec
potest quiescere (ostendebat autem Karthaginem
de excelso et pleno stellarum illustri et claro
quodam loco) ad quam tu oppugnandam nunc venis
paene miles? hanc hoc biennio consul evertes, eritque
cognomen id tibi per te partum, quod habes adhuc
a nobis hereditarium.   cum autem Karthaginem
deleveris, triumphum egeris censorque fueris et
obieris legatus Aegyptum, Syriam, Asiam, Graeciam,
deligere iterum consul absens bellumque maximum

---

[1] *ubi* MSS. ; *ut* Orelli.

---

[1] A reference to a passage in Ennius' *Annales* (probably
Book I) which is also referred to in *Acad.* II, 51 (*cum som-
niavit, ita narravit* : " *Visus Homerus adesse poeta* "), and 88.
[2] *i.e.*, Africanus.

X. Later, after I had been entertained with royal hospitality, we continued our conversation far into the night, the aged king talking of nothing but Africanus, and recollecting all his sayings as well as his deeds. When we separated to take our rest, I fell immediately into a deeper sleep than usual, as I was weary from my journey and the hour was late. The following dream came to me, prompted, I suppose, by the subject of our conversation; for it often happens that our thoughts and words have some such effect in our sleep as Ennius describes with reference to Homer,[1] about whom, of course, he frequently used to talk and think in his waking hours. I thought that Africanus stood before me, taking that shape which was familiar to me from his bust rather than from his person. Upon recognizing him I shuddered in terror, but he said:

"Courage, Scipio, have no fear, but imprint my words upon your memory.

XI. "Do you see yonder city, which, though forced by me into obedience to the Roman people, is renewing its former conflicts and cannot be at rest" (and from a lofty place which was bathed in clear starlight, he pointed out Carthage), "that city to which you now come to lay siege, with a rank little above that of a common soldier? Within two years you as consul shall overthrow it, thus winning by your own efforts the surname[2] which till now you have as an inheritance from me. But after destroying Carthage and celebrating your triumph, you shall hold the censorship; you shall go on missions to Egypt, Syria, Asia and Greece; you shall be chosen consul a second time in your absence; you shall bring a great war to a successful close; and you

conficies, Numantiam exscindes.[1] sed cum eris curru
in Capitolium invectus, offendes rem publicam consiliis perturbatam nepotis mei.

12 XII. Hic tu, Africane, ostendas oportebit patriae
lumen animi, ingenii consiliique tui. sed eius
temporis ancipitem video quasi fatorum viam. nam
cum aetas tua septenos octiens solis anfractus
reditusque converterit, duoque ii numeri, quorum
uterque plenus alter altera de causa habetur,
circuitu naturali summam tibi fatalem confecerint,
in te unum atque in tuum nomen se tota convertet
civitas, te senatus, te omnes boni, te socii, te Latini
intuebuntur, tu eris unus, in quo nitatur civitatis
salus, ac, ne multa, dictator rem publicam constituas
oportet, si impias propinquorum manus effugeris.

Hic cum exclamasset Laelius ingemuissentque
vehementius ceteri, leniter arridens Scipio: St!
quaeso, inquit, ne me e somno excitetis, et parumper
audite cetera.

13 XIII. Sed quo sis, Africane, alacrior ad tutandam
rem publicam, sic habeto: omnibus, qui patriam
conservaverint, adiuverint, auxerint, certum esse in
caelo definitum locum, ubi beati aevo sempiterno
fruantur; nihil est enim illi principi deo, qui omnem
mundum regit, quod quidem in terris fiat, acceptius
quam concilia coetusque hominum iure sociati, quae

---

[1] *exscindes* EF; *excindes* MPR; *excides* Orelli.

---

[1] For the career of Scipio the Younger, see Index.
[2] Tiberius Gracchus, son of the elder Scipio's daughter
Cornelia.

shall destroy Numantia.[1] But, after driving in state
to the Capitol, you shall find the commonwealth
disturbed by the designs of my grandson.[2]

XII. "Then, Africanus, it will be your duty to
hold up before the fatherland the light of your
character, your ability, and your wisdom. But at that
time I see two paths of destiny, as it were, opening
before you. For when your age has fulfilled seven
times eight returning circuits of the sun, and those
two numbers, each of which for a different reason is
considered perfect,[3] in Nature's revolving course have
reached their destined sum in your life, then the whole
State will turn to you and your name alone. The
senate, all good citizens, the allies, the Latins, will look
to you; you shall be the sole support of the State's
security, and, in brief, it will be your duty as dictator
to restore order in the commonwealth, if only you
escape the wicked hands of your kinsmen."[4]

Laelius cried aloud at this, and the rest groaned
deeply, but Scipio said with a gentle smile: Quiet,
please; do not wake me from my sleep; listen for a
few moments, and hear what followed.

XIII. "But, Africanus, be assured of this, so that
you may be even more eager to defend the commonwealth: all those who have preserved, aided, or
enlarged their fatherland have a special place prepared
for them in the heavens, where they may enjoy an
eternal life of happiness. For nothing of all that is
done on earth is more pleasing to that supreme God
who rules the whole universe than the assemblies
and gatherings of men associated in justice, which

---

[3] τέλεος ἀριθμός; compare Plato, *Timaeus* 39 D. The idea
of "perfect numbers" goes back to Pythagoras.
[4] There was a suspicion that Scipio's death (in 129 B.C.)
was due to the party of the Gracchi.

civitates appellantur; harum rectores et conservatores hinc profecti huc revertuntur.

14 XIV. Hic ego, etsi eram perterritus non tam
mortis metu quam insidiarum a meis, quaesivi tamen,
viveretne ipse et Paulus pater et alii, quos nos
extinctos arbitraremur.

Immo vero, inquit, hi vivunt, qui e corporum
vinculis tamquam e carcere evolaverunt, vestra vero,
quae dicitur, vita mors est. quin tu aspicis ad te
venientem Paulum patrem?

Quem ut vidi, equidem vim lacrimarum profudi,
ille autem me complexus atque osculans flere
15 prohibebat. XV. atque ego ut primum fletu re-
presso loqui posse coepi, Quaeso, inquam, pater
sanctissime atque optime, quoniam haec est vita,
ut Africanum audio dicere, quid moror in terris?
quin huc ad vos venire propero?

Non est ita, inquit ille. nisi enim deus is, cuius
hoc templum est omne, quod conspicis, istis te corporis custodiis liberaverit, huc tibi aditus patere non
potest. homines enim sunt hac lege generati, qui
tuerentur illum globum, quem in hoc templo medium
vides, quae terra dicitur, hisque[1] animus datus est
ex illis sempiternis ignibus, quae sidera et stellas
vocatis, quae globosae et rotundae, divinis animatae
mentibus, circulos suos orbesque conficiunt celeritate
mirabili. quare et tibi, Publi, et piis omnibus
retinendus animus est in custodia corporis nec
iniussu eius, a quo ille est vobis datus, ex hominum
vita migrandum est, ne munus humanum[2] adsig-

---

[1] *hisque* MSS.; *iisque* is often read.
[2] *humanum* lacking in Macrobius, and bracketed by
Halm, Baiter.

are called States. Their rulers and preservers come from that place, and to that place they return."

XIV. Though I was then thoroughly terrified, more by the thought of treachery among my own kinsmen than by the fear of death, nevertheless I asked him whether he and my father Paulus and the others whom we think of as dead, were really still alive.

"Surely all those are alive," he said, " who have escaped from the bondage of the body as from a prison ; but that life of yours, which men so call, is really death. Do you not see your father Paulus approaching you ? "

When I saw him I poured forth a flood of tears, but he embraced and kissed me, and forbade me to weep. XV. As soon as I had restrained my grief and was able to speak, I cried out : " O best and most blameless of fathers, since that is life, as I learn from Africanus, why should I remain longer on earth ? Why not hasten thither to you ? "

" Not so," he replied, " for unless that God, whose temple [1] is everything that you see, has freed you from the prison of the body, you cannot gain entrance there. For man was given life that he might inhabit that sphere called Earth, which you see in the centre of this temple ; and he has been given a soul out of those eternal fires which you call stars and planets, which, being round and globular bodies animated by divine intelligences, circle about in their fixed orbits with marvellous speed. Wherefore you, Publius, and all good men, must leave that soul in the custody of the body, and must not abandon human life except at the behest of him by whom it was given you, lest

[1] *Templum* originally meant a region of the sky marked off for purposes of divination.

16 natum a deo defugisse videamini. XVI. sed sic,
Scipio, ut avus hic tuus, ut ego, qui te genui,
iustitiam cole et pietatem, quae cum magna in
parentibus et propinquis, tum in patria maxima
est; ea vita via est in caelum et in hunc coetum
eorum, qui iam vixerunt et corpore laxati illum
incolunt locum, quem vides (erat autem is splendi-
dissimo candore inter flammas circus elucens), quem
vos, ut a Graiis accepistis, orbem lacteum nun-
cupatis.

Ex quo omnia mihi contemplanti praeclara cetera
et mirabilia videbantur. erant autem eae stellae,
quas numquam ex hoc loco vidimus, et eae magnitu-
dines omnium, quas esse numquam suspicati sumus,
ex quibus erat ea minima, quae ultima a caelo,
citima terris[1] luce lucebat aliena. stellarum autem
globi terrae magnitudinem facile vincebant. iam
ipsa terra ita mihi parva visa est, ut me imperii
nostri, quo quasi punctum eius attingimus, pae-
niteret.

17 XVII. Quam cum magis intuerer, Quaeso, inquit
Africanus, quousque humi defixa tua mens erit?
nonne aspicis, quae in templa veneris? novem tibi
orbibus vel potius globis conexa sunt omnia, quorum
unus est caelestis, extumus, qui reliquos omnes com-
plectitur, summus ipse deus arcens et continens ceteros; in quo sunt infixi illi, qui volvuntur, stellarum cursus sempiterni; cui subiecti sunt septem,
qui versantur retro contrario motu atque caelum; ex
quibus unum globum possidet illa, quam in terris

---

[1] *citima terris* MSS. ; *citima a terris* Madvig.

---

[1] The elder Scipio. [2] *i.e.*, the Milky Way.
[3] The Moon.

you appear to have shirked the duty imposed upon man by God. XVI. But, Scipio, imitate your grand-father[1] here; imitate me, your father; love justice and duty, which are indeed strictly due to parents and kinsmen, but most of all to the fatherland. Such a life is the road to the skies, to that gathering of those who have completed their earthly lives and been relieved of the body, and who live in yonder place which you now see" (it was the circle of light which blazed most brightly among the other fires), "and which you on earth, borrowing a Greek term, call the Milky Circle."[2]

When I gazed in every direction from that point, all else appeared wonderfully beautiful. There were stars which we never see from the earth, and they were all larger than we have ever imagined. The smallest of them was that farthest from heaven and nearest the earth which shone with a borrowed light.[3] The starry spheres were much larger than the earth; indeed the earth itself seemed to me so small that I was scornful of our empire, which covers only a single point, as it were, upon its surface.

XVII. As I gazed still more fixedly at the earth, Africanus said: "How long will your thoughts be fixed upon the lowly earth? Do you not see what lofty regions you have entered? These are the nine circles, or rather spheres, by which the whole is joined. One of them, the outermost, is that of heaven; it contains all the rest, and is itself the supreme God, holding and embracing within itself all the other spheres; in it are fixed the eternal revolving courses of the stars. Beneath it are seven other spheres which revolve in the opposite direction to that of heaven. One of these globes is that light

Saturniam nominant. deinde est hominum generi prosperus et salutaris ille fulgor, qui dicitur Iovis; tum rutilus horribilisque terris, quem Martium dicitis ; deinde subter mediam fere regionem sol obtinet, dux et princeps et moderator luminum reliquorum, mens mundi et temperatio, tanta magnitudine, ut cuncta sua luce lustret et compleat. hunc ut comites consequuntur Veneris alter, alter Mercurii cursus, in infimoque orbe luna radiis solis accensa convertitur. infra autem iam nihil est nisi mortale et caducum praeter animos munere deorum hominum generi datos, supra lunam sunt aeterna omnia. nam ea, quae est media et nona, tellus, neque movetur et infima est, et in eam feruntur omnia nutu suo pondera.

18   XVIII. Quae cum intuerer stupens, ut me recepi, Quid ? hic, inquam, quis est, qui conplet aures meas tantus et tam dulcis sonus?

Hic est, inquit, ille, qui intervallis disiunctus[1] inparibus, sed tamen pro rata parte ratione distinctis inpulsu et motu ipsorum orbium efficitur et acuta cum gravibus temperans varios aequabiliter concentus efficit ; nec enim silentio tanti motus incitari possunt, et natura fert, ut extrema ex altera parte graviter, ex altera autem acute sonent. quam ob causam summus ille caeli stellifer cursus, cuius conversio est

---

[1] *disiunctus* Macrobius and Favonius Eulogius, *Schol. Cic.* I, p. 412 ; *coniunctus* MSS.

---

[1] *i.e.,* between heaven and earth.
[2] For the astronomical system see Plato, *Republic* X, 616 B–617 C ; *Timaeus* 36 and 38. Most of these ideas appear to go back to the Pythagoreans (especially to Philolaus of Croton, a contemporary of Socrates).
[3] Compare Plato, *Republic* X, 617 B ; Aristotle, *De Caelo* II, 290 B.

which on earth is called Saturn's. Next comes the star called Jupiter's, which brings fortune and health to mankind. Beneath it is that star, red and terrible to the dwellings of man, which you assign to Mars. Below it and almost midway of the distance[1] is the Sun, the lord, chief, and ruler of the other lights, the mind and guiding principle of the universe, of such magnitude that he reveals and fills all things with his light. He is accompanied by his companions, as it were—Venus and Mercury in their orbits, and in the lowest sphere revolves the Moon, set on fire by the rays of the Sun. But below the Moon there is nothing except what is mortal and doomed to decay, save only the souls given to the human race by the bounty of the gods, while above the Moon all things are eternal. For the ninth and central sphere, which is the earth, is immovable and the lowest of all, and toward it all ponderable bodies are drawn by their own natural tendency downward."[2]

XVIII. After recovering from the astonishment with which I viewed these wonders, I said : "What is this loud and agreeable sound that fills my ears ? "[3]

"That is produced," he replied, "by the onward rush and motion of the spheres themselves; the intervals between them, though unequal, being exactly arranged in a fixed proportion, by an agreeable blending of high and low tones various harmonies are produced; for such mighty motions cannot be carried on so swiftly in silence; and Nature has provided that one extreme shall produce low tones while the other gives forth high. Therefore this uppermost sphere of heaven, which bears

concitatior, acuto et excitato movetur sono, gravissimo autem hic lunaris atque infimus; nam terra
nona inmobilis manens una sede semper haeret com-
plexa medium mundi locum. illi autem octo cursus,
in quibus eadem vis est duorum, septem efficiunt
distinctos intervallis sonos, qui numerus rerum
omnium fere nodus est; quod docti homines nervis
imitati atque cantibus aperuerunt sibi reditum in
hunc locum, sicut alii, qui praestantibus ingeniis in
19 vita humana divina studia coluerunt. hoc sonitu
oppletae aures hominum obsurduerunt; nec est ullus
hebetior sensus in vobis, sicut, ubi Nilus ad illa, quae
Catadupa nominantur, praecipitat[1] ex altissimis
montibus, ea gens, quae illum locum adcolit, propter
magnitudinem sonitus sensu audiendi caret. hic
vero tantus est totius mundi incitatissima conversione
sonitus, ut eum aures hominum capere non possint,
sicut intueri solem adversum nequitis, eiusque radiis
acies vestra sensusque vincitur.

Haec ego admirans referebam tamen oculos ad
20 terram identidem. XIX. Tum Africanus:

Sentio, inquit, te sedem etiam nunc hominum ac domum contemplari; quae si tibi parva, ut est, ita videtur,
haec caelestia semper spectato, illa humana contem-
nito. tu enim quam celebritatem sermonis hominum
aut quam expetendam consequi gloriam potes? vides

---

[1] *praecipitat* MPR¹T; *praecipitatur* EFR².

---

[1] The Cataracts of the Nile.

the stars, as it revolves more rapidly, produces a high, shrill tone, whereas the lowest revolving sphere, that of the Moon, gives forth the lowest tone; for the earthly sphere, the ninth, remains ever motionless and stationary in its position in the centre of the universe. But the other eight spheres, two of which move with the same velocity, produce seven different sounds,—a number which is the key of almost everything. Learned men, by imitating this harmony on stringed instruments and in song, have gained for themselves a return to this region, as others have obtained the same reward by devoting their brilliant intellects to divine pursuits during their earthly lives. Men's ears, ever filled with this sound, have become deaf to it; for you have no duller sense than that of hearing. We find a similar phenomenon where the Nile rushes down from those lofty mountains at the place called Catadupa;[1] the people who live near by have lost their sense of hearing on account of the loudness of the sound. But this mighty music, produced by the revolution of the whole universe at the highest speed, cannot be perceived by human ears, any more than you can look straight at the Sun, your sense of sight being overpowered by its radiance."

While gazing at these wonders, I was repeatedly turning my eyes back to earth. XIX. Then Africanus resumed :

" I see that you are still directing your gaze upon the habitation and abode of men. If it seems small to you, as it actually is, keep your gaze fixed upon these heavenly things, and scorn the earthly. For what fame can you gain from the speech of men, or what glory that is worth the seeking? You see that

habitari in terra raris et angustis in locis et in ipsis
quasi maculis, ubi habitatur, vastas solitudines
interiectas, eosque, qui incolunt[1] terram, non modo
interruptos ita esse, ut nihil inter ipsos ab aliis ad
alios manare possit, sed partim obliquos, partim
transversos, partim etiam adversos stare vobis ; a
quibus expectare gloriam certe nullam potestis.

21   XX. Cernis autem eandem terram quasi quibusdam redimitam et circumdatam cingulis, e quibus
duos maxime inter se diversos et caeli verticibus
ipsis ex utraque parte subnixos obriguisse pruina
vides, medium autem illum et maximum solis ardore
torreri.   duo sunt habitabiles, quorum australis ille,
in quo qui insistunt, adversa vobis urgent vestigia,
nihil ad vestrum genus ; hic autem alter subiectus
aquiloni, quem incolitis, cerne quam tenui vos parte
contingat.   omnis enim terra, quae colitur a vobis,
angustata[2] verticibus, lateribus latior, parva quaedam
insula est circumfusa illo mari, quod Atlanticum,
quod magnum, quem Oceanum appellatis in terris,
22 qui tamen tanto nomine quam sit parvus, vides.   ex
his ipsis cultis notisque terris num aut tuum aut
cuiusquam nostrum[3] nomen vel Caucasum hunc,
quem cernis, transcendere potuit vel illum Gangen
tranatare?   quis in reliquis orientis aut obeuntis

[1] *incolunt* Macrobius ; *incolant* MSS.
[2] *angustata* MSS. ; *angusta* Macrobius.
[3] *nostrum* MSS. ; *vestrum* Halm.

---

[1] *Obliqui* (ἄντοικοι) are the inhabitants of the other temperate zone of one's own hemisphere.   *Transversi* (περίοικοι) are
those of the same temperate zone of the other hemisphere.
Adversi (ἀντίποδες) are those of the other temperate zone of

the earth is inhabited in only a few portions, and those very small, while vast deserts lie between those inhabited patches, as we may call them; you see that the inhabitants are so widely separated that there can be no communication whatever among the different areas; and that some of the inhabitants live in parts of the earth that are oblique, transverse, and sometimes directly opposite your own;[1] from such you can expect nothing surely that is glory.

XX. " Besides, you will notice that the earth is surrounded and encircled by certain zones, of which the two that are most widely separated, and are supported by the opposite poles of heaven, are held in icy bonds, while the central and broadest zone is scorched by the heat of the sun. Two zones are habitable; of these the southern (the footsteps of whose inhabitants are opposite to yours)[2] has no connection whatever with your zone. Examine this northern zone which you inhabit, and you will see what a small portion of it belongs to you Romans. For that whole territory which you hold, being narrow from North to South, and broader from East to West, is really only a small island surrounded by that sea which you on the earth call the Atlantic, the Great Sea, or the Ocean. Now you see how small it is in spite of its proud name! Do you suppose that your fame or that of any of us could ever go beyond those settled and explored regions by climbing the Caucasus, which you see there, or by swimming the Ganges? What inhabitants of those distant lands of the rising or setting sun, or

the other hemisphere.   Compare Plato, *Timaeus* 63 A; Cicero, *Acad.* II, 123.
    [2] See section 20 : *adversi*, and note.

solis ultimis aut aquilonis austrive partibus tuum
nomen audiet? quibus amputatis cernis profecto
quantis in angustiis vestra se gloria dilatari velit.
ipsi autem, qui de nobis [1] loquuntur, quam loquentur
diu?

23   XXI. Quin etiam si cupiat proles illa futurorum
hominum deinceps laudes unius cuiusque nostrum a
patribus acceptas posteris prodere, tamen propter
eluviones exustionesque terrarum, quas accidere
tempore certo necesse est, non modo non [2] aeternam,
sed ne diuturnam quidem gloriam adsequi possumus.
quid autem interest ab iis, qui postea nascentur,
sermonem fore de te, cum ab iis nullus fuerit, qui
24 ante nati sunt?   XXII. qui nec pauciores et certe
meliores fuerunt viri, praesertim cum apud eos ipsos,
a quibus audiri nomen nostrum potest, nemo unius
anni memoriam consequi possit. homines enim
populariter annum tantum modo solis, id est unius
astri, reditu metiuntur; cum autem ad idem, unde
semel profecta sunt, cuncta astra redierint eandemque totius caeli discriptionem longis intervallis
rettulerint, tum ille vere vertens annus appellari
potest; in quo vix dicere audeo quam multa hominum saecula teneantur. namque ut olim deficere
sol hominibus exstinguique visus est, cum Romuli
animus haec ipsa in templa penetravit, quandoque
ab eadem parte sol eodemque tempore iterum defe-
cerit, tum signis omnibus ad principium stellisque

---

[1] *nobis* MSS. ; *vobis* Halm.
[2] *non modo non* MSS. ; *non modo* [*non*] Mueller.

---

[1] A Stoic doctrine ; compare Cicero, *De Nat. Deor.* II, 118 ;
Seneca, *Nat. Quaest.* III, 27 ff.

the extreme North or South, will ever hear your name? Leave out all these and you cannot fail to see what a narrow territory it is over which your glory is so eager to spread. And how long will even those who do talk of us now continue so to do?

XXI. "But even if future generations should wish to hand down to those yet unborn the eulogies of every one of us which they received from their fathers, nevertheless the floods and conflagrations[1] which necessarily happen on the earth at stated intervals would prevent us from gaining a glory which could even be long-enduring, much less eternal. But of what importance is it to you to be talked of by those who are born after you, when you were never mentioned by those who lived before you, [XXII] who were no less numerous and were certainly better men; especially as not one of those who may hear our names can retain any recollection for the space of a single year? For people commonly measure the year by the circuit of the sun, that is, of a single star alone; but when all the stars return to the place from which they at first set forth, and, at long intervals, restore the original configuration of the whole heaven, then that can truly be called a revolving year.[2] I hardly dare to say how many generations of men are contained within such a year; for as once the sun appeared to men to be eclipsed and blotted out, at the time when the soul of Romulus entered these regions, so when the sun shall again be eclipsed at the same point and in the same season, you may believe that all the planets and stars have returned to their original positions,

[2] For the "great year" see Plato, *Timaeus* 39; Cicero, *De Nat. Deor.* II, 51.

revocatis expletum annum habeto; cuius quidem anni nondum vicesimam partem scito esse conversam.

25   XXIII. Quocirca si reditum in hunc locum desperaveris, in quo omnia sunt magnis et praestantibus viris, quanti tandem est ista hominum gloria, quae pertinere vix ad unius anni partem exiguam potest? igitur alte spectare si voles atque hanc sedem et aeternam domum contueri, neque te sermonibus vulgi dedideris[1] nec in praemiis humanis spem posueris rerum tuarum; suis te oportet inlecebris ipsa virtus trahat ad verum decus, quid de te alii loquantur, ipsi videant, sed loquentur tamen.   sermo autem omnis ille et angustiis cingitur iis regionum, quas vides, nec umquam de ullo perennis fuit et obruitur hominum interitu et oblivione posteritatis extinguitur.

26   XXIV. Quae cum dixisset, Ego vero, inquam, Africane, siquidem bene meritis de patria quasi limes ad caeli aditum patet, quamquam a pueritia vestigiis ingressus patris et tuis decori vestro non defui, nunc tamen tanto praemio exposito enitar multo vigilantius.

Et ille : Tu vero enitere et sic habeto, non esse te mortalem, sed corpus hoc; nec enim tu is es, quem forma ista declarat, sed mens cuiusque is est quisque, non ea figura, quae digito demonstrari potest.   deum te igitur scito esse, siquidem est deus, qui viget, qui sentit, qui meminit, qui providet, qui tam regit et

---

[1] *dedideris* MSS. ; *dederis* Halm.

and that a year has actually elapsed. But be sure that a twentieth part of such a year has not yet passed.

XXIII. "Consequently, if you despair of ever returning to this place, where eminent and excellent men find their true reward, of how little value, indeed, is your fame among men, which can hardly endure for the small part of a single year? Therefore, if you will only look on high and contemplate this eternal home and resting place, you will no longer attend to the gossip of the vulgar herd or put your trust in human rewards for your exploits. Virtue herself, by her own charms, should lead you on to true glory. Let what others say of you be their own concern; whatever it is, they will say it in any case. But all their talk is limited to those narrow regions which you look upon, nor will any man's reputation endure very long, for what men say dies with them and is blotted out with the forgetfulness of posterity."

XXIV. When he had spoken thus, I said: "If indeed a path to heaven, as it were, is open to those who have served their country well, henceforth I will redouble my efforts, spurred on by so splendid a reward; though even from my boyhood I have followed in the footsteps of my father and yourself, and have not failed to emulate your glory."

He answered: "Strive on indeed, and be sure that it is not you that is mortal, but only your body. For that man whom your outward form reveals is not yourself; the spirit is the true self, not that physical figure which can be pointed out by the finger. Know, then, that you are a god, if a god is that which lives, feels, remembers, and foresees, and

moderatur et movet id corpus, cui praepositus est,
quam hunc mundum ille princeps deus; et ut mundum ex quadam parte mortalem ipse deus aeternus,
sic fragile corpus animus sempiternus movet.

27 XXV. Nam quod semper movetur, aeternum est;
quod autem motum adfert alicui, quodque ipsum
agitatur aliunde, quando finem habet motus, vivendi
finem habeat necesse est. solum igitur, quod sese
movet,[1] quia numquam deseritur a se, numquam ne
moveri quidem desinit; quin etiam ceteris, quae
moventur, hic fons, hoc principium est movendi.
principii autem nulla est origo; nam ex principio
oriuntur omnia, ipsum autem nulla ex re alia nasci
potest; nec enim esset id principium, quod gignere-
tur aliunde; quodsi numquam oritur, ne occidit
quidem umquam. nam principium exstinctum nec
ipsum ab alio renascetur nec ex se aliud creabit,
siquidem necesse est a principio oriri omnia. ita
fit, ut motus principium ex eo sit, quod ipsum a se
movetur; id autem nec nasci potest nec mori; vel
concidat omne caelum omnisque natura et consistat
necesse est nec vim ullam nanciscatur, qua a primo
inpulsa moveatur.

28 XXVI. Cum pateat igitur aeternum id esse, quod
a se ipso moveatur,[2] quis est, qui hanc naturam
animis esse tributam neget? inanimum est enim
omne, quod pulsu agitatur externo; quod autem est
animal, id motu cietur interiore et suo: nam haec

---

[1] *sese movet* T; *de se movet* PR; *de se movetur* EF; *se
ipsum movet* Macrobius.

which rules, governs, and moves the body over which it is set, just as the supreme God above us rules this universe. And just as the eternal God moves the universe, which is partly mortal, so an immortal spirit moves the frail body.

XXV. "For that which is always in motion is eternal, but that which communicates motion to something else, but is itself moved by another force, necessarily ceases to live when this motion ends. Therefore only that which moves itself never ceases its motion, because it never abandons itself; nay, it is the source and first cause of motion in all other things that are moved. But this first cause has itself no beginning, for everything originates from the first cause, while it can never originate from anything else; for that would not be a first cause which owed its origin to anything else. And since it never had a beginning, it will never have an end. For if a first cause were destroyed, it could never be reborn from anything else, nor could it bring anything else into being; since everything must originate from a first cause. Thus it follows that motion begins with that which is moved of itself; but this can neither be born nor die, or else all the heavens must fall and all nature perish, possessing no force from which they can receive the first impulse to motion.

XXVI. "Therefore, now that it is clear that what moves of itself is eternal, who can deny that this is the nature of spirits? For whatever is moved by an external impulse is spiritless; but whatever possesses a spirit is moved by an inner impulse of its own; for

---

[2] *quod a se ipso moveatur* MSS.; *quod ipsum se moveat* Macrobius.

est propria natura animi atque vis; quae si est una
ex omnibus, quae sese[1] moveat, neque nata certe
29 est et aeterna est.   hanc tu exerce optimis in
rebus! sunt autem optimae curae de salute patriae,
quibus agitatus et exercitatus animus velocius in
hanc sedem et domum suam pervolabit; idque ocius
faciet, si iam tum, cum erit inclusus in corpore,
eminebit foras et ea, quae extra erunt, contemplans
quam maxime se a corpore abstrahet.   namque
eorum animi, qui se corporis voluptatibus dediderunt
earumque se quasi ministros praebuerunt inpulsuque
libidinum voluptatibus oboedientium deorum et
hominum iura violaverunt, corporibus elapsi circum
terram ipsam volutantur nec hunc in locum nisi
multis exagitati saeculis revertuntur.

Ille discessit; ego somno solutus sum.

[1] *sese* MSS.; *se ipsa* Macrobius.

that is the peculiar nature and property of a spirit.
And as a spirit is the only force that moves itself, it
surely has no beginning and is immortal.[1] Use it,
therefore, in the best pursuits! And the best tasks
are those undertaken in defence of your native land ;
a spirit occupied and trained in such activities will
have a swifter flight to this, its proper home and
permanent abode. And this flight will be still more
rapid if, while still confined in the body, it looks
abroad, and, by contemplating what lies outside
itself, detaches itself as much as may be from the
body. For the spirits of those who are given over
to sensual pleasures and have become their slaves, as
it were, and who violate the laws of gods and men
at the instigation of those desires which are sub-
servient to pleasure—their spirits, after leaving their
bodies, fly about close to the earth, and do not
return to this place except after many ages of
torture."

He departed, and I awoke from my sleep.[2]

---

[1] Sections 27 and 28 are borrowed from Plato, *Phaedrus*
245 C–E. Compare also Cicero, *Tusc. Disp.* I, 53–55.

[2] This is the end of the work.

LIBRORUM DE RE PUBLICA INCERTORUM
FRAGMENTA

1. idque ipsa natura non invitaret solum, sed etiam cogeret. (*Nonius* p. 321. 17.)

2. Fanni, causa difficilis laudare puerum; non enim res laudanda, sed spes est. (*Servius ad Verg. Aen. VI* 877.)

3. Si fas endo plagas caelestum ascendere cuiquam est,

mi soli caeli maxima porta patet,

. . . est vero, Africane; nam et Herculi eadem ista porta patuit. (*Lactant, Inst. Div. I,* 18.)

4. Quoniam sumus ab ipsa calce eius interpellatione revocati. . . . .

cui nemo civis neque hostis quivit pro factis reddere opis [1] pretium. (*Seneca, Epist.* 108. 32 *sq.*)

5. Quicumque epulis et conviviis et sumptibus existimationem hominum sibi conciliant, palam ostendunt sibi verum decus, quod ex virtute ac dignitate nascitur, deficere. (*Anonymus Paradoxa Koronne apud Bielowsk. Pompeii Trogi fragm. p. XV sq.*)

6. leniter atque placide fides, non vi et impetu, concuti debere . . . . (*Cod. manuscr. n.* 458, p. 82 *biblioth. Ossolinianae.*)

7. Nullum est exemplum cui malimus adsimulare rem publicam. (*Diomedes I* p. 365. 20 *Keil.*)

8. foedifragos Afros. (*Schol. Crucq. ad Hor. Carm. IV* 8. 17.)

---

[1] *opis* Vahlen; *operae* MSS.; *par* Maehly.

UNPLACED FRAGMENTS OF THE REPUBLIC

1. . . . . and Nature herself would not only invite, but even compel this.

2. Fannius, it is a difficult matter to praise a boy; for praise must then be given to hope, not to achievement.

3. If fate let man ascend to heavenly heights
   To me alone the great gates open wide.[1]

. . . . Quite true, Africanus, for that same gate stood open to Hercules.

4. Since we have been recalled from the very goal itself by his interruption. . . . .

   A man to whom nor friend nor foe could give
   A just repayment for his deeds of might.[2]

5. All who attempt to win men's favour by banquets or dinners or extravagant entertainments show clearly that they lack true honour, which comes from virtue and merit.

6. Confidence ought to be won gradually and quietly, not by force or sudden attack.

7. There is no pattern to which we should prefer to make the State conform.

8. . . . . . treaty-breaking Africans . . . .

[1] Ennius put these words into the mouth of Africanus the Elder. It is thought that the complete epigram consisted of these two verses preceded by those quoted in *Tusc. Disp.* V, 49 :

   A sole exoriente supra Maeotis paludes
   Nemo est qui factis aequiperare queat.

[2] Another epigram of Ennius on Africanus. It is thought to have read :

   Hic est ille situs cui nemo, etc.

Compare *De Leg.* II, 57.

THE LAWS

INTRODUCTION TO THE DE LEGIBUS

THE *De Legibus* is a sequel to the *De Re Publica*;
Cicero's *Laws* are the laws of Cicero's *Republic.*[1] It
appears to have been begun soon after the *De Re
Publica* was finished, or perhaps even before the
latter had received its final preparation for publica-
tion. Certain passages point to the year 52 B.C.;[2] the
work was evidently discontinued during Cicero's
provincial governorship (51–50 B.C.) and the Civil War
(49–48 B.C.). In 46 B.C. Cicero's literary activity was
resumed; from then on until his death (43 B.C.) was the
period of his greatest production of rhetorical and
philosophic treatises. There is evidence that he
was working on the *De Legibus* in 46 B.C.,[3] and in the
following year also.[4] On the other hand, we know
that it had not been published when *De Divinatione*
was written in 44 B.C.,[5] and we have no evidence whatever that Cicero ever finished it, or that it was
published during his life. Yet the arguments adduced

---

[1] *De Leg.* I, 15; 20; II, 14; 23; III, 4; 12–13.

[2] The reference in II, 42 is evidently to Clodius' death
(Jan. **18,** 52 B.C.). See also A. Gudeman, *Zur Chronologie von
Ciceros De Legibus,* Berl. Philol. Woch. XII (1892), col.
930–32.

[3] *Ep. ad Fam.* IX, 2, 5.

[4] See R. Reitzenstein, *Drei Vermutungen zur Geschichte der
roemischen Litteratur,* Marburg, 1894, pp. 1–31.

[5] Cicero *De Divin.* II, 1.

to show that the work as we have it is actually in an unfinished state seem quite inconclusive.[1]

In the *De Legibus* Cicero used the plan which he finally rejected for the *De Re Publica*; he himself is the chief character, and Quintus and Atticus are the others. The time is one long summer day; the place is Cicero's estate at Arpinum. The conversation begins in a grove which contains the "Marian Oak";[2] the scene soon changes to the bank of the Liris.[3] Later the speakers go to an island in the Fibrenus,[4] where they remain throughout the conversation of the second and third books; during the conversation recorded in the lost fifth book they return to the bank of the Liris.[5]

The greater part of the first three books is extant. The first book is introductory, its subject being Law and Justice in general. In the second book Cicero proposes and explains the religious laws of his ideal State, and the third is devoted to the statement and defence of the laws which have to do primarily with the State officials, though the legislative and judicial powers of the State, as well as the executive, receive considerable attention. At the end of the third book, as we have it, Cicero proposes to take up a special subject related to the general contents of the book. This subject was probably the legal basis and limits of the powers of the State officials;[6] his treatment of it is lost.

[1] A. Reifferscheid, *Kritische Beitraege zu Cicero De Legibus,* Rhein. Mus. XVII (1862), pp. 269 ff. Compare R. Reitzenstein, *op. cit.*
[2] *De Leg.* I. 1.   [3] *De Leg.* I, 14.
[4] *De Leg.* II, 1–2; 6–7.
[5] Macrobius, *Sat.* VI, 4, 8 = Fragment 3 of *De Leg.*
[6] *De potestatum iure* (*De Leg.* III, 48–9).

INTRODUCTION

How many books the total work contained is doubtful. At least five must have been published, as we have a quotation from the fifth book.[1] The common opinion is that the work contained, or was to contain, six books, as did the *Republic*, but an ingenious argument has been advanced in favour of eight.[2] We cannot know, of course, what subjects were treated in the lost portion. It has been conjectured[3] from III, 47 that the subject of Book IV was the administration of justice (*De iudiciis*). Cicero also expresses his intention of treating the subject of education at a later point of the work (III, 29–30).

The dialogue form is used with greater success in the *De Legibus* than in any other of Cicero's works except the *De Re Publica*. In one passage he ridicules the custom of indicating a change of subject in the disquisition of the chief speaker by introducing a brief expression of agreement on the part of one of the other characters.[4] And in several cases the other speakers make it plain that they are in complete disagreement with the opinions expressed by Cicero; this was doubtless necessitated by the impossibility of ignoring the actual opinions of Quintus and Atticus, and it furnished Cicero with a convenient opportunity of meeting obvious criticisms of his own views.[5]

THE SOURCES.

Cicero's dependence on Plato for the general plan of the dialogue is as clear as in the case of the *De*

[1] See note 5, p. 290.
[2] By A. du Mesnil, in his edition, Leipzig, 1879, pp. 5–6.
[3] A. du Mesnil, *op. cit.*, p. 9.
[4] *De Leg.* III, 26.   [5] See *De Leg.* III, 19–26; 33–9.

Re Publica. He appears to have overlooked the fact that Plato's *Laws* was in no sense a sequel to his *Republic*; at any rate his own plan made such a relation between his two treatises necessary. He has imitated Plato [1] in placing the assumed date of the *Laws* in a later age than that of his previous work, in making himself the chief character, throwing off the mask of Scipio, as Plato did that of Socrates, in the number present, in the peripatetic character of the dialogue and the harmony of scene with subject, and in the fact that the conversation occupies a long (perhaps the longest) summer day. Cicero's departure from his custom of introducing his dialogues with a preface in his own person [2] may also be due to Plato's example.[3]

The source for the contents of Book I is much disputed. One view is that this book contains practically the same material as *De Re Publica* III, and that its source is therefore the same—Panaetius.[4] Other scholars favour the Academic philosopher Antiochus of Ascalon as the main source.[5] Our slight knowledge of the distinguishing character-

---

[1] Compare R. Hirzel, *Der Dialog*, Leipzig, 1895, I, pp. 473–6.

[2] *Ep. ad Att.* IV, 16, 2.

[3] Plato's *Republic* has a preface, whilst his *Laws* is so arranged as to make one superfluous; exactly the same thing is true of the corresponding works of Cicero.

[4] A. Schmekel, *Die Philosophie der mittleren Stoa*, Berlin, 1892, pp. 47–63; Ioh. Galbiatius (= G. Galbiati), *De fontibus M. Tullii Ciceronis librorum qui manserunt de re publica et de legibus quaestiones*, Milan, 1916, pp. 364–97.

[5] R. Hoyer, *De Antiocho Ascalonita*, Bonn, 1883, p. 15; R. Reitzenstein, *op. cit.*, p. 25; A. Laudien, *Die Composition und Quelle von Ciceros I Buch der Gesetze*, Hermes XLVI (1911), pp. 108 ff.

INTRODUCTION

istics of these philosophers makes a decision impossible; in fact we can by no means be certain that Cicero used a single Greek source for the whole argument.[1]

In the second and third books there is, of course, less question of Greek sources for any large part of the contents;[2] Roman law and the works of the Roman jurists[3] are the sources for the greater part of what is not original.

The work's greatest claim to our interest is the fact that it contains so much concrete information about Cicero's political ideals. While the *De Re Publica* and the first book of the *De Legibus* are general and philosophical, the second and third books of the latter treatise provide us with what would at present be called an actual constitution for an ideal State, with a detailed commentary on many of its provisions; this constitution, though based in general upon the actual law and custom of Rome, contains a considerable amount of original material.[4]

---

[1] A. Loercher, *Jahresbericht der Klass. Alt.* 162 (1913), pp. 129–34, believes that only §§ 22–32 come directly from a single Greek source, and that this passage was taken from Chrysippus.

[2] But compare *De Leg.* III, 13–14; F. Boesch, *De XII Tabularum Lege a Graecis petita*, Goettingen, 1893, pp. 16 ff.; T. Boegel, *Inhalt und Zerlegung des zweiten Buches von Cicero de Legibus*, Kreuzberg, 1907, pp. 12 ff. See also A. Loercher, *op. cit.*, pp. 134–44.

[3] Compare *De Leg.* II, 49.

[4] Compare C. W. Keyes, *Original Elements in Cicero's Ideal Constitution*, Amer. Jour. of Philol. XIII (1921), pp. 309–23.

INTRODUCTION

The Manuscripts.

The three important manuscripts of the *De Legibus*, all at Leyden, are :

    Vossianus 84, A.D. 800–1100 (A).
    Vossianus 86, A.D. 900–1200 (B).
    Heinsianus 118, A.D. 1000–1200 (H).

A and B are recognized as the best manuscripts,[1] but there has been a considerable amount of controversy as to the value of the variant readings of H.[2]

The manuscripts of minor importance (*dett.* = *deteriores*) are :

    Florentinus 118, A.D. 900–1100.
    Monacensis 528, eleventh century.
    Hadoardi Presbyteri Excerpta, A.D. 800–1000
      (selections only).

Editions.

I. Editions of Cicero's Works containing the *De Legibus* :

    A. Manutianus (printer), Milan, 1498.
    B. Ascensius (printer), Paris, 1511, 1521–22.
    M. Bentinus, Basle, 1528.
    P. Victorius, Venice, 1534–37.
    R. Stephanus, Paris, 1538–39.

---

[1] Both have been corrected ; the symbols A[1], A[2], B[1], and B[2] refer to the first and second hands.

[2] See J. Vahlen's second edition, prefaces ; C. F. W. Mueller's edition, p. xxxii ; H. Deiter, *De Ciceronis codice Leid.* 118, Emden, 1882 ; E. Schramm, *De Ciceronis libris de legibus recensendis*, Marburg, 1897.

INTRODUCTION

J. Camerarius, Basle, 1540.

P. Manutius (Aldine Press), Venice, 1540-46.

D. Lambinus, Paris, 1565-84.

J. A. Ernesti, Leipzig, 1737, 1820-24.

J. C. Orelli, Zuerich, 1826-38.

J. C. Orelli, G. Baiter, and C. Halm, Zuerich, 1845-62.

C. F. A. Nobbe, Leipzig, 1827, 1849, 1869.

R. Klotz, Leipzig, 1850-57, 1869-74.

J. G. Baiter and C. L. Kayser, Leipzig, 1860-69.

C. F. W. Mueller, Leipzig (Teubner), 1878–

II. Separate editions of the *De Legibus* :

A. Turnebus, Paris, 1538-57.

J. Davies, Cambridge, 1727, 1745.

J. A. Goerenz, Leipzig, 1796, 1809.

F. Wagner, Goettingen, 1804.

J. Davies and R. G. Rath, Halle, 1809, 1818.

G. H. Moser and F. Creuzer, Frankfort, 1824.

J. Bake, Leyden, 1842.

C. F. Feldhuegel, Zeitz, 1852-3.

W. D. Pearman. Cambridge, 1881.

J. Vahlen, Berlin, 1870, 1883.

A. du Mesnil, Leipzig, 1879.

G. Sichirollo, Padua, 1885.

P. E. Huschke (in *Iurisprudentiae Anteiustinianae quae supersunt*, fifth edition, pp. 18–84), Leipzig, 1886.

DE LEGIBUS

LIBER PRIMUS

1 I. *A.* Lucus quidem ille et haec Arpinatium quercus agnoscitur saepe a me lectus in Mario. si manet illa quercus, haec est profecto ; etenim est sane vetus.

Q. Manet vero, Attice noster, et semper manebit ; sata est enim ingenio. nullius autem agricolae cultu stirps tam diuturna quam poëtae versu seminari potest.

A. Quo tandem modo, Quinte, aut quale est istuc, quod poëtae serunt? mihi enim videris fratrem laudando suffragari tibi.

Q. Sit ita sane ; verum tamen, dum Latinae loquentur litterae, quercus huic loco non deerit, quae Mariana dicatur, eaque, ut ait Scaevola de fratris mei Mario,

> Canescet saeclis innumerabilibus ;

---

[1] A poem of Cicero, written in or previous to 59, if, as seems probable, the verse in *Ep. ad Att.* II. 15, 3 (April 59) is quoted from it.

[2] Quintus was also a poet, being known particularly as a writer of tragedies after Greek models. In 54 B.C., while serving under Caesar in Gaul, he composed four tragedies in sixteen days (*Ep. ad Quintum Fr.* III. 6, 7).

LAWS

BOOK I

I. *Atticus.* Surely I recognize that grove yonder and this oak tree of Arpinum as those of which I have read so often in the " Marius "; [1] if that famous oak still lives, this is certainly the same ; and in fact it is a very old tree.

Quintus. That oak lives indeed, my dear Atticus, and will live for ever ; for it was planted by the imagination. No tree nourished by a farmer's care can be so long-lived as one planted by a poet's verses.

A. How is that, Quintus ? What sort of planting is it that poets do ? It seems to me that while praising your brother you are putting in a word for yourself as well. [2]

Q. You may be right ; but for all that, as long as Latin literature shall live, there will not fail to be an oak tree on this spot, called the " Marian Oak," and this tree, as Scaevola says of my brother's " Marius," [3] will

Through countless ages come to hoary eld.

[3] This may mean that a Scaevola (see II, 47 and Index) actually made this statement about Cicero's poem, or that Scaevola, a character in Cicero's "Marius," spoke these words. Therefore the quotation may be from the "Marius," or possibly from an epigram of Scaevola's.

2 nisi forte Athenae tuae sempiternam in arce oleam
tenere potuerunt, aut, quod Homericus Ulixes Deli
se proceram et teneram palmam vidisse dixit, hodie
monstrant eandem; multaque alia multis locis
diutius commemoratione manent quam natura stare
potuerunt. quare "glandifera" illa quercus, ex qua
olim evolavit

> Nuntia fulva Iovis miranda visa figura,

nunc sit haec. sed cum eam tempestas vetustasve
consumpserit, tamen erit his in locis quercus, quam
Marianam quercum vocabunt.[1]

3 *A.* Non dubito id quidem; sed haec iam non[2] ex
te, Quinte, quaero, verum ex ipso poëta, tuine
versus hanc quercum severint, an ita factum de
Mario, ut scribis, acceperis.

M. Respondebo tibi equidem, sed non ante quam
mihi tu ipse responderis, Attice, certen non longe
a tuis aedibus inambulans post excessum suum
Romulus Proculo Iulio dixerit se deum esse et
Quirinum vocari templumque sibi dedicari in eo loco
iusserit, et verumne sit, ut[3] Athenis non longe
item a tua illa antiqua domo Orithyiam Aquilo
sustulerit; sic enim est traditum.

---

[1] *vocabunt* R. Klotz; *vocant* A B H.
[2] *non* H²; omitted in A B H¹.
[3] *ut* supplied by Rath; omitted in MSS.

---

[1] The Athenians claimed that the olive tree on the Acropolis
west of the Erechtheum had been planted by Athena and
was the parent stock of all the olive trees of Attica.

[2] See *Odyssey*, VI, 162–3, where Odysseus compares
Nausicaa to this palm tree.

[3] From the "Marius." The eastward flight of an eagle
after a successful struggle with a serpent was looked upon
as a good omen by Marius (*De Divin.* I, 106).

For I suppose you do not really believe that your
beloved Athens has been able to preserve in her
citadel an undying olive tree,[1] or that the tall and
graceful palm which Homer's Ulysses said that he
saw at Delos[2] is the one shown there to-day. And
in the same way many other objects in many different places live in men's thoughts for a longer
time than Nature could have kept them in existence.
Therefore let us assume that this tree is that
"acorn-laden" oak, from which once flew

> Jove's golden messenger of wondrous form.[3]

But when time or age shall have destroyed this
tree, still there will be an oak tree on this spot,
which men will call the "Marian Oak."

A. I have no doubt of that. But my next
question must be addressed not to you, Quintus,
but to the poet himself. Was it really your verses
that planted this oak tree, or were you following
a tradition that this incident happened to Marius
as you describe it?

Marcus. I will answer you, Atticus, but not until
you have yourself answered a question. Is it a fact
that Romulus, after his death, while wandering
about near the place where your house now stands,
met Proculus Julius, told him that he was a god,
and was called Quirinus, and ordered that a temple
be dedicated to him on that spot?[4] And is it true
that at Athens, likewise not far from your old home,[5]
Aquilo carried off Orithyia? For that is what
tradition tells us.

[4] See Livy, I. 16.
[5] In the south-eastern part of the city, near the river
Ilissus (Pausanias, I, 19; Plato, *Phaedrus* 229 B-C).

MARCUS TULLIUS CICERO

4 *A.* Quorsum tandem aut cur ista quaeris?

M. Nihil sane, nisi ne nimis diligenter inquiras in ea, quae isto modo memoriae sint prodita.

A. Atqui multa quaeruntur in Mario fictane an vera sint, et a non nullis, quod et in recenti memoria et in Arpinati homine versere, veritas a te postulatur.

M. Et mehercule ego me cupio non mendacem putari; sed tamen non nulli isti, Tite noster, faciunt imperite, qui in isto periculo non ut a poëta, sed ut a teste veritatem exigant; nec dubito quin idem et cum Egeria conlocutum Numam et ab aquila Tarquinio apicem inpositum putent.

5 *Q.* Intellego te, frater, alias in historia leges observandas putare, alias in poëmate.

M. Quippe, cum in illa omnia[1] ad veritatem, Quinte, referantur, in hoc ad delectationem pleraque; quamquam et apud Herodotum, patrem historiae, et apud Theopompum sunt innumerabiles fabulae.

II. *A.* Teneo quam optabam occasionem neque omittam.

M. Quam tandem, Tite?

A. Postulatur a te iam diu vel flagitatur potius historia. sic enim putant, te illam tractante effici

---

[1] *omnia* supplied by Vahlen; omitted in MSS.

---

[1] According to the tradition King Numa frequently met the goddess Egeria in a sacred grove (Livy I, 21).

[2] Before Tarquinius Priscus became king, it was said that an eagle whisked off his cap, circled about with loud cries, and then replaced it on his head, thus prophesying his future greatness (Livy I, 34).

A. What is your purpose or reason for asking such questions?

M. None at all, except to keep you from inquiring too critically into traditions which are handed down in that way.

A. Yet people ask, concerning many parts of the " Marius," whether they are fiction or fact; and certain persons, since you are dealing with recent events and a native of Arpinum, demand that you stick to the truth.

M. And I for my part have no desire to be thought to deal in falsehood; but all the same, my dear Titus, those "certain persons" whom you mention display their ignorance by demanding in such a matter the kind of truthfulness expected of a witness in court rather than of a poet. No doubt these same people believe that Numa talked with Egeria,[1] and that the cap was placed on Tarquinius' head by the eagle![2]

Q. As I understand it, then, my dear brother, you believe that different principles are to be followed in history and in poetry.

M. Certainly, Quintus; for in history the standard by which everything is judged is the truth, while in poetry it is generally the pleasure one gives; however, in the works of Herodotus, the Father of History, and in those of Theopompus, one finds innumerable fabulous tales.

II. *A.* I now have an opportunity which I have been wanting, and I shall not let it pass.

M. What do you mean, Titus?

A. There has long been a desire, or rather a demand, that you should write a history. For people think that, if you entered that field, we might rival

posse, ut in hoc etiam genere Graeciae nihil ceda-
mus. atque ut audias, quid ego ipse sentiam, non
solum mihi videris eorum studiis, qui litteris[1] de-
lectantur, sed etiam patriae debere hoc munus, ut
ea, quae salva per te est, per te eundem sit ornata.
dest[2] enim historia litteris nostris, ut et ipse intellego
et ex te persaepe audio. potes autem tu profecto
satis facere in ea, quippe cum sit opus, ut tibi
quidem videri solet, unum hoc oratorium maxime.
6 quam ob rem adgredere, quaesumus, et sume ad
hanc rem tempus, quae est a nostris hominibus
adhuc aut ignorata aut relicta. nam post annalis
pontificum maximorum, quibus nihil potest esse
ieiunius, si aut ad Fabium aut ad eum, qui tibi
semper in ore est, Catonem, aut ad Pisonem aut ad
Fannium aut ad Vennonium venias, quamquam ex
his alius alio plus habet virium, tamen quid tam
exile quam isti omnes? Fanni autem aetati coniunctus Antipater paulo inflavit vehementius habuit-
que vires agrestis ille quidem atque horridas sine
nitore ac palaestra, sed tamen admonere reliquos
potuit ut adcuratius scriberent. ecce autem succes-
sere huic belli : Clodius, Asellio ; nihil ad Coelium,
sed potius ad antiquorum languorem et inscitiam.
7 nam quid Macrum numerem ? cuius loquacitas habet
aliquid argutiarum, nec id tamen ex illa erudita

---

[1] *qui litteris* A[1] H ; *qui tuis litteris* A[2] B.
[2] *dest* Vahlen ; *at est* A ; *a te* B ; *adest* H ; *abest* is the common reading.

Greece in this branch of literature also. And to give you my own opinion, it seems to me that you owe this duty not merely to the desires of those who take pleasure in literature, but also to your country, in order that the land which you have saved you may also glorify. For our national literature is deficient in history, as I realize myself and as I frequently hear you say. But you can certainly fill this gap satisfactorily, since, as you at least have always believed,[1] this branch of literature is closer than any other to oratory. Therefore take up the task, we beg of you, and find the time for a duty which has hitherto been either overlooked or neglected by our countrymen. For after the annals of the chief pontiffs, which are records of the driest possible character, when we come to Fabius, or to Cato (whose name is always on your lips), or to Piso, Fannius, or Vennonius, although one of these may display more vigour than another, yet what could be more lifeless than the whole group? Fannius' contemporary, Antipater, to be sure, blew a somewhat more forceful strain, and showed some power, though of a rough and rustic character, lacking in polish and the skill that comes from training; nevertheless he might have served as a warning to his successors that they should take greater pains with their writing. But lo and behold, his successors were those fine specimens, Clodius and Asellio! These two are not to be compared with Coelius, but rather with the feebleness and clumsiness of our earlier historians. And why should I even mention Macer? His long-winded style shows indeed some little acumen (though borrowed not

---

[1] See Cicero, *De Oratore* II, 62.

Graecorum copia, sed ex librariolis Latinis, in orationibus autem multas ineptias, elatio summam inpudentiam.[1] Sisenna, eius amicus, omnes adhuc nostros scriptores, nisi qui forte nondum ediderunt, de quibus existimare non possumus, facile superavit. is tamen neque orator in numero vestro umquam est habitus et in historia puerile quiddam consectatur, ut unum Clitarchum neque praeterea quemquam de Graecis legisse videatur, eum tamen velle dumtaxat imitari ; quem si adsequi posset, aliquantum ab optumo tamen abesset. quare tuum est munus hoc, a te expectatur, nisi quid Quinto videtur secus.

8   III. *Q.* Mihi vero nihil, et saepe de isto conlocuti sumus. sed est quaedam inter nos parva dissensio.

A. Quae tandem?

Q. A quibus temporibus scribendi capiat exordium. ego enim ab ultimis censeo, quoniam illa sic scripta sunt, ut ne legantur quidem, ipse autem aequalem aetatis suae memoriam deposcit, ut ea conplectatur, quibus ipse interfuit.

A. Ego vero huic potius adsentior. sunt enim maxumae res in hac memoria atque aetate nostra ; tum autem hominis amicissimi, Cn. Pompei, laudes inlustrabit, incurret etiam in illum divinum [2] et memo-

---

[1] *multas ineptias, elatio summam inpudentiam* Vahlen; *multas ineptus datio summam inpudentiam* A[1] B[1] H ; *multus et ineptus,* etc., A[2] B[2]; *multa set inepta elatio, summa inpudentia* Mommsen.

[2] *divinum* supplied by Vahlen ; omitted in MSS.

---

[1] This appears to be Cicero's meaning, but the text is uncertain.

from the Greeks' wealth of knowledge, but from the
Roman copyists), but his speeches contain many
absurdities, and his elevated passages are exaggerated beyond all bounds.[1] His friend Sisenna has
easily surpassed all our other historians up to the
present time, with the exception of those whose
works may not yet have been published, and therefore cannot be estimated. Yet he has never been
considered an orator of your rank, and in his
historical writing he has an almost childish purpose
in view, for it seems that Clitarchus is absolutely
the only Greek author whom he has read, and that
his sole desire is to imitate him. And even if he
had succeeded in this, he would still be considerably
below the highest standards. Therefore this task
is yours; its accomplishment is expected of you —
that is, if Quintus agrees with me.

III. *Q.* Indeed I agree perfectly, and Marcus and
I have frequently discussed the matter. But there
is one small point on which we disagree.

A. What is that?

Q. The question of the period at which he should
begin his history. I think it should be the earliest,
for the records of that age have been written in
such a style that they are never read at all. But
he prefers to write of his own lifetime, in order to
include those events in which he himself has taken
part.

A. Indeed I agree rather with him. For most
important events have taken place within the
memory of our generation; besides, he will be
able to glorify the deeds of his dear friend Gnaeus
Pompeius, and to include a description of the
illustrious and memorable year of his own consul-

rabilem annum suum ; quae ab isto malo praedicari quam, ut aiunt, de Remo et Romulo.

M. Intellego equidem a me istum laborem iam diu postulari, Attice ; quem non recusarem, si mihi ullum tribueretur vacuum tempus et liberum ; neque enim occupata opera neque inpedito animo res tanta suscipi potest ; utrumque opus est, et cura vacare et negotio.

9   *A.* Quid ad cetera, quae scripsisti plura quam quisquam e nostris ? quod tibi tandem tempus vacuum fuit concessum ?

M. Subsiciva quaedam **tempora** incurrunt, quae ego perire non patior, ut, si qui dies ad rusticandum dati sint, ad eorum numerum adcommodentur quae scribimus. historia vero nec institui potest nisi praeparato otio nec exiguo tempore absolvi, et ego animi pendere soleo, cum semel quid orsus sum,[1] si traducor alio, neque tam facile interrupta contexo quam absolvo instituta.

10   *A.* Legationem aliquam nimirum ista oratio postulat aut eius modi quampiam cessationem liberam atque otiosam.

M. Ego vero aetatis potius vacationi confidebam, cum praesertim non recusarem quo minus more patrio sedens in solio consulentibus responderem

---

   [1] *sum* supplied by Halm ; omitted in MSS.

---

   [1] An expression used for anything out of date or "antediluvian."

   [2] *Subsicivus* was originally a technical term used by surveyors to refer to small pieces of land which were "left over" in their surveys. Later it came to signify "leftovers" or "odds and ends" of any kind.

   [3] Evidently the reference is to a "free embassy" (*libera legatio*), which entitled its recipient to all the privileges of an ambassador, but left him free of official duties. See Book III, 9 and 18.

ship. I should rather have him write of these events than "of Romulus and Remus," as the saying is.[1]

M. Certainly I realize that the accomplishment of this task has long been demanded of me, Atticus. And I should not refuse to undertake it, if I were granted any unoccupied or leisure time. But so great a task cannot be undertaken when one's time is filled or his attention distracted; one must be free from both work and worry.

A. What of those other works that you have produced in greater numbers than any other of our countrymen? What leisure time was granted you for those?

M. Odds and ends of time,[2] as I may call them, are sometimes available, which I do not allow to go to waste. For example, if a few days are free for a vacation in the country, the length of the composition I undertake is adapted to the time at my disposal. But an historical work cannot be commenced unless a period of leisure is arranged for in advance, nor can it be completed in a short time; and it usually disturbs my train of thought, when I have once begun a task, if I am forced to turn my attention elsewhere; nor do I find it so easy to resume an interrupted task as I do to complete at once whatever I have undertaken.

A. This statement seems to call for your appointment on an embassy,[3] or some similar holiday that will give you absolute and entire freedom.

M. I have been counting rather upon the leisure to which age entitles one, especially as I should not refuse to sit in the counsellor's chair in accordance with our ancestral custom and advise clients, thus

senectutisque non inertis grato atque honesto fungerer munere. sic enim mihi liceret et isti rei, quam desideras, et multis uberioribus atque maioribus operae quantum vellem dare.

11 IV. *A.* Atqui vereor, ne istam causam nemo noscat tibique semper dicendum sit, et eo magis, quod te ipse mutasti et aliud dicendi instituisti genus, ut, quem ad modum Roscius, familiaris tuus, in senectute numeros in cantu . . . ¹ cecinerat ipsasque tardiores fecerat tibias, sic tu a contentionibus, quibus summis uti solebas, cotidie relaxes aliquid, ut iam oratio tua non multum a philosophorum lenitate absit; quod sustinere cum vel summa senectus posse videatur, nullam tibi a causis vacationem video dari.

12 *Q.* At mehercule ego arbitrabar posse id populo nostro probari, si te ad ius respondendum dedisses. quam ob rem, cum placebit, experiendum tibi censeo.²

M. Siquidem, Quinte, nullum esset in experiundo periculum; sed vereor ne, dum minuere velim laborem, augeam atque ad illam causarum operam, ad quam ego numquam nisi paratus et meditatus accedo, adiungatur haec iuris interpretatio, quae non tam mihi molesta sit propter laborem, quam quod

---

¹ Vahlen suggests *remissius quam ante* to fill the gap; *in cantu remiserat* Lambinus.

² *censeo. M. Siquidem* Garatoni; *censeo id siquidem* A B H; *id censeo. M. Siquidem* Turnebus.

---

¹ *i.e.*, while withdrawing from active work as a pleader in court, he hoped to continue the old Roman practice of giving advice to clients.

² Evidently such a change in style as would make appropriate a quieter and perhaps slower delivery.

³ This appears to be Cicero's meaning; see critical note.

performing the pleasant and honourable duties of a not inactive old age.[1] For under such conditions it would be possible for me to give as much attention as I wished to this task which you require of me, and to many other activities even more fruitful and important.

IV. *A.* Yet I fear that no one would recognize such an excuse for leisure, and that you would always be having to make speeches, especially since you have changed your methods and adopted a different style of oratory.[2] For just as your friend Roscius in his old age rendered the recitatives [more softly][3] and even had the flutes adopt a slower tempo, so you are moderating somewhat, day by day, those passionate outbursts which used to be customary with you, and consequently your present manner is not very different from the deliberate speech of the philosophers. So, since this style is not, it would seem, too strenuous for even extreme old age, I observe that no rest from the pleading of cases is being granted to you.

Q. But I have certainly been thinking that our people might approve of your devoting yourself to the duties of a counsellor at law. Therefore, as soon as you think proper, I believe you should make the experiment.

M. Yes, Quintus, if there were no danger in such an experiment. But I fear that, while endeavouring to lessen my labour, I may only increase it, and find that, in addition to my usual pleading of cases, which I never attempt without preparation and careful thought, this interpretation of the law is imposed upon me. The latter task would not be so irksome to me on account of the labour involved

dicendi cogitationem auferat; sine qua ad nullam
maiorem umquam causam sum ausus accedere.

13   *A.* Quin igitur ista ipsa explicas nobis his sub-
sicivis, ut ais, temporibus et conscribis de iure civili
subtilius quam ceteri ?   nam a primo tempore aetatis
iuri studere te memini, cum ipse etiam ad Scaevolam
ventitarem, neque umquam mihi visus es ita te ad
dicendum dedisse, ut ius civile contemneres.

M. In longum sermonem me vocas, Attice ; quem
tamen, nisi Quintus aliud quid nos agere mavult,
suscipiam et, quoniam vacui sumus, dicam.

Q. Ego vero libenter audierim ; quid enim agam
potius aut in quo melius hunc consumam diem ?

14   *M.* Quin igitur ad illa spatia nostra sedesque
pergimus ? ubi, cum satis erit ambulatum, requiesce-
mus, nec profecto nobis delectatio derit aliud ex alio
quaerentibus.

A. Nos vero, et hac quidem ad Lirem,[1] si placet,
per ripam et umbram. sed iam ordire explicare,
quaeso, de iure civili quid sentias.

M. Egone ? summos fuisse in civitate nostra viros,
qui id interpretari populo et responsitare soliti sint,
sed eos magna professos in parvis esse versatos.

---

[1] *ad Lirem* Bake ; *adirem* AB   *adire* H

as because it would deprive me of the opportunity
to think over my speeches in advance, without which
preparation I have never been bold enough to speak
in any important case.

A. Why do you not, then, in the present "odds and
ends of time," as you call them, expound this very
subject to us, and compose a treatise on the civil
law, going into it more deeply than your predeces-
sors? For I remember that you were interested in
law even in your early youth, when I too was study-
ing with Scaevola, and it has never seemed to me
that you have become so absorbed in oratory as to
turn your back completely upon the civil law.

M. You are urging me to a long discussion,
Atticus, but nevertheless I will undertake it, unless
Quintus prefers some other occupation; and, as we
are at leisure, I will state my views on this topic.

Q. I should be very glad to listen to you; for
what occupation could I prefer, or how could I spend
the day more profitably?

M. Then let us go to those promenades and seats
of ours, so that when we have enough of walking,
we may rest. Surely we shall not lack entertainment as we take up one question after another.

A. We agree; and indeed, if you approve, we
might walk here by the Liris, in the shade along
its bank. But kindly begin without delay the statement of your opinions on the civil law.

M. My opinions? Well then, I believe that
there have been most eminent men in our State
whose customary function it was to interpret the
law to the people and answer questions in regard
to it, but that these men, though they have made
great claims, have spent their time on unimportant

quid enim est tantum, quantum ius civitatis? quid
autem tam exiguum, quam est munus hoc eorum,
qui consuluntur? quamquam est populo necessarium. nec vero eos, qui ei muneri praefuerunt,
universi iuris fuisse expertis existimo, sed hoc civile,
quod vocant, eatenus exercuerunt, quoad populo
praestare voluerunt. id autem in cognitione tenue
est, in usu necessarium. quam ob rem quo me vocas
aut quid hortaris? ut libellos conficiam de stillicidio-
rum ac de parietum iure? an ut stipulationum et
iudiciorum formulas conponam? quae et conscripta a
multis sunt diligenter et sunt humiliora quam illa,
quae a nobis expectari puto.

15　　V. *A.* Atqui si quaeris[1] ego quid expectem, quoniam scriptum est a te de optimo rei publicae statu,
consequens esse videtur ut scribas tu idem de legibus; sic enim fecisse video Platonem illum tuum,
quem tu admiraris, quem omnibus anteponis, quem
maxime diligis.

　　M. Visne igitur, ut ille Cretae cum Clinia et
cum Lacedaemonio Megillo aestivo, quem ad modum describit, die in cupressetis Gnosiorum et
spatiis silvestribus crebro insistens, interdum ad-
quiescens de institutis rerum publicarum ac de
optimis legibus disputat, sic nos inter has pro-
cerissimas populos in viridi opacaque ripa inambu-
lantes, tum autem residentes quaeramus isdem

---

[1] *quaeris* Rath; *quaeres* AB; *queres* H.

---

[1] The *De Re Publica.*
[2] For the relation of Cicero's treatises to Plato's *Republic*
and *Laws*, see Introduction to *De Re Pub.*, pp. 6–7; Introduction to *De Leg.*, pp. 291–292.

details. What subject indeed is so vast as the law
of the State? But what is so trivial as the task of
those who give legal advice? It is, however,
necessary for the people. But, while I do not consider that those who have applied themselves to
this profession have lacked a conception of universal
law, yet they have carried their studies of this civil
law, as it is called, only far enough to accomplish
their purpose of being useful to the people. Now
all this amounts to little so far as learning is concerned, though for practical purposes it is indispensable. What subject is it, then, that you are
asking me to expound? To what task are you
urging me? Do you want me to write a treatise
on the law of eaves and house-walls? Or to compose formulas for contracts and court procedure?
These subjects have been carefully treated by many
writers, and are of a humbler character, I believe,
than what is expected of me.

V. *A.* Yet if you ask what I expect of you, I
consider it a logical thing that, since you have already
written a treatise on the constitution of the ideal
State,[1] you should also write one on its laws. For
I note that this was done by your beloved Plato,[2]
whom you admire, revere above all others, and love
above all others.

M. Is it your wish, then, that, as he discussed the
institutions of States and the ideal laws with Clinias
and the Spartan Megillus in Crete on a summer day
amid the cypress groves and forest paths of Cnossus,
sometimes walking about, sometimes resting—you
recall his description—we, in like manner, strolling
or taking our ease among these stately poplars on
the green and shady river bank, shall discuss the

de rebus aliquid uberius, quam forensis usus
desiderat?

16   *A.* Ego vero ista audire cupio.

   M. Quid ait Quintus?

   Q. Nulla de re magis.

   M. Et recte quidem. nam sic habetote, nullo in
genere disputando posse ita[1] patefieri, quid sit
homini a natura tributum, quantam vim rerum
optimarum mens humana contineat, cuius muneris
colendi efficiendique causa nati et in lucem editi
simus, quae sit coniunctio hominum, quae naturalis
societas inter ipsos; his enim explicatis fons legum
et iuris inveniri potest.

17   *A.* Non ergo a praetoris edicto, ut plerique nunc,
neque a duodecim tabulis, ut superiores, sed penitus
ex intima philosophia hauriendam iuris disciplinam
putas?

   M. Non enim id quaerimus hoc sermone, Pomponi, quem ad modum caveamus in iure aut quid de
quaque consultatione respondeamus. sit ista res
magna, sicut est, quae quondam a multis claris viris,
nunc ab uno summa auctoritate et scientia susti-
netur, sed nobis ita conplectenda in hac disputatione
tota causa est universi iuris ac legum, ut hoc civile,
quod dicimus, in parvum quendam et angustum
locum concludatur. natura enim iuris explicanda

---

   [1] *posse ita* Vahlen; *honesta* A B H.

---

   [1] Evidently Servius Sulpicius Rufus, Cicero's friend and
professional rival, consul in 51 B.C. He was the author of a
large number of legal treatises (Cicero, *Brutus*, 152).

same subjects along somewhat broader lines than the practice of the courts calls for?

A. I should certainly like to hear such a conversation.

M. What does Quintus say?

Q. No other subject would suit me better.

M. And you are wise, for you must understand that in no other kind of discussion can one bring out so clearly what Nature's gifts to man are, what a wealth of most excellent possessions the human mind enjoys, what the purpose is, to strive after and accomplish which we have been born and placed in this world, what it is that unites men, and what natural fellowship there is among them. For it is only after all these things have been made clear that the origin of Law and Justice can be discovered.

A. Then you do not think that the science of law is to be derived from the praetor's edict, as the majority do now, or from the Twelve Tables, as people used to think, but from the deepest mysteries of philosophy?

M. Quite right; for in our present conversation, Pomponius, we are not trying to learn how to protect ourselves legally, or how to answer clients' questions. Such problems may be important, and in fact they are; for in former times many eminent men made a specialty of their solution, and at present one person[1] performs this duty with the greatest authority and skill. But in our present investigation we intend to cover the whole range of universal Justice and Law in such a way that our own civil law, as it is called, will be confined to a small and narrow corner. For we must explain the

nobis est eaque ab hominis repetenda natura, considerandae leges, quibus civitates regi debeant, tum haec tractanda, quae conposita sunt et descripta iura et iussa populorum, in quibus ne nostri quidem populi latebunt quae vocantur iura civilia.

18   VI. *Q.* Alte vero et, ut oportet, a capite, frater, repetis quod quaerimus; et qui aliter ius civile tradunt non tam iustitiae quam litigandi tradunt vias.

M. Non ita est, Quinte, ac potius ignoratio iuris litigiosa est quam scientia.   sed hoc posterius; nunc iuris principia videamus.

Igitur doctissimis viris proficisci placuit a lege, haud scio an recte, si modo, ut idem definiunt, lex est ratio summa insita in natura, quae iubet ea, quae facienda sunt, prohibetque contraria.   eadem ratio cum est in hominis mente confirmata et confecta,[1]

19 lex est.   itaque arbitrantur prudentiam esse legem, cuius ea vis sit, ut recte facere iubeat, vetet delinquere; eamque rem illi Graeco putant nomine a[2] suum cuique tribuendo appellatam, ego nostro a legendo; nam ut illi aequitatis, sic nos dilectus vim in lege ponimus, et proprium tamen utrumque legis est.   quod si ita recte dicitur, ut mihi quidem plerumque videri solet, a lege ducendum est iuris

---

[1] *confecta* A B H ; *perfecta* Vahlen (cf. § 27 extr.).
[2] *a* added by Turnebus ; omitted in MSS.

---

[1] Νόμος is derived by Cicero from νέμω, " to distribute," *lex* from *lego*, "to choose."

nature of Justice, and this must be sought for in the
nature of man; we must also consider the laws by
which States ought to be governed; then we must
deal with the enactments and decrees of nations
which are already formulated and put in writing;
and among these the civil law, as it is called, of the
Roman people will not fail to find a place.

VI. *Q.* You probe deep, and seek, as you should,
the very fountain-head, to find what we are after,
brother. And those who teach the civil law in any
other way are teaching not so much the path of
justice as of litigation.

M. There you are mistaken, Quintus, for it is rather
ignorance of the law than knowledge of it that leads to
litigation. But that will come later; now let us
investigate the origins of Justice.

Well then, the most learned men have determined
to begin with Law, and it would seem that they are
right, if, according to their definition, Law is the
highest reason, implanted in Nature, which commands
what ought to be done and forbids the opposite.
This reason, when firmly fixed and fully developed
in the human mind, is Law. And so they believe
that Law is intelligence, whose natural function it is
to command right conduct and forbid wrongdoing.
They think that this quality has derived its name in
Greek from the idea of granting to every man his
own, and in our language I believe it has been
named from the idea of choosing.[1] For as they have
attributed the idea of fairness to the word law, so we
have given it that of selection, though both ideas
properly belong to Law. Now if this is correct, as I
think it to be in general, then the origin of Justice
is to be found in Law, for Law is a natural force; it

exordium; ea est enim naturae vis, ea mens ratio-
que prudentis, ea iuris atque iniuriae regula. sed
quoniam in populari ratione omnis nostra versatur
oratio, populariter interdum loqui necesse erit et
appellare eam legem, quae scripta sancit, quod vult,
aut iubendo aut prohibendo,[1] ut vulgus appellat.
constituendi vero iuris ab illa summa lege capiamus
exordium, quae saeclis omnibus ante nata est quam
scripta lex ulla aut quam omnino civitas constituta.

20 *Q.* Commodius vero et ad rationem instituti
sermonis sapientius.

M. Visne ergo ipsius iuris ortum a fonte repe-
tamus? quo invento non erit dubium quo sint haec
referenda quae quaerimus.

Q. Ego vero ita esse faciendum censeo.

A. Me quoque adscribe fratris sententiae.

M. Quoniam igitur eius rei publicae, quam optumam esse docuit in illis sex libris Scipio, tenendus
est nobis et servandus status omnesque leges ad-
commodandae ad illud civitatis genus, serendi etiam
mores nec scriptis omnia sancienda, repetam stirpem
iuris a natura, qua duce nobis omnis est disputatio
explicanda.

A. Rectissime, et quidem ista duce errari nullo
pacto potest.

21 VII. *M.* Dasne igitur hoc nobis, Pomponi (nam
Quinti novi sententiam), deorum inmortalium vi,

---

[1] *aut prohibendo* added by Baiter; omitted in MSS. *aut vetando* was formerly the common reading.

---

[1] The *De Re Publica.*

is the mind and reason of the intelligent man, the standard by which Justice and Injustice are measured. But since our whole discussion has to do with the reasoning of the populace, it will sometimes be necessary to speak in the popular manner, and give the name of law to that which in written form decrees whatever it wishes, either by command or prohibition. For such is the crowd's definition of law. But in determining what Justice is, let us begin with that supreme Law which had its origin ages before any written law existed or any State had been established.

Q. Indeed that will be preferable and more suitable to the character of the conversation we have begun.

M. Well, then, shall we seek the origin of Justice itself at its fountain-head? For when that is discovered we shall undoubtedly have a standard by which the things we are seeking may be tested.

Q. I think that is certainly what we must do.

A. Put me down also as agreeing with your brother's opinion.

M. Since, then, we must retain and preserve that constitution of the State which Scipio proved to be the best in the six books[1] devoted to the subject, and all our laws must be fitted to that type of State, and since we must also inculcate good morals, and not prescribe everything in writing, I shall seek the root of Justice in Nature, under whose guidance our whole discussion must be conducted.

A. Quite right. Surely with her as our guide, it will be impossible for us to go astray.

VII. *M.* Do you grant us, then, Pomponius (for I am aware of what Quintus thinks), that it is by the might of the immortal gods, or by their nature,

natura, ratione, potestate, mente, numine, sive quod
est aliud verbum, quo planius significem quod volo,
naturam omnem regi ? nam si hoc non probas, ab
eo nobis causa ordienda est potissimum.

A. Do sane, si postulas ; etenim propter hunc
concentum avium strepitumque fluminum non vereor
condiscipulorum ne quis exaudiat.

M. Atqui cavendum est ; solent enim, id quod
virorum bonorum est, admodum irasci, nec vero
ferent, si audierint te primum caput libri optimi
prodidisse, in quo scripsit "nihil curare deum nec
sui nec alieni."

22   *A.* Perge, quaeso ; nam id, quod tibi concessi,
quorsus pertineat expecto.

M. Non faciam longius ; huc enim pertinet,
animal hoc providum, sagax, multiplex, acutum,
memor, plenum rationis et consilii, quem vocamus
hominem, praeclara quadam condicione generatum
esse a supremo deo ; solum est enim ex tot animantium generibus atque naturis particeps rationis et
cogitationis, cum cetera sint omnia expertia. quid
est autem non dicam in homine, sed in omni caelo
atque terra ratione divinius ? quae cum adolevit
23 atque perfecta est, nominatur rite sapientia. est
igitur, quoniam nihil est ratione melius eaque est [1]
et in homine et in deo, prima homini cum deo
rationis societas ; inter quos autem ratio, inter eos-

---

[1] *est* supplied by Madvig ; omitted in MSS.

---

[1] Atticus was an Epicurean.
[2] Epicurus. Cf. Diogenes Laertius, X. 139: Τὸ μακάριον
καὶ ἄφθαρτον οὔτ' αὐτὸ πράγματ' ἔχει οὔτ' ἄλλῳ παρέχει.
"What is happy and immortal has no troubles of its own,
nor does it make trouble for another." Compare Lucretius
II, 646–8 ; Horace, *Sat.* I, 5, 101.

reason, power, mind, will, or any other term which may make my meaning clearer, that all Nature is governed? For if you do not admit it, we must begin our argument with this problem before taking up anything else.

A. Surely I will grant it, if you insist upon it, for the singing of the birds about us and the babbling of the streams relieve me from all fear that I may be overheard by any of my comrades in the School.[1]

M. Yet you must be careful; for it is their way to become very angry at times, as virtuous men will; and they will not tolerate your treason, if they hear of it, to the opening passage of that excellent book, in which the author[2] has written, "God troubles himself about nothing, neither his own concerns nor those of others."

A. Continue, if you please, for I am eager to learn what my admission will lead to.

M. I will not make the argument long. Your admission leads us to this: that animal which we call man, endowed with foresight and quick intelligence, complex, keen, possessing memory, full of reason and prudence, has been given a certain distinguished status by the supreme God who created him; for he is the only one among so many different kinds and varieties of living beings who has a share in reason and thought, while all the rest are deprived of it. But what is more divine, I will not say in man only, but in all heaven and earth, than reason? And reason, when it is full grown and perfected, is rightly called wisdom. Therefore, since there is nothing better than reason, and since it exists both in man and God, the first common possession of man and God is reason. But those who have reason in common

dem etiam recta ratio communis [1] est; quae cum
sit lex, lege quoque consociati homines cum dis
putandi sumus. inter quos porro est communio
legis, inter eos communio iuris est; quibus autem
haec sunt inter eos communia, et civitatis eiusdem
habendi sunt. si vero isdem imperiis et potestatibus
parent, multo iam magis; parent autem huic cae-
lesti descriptioni mentique divinae et praepotenti
deo; ut iam universus hic mundus sit [2] una civitas
communis deorum atque hominum existimanda.

Et quod in civitatibus ratione quadam, de qua
dicetur idoneo loco, agnationibus familiarum distin-
guuntur status, id in rerum natura tanto est magnifi-
centius tantoque praeclarius, ut homines deorum ag-
24 natione et gente teneantur. VIII. nam cum de natura
hominis quaeritur, disputari solet (et [3] nimirum ita est,
ut disputatur) perpetuis cursibus conversionibusque [4]
caelestibus extitisse quandam maturitatem serendi
generis humani, quod sparsum in terras atque satum
divino auctum sit animorum munere, cumque alia,
quibus cohaererent homines, e mortali genere sump-
serint, quae fragilia essent et caduca, animum esse
ingeneratum a deo. ex quo vere vel agnatio nobis
cum caelestibus vel genus vel stirps appellari potest.
itaque ex tot generibus nullum est animal praeter

---

[1] *ratio communis* Stephanus; *ratio et communis* A B H;
Vahlen conjectures *ratio par et communis.*
[2] *sit* added by Vahlen; omitted in MSS.
[3] *et* added by Lambinus; omitted in MSS.
[4] *-que* added by Ernst; omitted in MSS.

---

[1] The discussion referred to is lost. See Introduction, pp.
290–291.

must also have right reason in common. And since
right reason is Law, we must believe that men have
Law also in common with the gods. Further, those
who share Law must also share Justice; and those
who share these are to be regarded as members of
the same commonwealth. If indeed they obey the
same authorities and powers, this is true in a far
greater degree; but as a matter of fact they do obey
this celestial system, the divine mind, and the God of
transcendent power. Hence we must now conceive
of this whole universe as one commonwealth of which
both gods and men are members.

And just as in States distinctions in legal status
are made on account of the blood relationships of
families, according to a system which I shall take up
in its proper place,[1] so in the universe the same
thing holds true, but on a scale much vaster and
more splendid, so that men are grouped with Gods
on the basis of blood relationship and descent.
VIII. For when the nature of man is examined,
the theory is usually advanced (and in all probability
it is correct) that through constant changes and
revolutions in the heavens, a time came which was
suitable for sowing the seed of the human race.
And when this seed was scattered and sown over the
earth, it was granted the divine gift of the soul. For
while the other elements of which man consists were
derived from what is mortal, and are therefore fragile
and perishable, the soul was generated in us by God.
Hence we are justified in saying that there is a blood
relationship between ourselves and the celestial
beings; or we may call it a common ancestry or
origin. Therefore among all the varieties of living
beings, there is no creature except man which has

hominem, quod habeat notitiam aliquam dei, ipsisque
in hominibus nulla gens est neque tam mansueta
neque tam fera, quae non, etiamsi ignoret qualem
25 habere deum deceat, tamen habendum sciat. ex
quo efficitur illud, ut is agnoscat deum, qui unde
ortus sit quasi recordetur et [1] agnoscat.

Iam vero virtus eadem in homine ac deo est
neque alio ullo in genere praeterea; est autem
virtus nihil aliud nisi perfecta et ad summum perducta
natura; est igitur homini cum deo similitudo. quod
cum ita sit, quae tandem esse potest propior certiorve
cognatio? itaque ad hominum commoditates et usus
tantam rerum ubertatem natura largita est, ut ea, quae
gignuntur, donata consulto nobis, non fortuito nata
videantur, nec solum ea, quae frugibus atque bacis terrae fetu profunduntur, sed etiam pecudes, quod perspicuum sit, partim esse ad usum hominum, partim ad
26 fructum, partim ad vescendum procreatas. artes vero
innumerabiles repertae sunt docente natura; quam
imitata ratio res ad vitam necessarias sollerter consecuta est. IX. ipsum autem hominem eadem natura
non solum celeritate mentis ornavit, sed et sensus
tamquam satellites adtribuit ac nuntios et rerum
plurimarum obscuras nec satis [2] . . . intellegentias
enudavit quasi fundamenta quaedam scientiae figu-
ramque corporis habilem et aptam ingenio humano
dedit. nam cum ceteras animantes abiecisset ad

---

[1] *et* added by Turnebus; omitted in MSS.
[2] *apertas* supplied by Lambinus; *claras* by Madvig;
inlustratas by Beier (cf. § 59 extr.).

any knowledge of God, and among men themselves there is no race either so highly civilized or so savage as not to know that it must believe in a god, even if it does not know in what sort of god it ought to believe. Thus it is clear that man recognizes God because, in a way, he remembers and recognizes the source from which he sprang.

Moreover, virtue exists in man and God alike, but in no other creature besides; virtue, however, is nothing else than Nature perfected and developed to its highest point; therefore there is a likeness between man and God. As this is true, what relationship could be closer or clearer than this one? For this reason, Nature has lavishly yielded such a wealth of things adapted to man's convenience and use that what she produces seems intended as a gift to us, and not brought forth by chance; and this is true, not only of what the fertile earth bountifully bestows in the form of grain and fruit, but also of the animals; for it is clear that some of them have been created to be man's slaves, some to supply him with their products, and others to serve as his food. Moreover innumerable arts have been discovered through the teachings of Nature; for it is by a skilful imitation of her that reason has acquired the necessities of life. IX. Nature has likewise not only equipped man himself with nimbleness of thought, but has also given him the senses, to be, as it were, his attendants and messengers; she has laid bare the obscure and none too [obvious] meanings of a great many things, to serve as the foundations of knowledge, as we may call them; and she has granted us a bodily form which is convenient and well suited to the human mind. For while she has

pastum, solum hominem erexit et ad caeli quasi
cognationis domiciliique pristini conspectum excitavit ; tum speciem ita formavit oris, ut in ea penitus
27 reconditos mores effingeret ; nam et oculi nimis
arguti, quem ad modum animo affecti simus, loquuntur, et is, qui appellatur vultus, qui nullo in
animante esse praeter hominem potest, indicat
mores, cuius vim Graeci norunt, nomen omnino non
habent. omitto opportunitates habilitatesque reliqui
corporis, moderationem vocis, orationis vim, quae
conciliatrix est humanae maxime societatis ; neque
enim omnia sunt huius disputationis ac temporis, et
hunc locum satis, ut mihi videtur, in iis libris,
quos legistis, expressit Scipio. nunc, quoniam
hominem, quod principium reliquarum rerum esse
voluit, generavit et ornavit deus, perspicuum sit
illud, ne omnia disserantur, ipsam per se naturam
longius progredi ; quae etiam nullo docente profecta
ab iis, quorum ex prima et inchoata intellegentia
genera cognovit, confirmat ipsa per se rationem et
perficit.

28   X. *A.* Dii inmortales, quam tu longe iuris principia
repetis ! atque ita, ut ego non modo ad illa non pro-
perem, quae expectabam a te de iure civili, sed facile

---

[1] Cicero appears to be referring both to facial expression
as a mirror of momentary emotion and to the countenance,
vultus, as an index to the character.

[2] The *De Re Publica.*

bent the other creatures down toward their food, she
has made man alone erect, and has challenged
him to look up toward heaven, as being, so to speak,
akin to him, and his first home. In addition, she
has so formed his features as to portray therein the
character that lies hidden deep within him; for not
only do the eyes declare with exceeding clearness
the innermost feelings of our hearts, but also the
countenance, as we Romans call it, which can be
found in no living thing save man, reveals the
character.[1] (The Greeks are familiar with the meaning which this word "countenance" conveys, though
they have no name for it.) I will pass over the
special faculties and aptitudes of the other parts of
the body, such as the varying tones of the voice and
the power of speech, which is the most effective
promoter of human intercourse; for all these things
are not in keeping with our present discussion or the
time at our disposal; and besides, this topic has been
adequately treated, as it seems to me, by Scipio in
the books which you have read.[2] But, whereas God
has begotten and equipped man, desiring him to
be the chief of all created things, it should now
be evident, without going into all the details, that
Nature, alone and unaided, goes a step farther; for,
with no guide to point the way, she starts with
those things whose character she has learned through
the rudimentary beginnings of intelligence, and,
alone and unaided, strengthens and perfects the
faculty of reason.

X. *A.* Ye immortal gods, how far back you go to
find the origins of Justice! And you discourse so
eloquently that I not only have no desire to hasten
on to the consideration of the civil law, concerning

patiar te hunc diem vel totum in isto sermone con-
sumere; sunt enim haec maiora, quae aliorum causa
fortasse conplecteris, quam ipsa illa, quorum haec
causa praeparantur.

M. Sunt haec quidem magna, quae nunc breviter
attinguntur, sed omnium, quae in hominum doctorum
disputatione versantur, nihil est profecto praestabilius
quam plane intellegi nos ad iustitiam esse natos,
neque opinione, set natura constitutum esse ius. id
iam patebit, si hominum inter ipsos societatem con-
29 iunctionemque perspexeris. nihil est enim unum uni
tam simile, tam par, quam omnes inter nosmet ipsos
sumus. quodsi depravatio consuetudinum, si opinio-
num vanitas non inbecillitatem animorum torqueret
et flecteret quocumque coepisset, sui nemo ipse tam
similis esset quam omnes essent omnium. itaque,
quaecumque est hominis definitio, una in omnis
30 valet; quod argumenti satis est nullam dissimilitu-
dinem esse in genere; quae si esset, non una omnis
definitio contineret; etenim ratio, qua una praestamus
beluis, per quam coniectura valemus, argumentamur,
refellimus, disserimus, conficimus aliquid, concludi-
mus, certe est communis, doctrina differens, discendi
quidem facultate par. nam et sensibus eadem omnia
conprehenduntur, et ea, quae movent sensus, itidem
movent omnium, quaeque in animis inprimuntur, de

---

[1] Apparently a paradox, designed to enforce a funda-
mental truth with emphasis. It seems merely to mean
"men would all be exactly alike."

which I was expecting you to speak, but I should
have no objection to your spending even the entire
day on your present topic; for the matters which
you have taken up, no doubt, merely as preparatory
to another subject, are of greater import than the
subject itself to which they form an introduction.

M. The points which are now being briefly touched
upon are certainly important; but out of all the
material of the philosophers' discussions, surely there
comes nothing more valuable than the full realization that we are born for Justice, and that right is
based, not upon men's opinions, but upon Nature.
This fact will immediately be plain if you once get
a clear conception of man's fellowship and union
with his fellow-men. For no single thing is so like
another, so exactly its counterpart, as all of us are to
one another. Nay, if bad habits and false beliefs
did not twist the weaker minds and turn them in
whatever direction they are inclined, no one would
be so like his own self as all men would be like
all others.[1] And so, however we may define man,
a single definition will apply to all. This is a
sufficient proof that there is no difference in kind
between man and man; for if there were, one definition could not be applicable to all men; and indeed
reason, which alone raises us above the level of the
beasts and enables us to draw inferences, to prove
and disprove, to discuss and solve problems, and to
come to conclusions, is certainly common to us all,
and, though varying in what it learns, at least in the
capacity to learn it is invariable. For the same things
are invariably perceived by the senses, and those
things which stimulate the senses, stimulate them
in the same way in all men; and those rudimentary

quibus ante dixi, inchoatae intellegentiae, similiter
in omnibus inprimuntur, interpresque mentis oratio
verbis discrepat sententiis congruens ; nec est quisquam gentis ullius, qui ducem nactus ad virtutem
pervenire non possit.

31   XI. Nec solum in rectis, sed etiam in pravitatibus
insignis est humani generis similitudo. nam et
voluptate capiuntur omnes, quae etsi est inlecebra
turpitudinis, tamen habet quiddam simile naturalis
boni ; levitate est enim et suavitate delectans ; sic
ab errore mentis tamquam salutare aliquid adscisci-
tur ; similique inscitia mors fugitur quasi dissolutio
naturae, vita expetitur, quia nos, in quo nati sumus,
continet, dolor in maximis malis ducitur cum sua
asperitate, tum quod naturae interitus videtur sequi ;
32 propterque honestatis et gloriae similitudinem beati,
qui honorati sunt, videntur, miseri autem, qui sunt
inglorii. molestiae, laetitiae, cupiditates, timores
similiter omnium mentes pervagantur, nec, si opiniones aliae sunt apud alios, idcirco, qui canem et
faelem ut deos colunt, non eadem superstitione qua
ceterae gentes conflictantur. quae autem natio non
comitatem, non benignitatem, non gratum animum
et beneficii memorem diligit? quae superbos, quae

330

beginnings of intelligence to which I have referred, which are imprinted on our minds, are imprinted on all minds alike ; and speech, the mind's interpreter, though differing in the choice of words, agrees in the sentiments expressed. In fact, there is no human being of any race who, if he finds a guide, cannot attain to virtue.

XI. The similarity of the human race is clearly marked in its evil tendencies as well as in its goodness. For pleasure also attracts all men ; and even though it is an enticement to vice, yet it has some likeness to what is naturally good. For it delights us by its lightness and agreeableness; and for this reason, by an error of thought, it is embraced as something wholesome. It is through a similar misconception that we shun death as though it were a dissolution of nature, and cling to life because it keeps us in the sphere in which we were born ; and that we look upon pain as one of the greatest of evils, not only because of its cruelty, but also because it seems to lead to the destruction of nature. In the same way, on account of the similarity between moral worth and renown, those who are publicly honoured are considered happy, while those who do not attain fame are thought miserable. Troubles, joys, desires, and fears haunt the minds of all men without distinction, and even if different men have different beliefs, that does not prove, for example, that it is not the same quality of superstition that besets those races which worship dogs and cats as gods, as that which torments other races. But what nation does not love courtesy, kindliness, gratitude, and remembrance of favours bestowed ? What people does not hate and despise

maleficos, quae crudeles, quae ingratos non asper-
natur, non odit ? quibus ex rebus cum omne genus
hominum sociatum inter se esse intellegatur, illud
extremum est, quod recte vivendi ratio meliores
efficit.

Quae si adprobatis, pergam ad reliqua ; sin quid
requiritis, id explicemus prius.

A. Nos vero nihil, ut pro utroque respondeam.

33 XII. *M.* Sequitur igitur ad participandum alium
alio communicandumque inter omnes ius nos natura
esse factos. atque hoc in omni hac disputatione sic
intellegi volo, quod dicam naturam . . .[1] esse,
tantam autem esse corruptelam malae consuetudinis,
ut ab ea tamquam igniculi extinguantur a natura
dati exorianturque et confirmentur vitia contraria.
quodsi, quo modo est natura, sic iudicio homines
"humani," ut ait poeta, "nihil a se alienum putarent," coleretur ius aeque ab omnibus. quibus
enim ratio natura data est, isdem etiam recta ratio
data est, ergo et lex, quae est recta ratio in iubendo
et vetando ; si lex, ius quoque ; et omnibus ratio ;
ius igitur datum est omnibus. recteque Socrates
exsecrari eum solebat, qui primus utilitatem a iure

---

[1] *quod dicam naturam esse* ABH. *ingenitum nobis natura*
is conjectured by Vahlen to fill the gap which he assumes at
this point. *volo, ius quod dicam natura esse* is the common
reading ; it depends on emendations by Pearce and Turnebus.

---

[1] Terence, *Heaut. Timor.* 77.

the haughty, the wicked, the cruel, and the ungrateful? Inasmuch as these considerations prove to us that the whole human race is bound together in unity, it follows, finally, that knowledge of the principles of right living is what makes men better.

If you approve of what has been said, I will go on to what follows. But if there is anything that you care to have explained, we will take that up first.

A. We have no questions, if I may speak for both of us.

XII. *M.* The next point, then, is that we are so constituted by Nature as to share the sense of Justice with one another and to pass it on to all men. And in this whole discussion I want it understood that what I shall call Nature is [that which is implanted in us by Nature]; that, however, the corruption caused by bad habits is so great that the sparks of fire, so to speak, which Nature has kindled in us are extinguished by this corruption, and the vices which are their opposites spring up and are established. But if the judgments of men were in agreement with Nature, so that, as the poet says, they considered "nothing alien to them which concerns mankind,"[1] then Justice would be equally observed by all. For those creatures who have received the gift of reason from Nature have also received right reason, and therefore they have also received the gift of Law, which is right reason applied to command and prohibition. And if they have received Law, they have received Justice also. Now all men have received reason; therefore all men have received Justice. Consequently Socrates was right when he cursed, as he often did, the man who first separated utility from Justice; for this

34 seiunxisset; id enim querebatur caput esse exitiorum
omnium. unde enim illa Pythagorea[1] vox de
amicitia?[2] . . . . locus. ex quo perspicitur, cum
hanc benivolentiam tam late longeque[3] diffusam vir
sapiens in aliquem pari virtute praeditum contu-
lerit, tum illud effici, quod quibusdam incredibile videatur, sit autem necessarium, ut nihilo sepse plus
quam alterum diligat; quid enim est, quod differat,
cum sint cuncta paria? quodsi interesse quippiam
tantulum modo potuerit in amicitia;[4] amicitiae nomen
iam occiderit, cuius est ea vis, ut, simul atque sibi
aliquid alter maluerit, nulla sit.

Quae praemuniuntur omnia reliquo sermoni
disputationique nostrae, quo facilius ius in natura
esse positum intellegi possit. de quo cum perpauca
dixero, tum ad ius civile veniam, ex quo haec omnis
est nata oratio.

35 XIII. Q. Tu vero iam perpauca scilicet; ex iis
enim quae dixisti Attico[5] videtur, mihi quidem certe,
ex natura ortum esse ius.

A. An mihi aliter videri possit, cum haec iam
perfecta sint, primum quasi muneribus deorum nos

---

[1] *Pythagorea* is the common reading. *Phytagoraeia* A;
Pithagoreia B; *Phitagorea* H; Vahlen conjectures *Pythagorae
iam trita vox.*

[2] Vahlen assumes a gap here, and conjectures *amicitia?*
(*nimirum huic communioni est in hominum societate, non
solum in amicitia*) *locus.*

[3] *longeque diffusam* A[2]; *longe diffusam* A[1] B H.

[4] *amicitia* supplied by Vahlen; omitted in MSS.

[5] *Attico* A[1] B[1] H; *Attice* A[2] B[2]; *effici videtur* Haupt.

---

[1] Clement of Alexandria (*Stromata* II, 21, 3) tells us that
this statement about Socrates was made by Cleanthes, second
head of the Stoic school (about 250 B.C.).

separation, he complained, is the source of all mischief.[1] For what gave rise to Pythagoras' famous words about friendship?[2] . . . From this it is clear that, when a wise man shows toward another endowed with equal virtue the kind of benevolence which is so widely diffused among men, that will then have come to pass which, unbelievable as it seems to some, is after all the inevitable result—namely, that he loves himself no whit more than he loves another. For what difference can there be among things which are all equal? But if the least distinction should be made in friendship, then the very name of friendship would perish forthwith; for its essence is such that, as soon as either friend prefers anything for himself, friendship ceases to exist.

Now all this is really a preface to what remains to be said in our discussion, and its purpose is to make it more easily understood that Justice is inherent in Nature. After I have said a few words more on this topic, I shall go on to the civil law, the subject which gives rise to all this discourse.

XIII. Q. You certainly need to say very little more on that head, for from what you have already said, Atticus is convinced, and certainly I am, that Nature is the source of Justice.

A. How can I help being convinced, when it has just been proved to us, first, that we have been

---

[2] Whether the quotation from Pythagoras was given by Cicero or not we cannot tell, nor can we be sure what "famous words" are referred to. The well-known sayings, κοινὰ τὰ τῶν φίλων, "the possessions of friends are owned in common," and τὸν φίλον ἄλλον ἑαυτόν, "a friend is a second self," are credited to him, as well as several other aphorisms on the subject. (See Porphyrius, *De Vita Pythag.* § 33.)

esse instructos et ornatos, secundo autem loco unam esse hominum inter ipsos vivendi parem communemque rationem, deinde omnes inter se naturali quadam indulgentia et benivolentia, tum etiam societate iuris contineri? quae cum vera esse recte, ut arbitror, concesserimus, qui iam licet nobis a natura leges et iura seiungere?

36 *M.* Recte dicis, et res se sic habet. verum philosophorum more, non veterum quidem illorum, sed eorum, qui quasi officinas instruxerunt sapientiae, quae fuse olim disputabantur ac libere, ea nunc articulatim distincta dicuntur; nec enim satis fieri censent huic loco, qui nunc est in manibus, nisi separatim hoc ipsum, natura[1] esse ius, disputarint.

A. Et scilicet tua libertas disserendi amissa est, aut tu is es, qui in disputando non tuum iudicium sequare, set auctoritati aliorum pareas!

37 *M.* Non semper, Tite; sed iter huius sermonis quod sit vides: ad res publicas firmandas et ad stabiliendas urbes sanandosque[2] populos omnis nostra pergit oratio. quocirca vereor committere, ut non bene provisa et diligenter explorata principia ponantur, nec tamen ut omnibus probentur (nam id fieri

---

[1] *natura* Turnebus; *naturae* A B H.
[2] *-que* added by Feldhuegel; omitted in MSS.

---

[1] It was particularly the Stoics who laid stress on the exact subdivision of philosophic problems and the systematic discussion of every point separately.

provided and equipped with what we may call the gifts of the gods; next, that there is only one principle by which men may live with one another, and that this is the same for all, and possessed equally by all; and, finally, that all men are bound together by a certain natural feeling of kindliness and good-will, and also by a partnership in Justice? Now that we have admitted the truth of these conclusions, and rightly, I think, how can we separate Law and Justice from Nature?

M. Quite right; that is exactly the situation. But we are following the method of the philosophers —not those of former times, but those who have built workshops, so to speak, for the production of wisdom. Those problems which were formerly argued loosely and at great length they now discuss systematically, taking them up point by point;[1] and they do not think that a treatment of the topic which we are now considering is complete unless a separate discussion is devoted to the particular point that Justice springs from Nature.

A. And, of course, you have lost your independence in discussion, or else you are the kind of man not to follow your own judgment in a debate, but meekly to accept the authority of others!

M. I do not always do that, Titus. But you see the direction this conversation is to take; our whole discourse is intended to promote the firm foundation of States, the strengthening of cities, and the curing of the ills of peoples. For that reason I want to be especially careful not to lay down first principles that have not been wisely considered and thoroughly investigated. Of course I cannot expect that they will be universally accepted, for that is impossible;

non potest), sed ut eis, qui omnia recta atque honesta
per se expetenda duxerunt et aut nihil omnino in
bonis numerandum, nisi quod per se ipsum laudabile
esset, aut certe nullum habendum magnum bonum,
38 nisi quod vere laudari sua sponte posset,—iis omnibus, sive in Academia vetere cum Speusippo, Xeno-
crate, Polemone manserunt, sive Aristotelem et
Theophrastum cum illis congruentis re, genere docendi paulum differentis secuti sunt, sive, ut Zenoni visum
est, rebus non commutatis inmutaverunt vocabula,
sive etiam Aristonis difficilem atque arduam, sed iam
tamen fractam et convictam sectam secuti sunt, ut
virtutibus exceptis atque vitiis cetera in summa aequa-
litate ponerent,—iis omnibus haec, quae dixi, pro-
39 bentur. sibi autem indulgentis et corpori deservientis
atque omnia, quae sequantur in vita quaeque fugiant,
voluptatibus et doloribus ponderantis, etiamsi vera
dicunt (nihil enim opus est hoc loco litibus), in hortulis suis iubeamus dicere atque etiam ab omni societate rei publicae, cuius partem nec norunt ullam
neque umquam nosse voluerunt, paulisper facessant
rogemus. perturbatricem autem harum omnium rerum Academiam, hanc ab Arcesila et Carneade re-

---

[1] Speusippus, Xenocrates, and Polemon were Plato's successors in the leadership of the Academy. Aristotle and
Theophrastus were respectively the founder and the second
head of the Peripatetic school. Zeno was the founder of the
Stoic school. Aristo of Chios was an unorthodox Stoic.
[2] The Epicureans are meant.

but I do look for the approval of all who believe
that everything which is right and honourable is to
be desired for its own sake, and that nothing
whatever is to be accounted a good unless it is
praiseworthy in itself, or at least that nothing should
be considered a great good unless it can rightly be
praised for its own sake. Of all such, I say, I expect
the approval, whether they have remained in the
Old Academy with Speusippus, Xenocrates, and
Polemon ; or have followed Aristotle and Theophrastus, who agree with the school just mentioned
in doctrine, though differing slightly from it in mode
of presentation ; or, in agreement with Zeno, have
changed the terminology without altering the ideas ;
or even if they have followed the strict and severe
sect of Aristo, now broken up and refuted, and
believe everything except virtue and vice to be on
an absolute equality.[1] So far, however, as those
philosophers [2] are concerned who practise self-indul-
gence, are slaves to their own bodies, and test the
desirability or undesirability of everything on the
basis of pleasure and pain, let us, even if they are
right (for there is no need to quarrel with them
here), bid them carry on their discussions in their
own gardens,[3] and even request them to abstain for a
while from taking any part in matters affecting the
State, which they neither understand nor have ever
wished to understand. And let us implore the
Academy—the new one,[4] formed by Arcesilaus and

---

[3] Epicurus' pupils met in his garden at Athens.

[4] Arcesilaus and Carneades were considered the founders of
a " New Academy," as they had introduced scepticism into
the Academic teachings. It is to this scepticism that Cicero
refers here.

centem, exoremus ut sileat; nam si invaserit in haec,
quae satis scite nobis instructa et composita videntur,
nimias edet ruinas; quam quidem ego placare cupio,
summovere non audeo.

40   XIV.[1] . . . . nam et in iis sine illius [2] suffimentis
expiati sumus; at vero scelerum in homines atque in
deos [3] inpietatum nulla expiatio est.   itaque poenas
luunt non tam iudiciis (quae quondam nusquam
erant, hodie multifariam nulla sunt, ubi sunt, tamen
persaepe falsa sunt), set ut eos agitent insectenturque [4]
furiae non ardentibus taedis, sicut in fabulis, sed
angore conscientiae fraudisque cruciatu.

Quodsi homines ab iniuria poena, non natura
arcere deberet, quaenam sollicitudo vexaret impios
sublato suppliciorum metu? quorum tamen nemo
tam audax umquam fuit, quin aut abnueret a se
commissum esse facinus aut iusti sui doloris causam
aliquam fingeret defensionemque facinoris a naturae
iure aliquo quaereret. quae si appellare audent
impii, quo tandem studio colentur a bonis? quodsi
poena, si metus supplici, non ipsa turpitudo deterret

---

[1] There is evidently a gap of considerable length at this
point.
[2] *illius* A B H; *ullius* Turnebus; *ullis* Camerarius; *illis*
is suggested by Vahlen.
[3] *in deos* added by Reifferscheid; omitted in MSS.
[4] *aqitent* A B; *agitant* H. *insectenturque* dett.; *insectanturque*
A B H.   Bake reads *sed eos agitant insectanturque.*

---

[1] It is impossible to say who, if anyone, is referred to (see
critical note). After the gap Cicero appears to be concluding
some remarks on the expiation of slight offences. He immediately goes on to state the impossibility of expiating
really serious wrongdoing.

Carneades—to be silent, since it contributes nothing but confusion to all these problems ; for if it should attack what we think we have constructed and arranged so beautifully, it would play too great havoc with it ; at the same time I should like to win over this school, and so do not dare to banish it from the discussion. . . .

XIV. . . . . for even in these matters we conducted the expiation without the use of his incense ;[1] but there is really no expiation for crimes against men or sacrilege against the gods. And so men pay the penalty, not so much through decisions of the courts (for once there were no courts anywhere, and to-day there are none in many lands ; and where they do exist, they often act unjustly after all) ; but guilty men are tormented and pursued by the Furies, not with blazing torches, as in the tragedies,[2] but with the anguish of remorse and the torture of a guilty conscience.

But if it were a penalty and not Nature that ought to keep men from injustice, what anxiety would there be to trouble the wicked when the danger of punishment was removed ? But in fact there has never been a villain so brazen as not to deny that he had committed a crime, or else invent some story of just anger to excuse its commission, and seek justification for his crime in some natural principle of right. Now if even the wicked dare to appeal to such principles, how jealously should they be guarded by the good ! But if it is a penalty, the fear of punishment, and not the

[2] Aeschylus' *Eumenides*, for example, where the Furies pursue Orestes. The torches may possibly be referred to in *Eum.* 1005 and 1021.

ab iniuriosa facinerosaque vita, nemo est iniustus,
41 aut incauti potius habendi sunt inprobi; tum autem,
qui non ipso honesto movemur ut boni viri simus,
sed utilitate aliqua atque fructu, callidi sumus, non
boni; nam quid faciet is homo in tenebris, qui nihil
timet nisi testem et iudicem? quid in deserto quo
loco nactus, quem multo auro spoliare possit,
inbecillum atque solum? noster quidem hic natura
iustus vir ac bonus etiam conloquetur, iuvabit, in
viam deducet; is vero, qui nihil alterius causa facit
et metitur[1] suis commodis omnia, videtis, credo,
quid sit acturus; quodsi negabit se illi vitam erep-
turum et aurum ablaturum, numquam ob eam
causam negabit, quod id natura turpe iudicet, sed
quod metuat, ne emanet, id est ne malum habeat.
o rem dignam, in qua non modo docti, sed etiam
agrestes erubescant!

42   XV. Iam vero illud stultissimum, existimare omnia iusta esse, quae sita sint in populorum institutis
aut legibus. etiamne si quae leges sint tyrannorum?
si triginta illi Athenis leges inponere voluissent, aut
si omnes Athenienses delectarentur tyrannicis legibus, num idcirco eae leges iustae haberentur?
nihilo, credo, magis illa, quam interrex noster tulit,

---

[1] *facit et metitur* Victorius; *facit et mentietur* A; *facti et
mentietur* B[1]; *faciet et mentietur* B[2]; *faciet emetietur* H; *faciet
mentietur* dett.

---

[1] See *De Re Pub.* I, 44.
[2] This evidently refers to a law proposed by L. Valerius
Flaccus in 82 B.C. with reference to Sulla's dictatorship. Cf.
Cicero, *De Lege Agraria* III, 4; *Act.* II *in Verrem* III, 82.

wickedness itself, that is to keep men from a life of wrongdoing and crime, then no one can be called unjust, and wicked men ought rather to be regarded as imprudent; furthermore, those of us who are not influenced by virtue itself to be good men, but by some consideration of utility and profit, are merely shrewd, not good. For to what lengths will that man go in the dark who fears nothing but a witness and a judge? What will he do if, in some desolate spot, he meets a helpless man, unattended, whom he can rob of a fortune? Our virtuous man, who is just and good by nature, will talk with such a person, help him, and guide him on his way; but the other, who does nothing for another's sake, and measures every act by the standard of his own advantage—it is clear enough, I think, what he will do! If, however, the latter does deny that he would kill the man and rob him of his money, he will not deny it because he regards it as a naturally wicked thing to do, but because he is afraid that his crime may become known—that is, that he may get into trouble. Oh, what a motive, that might well bring a blush of shame to the cheek, not merely of the philosopher, but even of the simple rustic!

XV. But the most foolish notion of all is the belief that everything is just which is found in the customs or laws of nations. Would that be true, even if these laws had been enacted by tyrants? If the well-known Thirty[1] had desired to enact a set of laws at Athens, or if the Athenians without exception were delighted by the tyrants' laws, that would not entitle such laws to be regarded as just, would it? No more, in my opinion, should that law be considered just which a Roman interrex[2]

ut dictator, quem vellet civium, aut indicta[1] causa
inpune posset occidere. est enim unum ius, quo
devincta est hominum societas, et quod lex constituit una; quae lex est recta ratio imperandi atque
prohibendi; quam qui ignorat, is est iniustus, sive
est illa scripta uspiam sive nusquam.

Quodsi iustitia est obtemperatio scriptis legibus
institutisque populorum, et si, ut eidem dicunt,
utilitate omnia metienda sunt, negleget leges easque
perrumpet, si poterit, is, qui sibi eam rem fructuosam
putabit fore. ita fit, ut nulla sit omnino iustitia, si
neque natura est, eaque quae propter[2] utilitatem
43 constituitur, utilitate illa convellitur. atque si natura confirmatura ius non erit, tollantur[3] . . .; ubi
enim liberalitas, ubi patriae caritas, ubi pietas, ubi
aut bene merendi de altero aut referendae gratiae
voluntas poterit existere? nam haec nascuntur ex
eo, quia natura propensi sumus ad diligendos
homines, quod fundamentum iuris est. neque solum
in homines obsequia, sed etiam in deos caerimoniae
religionesque tolluntur, quas non metu, sed ea
coniunctione, quae est homini cum deo, conser
vandas puto. XVI. quodsi populorum iussis, si prin
cipum decretis, si sententiis iudicum iura consti
tuerentur, ius esset latrocinari, ius adulterare, iu

---

[1] *civium aut indicta* B H; *civium vindicta* A: *civium
indemnatum aut indicta* is conjectured by Vahlen.
[2] *eaque quae propter* dett.; *eaque propter* A H; *aeaqua
propter* B.
[3] *erit tollantur* A B H; *erit virtutes omnes tollentur* dett
Although probably only a conjecture, the reading of the dett
seems to complete the sense accurately.

proposed, to the effect that a dictator might put to death with impunity any citizen he wished, even without a trial. For Justice is one; it binds all human society, and is based on one Law, which is right reason applied to command and prohibition. Whoever knows not this Law, whether it has been recorded in writing anywhere or not, is without Justice.

But if Justice is conformity to written laws and national customs, and if, as the same persons claim, everything is to be tested by the standard of utility, then anyone who thinks it will be profitable to him will, if he is able, disregard and violate the laws. It follows that Justice does not exist at all, if it does not exist in Nature, and if that form of it which is based on utility can be overthrown by that very utility itself. And if Nature is not to be considered the foundation of Justice, that will mean the destruction [of the virtues on which human society depends]. For where then will there be a place for generosity, or love of country, or loyalty, or the inclination to be of service to others or to show gratitude for favours received? For these virtues originate in our natural inclination to love our fellow-men, and this is the foundation of Justice. Otherwise not merely consideration for men but also rites and pious observances in honour of the gods are done away with; for I think that these ought to be maintained, not through fear, but on account of the close relationship which exists between man and God. XVI. But if the principles of Justice were founded on the decrees of peoples, the edicts of princes, or the decisions of judges, then Justice would sanction robbery and adultery and

testamenta falsa supponere, si haec suffragiis aut
44 scitis multitudinis probarentur. quae si tanta potestas est stultorum sententiis atque iussis, ut eorum
suffragiis rerum natura vertatur, cur non sanciunt,
ut, quae mala perniciosaque sunt, habeantur pro
bonis et salutaribus? aut cum[1] ius ex iniuria lex
facere possit, bonum eadem facere non possit ex
malo? atqui nos legem bonam a mala nulla alia nisi
naturae norma dividere possumus; nec solum ius et
iniuria natura diiudicatur, sed omnino omnia honesta
et turpia. nam ut communis[2] intellegentia nobis
notas res efficit easque in animis nostris inchoavit,
45 honesta in virtute ponuntur, in vitiis turpia. ea
autem in opinione existimare, non in natura posita
dementis est. nam nec arboris nec equi virtus quae
dicitur, in quo abutimur nomine, in opinione sita est
sed in natura; quod si ita est, honesta quoque et
turpia natura diiudicanda sunt. nam si opinione
universa virtus, eadem eius etiam partes probarentur; quis igitur prudentem et, ut ita dicam
catum non ex ipsius habitu sed ex aliqua re externa
iudicet? est enim virtus perfecta ratio, quod certe
in natura est; igitur omnis honestas eodem modo
XVII. nam ut vera et falsa, ut consequentia et contraria sua sponte, non aliena iudicantur, sic constans

---

[1] *aut cum* A [2] B[2] H; *aut quom* B[1]; *autem quom* A[1]; *ac
quom* Vahlen; *aut cur* Bake.
[2] *nam ut communis* C. F. W. Mueller; *nam et communi*
A B H: *nam et ut communis* Vahlen.

---

[1] *i.e.*, the proper excellence of anything (ἀρετή).
346

forgery of wills, in case these acts were approved by
the votes or decrees of the populace.   But if so
great a power belongs to the decisions and decrees
of fools that the laws of Nature can be changed
by their votes, then why do they not ordain that
what is bad and baneful shall be considered good
and salutary?   Or, if a law can make Justice out of
Injustice, can it not also make good out of bad?
But in fact we can perceive the difference between
good laws and bad by referring them to no other
standard than Nature; indeed, it is not merely
Justice and Injustice which are distinguished by
Nature, but also and without exception things which
are honourable and dishonourable.   For since an
intelligence common to us all makes things known
to us and formulates them in our minds, honourable
actions are ascribed by us to virtue, and dishonourable actions to vice; and only a madman would
conclude that these judgments are matters of
opinion, and not fixed by Nature.   For even what
we, by a misuse of the term, call the virtue[1] of a
tree or of a horse, is not a matter of opinion, but is
based on Nature.   And if that is true, honourable
and dishonourable actions must also be distinguished
by Nature.   For if virtue in general is to be tested
by opinion, then its several parts must also be so
tested; who, therefore, would judge a man of
prudence and, if I may say so, hard common sense,
not by his own character but by some external
circumstance?   For virtue is reason completely
developed; and this certainly is natural; therefore
everything honourable is likewise natural.   XVII.
For just as truth and falsehood, the logical and
illogical, are judged by themselves and not by

et perpetua ratio vitae, quae virtus est, itemque
inconstantia, quod est vitium, sua natura[1] . . . .
46 probavit, nos ingenia iuvenum non item? an ingenia natura, virtutes et vitia, quae existunt ab
ingeniis, aliter iudicabuntur? an ea non aliter,
honesta et turpia non ad naturam referri necesse
erit? quod laudabile bonum est, in se habeat quod
laudetur necesse est; ipsum enim bonum non est
opinionibus, sed natura. nam ni ita esset, beati
quoque opinione essent; quo quid dici potest stul-
tius? quare cum et bonum et malum natura iudicetur et ea sint principia naturae, certe honesta quoque et turpia simili ratione diiudicanda et ad
47 naturam referenda sunt. sed perturbat nos opinio-
num varietas hominumque dissensio, et quia non
idem contingit in sensibus, hos natura certos
putamus, illa, quae aliis sic, aliis secus nec isdem
semper uno modo videntur, ficta esse dicimus; quod
est longe aliter. nam sensus nostros non parens,
non nutrix, non magister, non poëta, non scena
depravat, non multitudinis consensus abducit; at
vero[2] animis omnes tenduntur insidiae vel ab iis,

[1] *natura probavit* A B H; *natura probabit* dett. ; Vahlen
conjectures *natura* (*iudicabitur. an agricola surculi ingenium
natura*) *probabit.*

[2] *abducit at vero* A[1] H ; *abducit ad vero* B ; *abducit a vero*
A[2]. The latter is the common reading, but *abducit at vero*
appears to have stood in the MSS. originally.

anything else, so the steadfast and continuous use of reason in the conduct of life, which is virtue, and also inconstancy, which is vice, [are judged] by their own nature

[Or, when a farmer judges the quality of a tree by nature,] shall we not use the same standard in regard to the characters of young men? Then shall we judge character by Nature, and judge virtue and vice, which result from character, by some other standard? But if we adopt the same standard for them, must we not refer the honourable and the base to Nature also? Whatever good thing is praiseworthy must have within itself something which deserves praise, for goodness itself is good by reason not of opinion but of Nature. For, if this were not true, men would also be happy by reason of opinion; and what statement could be more absurd than that? Wherefore since both good and evil are judged by Nature and are natural principles, surely honourable and base actions must also be distinguished in a similar way and referred to the standard of Nature. But we are confused by the variety of men's beliefs and by their disagreements, and because this same variation is not found in the senses, we think that Nature has made these accurate, and say that those things about which different people have different opinions and the same people not always identical opinions are unreal. However, this is far from being the case. For our senses are not perverted by parent, nurse, teacher, poet, or the stage, nor led astray by popular feeling; but against our minds all sorts of plots are constantly being laid, either by those whom I have just mentioned, who, taking possession of them

349

quos modo enumeravi, qui teneros et rudes cum
acceperunt, inficiunt et flectunt, ut volunt, vel ab ea,
quae penitus in omni sensu inplicata insidet, imi-
tatrix boni, voluptas, malorum autèm mater omnium ;
cuius blanditiis corrupti, quae natura bona sunt, quia
dulcedine hac et scabie carent, non cernunt satis.

48   XVIII. Sequitur, ut conclusa mihi iam haec sit
omnis oratio, id quod ante oculos ex iis est, quae
dicta sunt, et ius et omne honestum sua sponte esse
expetendum ; etenim omnes viri boni ipsam aequitatem et ius ipsum amant, nec est viri boni errare et
diligere, quod per se non sit diligendum ; per se
igitur ius est expetendum et colendum ; quodsi ius,
etiam iustitia ; sin ea, reliquae quoque virtutes per
se colendae sunt. quid ? liberalitas gratuitane est
an mercennaria ? si sine praemio benignus est, gra-
tuita, si cum mercede, conducta ; nec est dubium,
quin is, qui liberalis benignusve dicitur, officium, non
fructum sequatur ; ergo item iustitia nihil expetit
praemii, nihil pretii ; per se igitur expetitur. eademque omnium virtutum causa atque sententia est.

49   Atque etiam si emolumentis, non suapte vi[1] virtus
expetitur, una erit virtus, quae malitia rectissime
dicetur ; ut enim quisque maxume ad suum commo-

----

[1] *vi* supplied by Moser ; omitted in MSS.

----

[1] Evidently *malitia* has here its literal meaning (= κακία)
and is the opposite of *virtus*. Later Cicero decides to use
vitiositas or *vitium* in this sense instead of *malitia*. (*Tusc.
Disp.* IV, 34 ; *De Fin.* III, 39–40.)

while still tender and unformed, colour and bend them as they wish, or else by that enemy which lurks deep within us, entwined in our every sense—that counterfeit of good, which is, however, the mother of all evils—pleasure. Corrupted by her allurements, we fail to discern clearly what things are by Nature good, because the same seductiveness and itching does not attend them.

XVIII. To close now our discussion of this whole subject, the conclusion, which stands clearly before our eyes from what has already been said, is this: Justice and all things honourable are to be sought for their own sake. And indeed all good men love fairness in itself and Justice in itself, and it is unnatural for a good man to make such a mistake as to love what does not deserve love for itself alone. Therefore Justice must be sought and cultivated for her own sake; and if this is true of Justice, it is also true of equity; and if this is the case with equity, then all the other virtues are also to be cherished for their own sake. What of generosity? Is it disinterested or does it look to a recompense? If a man is kind without any reward, then it is disinterested; but if he receives payment, then it is hired. It cannot be doubted that he who is called generous or kind answers the call of duty, not of gain. Therefore equity also demands no reward or price; consequently it is sought for its own sake. And the same motive and purpose characterize all the virtues.

In addition, if it be true that virtue is sought for the sake of other benefits and not for its own sake, there will be only one virtue, which will most properly be called a vice.[1] For in proportion as anyone

351

dum refert, quaecumque agit, ita minime est vir
bonus, ut qui virtutem praemio metiuntur, nullam
virtutem nisi malitiam putent. ubi enim beneficus,
si nemo alterius causa benigne facit? ubi gratus, si
non eum ipsi[1] cernunt grati, cui referunt gratiam?
ubi illa sancta amicitia, si non ipse amicus per se
amatur toto pectore, ut dicitur? qui etiam dese-
rendus et abiciendus est desperatis emolumentis et
fructibus; quo quid potest dici immanius? quodsi
amicitia per se colenda est, societas quoque hominum
et aequalitas et iustitia per se expetenda; quod ni
ita est, omnino iustitia nulla est; id enim iniustissi-
mum ipsum est, iustitiae mercedem quaerere.   XIX.
50 quid vero de modestia, quid de temperantia, quid de
continentia, quid de verecundia, pudore pudicitiaque
dicemus? infamiaene metu non esse petulantis an
legum et iudiciorum? innocentes ergo et verecundi
sunt, ut bene audiant, et ut rumorem bonum colli-
gant, erubescunt; pudet etiam loqui de pudicitia.
at me istorum philosophorum pudet, qui ullum
iudicium vitare nisi vitio ipso vitato honestum[2]
putant.

[1] *ipsi* A B H; *ipsum* dett.
[2] *ullum iudicium vitare nisi vitio ipso vitato honestum*
Eussner; *ullum iuditium vitare nisi vicio ipso mutatum* A;
illum iudicium vitare nisi vitio ipso nutatum B; *nullum
iudicium vitare nisi vitio ipso notatum* H, Vahlen.

---

[1] The meaning of this sentence is doubtful; the text is
probably corrupt.
[2] Cicero states in *Tusc. Disp.* III, 16 that he uses three
different Latin terms, *i.e.*, *temperantia, moderatio,* and *modestia,*
to translate σωφροσύνη.

makes his own advantage absolutely the sole standard
of all his actions, to that extent he is absolutely not
a good man ; therefore those who measure virtue by
the reward it brings believe in the existence of no
virtue except vice.   For where shall we find a kindly
man, if no one does a kindness for the sake of anyone
else than himself ? Who can be considered grateful,
if even those who repay favours have no real consideration for those to whom they repay them ?[1]
What becomes of that sacred thing, friendship, if
even the friend himself is not loved for his own sake,
" with the whole heart," as people say ?   Why,
according to this theory, a friend should even be
deserted and cast aside as soon as there is no longer
hope of benefit and profit from his friendship !   But
what could be more inhuman than that ?   If, on the
other hand, friendship is to be sought for its own
sake, then the society of our fellow-men, fairness,
and Justice, are also to be sought for their own sake.
If this is not the case then there is no such thing as
Justice at all, for the very height of injustice is to
seek pay for Justice.   XIX. But what shall we say
of sobriety, moderation, and self-restraint ;[2] of
modesty, self-respect, and chastity ?   Is it for fear of
disgrace that we should not be wanton, or for fear of
the laws and the courts?   In that case men are
innocent and modest in order to be well spoken of,
and they blush in order to gain a good reputation !
I am ashamed even to mention chastity !   Or rather
I am ashamed of those philosophers who believe it
honourable to avoid condemnation for a crime without having avoided the crime itself.[3]

[3] The text is uncertain and the meaning doubtful.

51 Quid enim? possumus eos, qui a stupro arcentur infamiae metu, pudicos dicere, cum ipsa infamia propter rei turpitudinem consequatur? nam quid aut laudari rite aut vituperari potest, si ab eius natura recesseris, quod aut laudandum aut vituperandum putes? an corporis pravitates, si erunt perinsignes, habebunt aliquid offensionis, animi deformitas non habebit? cuius turpitudo ex ipsis vitiis facillime percipi[1] potest; quid enim foedius avaritia, quid inmanius libidine, quid contemptius timiditate, quid abiectius tarditate et stultitia dici potest? quid ergo? eos, qui singulis vitiis excellunt aut etiam pluribus, propter damna aut detrimenta aut cruciatus aliquos miseros esse dicimus an propter vim turpitudinemque vitiorum? quod item ad contrariam laudem

52 in virtutem dici potest. postremo, si propter alias res virtus expetitur, melius esse aliquid quam virtutem necesse est; pecuniamne igitur an honores, an formam, an valetudinem? quae et, cum adsunt, perparva sunt, et, quam diu adfutura sint, certum sciri nullo modo potest; an, id quod turpissimum dictu est, voluptatem? at in ea quidem spernenda et repudianda virtus vel maxime cernitur.

Sed videtisne, quanta series rerum sententiarumque sit, atque ut ex alio alia nectantur? quin labebar longius, nisi me retinuissem.

---

[1] percipi ABH ; *perspici* dett., Madvig.

And what shall we say of this? Is it possible for us to call those chaste who are kept from lewdness by the fear of disgrace, when the disgrace itself results from the inherent vileness of the deed? For what can properly be either praised or blamed, if you have disregarded the nature of the thing which in your opinion deserves praise or blame? Are bodily defects, if very conspicuous, to offend us, but not a deformity of character? And yet the baseness of this latter can easily be perceived from the very vices which result from it. For what can be thought of that is more loathsome than greed, what more inhuman than lust, what more contemptible than cowardice, what more degraded than stupidity and folly? Well, then, shall we say that those who are sunk deepest in a single vice, or in several, are wretched on account of any penalties or losses or tortures which they incur, or on account of the base nature of the vices themselves? And the same argument can be applied conversely to the praise accorded to virtue. Finally, if virtue is sought on account of other advantages, there must necessarily be something better than virtue. Is it money, then, or public office, or beauty, or health? But these things amount to very little when we possess them, and we can have no certain knowledge as to how long they will remain with us. Or is it—the very mention of such a thing is shameful—is it pleasure? But it is precisely in scorning and repudiating pleasure that virtue is most clearly discerned.

Well, do you see what a series of subjects and ideas we have before us, and how closely they are connected one with another? Indeed, if I had not forced myself to stop, I should have been led on still further.

XX. *Q.* Quo tandem? libenter enim, frater, quod istam orationem tecum prolaberer.[1]

M. Ad finem bonorum, quo referuntur et cuius apiscendi causa sunt facienda omnia, controversam rem et plenam dissensionis inter doctissimos, sed aliquando iam iudicandam.

53　　*A.* Qui istuc fieri potest L. Gellio mortuo?

M. Quid tandem id ad rem?

A. Quia me Athenis audire ex Phaedro meo memini Gellium, familiarem tuum, cum pro consule ex praetura in Graeciam venisset essetque[2] Athenis, philosophos, qui tum erant, in locum unum convocasse ipsisque magno opere auctorem fuisse, ut aliquando controversiarum aliquem facerent modum; quodsi essent eo animo, ut nollent aetatem in litibus conterere, posse rem convenire; et simul operam suam illis esse pollicitum, si posset inter eos aliquid convenire.

M. Ioculare istuc quidem, Pomponi, et a multis saepe derisum; sed ego plane vellem me arbitrum inter antiquam Academiam et Zenonem datum.

A. Quo tandem istuc modo?

M. Quia de re una solum dissident, de ceteris mirifice congruunt.

A. Ain tandem? unane est solum dissensio?

54　　*M.* Quae quidem ad rem pertineat, una, quippe

---

[1] The text of this clause is evidently corrupt, but its meaning is clear.

[2] *venisset essetque Athenis* Vahlen; *venissetque Athenis* ABH.

XX. Q. To what subject, pray? For, my dear brother, I should be overjoyed to follow you along the path of such a discussion.

M. To the highest good, the standard of all our actions, toward the attainment of which they should all be directed. This is a subject over which there is much controversy and disagreement among the most learned men; but the time has finally come for the question to be settled.

A. How can this be done, now that Lucius Gellius is dead?

M. What can his death have to do with it?

A. Well, I remember that my friend Phaedrus, when I was in Athens, told me the following story about your friend Gellius. When, after his praetorship, he went to Greece as proconsul and had arrived at Athens, he called together the philosophers who were there at the time, and urgently advised them to come at length to some settlement of their controversies. He said, if they really desired not to waste their lives in argument, that the matter might be settled; and at the same time he promised his own best efforts to aid them in coming to some agreement.

M. It was said in jest, Pomponius, and has often raised a laugh: but I should really like to be appointed arbiter between the Old Academy and Zeno.

A. How is that?

M. Because they differ on only one point; about everything else they are in remarkably perfect agreement.

A. Is that so? Is there only a single difference?

M. Yes, only one in any essential matter. For the

357

cum antiqui omne, quod secundum naturam esset,
quo iuvaremur in vita, bonum esse decreverint, hic
nihil,[1] nisi quod honestum esset, putarit bonum.

A. Parvam vero controversiam dicis, at non eam,
quae dirimat omnia '

M. Probe quidem sentires, si re ac non verbis
dissiderent.

XXI. *A.* Ergo adsentiris Antiocho, familiari meo
(magistro enim non audeo dicere) quocum vixi, et
qui me ex nostris paene convellit hortulis deduxitque
in Academiam perpauculis passibus.

M. Vir iste fuit ille quidem[2] prudens et acutus
et in suo genere perfectus mihique, ut scis, familiaris;
cui tamen ego adsentiar in omnibus necne mox
videro; hoc dico, controversiam totam istam posse
sedari.

55 *A.* Qui istuc tandem vides?

M. Quia, si, ut Chius Aristo dixit,[3] solum bonum
esse quod honestum esset, malumque quod turpe,
ceteras res omnis plane paris ac ne minimum quidem
utrum adessent an abessent interesse, valde a Xeno-
crate et Aristotele et ab illa Platonis familia discre-
paret essetque inter eos de re maxima et de omni
vivendi ratione dissensio; nunc vero, cum decus,
quod antiqui summum bonum esse dixerant, hic

---

[1] *nihil* supplied by Lambinus; omitted in MSS.
[2] *ille quidem prudens* dett.; *ille prudens* ABH.
[3] *dixit* ABH; *dixisset* Madvig.

---

[1] *i.e.*, there is not a *small* difference, but *no* real difference.

members of the Old Academy concluded that everything which is in accordance with nature and which
helps us in the conduct of life, is a good, while Zeno
thought that nothing is a good except what is
honourable.

A. It is a small matter indeed to quarrel about;
surely you do not mean that this can break off all
relations between them !

M. You would be exactly right, if it were in
things and not in words that they differed.[1]

XXI. *A.* Then you agree with my friend Antiochus (for I do not dare to call him my teacher),
with whom I once lived; he almost tore me away
from our gardens and led me within a few steps of
the Academy.

M. He was truly a wise man and astute, and in
his own specialty perfect; and he was my friend, as
you know. Whether, for all that, I am in entire
agreement with him or not, we shall soon see; at
any rate, I maintain that this whole dispute can be
settled.

A. Why do you think that possible ?

M. For the following reasons. If Zeno, like Aristo
of Chios, had said that what is honourable is the
sole good, and what is disgraceful the sole evil, and
that everything else is on an absolutely equal plane,
its presence or absence being entirely a matter of
indifference, then he would differ widely from
Xenocrates, Aristotle and the whole Platonic school,
and there would be a disagreement between them
in regard to a most important matter which involves
the whole philosophy of human life. As it is, however, the Old Academy held that honour is the
highest good, while Zeno considers it the sole good,

solum bonum dicat, itemque dedecus illi summum
malum, hic solum, divitias, valetudinem, pulchritu-
dinem commodas res appellet, non bonas, paupertatem, debilitatem, dolorem incommodas, non malas,
sentit idem quod Xenocrates, quod Aristoteles,
loquitur alio modo. ex hac autem non rerum, sed
verborum discordia controversia est nata de finibus;
in qua, quoniam usus capionem duodecim tabulae
intra quinque pedes esse noluerunt, depasci veterem
possessionem Academiae ab hoc acuto homine non
sinemus, nec Mamilia lege singuli, sed e duodecim
tres arbitri finis regemus.

56   *Q.* Quamnam igitur sententiam dicimus?

M. Requiri placere terminos, quos Socrates pegerit,
iisque parere.

Q. Praeclare, frater, iam nunc a te verba usur-
pantur civilis iuris et legum, quo de genere expecto
disputationem tuam. nam ista quidem magna diiu-
dicatio est, ut ex te ipso saepe cognovi; sed certe
ita res se habet, ut ex natura vivere summum bonum
sit, id est vita modica et apta virtute perfrui aut
naturam sequi et eius quasi lege vivere, id est nihil,
quantum in ipso sit, praetermittere, quo minus ea,
quae natura postulet, consequatur, quod inter haec

---

[1] This strip was left free for the turning of the plough, and
as a path. Ownership of it could never be acquired by a
"squatter." This sentence is connected with the previous
one by a play on words; *finis* means both "end" and
"boundary."

[2] *i.e.* Zeno.

[3] See Cicero, *De Fin.* IV, 14. The discussion of this
topic is broken off abruptly at this point, but it is taken up
in detail in *De Fin.* IV.

and likewise dishonour is the greatest evil according
to the Academy, but the sole evil according to him ;
for he calls wealth, health, and beauty advantages
instead of goods, and poverty, ill-health, and pain
disadvantages instead of evils. Therefore Zeno holds
the same belief as Xenocrates and Aristotle, but
states it in a different way. Yet, out of this disagreement, which is one of words, not of things, a controversy about the ends of conduct has arisen. Now
since the Twelve Tables have provided that ownership of a five-foot strip along a boundary line [1] can
never be acquired by possession, we shall not allow
the exclusive rights to the ancient estate of the
Academy to be acquired by this astute person,[2] but
in fixing the boundaries we shall follow the pre-
scription of the Twelve Tables, which require three
arbiters, instead of those of the Mamilian Law,
which calls for only one.

Q. What decision shall we make, then ?

M. That the boundary which Socrates set up is to
be searched for and respected.[3]

Q. At this very moment, my dear brother, you are
already making excellent use of the terms of the
civil law and the statutes, your discussion of which
I am awaiting. For although the settlement of the
disagreement you have mentioned is important, as I
have often heard you remark, yet it is undoubtedly
true that to live in accordance with Nature is the
highest good. That signifies the enjoyment of a
life of due measure based upon virtue, or following
Nature and living according to her law, if I may call
it so ; in other words, to spare no effort, so far as in
us lies, to accomplish what Nature demands ; among
these demands being her wish that we live by virtue

velit virtute tamquam lege vivere. quapropter hoc
diiudicari nescio an numquam, sed hoc sermone certe
non potest, siquidem id, quod suscepimus, perfecturi
sumus.

57 XXII. *A.* At ego huc declinabam nec invitus.

Q. Licebit alias; nunc id agamus, quod coepimus,
cum praesertim ad id nihil pertineat haec de summo
malo bonoque dissensio.

M. Prudentissime, Quinte, dicis; nam quae a me
adhuc dicta sunt, . . .[1]

Q. . . . te Lycurgi leges neque Solonis neque
Charondae neque Zaleuci nec nostras duodecim
tabulas nec plebiscita desidero, sed te existimo cum
populis, tum etiam singulis hodierno sermone leges
vivendi et disciplinam daturum.

58 *M.* Est huius vero disputationis, Quinte, proprium
id, quod expectas, atque utinam esset etiam facultatis
meae! sed profecto ita se res habet, ut, quoniam
vitiorum emendatricem legem esse oportet com-
mendatricemque virtutum, ab ea vivendi doctrina
ducatur. Ita fit ut mater omnium bonarum rerum
sit[2] sapientia, cuius amore Graeco verbo philosophia
nomen invenit, qua nihil a dis inmortalibus uberius,
nihil florentius, nihil praestabilius hominum vitae
datum est. haec enim una nos cum ceteras res

---

[1] The last words of M.'s and the first of Q.'s speech are
missing. Vahlen conjectures *neque vero a te* as the words
immediately preceding *Lycurgi.*

[2] *sit* is commonly supplied; omitted in MSS.

---

[1] Quintus is urging his brother to return to the subject of
the law. He attempts to demonstrate, by presenting a
résumé of the conclusions reached, that a sufficient philosophical foundation for its consideration has been laid.

as our law.   Therefore, though it may be possible to
decide the controversy referred to at some future
time, we shall surely be unable to do so in this
conversation; at any rate, if we are to accomplish
what we set out to do.[1]

XXII. *A.* Yet I for my part was following this
digression with pleasure.

Q. We can go further with it on some other
occasion; at present let us keep to the subject with
which we began, as this controversy about the
greatest good and the greatest evil certainly has
nothing to do with it.

M. Your suggestion is a sensible one, Quintus;
for what I have said so far [suffices for our present
purpose].

Q. . . . . [and indeed] it is not the laws of
Lycurgus or Solon or Charondas or Zaleucus, or our
own Twelve Tables or the resolutions of the Plebeian
Assembly, that I require of you, but I believe that
you will lay down in to-day's discussion the laws of
life and a system of training for both nations and
individuals.

M. What you look for, Quintus, certainly belongs
to our discussion; I only wish it were in my power
to accomplish it adequately!   But it is certainly
true that, since Law ought to be a reformer of vice
and an incentive to virtue, the guiding principles of
life may be derived from it.   It is therefore true
that wisdom is the mother of all good things; and
from the Greek expression meaning "the love of
wisdom" philosophy has taken its name.   And
philosophy is the richest, the most bounteous, and
the most exalted gift of the immortal gods to
humanity.   For she alone has taught us, in addition

omnes, tum, quod est difficillimum, docuit, ut nosmet
ipsos nosceremus ; cuius praecepti tanta vis et tanta
sententia est, ut ea non homini cuipiam, sed
59 Delphico deo tribueretur. nam qui se ipse norit,
primum aliquid se habere sentiet divinum ingeni-
umque in se suum sicut simulacrum aliquod dicatum
putabit tantoque munere deorum semper dignum
aliquid et faciet et sentiet et, cum se ipse perspexerit
totumque temptarit, intelleget, quem ad modum a
natura subornatus in vitam venerit quantaque instrumenta habeat ad obtinendam adipiscendamque
sapientiam, quoniam principio rerum omnium quasi
adumbratas intellegentias animo ac mente conceperit,
quibus inlustratis sapientia duce bonum virum et ob
60 eam ipsam causam cernat se beatum fore. XXIII. nam
cum animus cognitis perceptisque virtutibus a corporis obsequio indulgentiaque discesserit volupta-
temque sicut labem aliquam dedecoris oppresserit
omnemque mortis dolorisque timorem effugerit socie-
tatemque caritatis coierit cum suis omnisque natura
coniunctos suos duxerit cultumque deorum et puram
religionem susceperit et exacuerit illam, ut oculorum,
sic ingenii aciem ad bona seligenda et reicienda
contraria, quae virtus ex providendo est appellata
prudentia, quid eo dici aut cogitari poterit beatius ?
61 idemque cum caelum, terras, maria rerumque omnium
naturam perspexerit, eaque unde generata, quo re-

---

[1] Compare *De Re Pub.* VI, 1.

to all other wisdom, that most difficult of all things
—to know ourselves. This precept is so important
and significant that the credit for it is given, not to
any human being, but to the god of Delphi. For he
who knows himself will realize, in the first place,
that he has a divine element within him, and will
think of his own inner nature as a kind of consecrated image of God ; and so he will always act and
think in a way worthy of so great a gift of the gods,
and, when he has examined and thoroughly tested
himself, he will understand how nobly equipped by
Nature he entered life, and what manifold means he
possesses for the attainment and acquisition of wisdom. For from the very first he began to form in
his mind and spirit shadowy concepts, as it were, of
all sorts, and when these have been illuminated
under the guidance of wisdom, he perceives that he
will be a good man, and, for that very reason, happy.
XXIII. For when the mind, having attained to a
knowledge and perception of the virtues, has
abandoned its subservience to the body and its
indulgence of it, has put down pleasure as if it were
a taint of dishonour, has escaped from all fear of
death or pain, has entered into a partnership of love
with its own, recognizing as its own all who are
joined to it by Nature ; when it has taken up the
worship of the gods and pure religion, has sharpened
the vision both of the eye and of the mind so that
they can choose the good and reject the opposite—a
virtue which is called prudence because it foresees [1]
—then what greater degree of happiness can be
described or imagined ? And further, when it has
examined the heavens, the earth, the seas, the nature
of the universe, and understands whence all these

cursura, quando, quo modo obitura, quid in iis mortale
et caducum, quid divinum aeternumque sit, viderit
ipsumque ea moderantem et regentem paene prende-
rit seseque non omnis[1] circumdatum moenibus popularem alicuius definiti loci, set civem totius mundi
quasi unius urbis agnoverit, in hac ille magnificentia
rerum atque in hoc conspectu et cognitione naturae,
dii inmortales, quam se ipse noscet, quod Apollo
praecepit Pythius! quam contemnet, quam despiciet,
quam pro nihilo putabit ea, quae volgo dicuntur
62 amplissima! XXIV. atque haec omnia quasi saepi-
mento aliquo vallabit disserendi ratione, veri et falsi
iudicandi scientia et arte quadam intellegendi quid
quamque rem sequatur, et quid sit cuique contrarium. cumque se ad civilem societatem natum
senserit, non solum illa subtili disputatione sibi
utendum putabit, sed etiam fusa latius perpetua
oratione, qua regat populos, qua stabiliat leges, qua
castiget inprobos, qua tueatur bonos, qua laudet
claros viros, qua praecepta salutis et laudis apte ad
persuadendum edat suis civibus, qua hortari ad
decus, revocare a flagitio, consolari possit adflictos
factaque et consulta fortium et sapientium cum
inproborum ignominia sempiternis monumentis prodere. quae cum tot res tantaeque sint, quae inesse

---

[1] *omnis* AB; *homines* H. *Omnis* is of course corrupt.
Vahlen conjectures *communibus.*

---

[1] Cicero's philosophical works, though in the dialogue
form, make little use of dialectic (*illa subtilis disputatio*), but
employ for the most part the continuous discourse characteristic of an essay or speech (*perpetua oratio*). His meaning

things came and whither they must return, when and
how they are destined to perish, what part of them
is mortal and transient and what is divine and
eternal; and when it almost lays hold of the ruler
and governor of the universe, and when it realizes
that it is not shut in by [narrow] walls as a resident
of some fixed spot, but is a citizen of the whole
universe, as it were of a single city—then in the
midst of this universal grandeur, and with such a
view and comprehension of nature, ye immortal gods,
how well it will know itself, according to the precept
of the Pythian Apollo! How it will scorn and
despise and count as naught those things which the
crowd calls splendid! XXIV. And in defence of all
this, it will erect battlements of dialectic, of the
science of distinguishing the true from the false, and
of the art, so to speak, of understanding the consequences and opposites of every statement. And
when it realizes that it is born to take part in the life
of a State, it will think that it must employ not
merely the customary subtle method of debate, but
also the more copious continuous style,[1] considering,
for example, how to rule nations, establish laws,
punish the wicked, protect the good, honour those
who excel, publish to fellow-citizens precepts conducive to their well-being and credit, so designed as
to win their acceptance; how to arouse them to
honourable actions, recall them from wrong-doing,
console the afflicted, and hand down to everlasting
memory the deeds and counsels of brave and wise
men, and the infamy of the wicked. So many and
so great are the powers which are perceived to exist

here seems to be that the latter is better suited for instruct-
ing and convincing one's fellow-citizens,

in homine perspiciantur ab iis, qui se ipsi velint nosse, earum parens est educatrixque sapientia.

A. Laudata quidem a te graviter et vere; sed quorsus hoc pertinet?

63   *M.* Primum ad ea, Pomponi, de quibus acturi iam sumus, quae tanta esse volumus; non enim erunt, nisi ea fuerint, unde illa manant, amplissima. deinde facio et lubenter et, ut spero, recte, quod eam, cuius studio teneor quaeque me eum, quicumque sum, effecit, non possum silentio praeterire.

A. Vero facis et merito et pie, fuitque id, ut dicis, in hoc sermone faciundum.

---

[1] *i.e.* philosophy.

in man by those who desire to know themselves;
and their parent and their nurse is wisdom.[1]

A. Your praise of wisdom is indeed impressive and
true; but what is its purpose?

M. In the first place, Pomponius, it has to do with
the subjects of which we are about to treat, which
we desire shall assume an equally lofty character;
for these matters cannot possess great dignity unless
the sources from which they are derived possess it
also. Secondly, I both take pleasure in praising wisdom, and do so, I believe, rightly, because, devoted
as I am to its study, and since it has made me all I
am, whatever that may be, I cannot pass over it in
silence.

A. Indeed wisdom deserves this tribute from you,
and it was your duty, as you say, to include it in
your discussion.

DE LEGIBUS

LIBER SECUNDUS

1   I. *A.* SED visne, quoniam et satis iam ambulatum
est et tibi aliud dicendi initium sumendum est,
locum mutemus et in insula, quae est in Fibreno
(nam, opinor, id[1] illi alteri flumini nomen est), sermoni reliquo demus operam sedentes?

M. Sane quidem ; nam illo loco libentissime soleo
uti, sive quid mecum ipse cogito sive aut quid scribo
aut lego.

2   *A.* Equidem, qui nunc potissimum huc venerim,
satiari non queo magnificasque villas et pavimenta
marmorea et laqueata tecta contemno ; ductus vero
aquarum, quos isti Nilos et Euripos vocant, quis non,
cum haec videat, inriserit ? itaque, ut tu paulo ante
de lege et de iure disserens ad naturam referebas
omnia, sic in his ipsis rebus, quae ad requietem animi
delectationemque quaeruntur, natura dominatur.
quare antea mirabar (nihil enim his in locis nisi saxa
et montes cogitabam, itaque ut facerem, et orationibus inducebar tuis et versibus), sed mirabar, ut dixı
te tam valde hoc loco delectari ; nunc contra miror
te, cum Roma absis, usquam potius esse.

---

[1] *id* supplied by Davies ; omitted in MSS.

---

[1] Euripus is the strait between Euboea and Boeotia, west
of Chalcis.

LAWS

BOOK II

I. *A.* As we have now had a sufficiently long walk,
and you are about to begin a new part of the discussion, shall we not leave this place and go to the
island in the Fibrenus (for I believe that is the name
of the other river), and sit there while we finish the
conversation?

M. By all means; for that island is a favourite
haunt of mine for meditation, writing and reading.

A. Indeed I cannot get enough of this place,
especially as I have come at this season of the year,
and I scorn luxurious country-places, marble walks
and panelled ceilings. Take those artificial streams
which some of our friends call " Niles " or " Euripi " [1]
—who, after seeing what we have before us, would
not laugh at them? And so, just as you, a moment
ago, in your discussion of law and justice, traced
everything back to Nature, in the same way Nature
is absolutely supreme in the things that men seek
for the recreation and delight of the soul. Hence I
used to be surprised (for I had the idea that there
was nothing in this vicinity except rocks and mountains, and both your speeches and poems encouraged
me in that opinion)—I was surprised, I say, that you
enjoyed this place so much; now, on the other hand,
I wonder that you ever prefer to go elsewhere, when
you leave Rome.

3   *M.* Ego vero, cum licet pluris dies abesse, praesertim hoc tempore anni, et amoenitatem hanc[1]
et salubritatem sequor ; raro autem licet. sed nimirum me alia quoque causa delectat, quae te non
attingit ita.

A. Quae tandem ista causa est ?

M. Quia, si verum dicimus, haec est mea et huius
fratris mei germana patria ; hic enim orti stirpe anti-
quissima sumus, hic sacra, hic genus, hic maiorum
multa vestigia. quid plura ? hanc vides villam, ut
nunc quidem est, lautius aedificatum patris nostri
studio, qui cum esset infirma valetudine, hic fere
aetatem egit in litteris. sed hoc ipso in loco, cum
avus viveret et antiquo more parva esset villa, ut illa
Curiana in Sabinis, me scito esse natum. quare
inest nescio quid et latet in animo ac sensu meo,
quo me plus hic locus fortasse delectet, siquidem
etiam ille sapientissimus vir, Ithacam ut videret,
inmortalitatem scribitur repudiasse.

4   II. *A.* Ego vero tibi istam iustam causam puto,
cur huc libentius venias atque hunc locum diligas ;
quin ipse, vere dicam, sum illi villae amicior modo
factus atque huic omni solo, in quo tu ortus et pro-
creatus es ; movemur enim nescio quo pacto locis
ipsis, in quibus eorum, quos diligimus aut admiramur,
adsunt vestigia. me quidem ipsae illae nostrae

---

[1] *amoenitatem hanc et salubritatem* [*hanc*] Vahlen ; *amoenitatem hanc et salubritatem hanc* AB ; *amoenitatem et salubritatem hanc* H.

---

[1] Manius Curius Dentatus. For other references to his
simple country home see Cicero, *De Senec.* 55, and Plutarch,
Cato 2.

[2] Odysseus preferred his return home to an immortal life
with the nymph Calypso (*Odyssey* I, 55–59 ; V, 135–6).

M. Indeed, whenever it is possible for me to be out of town for several days, especially at this time of the year, I do come to this lovely and healthful spot ; it is rarely possible, however. But I suppose that the place gives me additional pleasure on account of a circumstance which cannot have the same effect on you.

A. What circumstance is that ?

M. To tell you the truth, this is really my own fatherland, and that of my brother, for we are descended from a very ancient family of this district ; here are our ancestral sacred rites and the origin of our race ; here are many memorials of our forefathers. What more need I say ? Yonder you see our homestead as it is now—rebuilt and extended by my father's care ; for, as he was an invalid, he spent most of his life in study here. Nay, it was on this very spot, I would have you know, that I was born, while my grandfather was alive and when the homestead, according to the old custom, was small, like that of Curius[1] in the Sabine country. For this reason a lingering attachment for the place abides in my mind and heart, and causes me perhaps to feel a greater pleasure in it ; and indeed, as you remember, that exceedingly wise man[2] is said to have refused immortality that he might see Ithaca once more.

II. *A.* I think you certainly have good reason for preferring to come here and for loving this place. Even I myself, to tell you the truth, have now become more attached to the homestead yonder and to this whole countryside from the fact that it is the place of your origin and birth ; for we are affected in some mysterious way by places about which cluster memories of those whom we love and admire. Even

Athenae non tam operibus magnificis exquisitisque
antiquorum artibus delectant quam recordatione
summorum virorum, ubi quisque habitare, ubi sedere,
ubi disputare sit solitus, studioseque eorum etiam
sepulchra contemplor.   quare istum, ubi tu es natus,
plus amabo posthac locum.

M. Gaudeo igitur me incunabula paene mea tibi
ostendisse.

5 *A.* Equidem me cognosse admodum gaudeo.   sed
illud tamen quale est, quod paulo ante dixisti, hunc
locum, id enim [1] ego te accipio dicere Arpinum,
germanam patriam esse vestram? numquid duas
habetis patrias? an est una illa patria communis?
nisi forte sapienti illi Catoni fuit patria non Roma,
sed Tusculum.

M. Ego mehercule et illi et omnibus municipibus
duas esse censeo patrias, unam naturae, alteram
civitatis,[2] ut ille Cato, cum esset Tusculi natus, in
populi Romani civitatem susceptus est; ita, cum
ortu Tusculanus esset, civitate Romanus, habuit
alteram loci patriam, alteram iuris ; ut vestri Attici,
prius quam Theseus eos demigrare ex agris et in
astu, quod appellatur, omnis se conferre iussit, et sui
erant iidem et Attici, sic nos et eam patriam ducimus,
ubi nati, et illam, a qua excepti [3] sumus.   sed
necesse est caritate eam praestare, qua rei publicae

---

[1] *id enim* Goerenz ; *idem* ABH.

[2] *unam naturae, alteram civitatis* dett. ; *unam naturam
civitatis* ABH.

[3] *et illam a qua excepti* Bake ; *et illam qua excepti* dett.
these words omitted in ABH.

---

[1] The legend is that Attica had contained several city-
states, which Theseus united, making all the inhabitants of

in our beloved Athens, it is not so much the stately buildings and the exquisite works of ancient art which delight me, as the recollection of its peerless men—where they each used to live, to sit, and to carry on their discussions; and I even love to gaze upon their tombs. Therefore in the future I shall be even more fond of this spot because you were born here.

M. I am glad, then, that I have shown you what I may call my cradle.

A. And I am very glad to have become acquainted with it. But what did you really mean by the statement you made a while ago, that this place, by which I understand you to refer to Arpinum, is your own fatherland? Have you then two fatherlands? Or is our common fatherland the only one? Perhaps you think that the wise Cato's fatherland was not Rome but Tusculum?

M. Surely I think that he and all natives of Italian towns have two fatherlands, one by nature and the other by citizenship. Cato, for example, though born in Tusculum, received citizenship in Rome, and so, as he was a Tusculan by birth and a Roman by citizenship, had one fatherland which was the place of his birth, and another by law; just as the people of your beloved Attica, before Theseus [1] commanded them all to leave the country and move into the city (the *astu*, as it is called), were at the same time citizens of their own towns and of Attica, so we consider both the place where we were born our fatherland, and also the city into which we have been adopted. But that fatherland must stand first in our affection in which the name of republic signi-

the country Athenians (Thucydides, II, 15; Plutarch, *Theseus* 24).

nomen universae civitatis est ;[1] pro qua mori et cui
nos totos dedere et in qua nostra omnia ponere et
quasi consecrare debemus. dulcis autem non multo
secus est ea, quae genuit, quam illa, quae excepit.
itaque ego hanc meam esse patriam prorsus numquam
negabo, dum illa sit maior, haec in ea contineatur[2]
. . . habet civitates set unam illas civitatem putat.

6 III. *A.* Recte igitur Magnus ille noster me au-
diente posuit in iudicio, cum pro Ampio tecum simul
diceret, rem publicam nostram iustissimas huic
municipio gratias agere posse, quod ex eo duo sui
conservatores extitissent ; uti iam videar adduci hanc
quoque, quae te procrearit, esse patriam tuam.

Sed ventum in insulam est ; hac vero nihil est
amoenius. etenim[3] hoc quasi rostro finditur Fibrenus
et divisus aequaliter in duas partes latera haec ad-
luit rapideque dilapsus cito in unum confluit et tantum conplectitur quod satis sit modicae palaestrae
loci. quo effecto, tamquam id habuerit operis ac muneris, ut hanc nobis efficeret sedem ad disputandum,
statim praecipitat in Lirem et, quasi in familiam pa-
triciam venerit, amittit nomen obscurius Liremque
multo gelidiorem facit ; nec enim ullum hoc frigidius

---

[1] *qua,* etc. : the text is evidently faulty, though the
general meaning is clear.

[2] *contineatur* : [*et eodem modo omnis municeps duas ut mihi
videtur*] *habet civitatis set unam illas civitatem putat* suggested
by Vahlen ; *contineatur habet civitatis et unam illam civitatem
putat* ABH.

[3] *etenim* Lambinus : *ut enim* ABH.

---

[1] This translation follows Vahlen's suggestion as to the
text. But we might accept the manuscript reading and
render : [every native of an Italian town] has [two] citizenships, but considers that (greater one) his only citizenship.

[2] Evidently Marius and Cicero.

fies the common citizenship of all of us. For her it is our duty to die, to her to give ourselves entirely, to place on her altar, and, as it were, to dedicate to her service, all that we possess. But the fatherland which was our parent is not much less dear to us than the one which adopted us. Thus I shall never deny that my fatherland is here, though my other fatherland is greater and includes this one within it ; [and in the same way every native of an Italian town, in my opinion,] has [two] citizenships but thinks of them as one citizenship.[1]

III. *A.* Indeed, then, our friend Pompey the Great was right, when he was defending Ampius in company with you, and stated in court, in my hearing, that our republic most surely owed a debt of gratitude to this municipality, because two of her saviours had come from it.[2] Thus I am now inclined to share your view that this town which brought you forth is also your fatherland.

But here we are on the island ; surely nothing could be more lovely. It cuts the Fibrenus like the beak of a ship, and the stream, divided into two equal parts, bathes these banks, flows swiftly past, and then comes quickly together again, leaving only enough space for a wrestling ground[3] of moderate size. Then after accomplishing this, as if its only duty and function were to provide us with a seat for our discussion, it immediately plunges into the Liris, and, as if it had entered a patrician family, loses its less famous name, and makes the water of the Liris much colder. For, though I have visited many, I have never come upon a river which was colder

---

[3] The word *palaestra* is often used, in both Greek and Latin, of a school or a place for discussion.

flumen attigi, cum ad multa accesserim, ut vix pede
temptare id possim, quod in Phaedro Platonis facit
Socrates.

7 *M.* Est vero ita ; sed tamen huic amoenitati,
quem ex Quinto saepe audio, Thyamis Epirotes tuus
ille nihil, opinor, concesserit.

Q. Est ita ut dicis ; cave enim putes Attici nostri
Amalthio platanisque illis quicquam esse praeclarius.

Sed, si videtur, considamus hic in umbra atque ad
eam partem sermonis, ex qua egressi sumus, rever-
tamur.

M. Praeclare exigis, Quinte (at ego effugisse
arbitrabar), et tibi horum nihil deberi potest.

Q. Ordire igitur ; nam hunc tibi totum dicamus
diem.

M. " A Iove Musarum primordia,'' sicut in Ara-
tio carmine orsi sumus.

Q. Quorsum istuc ?

M. Quia nunc item ab eodem et a ceteris dis
inmortalibus sunt nobis agendi capienda primordia.

8 *Q.* Optime vero, frater, et fieri sic decet.

IV. *M.* Videamus igitur rursus, prius quam adgre-
diamur ad leges singulas, vim naturamque legis, ne,
cum referenda sint ad eam nobis omnia, labamur
interdum errore sermonis ignoremusque vim rationis
eius, qua iura nobis definienda sint.

Q. Sane quidem hercle, et est ista recta docendi
via.

M. Hanc igitur video sapientissimorum fuisse

---

[1] *Phaedrus*, 230 B.
[2] Atticus had an estate in Epirus on the river Thyamis,
which empties into the sea opposite Corcyra. The *Amaltheum*
there was probably a temple to the nymph Amalthea (Cicero,
Ep. ad. Att. I, 13, 1 ; I, 16, 15–18).

than this one; so that I could hardly bear to try its
temperature with my foot, as Socrates did in Plato's
Phaedrus.[1]

M. You are quite right, but I suppose your beloved
Thyamis in Epirus, of which Quintus often tells me,
is fully equal to this river in loveliness.

Q. That is true; for you must not imagine that
anything is finer than our friend Atticus' Amaltheum
and the plane trees there.[2]

But, if you please, let us sit down here in the
shade and return to that point in our conversation
where we left off.

M. You do well to remind me of it, Quintus
(though I thought I had escaped), and it is clear
that I must pay you my debt in full.

Q. Begin then; for we grant you the entire day.

M. "With Jupiter the Muses commence their
song," to quote from my version of Aratus' poem.[3]

Q. What is the point of that quotation?

M. That here likewise we must commence our
discussion with Jupiter and the other immortal
gods.

Q. Well done, brother; that is indeed fitting.

IV. M. Once more, then, before we come to the
individual laws, let us look at the character and
nature of Law, for fear that, though it must be the
standard to which we refer everything, we may now
and then be led astray by an incorrect use of terms,
and forget the rational principles on which our laws
must be based.

Q. Quite so, that is the correct method of exposition.

M. Well, then, I find that it has been the opinion

[3] Aratus' *Phaenomena* (see *De Re Pub.* I, 22).

sententiam, legem neque hominum ingeniis excogitatam nec scitum aliquod esse populorum, sed aeternum quiddam, quod universum mundum regeret imperandi prohibendique sapientia. ita principem legem illam et ultimam mentem esse dicebant omnia ratione aut cogentis aut vetantis dei ; ex quo illa lex, quam di humano generi dederunt, recte est laudata ; est enim ratio mensque sapientis ad iubendum et ad deterrendum idonea.

9 *Q.* Aliquotiens iam iste locus a te tactus est ; sed ante quam ad populares leges venias, vim istius caelestis legis explana, si placet, ne aestus nos consuetudinis absorbeat et ad sermonis morem usitati trahat.

M. A parvis enim, Quinte, didicimus "si in ius vocat" atque eius modi leges alias nominare. sed vero intellegi sic oportet, et hoc et alia iussa ac vetita populorum vim habere ad recte facta vocandi et a peccatis avocandi, quae vis non modo senior est quam aetas populorum et civitatium, sed aequalis illius caelum atque terras tuentis et regentis dei.

10 neque enim esse mens divina sine ratione potest, nec ratio divina non hanc vim in rectis pravisque sanciendis habet, nec, quia nusquam erat scriptum, ut contra omnis hostium copias in ponte unus adsisteret a tergoque pontem interscindi iuberet, idcirco minus Coclitem illum rem gessisse tantam fortitudinis lege

---

[1] From the Law of the Twelve Tables (see *De Re Pub.* II, 61).

of the wisest men that Law is not a product of
human thought, nor is it any enactment of peoples,
but something eternal which rules the whole universe
by its wisdom in command and prohibition. Thus
they have been accustomed to say that Law is the
primal and ultimate mind of God, whose reason
directs all things either by compulsion or restraint.
Wherefore that Law which the gods have given to
the human race has been justly praised ; for it is the
reason and mind of a wise lawgiver applied to command and prohibition.

Q. You have touched upon this subject several
times before. But before you come to the laws of
peoples, please make the character of this heavenly
Law clear to us, so that the waves of habit may not
carry us away and sweep us into the common mode
of speech on such subjects.

M. Ever since we were children, Quintus, we
have learned to call, "If one summon another to
court," [1] and other rules of the same kind, laws.
But we must come to the true understanding of the
matter, which is as follows : this and other commands
and prohibitions of nations have the power to summon
to righteousness and away from wrong-doing ; but
this power is not merely older than the existence of
nations and States, it is coeval with that God who
guards and rules heaven and earth. For the divine mind
cannot exist without reason, and divine reason cannot
but have this power to establish right and wrong.
No written law commanded that a man should take
his stand on a bridge alone, against the full force of
the enemy, and order the bridge broken down
behind him ; yet we shall not for that reason suppose
that the heroic Cocles was not obeying the law of

atque imperio putabimus, nec, si regnante L. Tarquinio nulla erat Romae scripta lex de stupris, idcirco non contra illam legem sempiternam Sex. Tarquinius vim Lucretiae, Tricipitini filiae, attulit. erat enim ratio profecta a rerum natura et ad recte faciendum inpellens et a delicto avocans, quae non tum denique incipit lex esse, cum scripta est, sed tum, cum orta est ; orta autem est simul cum mente divina. quam ob rem lex vera atque princeps apta ad iubendum et ad vetandum ratio est recta summi Iovis.

11   V. *Q.* Adsentior, frater, ut, quod est recte verumque, aeternum quoque[1] sit neque cum litteris, quibus scita scribuntur, aut oriatur aut occidat.

M. Ergo ut illa divina mens summa lex est, item, cum in homine est perfecta[2] . . . in mente sapientis ; quae sunt autem varie et ad tempus descriptae populis, favore magis quam re legum nomen tenent. omnem enim legem, quae quidem recte lex appellari possit, esse laudabilem quibusdam talibus argumentis docent : constat profecto ad salutem civium civitatiumque incolumitatem vitamque hominum quietam et beatam inventas esse leges, eosque, qui primum eius modi scita sanxerint, populis ostendisse ea se scripturos atque laturos, quibus illi adscitis susceptis-

---

[1] *aeternum quoque* supplied by Vahlen : omitted in MSS.

[2] *perfecta* (*ratio, lex est ; ea vero est perfecta*) *in mente sapientis* suggested by Vahlen ; *perfecta in mente sapientis* ABH ; *perfecta in mente sapientis* (*est*) Rath.

---

[1] This conjectural rendering follows Vahlen's suggestion for filling in the gap.

bravery and following its decrees in doing so noble a
deed. Even if there was no written law against
rape at Rome in the reign of Lucius Tarquinius, we
cannot say on that account that Sextus Tarquinius
did not break that eternal Law by violating Lucretia,
the daughter of Tricipitinus! For reason did exist,
derived from the Nature of the universe, urging men
to right conduct and diverting them from wrong-
doing, and this reason did not first become Law
when it was written down, but when it first came
into existence ; and it came into existence simultane-
ously with the divine mind. Wherefore the true
and primal Law, applied to command and prohibition,
is the right reason of supreme Jupiter.

V. *Q.* I agree with you, brother, that what is
right and true is also eternal, and does not begin
or end with written statutes.

M. Therefore, just as that divine mind is the
supreme Law, so, when [reason] is perfected in
man, [that also is Law ; and this perfected reason
exists] in the mind of the wise man ;[1] but those
rules which, in varying forms and for the need of
the moment, have been formulated for the guidance
of nations, bear the title of laws rather by favour
than because they are really such. For every law
which really deserves that name is truly praiseworthy, as they prove by approximately the following arguments. It is agreed, of course, that laws
were invented for the safety of citizens, the preservation of States, and the tranquillity and happiness of human life, and that those who first put
statutes of this kind in force convinced their people
that it was their intention to write down and put
into effect such rules as, once accepted and adopted,

383

que honeste beateque viverent; quaeque ita conposita
sanctaque essent, eas leges videlicet nominarent.
ex quo intellegi par est eos, qui perniciosa et iniusta
populis iussa descripserint, cum contra fecerint
quam polliciti professique sint, quidvis potius tulisse
quam leges; ut perspicuum esse possit in ipso nomine
legis interpretando inesse vim et sententiam iusti et
12 veri legendi. quaero igitur a te, Quinte, sicut illi
solent : quo si civitas careat, ob eam ipsam causam,
quod eo careat, pro nihilo habenda sit, id estne
numerandum in bonis ?

Q. Ac maxumis quidem.

M. Lege autem carens civitas estne ob id[1] ipsum
habenda nullo loco ?

Q. Dici aliter non potest.

M. Necesse est igitur legem haberi in rebus
optimis.

Q. Prorsus adsentior.

13 *M.* Quid, quod multa perniciose, multa pestifere
sciscuntur in populis? quae non magis legis nomen
adtingunt, quam si latrones aliquas consessu suo
sanxerint. nam neque medicorum praecepta dici
vere possunt, si quae inscii inperitique pro salutaribus
mortifera conscripserunt, neque in populo lex, cui-
cuimodi fuerit illa, etiamsi perniciosum aliquid
populus acceperit. ergo est lex iustorum iniusto-
rumque distinctio ad illam antiquissimam et rerum
omnium principem expressa naturam, ad quam leges

---

[1] *id* supplied by Lambinus; omitted in MSS.

---

[1] Cicero derives *lex,* "law," from *legere,* "to choose."
Compare I, 19.
[2] In these words Cicero introduces a bit of genuine
dialectic. Compare *De Re Pub.* I, 59-61.

would make possible for them an honourable and
happy life; and when such rules were drawn up
and put in force, it is clear that men called them
"laws." From this point of view it can be readily
understood that those who formulated wicked and
unjust statutes for nations, thereby breaking their
promises and agreements, put into effect anything
but "laws." It may thus be clear that in the very
definition of the term "law" there inheres the idea
and principle of choosing what is just and true.[1] I
ask you then, Quintus, according to the custom of
the philosophers:[2] if there is a certain thing, the
lack of which in a State compels us to consider it
no State at all, must we consider this thing a good?

Q. One of the greatest goods, certainly.

M. And if a State lacks Law, must it for that
reason be considered no State at all?

Q. It cannot be denied.

M. Then Law must necessarily be considered one
of the greatest goods.

Q. I agree with you entirely.

M. What of the many deadly, the many pestilential
statutes which nations put in force? These no more
deserve to be called laws than the rules a band of
robbers might pass in their assembly. For if ignorant
and unskilful men have prescribed deadly poisons
instead of healing drugs, these cannot possibly be
called physicians' prescriptions; neither in a nation
can a statute of any sort be called a law, even
though the nation, in spite of its being a ruinous
regulation, has accepted it. Therefore Law is the
distinction between things just and unjust, made in
agreement with that primal and most ancient of all
things, Nature; and in conformity to Nature's

hominum diriguntur, quae supplicio inprobos adficiunt, defendunt ac tuentur bonos.

VI. *Q.* Praeclare intellego nec vero iam aliam esse ullam legem puto non modo habendam, sed ne appellandam quidem.

14 *M.* Igitur tu Titias et Apuleias leges nullas putas?

Q. Ego vero ne Livias quidem.

M. Et recte, quae praesertim uno versiculo senatus puncto temporis sublatae sint; lex autem illa, cuius vim explicavi, neque tolli neque abrogari potest.

Q. Eas tu igitur leges rogabis videlicet, quae numquam abrogentur?

M. Certe, si modo acceptae a duobus vobis erunt. sed, ut vir doctissimus fecit Plato atque idem gravissimus philosophorum omnium, qui princeps de re publica conscripsit idemque separatim de legibus eius, id mihi credo esse faciundum, ut, prius quam ipsam legem recitem, de eius legis laude dicam. quod idem et Zaleucum et Charondam fecisse video, cum quidem illi non studii et delectationis, sed rei publicae causa leges civitatibus suis scripserunt. quos imitatus Plato videlicet hoc quoque legis putavit esse, persuadere aliquid, non omnia vi ac minis cogere.

15 *Q.* Quid, quod Zaleucum istum negat ullum fuisse Timaeus?

---

[1] These were agrarian and grain laws, proposed (1) by the tribune Sextus Titius in 99 B.C., (2) by the tribune Lucius Apuleius Saturninus in 100 B.C., and (3) by the tribune Marcus Livius Drusus in 91 B.C.

[2] See Diodor. Sicul. XII, 19, 3–21, 3.

[3] See Diodor. Sicul. XII, 11, 3–19, 2.

standard are framed those human laws which inflict punishment upon the wicked but defend and protect the good.

VI. *Q.* I understand you completely, and believe that from now on we must not consider or even call anything else a law.

M. Then you do not think the Titian or Apuleian Laws were really laws at all?

Q. No; nor the Livian Laws either.[1]

M. And you are right, especially as the Senate repealed them in one sentence and in a single moment. But the Law whose nature I have explained can neither be repealed nor abrogated.

Q. Then the laws you intend to propose will, of course, be the kind that will never be repealed?

M. Certainly, if only they are accepted by both of you. But I think that I should follow the same course as Plato, who was at the same time a very learned man and the greatest of all philosophers, and who wrote a book about the Republic first, and then in a separate treatise described its Laws. Therefore, before I recite the law itself, I will speak in praise of that law. I note that Zaleucus[2] and Charondas[3] did the same thing, though they wrote their laws, not for the interest and pleasure of doing so, but for actual use in their own States. Clearly Plato[4] agreed with their opinion that it was also the function of Law to win some measure of approval, and not always compel by threats of force.

Q. What do you think of Timaeus' denial of Zaleucus' existence?

---

[4] The doctrine that the power of persuasion is to be added to that of compulsion is discussed by Plato in *Laws* IV, 718 B–723 D.

M. At ait[1] Theophrastus, auctor haud deterior mea quidem sententia (meliorem multi nominant); commemorant vero ipsius cives, nostri clientes, Locri. sed sive fuit sive non fuit, nihil ad rem; loquimur quod traditum est.

VII. Sit igitur hoc iam a principio persuasum civibus, dominos esse omnium rerum ac moderatores deos, eaque, quae gerantur, eorum geri iudicio ac numine, eosdemque optime de genere hominum mereri et, qualis quisque sit, quid agat, quid in se admittat, qua mente, qua pietate colat religiones, intueri piorumque et impiorum habere rationem; 16 his enim rebus inbutae mentes haud sane abhorrebunt ab utili aut a vera sententia. quid est enim verius quam neminem esse oportere tam stulte adrogantem, ut in se rationem et mentem putet inesse, in caelo mundoque non putet, aut ut ea, quae vix summa ingenii ratione comprehendantur, nulla[2] ratione moveri putet? quem vero astrorum ordines, quem dierum noctiumque vicissitudines, quem mensum temperatio quemque ea, quae gignuntur nobis ad fruendum, non gratum esse cogunt, hunc hominem omnino numerari qui decet? cumque omnia, quae rationem habent, praestent iis, quae sint rationis expertia, nefasque sit dicere ullam rem praestare naturae omnium rerum, rationem inesse in ea confi-

---

[1] *ait* supplied by Mueller; omitted in MSS.

[2] *ratione comprehendantur, nulla* supplied by Vahlen; omitted in MSS.; *ratione comprehendat, nulla* Victorius.

---

[1] Cicero was their official representative at Rome (Cicero, *Pro Plancio* 97).

M. Well, Theophrastus affirms it, and he is just as trustworthy an authority, in my opinion (indeed, many rate him higher); and, in fact, my protégés,[1] the Locrians, his own fellow-citizens, still tell of Zaleucus. But whether he ever existed or not has nothing to do with the case; my statement merely follows the tradition.

VII. So in the very beginning we must persuade our citizens that the gods are the lords and rulers of all things, and that what is done, is done by their will and authority; that they are likewise great benefactors of man, observing the character of every individual, what he does, of what wrong he is guilty, and with what intentions and with what piety he fulfils his religious duties; and that they take note of the pious and the impious. For surely minds which are imbued with such ideas will not fail to form true and useful opinions. Indeed, what is more true than that no one ought to be so foolishly proud as to think that, though reason and intellect exist in himself, they do not exist in the heavens and the universe, or that those things which can hardly be understood by the highest reasoning powers of the human intellect are guided by no reason at all? In truth, the man that is not driven to gratitude by the orderly courses of the stars, the regular alternation of day and night, the gentle progress of the seasons, and the produce of the earth brought forth for our sustenance—how can such an one be accounted a man at all? And since all things that possess reason stand above those things which are without reason, and since it would be sacrilege to say that anything stands above universal Nature, we must admit that reason is inherent in Nature.

389

tendum est. utilis esse autem has opiniones quis
neget, cum intellegat quam multa firmentur iure
iurando, quantae saluti sint foederum religiones,
quam multos divini supplici metus a scelere revocarit,
quamque sancta sit societas civium inter ipsos diis inmortalibus interpositis tum iudicibus, tum[1] testibus?

Habes legis prooemium; sic enim haec appellat
Plato.

17   Q. Habeo vero, frater, et in hoc admodum delector,
quod in aliis rebus aliisque sententiis versaris atque
ille. nihil enim tam dissimile quam vel ea, quae
ante dixisti, vel hoc ipsum de deis exordium; unum
illud mihi videris imitari, orationis genus.

M. Velle fortasse; quis enim id potest aut umquam
poterit imitari? nam sententias interpretari per-
facile est; quod quidem ego facerem, nisi plane
esse vellem meus. quid enim negotii est eadem
prope verbis isdem conversa dicere?

Q. Prorsus adsentior; verum, ut modo tute dixisti,
te esse malo tuum. sed iam exprome, si placet, istas
leges de religione.

18   M. Expromam equidem, ut potero, et, quoniam
et locus et sermo familiaris est, legum leges voce
proponam.

Q. Quidnam id est?

M. Sunt certa legum verba, Quinte, neque ita
prisca, ut in veteribus duodecim sacratisque legibus,
et tamen, quo plus auctoritatis habeant, paulo anti-

---

[1] *tum* supplied in editions; omitted in MSS.

---

[1] Plato, *Laws* IV, 722 D.
[2] The *Sacratae Leges* were thought to have originated in
the earliest days of the Republic; they gave inviolability to
the plebeian tribunes.

Who will deny that such beliefs are useful when he remembers how often oaths are used to confirm agreements, how important to our well-being is the sanctity of treaties, how many persons are deterred from crime by the fear of divine punishment, and how sacred an association of citizens becomes when the immortal gods are made members of it, either as judges or as witnesses?

There you have the proem to the law; for that is the name given to it by Plato.[1]

Q. There it is indeed, brother, and I am particularly pleased that you have taken up different subjects and presented different ideas from his. For nothing could be more unlike his treatment than your previous remarks, and also this preface in regard to the gods. In just one thing you do seem to me to imitate him—in the style of your language.

M. Wish to do so, possibly; for who can or ever will be able to imitate him in this? It is very easy to translate another man's ideas, and I might do that, if I did not fully wish to be myself. For what difficulty is there in presenting the same thoughts rendered in practically the same phrases?

Q. I agree with you entirely. I certainly prefer that you be independent, as you have just said. But, if you please, let us hear your laws concerning religion.

M. I will present them as well as I can, and, since the place and the conversation are private, I will recite my laws in the legal style.

Q. What do you mean by that?

M. There is a certain legal language, Quintus, not so antiquated as that of our ancient Twelve Tables and Sacred Laws,[2] and yet, to give greater authority, a little more archaic than the language

quiora quam hic sermo est. eum morem igitur cum brevitate, si potuero, consequar. leges autem a me edentur non perfectae (nam esset infinitum), sed ipsae summae rerum atque sententiae.

Q. Ita vero necesse est ; quare audiamus.

19 VIII. *M. Ad divos adeunto caste, pietatem adhibento, opes amovento. qui secus faxit, deus ipse vindex erit.*

Separatim nemo habessit deos neve novos neve advenas nisi publice adscitos ; privatim colunto, quos rite a patribus cultos acceperint.[1]

In urbibus[2] *delubra habento ; lucos in agris habento et Larum sedes.*

Ritus familiae patrumque servanto.

Divos et eos, qui caelestes semper habiti, colunto et ollos, quos endo caelo merita locaverint, Herculem, Liberum, Aesculapium, Castorem, Pollucem, Quirinum, ast olla, propter quae datur homini ascensus in caelum, Mentem, Virtutem, Pietatem, Fidem, earumque laudum delubra sunto, ne uncula vitiorum.

Sacra sollemnia obeunto.

Feriis iurgia amovento easque in famulis operibus patratis habento, idque[3] *ut ita cadat in annuis anfractibus descriptum esto. certasque fruges certasque bacas sacerdotes publice libanto ; hoc certis sacrificiis ac die-*

[1] *cultos acceperint* supplied by Madvig ; omitted in MSS.
[2] *In urbibus* supplied (from § 26) by Stephanus ; omitted in MSS.
[3] *idque* Halm ; *itaque* AB²H ; *itque* B¹.

---

[1] After reciting his laws, Cicero proceeds to explain them. His commentary begins in section 24.

of the present day. That style, together with its brevity, I will follow as far as I can. But I shall not present my laws in complete form, for that would be an infinite task, but shall give only the gist and substance of their provisions.

Q. That is the only possible way: therefore let us hear them.

VIII. M.[1] *They shall approach the gods in purity, bringing piety, and leaving riches behind. Whoever shall do otherwise, God Himself will deal out punishment to him.*

No one shall have gods to himself, either new gods or alien gods, unless recognized by the State. Privately they shall worship those gods whose worship they have duly received from their ancestors.

In cities they shall have shrines; they shall have groves in the country and homes for the Lares.

They shall preserve the rites of their families and their ancestors.

They shall worship as gods both those who have always been regarded as dwellers in heaven, and also those whose merits have admitted them to heaven; Hercules, Liber, Aesculapius, Castor, Pollux, Quirinus; also those qualities through which an ascent to heaven is granted to mankind: Intellect, Virtue, Piety, Good Faith. To their praise there shall be shrines, but none for the vices.

They shall perform the established rites.

On holidays they shall refrain from law-suits; these they shall celebrate together with their slaves after their tasks are done. Let holidays be so arranged as to fall at regularly recurring breaks in the year. The priest shall offer on behalf of the State the prescribed grains and the prescribed fruits; this shall be done according to prescribed rites and on prescribed days;

20 *bus ; itemque alios ad dies ubertatem lactis feturaeque*
servanto ; idque ne committi possit, ad eam rem, rationem
cursus annuos sacerdotes finiunto ; quaeque quoique divo
decorae grataeque sint hostiae providento.

Divisque aliis alii[1] sacerdotes, omnibus pontifices,
singulis flamines sunto. virginesque Vestales in urbe
custodiunto ignem foci publici sempiternum.

Quoque haec privatim et publice modo rituque fiant,
discunto ignari a publicis sacerdotibus. eorum autem
genera sunto tria, unum, quod praesit caerimoniis et
sacris, alterum, quod interpretetur fatidicorum et vatium
ecfata incognita, quorum senatus populusque asciverit ;
interpretes autem Iovis optumi maxumi, publici augures,
21 *signis et auspiciis postera[2] vidento, disciplinam tenento ;*
sacerdotesque vineta virgetaque et salutem populi augu-
ranto, quique agent rem duelli quique popularem, au-
spicium praemonento ollique obtemperanto, divorumque
iras providento iisque[3] apparento caelique fulgora
regionibus ratis temperanto, urbemque et agros et templa
liberata et effata habento. quaeque augur iniusta nefasta,
vitiosa dira defixerit, inrita infectaque sunto ; quique non
paruerit, capital esto.

IX. *Foederum pacis belli indotiarum oratorum*
fetiales iudices nontii sunto ;[4] bella disceptanto.[5]

---

[1] *alii* supplied in Ed. Ascensiana ; omitted in MSS.
[2] *postera* Lambinus or Manutius ; *postea* ABH.
[3] *iisque* AB[2] ; *sisque* B[1]H.
[4] *iudices nontii sunto* Vahlen ; *iudices non sunto* ABH ; *ius noscunto* Madvig.
[5] *disceptanto* Ed. Ascensiana ; *disceptatis* ABH.

---

[1] Milk, wine, and honey were offered to Ceres and other
divinities (Vergil, *Georgics* I, 344). For the "offspring,"
compare § 29.
[2] The Etruscans divided the sky into sixteen regions for
this purpose (Cicero, *De Divin.* II, 42).

likewise for other days they shall reserve the plenteous offerings of the milk and the offspring.[1] *And so that no violation of these customs shall take place, the priests shall determine the mode and the annual circuit of such offerings ; and they shall prescribe the victims which are proper and pleasing to each of the gods.*

The several gods shall have their several priests, the gods all together their pontiffs, and the individual gods their flamens. The Vestal Virgins shall guard the eternal fire on the public hearth of the city.

Those who are ignorant as to the methods and rites suitable to these public and private sacrifices shall seek instruction from the public priests. Of them there shall be three kinds : one to have charge of ceremonies and sacred rites ; another to interpret those obscure sayings of soothsayers and prophets which shall be recognized by the Senate and the people ; and the interpreters of Jupiter the Best and Greatest, namely the public augurs, shall foretell the future from portents and auspices. and maintain their art. And the priests shall observe the omens in regard to vineyards and orchards and the safety of the people ; those who carry on war or affairs of State shall be informed by them beforehand of the auspices and shall obey them ; the priests shall foresee the wrath of the gods and yield to it ; they shall observe flashes of lightning in fixed regions of the sky,[2] *and shall keep free and unobstructed the city and fields and their places of observation. Whatever an augur shall declare to be unjust, unholy, pernicious, or ill-omened, shall be null and void ; and whosoever yields not obedience shall be put to death.*

IX. The fetial priests shall be judges and messengers for treaties, peace and war, truces, and embassies ; they shall make the decisions in regard to war.

MARCUS TULLIUS CICERO

Prodigia portenta ad Etruscos aruspices,[1] *si senatus iussit, deferunto, Etruriaque principis disciplinam doceto. quibus divis creverint, procuranto, idemque fulgora atque obstita pianto.*

Nocturna mulierum sacrificia ne sunto praeter olla, quae pro populo rite fient ; neve quem initianto nisi, ut adsolet, Cereri Graeco sacro.

22 *Sacrum commissum, quod neque expiari poterit, impie commissum esto ; quod expiari poterit, publici sacerdotes expianto.*

Loedis publicis quod sine curriculo et sine certatione corporum fiat, popularem laetitiam in cantu et fidibus et tibiis moderanto eamque cum divum honore iungunto.

Ex patriis ritibus optuma colunto.

Praeter Idaeae matris famulos, eosque iustis diebus, ne quis stipem cogito.

Sacrum sacrove commendatum qui clepsit rapsitve parricida esto.

Periurii poena divina exitium, humana dedecus.

Incestum pontifices supremo supplicio sanciunto.

Impius ne audeto placare donis iram deorum.

Caute vota reddunto ; poena violati iuris esto.

---

[1] *Etruscos aruspices* Turnebus : *Etruscos et aruspices* ABH.

---

[1] The solemn rites of Bona Dea, from which men were strictly excluded.

[2] Evidently the Eleusinian mysteries as practised at Rome. Compare § 35

[3] *i.e.* athletic games.

[4] *i.e.* Cybele, whose worship had been introduced into Rome in 204 B.C. The *Ludi Megalenses* were celebrated in her

Prodigies and portents shall be referred to the Etruscan soothsayers, if the Senate so decree ; Etruria shall instruct her leading men in this art. They shall make expiatory offerings to whatever gods they decide upon, and shall perform expiations for flashes of lightning and for whatever shall be struck by lightning.

No sacrifices shall be performed by women at night except those offered for the people in proper form ; [1] *nor shall anyone be initiated except into the Greek rites of Ceres,* [2] *according to the custom.*

Sacrilege which cannot be expiated shall be held to be impiously committed ; that which can be expiated shall be atoned for by the public priests.

At the public games which are held without chariot races or the contest of body with body, [3] *the public pleasure shall be provided for with moderation by song to the music of harp and flute, and this shall be combined with honour to the gods.*

Of the ancestral rites the best shall be preserved.

No one shall ask for contributions except the servants of the Idean Mother, [4] *and they only on the appointed days.*

Whoever steals or carries off what is sacred or anything entrusted to what is sacred shall be considered as equal in guilt to a parricide.

For the perjurer the punishment from the gods is destruction ; the human punishment shall be disgrace.

The pontiffs shall inflict capital punishment on those guilty of incest.

No wicked man shall dare to appease the wrath of the gods with gifts.

Vows shall be scrupulously performed ; there shall be a penalty for the violation of the law.

honour, but Roman citizens were not allowed to enter her priesthood ; note the word *famuli*, "house-slaves."

Ne quis[1] *agrum consecrato. auri, argenti, eboris sacrandi modus esto.*

Sacra privata perpetua manento.

Deorum Manium iura sancta sunto. suos[2] *leto datos divos habento ; sumptum in ollos luctumque minuunto.*

23　X. *Q.* Conclusa quidem est a te, frater,[3] magna lex sane quam brevi ; sed, ut mihi quidem videtur, non multum discrepat ista constitutio religionum a legibus Numae nostrisque moribus.

M. An censes, cum in illis de re publica libris persuadere videatur Africanus omnium rerum publicarum nostram veterem illam fuisse optumam, non necesse esse optumae rei publicae leges dare consentaneas ?

Q. Immo prorsus ita censeo.

M. Ergo adeo expectate leges, quae genus illud optumum rei publicae contineant, et, si quae forte a me hodie rogabuntur, quae non sint in nostra re publica nec fuerint, tamen erunt fere in more maiorum, qui tum ut lex valebat.

24　*A.* Suade igitur, si placet, istam ipsam legem, ut ego " utei tu rogas "[4] possim dicere.

M. Ain tandem, Attice ?　non es dicturus aliter ?

A. Prorsus maiorem quidem rem nullam sciscam aliter, in minoribus, si voles, remittam hoc tibi.

---

[1] *esto. Ne quis* Stephanus ; *esto quocirca ne quis* ABH.

[2] *suos* Davies (cf. § 55) ; *nos* ABH, Vahlen ; *bonos* Urlichs (cf. § 27).　Cf. also St. Augustine, *De Civ. Dei VIII,* 26.

[3] *est a te, frater, magna* Vahlen ; *est alter magna* A¹B¹H¹ ; *est p alte magna* A² ; *est pte alter magna* B² ; *est altera magna* H² ; *est a te permagna* Mueller.

[4] *utei tu rogas* Davies ; *ut et tu rogas* ABH ; *uti rogas* Turnebus.

---

[1] This rendering depends upon a conjectural emendation ; see critical note. The reference is to the *Dii Manes.*

No one shall consecrate a field ; the consecration of gold, silver, and ivory shall be confined to reasonable limits.

The sacred rites of families shall remain for ever.

The rights of the gods of the lower world shall be sacred. Kinsfolk[1] *who are dead shall be considered gods ; the expenditure and mourning for them shall be limited.*

X. Q. My dear brother, how quickly you have completed this important body of law ! However, it seems to me that this religious system of yours does not differ a great deal from the laws of Numa and our own customs.

M. Do you not think, then, since Scipio in my former work on the Republic offered a convincing proof that our early State was the best in the world, that we must provide that ideal State with laws which are in harmony with its character ?

Q. Certainly I think so.

M. Then you must expect such laws as will establish that best type of State. And if I chance to propose any provisions to-day which do not exist now and never have existed in our State, they will nevertheless be found for the most part among the customs of our ancestors, which used to have the binding force of law.

A. Then present the arguments in favour of this law of yours, so that I may have the opportunity of saying, " As you propose."

M. Do you mean that, Atticus ? You will not dissent ?

A. There are certainly no matters of importance in regard to which I shall disagree ; on minor points I will yield to your judgment, if you like.

399

Q. Atque mea quidem eadem[1] sententia est.

M. At, ne longum fiat, videte.

A. Utinam quidem! quid enim agere malumus?

M. Caste iubet lex *adire ad deos,* animo videlicet, in quo sunt omnia; nec tollit castimoniam
corporis, sed hoc oportet intellegi, cum multum
animus corpori praestet observeturque, ut casta corpora adhibeantur, multo esse in animis id servan-
dum magis. nam illud vel aspersione aquae vel
dierum numero tollitur; animi labes nec diuturnitate
evanescere nec amnibus ullis elui potest.

25　Quod autem *pietatem adhiberi, opes amoveri* iubet,
significat probitatem gratam esse deo, sumptum esse
removendum. quid enim? paupertatem cum divitiis
etiam inter homines esse aequalem velimus, cur eam
sumptu ad sacra addito deorum aditu arceamus,
praesertim cum ipsi deo nihil minus gratum futurum
sit quam non omnibus patere ad se placandum et
colendum viam?

Quod autem non iudex, sed *deus ipse vindex* constituitur, praesentis poenae metu religio confirmari
videtur.

Suosque deos aut novos aut alienigenas coli con-
fusionem habet religionum et ignotas caerimonias
26　nostris[2] sacerdotibus. nam *a*[3] *patribus acceptos*

---

[1] *eadem* supplied by Madvig; omitted in MSS.
[2] *nostris* Davies; *nos* ABH.
[3] *a* supplied by Aldus; omitted in MSS.

Q. That is my view, also.

M. But I warn you that my arguments may be lengthy.

A. Indeed, I hope they will be! For what better can we find to do?

M. The law commands us to *approach the gods in purity*—that is, purity of mind, for everything is included in that. This does not remove the requirement of bodily purity; but it ought to be understood that, since the mind is much superior to the body, and the requirement of bodily purity is observed, we ought to be much more careful about the mind. For in the former case impurity is removed by the sprinkling of water or the passage of a certain number of days, but a mental stain can neither be blotted out by the passage of time nor washed away by any stream.

The rule that *piety shall be brought, but riches left behind*, means that uprightness is pleasing to God, but that great expenditure is to be avoided. For indeed, since we desire that poverty shall be equal to riches even among men, why should we exclude it from the presence of the gods by adding costliness to our rites, especially since nothing would be less pleasing to God himself than that the pathway to his favour and to his worship should not be open to all alike?

The provision that no human judge, but *God Himself, is to punish the disobedient* would seem to strengthen the power of religion through the fear of immediate punishment.

The worship of *private gods, whether new or alien*, brings confusion into religion and introduces ceremonies unknown to our priests. For *the gods handed*

deos ita placet *coli,* si huic legi paruerint ipsi patres.

Delubra esse in urbibus censeo, nec sequor magos Persarum, quibus auctoribus Xerxes inflammasse templa Graeciae dicitur, quod parietibus includerent deos, quibus omnia deberent esse patentia ac libera, quorumque hic mundus omnis templum esset et domus.   XI. melius Graii atque nostri, qui ut augerent pietatem in deos, easdem illos urbis quas nos incolere voluerunt; adfert enim haec opinio religionem utilem civitatibus, siquidem et illud bene dictum est a Pythagora, doctissimo viro, tum maxume et pietatem et religionem versari in animis, cum rebus divinis operam daremus, et quod Thales, qui sapientissimus in septem fuit, homines existimare oportere omnia, quae [1] cernerent, deorum esse plena ; fore enim omnis castiores, veluti cum in fanis essent, maxime religiosos.[2]   est enim quaedam opinione species deorum in oculis, non solum in mentibus.

27 eandemque rationem *luci* habent *in agris.*   neque ea, quae a maioribus prodita est cum dominis, tum famulis posita in fundi villaeque conspectu, religio *Larum,* repudianda est.

Iam *ritus familiae patrumque servare* id est, quoniam antiquitas proxume accedit ad deos, a dis quasi traditam religionem tueri.

---

[1] *quae* supplied in an old edition ; omitted in MSS.
[2] *religiosos* A[1]H ; *religiosus* A[2]B ; *religiosis* Lambinus.

---

[1] Compare Herodotus, I, 131 ; VIII, 109 ; Cicero, *De Nat. Deor.* I, 115 ; *De Re Pub.* III, 14.

[2] βέλτιστοι γιγνόμεθα πρὸς τοὺς θεοὺς βαδίζοντες, Plutarch, *De Superstitione* 9, 169 E.

[3] Θαλῆς ῷήθη πάντα πλήρη θεῶν εἶναι, Aristotle, *De Anima* I, 411 A ; compare Diogenes Laertius, I, 1, 27.

[4] Compare Cicero, *De Nat. Deor.* II, 62.

down to us by our fathers should be worshipped only in case our fathers themselves obeyed this law.

I propose that that *there shall be shrines in cities,* on this point not following the Persian Magi, in accordance with whose advice Xerxes is said to have burned the temples of Greece [1] on the ground that the Greeks shut up the gods within walls, whereas all places consecrated to them ought to be open and free, seeing that this whole universe is their temple and home. XI. The Greeks and Romans have done a better thing : for it has been our wish, to the end that we may promote piety toward the gods, that they should dwell in our cities with us. For this idea encourages a religious attitude that is useful to States, if there is truth in the saying of Pythagoras,[2] a most learned man, that piety and religious feeling are most prominent in our minds while we are performing religious rites, and in the saying of Thales,[3] the wisest of the Seven, that men ought to believe that everything they see is filled with the gods, for all would then be purer, just as they feel the power of religion most deeply when they are in temples. For it is believed that perception of the gods is possible to our eyes as well as to our minds. *The groves in the country* have the same purpose. Nor is the worship of the *Lares,*[4] handed down by our ancestors, established in sight of farm and homestead, and shared by slaves as well as masters, to be rejected.

Next, *the preservation of the rites of the family and of our ancestors* means preserving the religious rites which, we can almost say, were handed down to us by the gods themselves, since ancient times were closest to the gods.

MARCUS TULLIUS CICERO

Quod autem *ex hominum genere consecratos, sicut Herculem et ceteros, coli* lex iubet, indicat omnium quidem animos inmortalis esse, sed fortium bonorum-
28 que divinos. bene vero, quod *Mens, Pietas, Virtus, Fides* consecratur manu; quarum omnium Romae dedicata publice templa sunt, ut, illa qui habeant (habent autem omnes boni), deos ipsos in animis suis conlocatos putent. nam illud vitiosum, Athenis quod Cylonio scelere expiato Epimenide Crete suadente fecerunt Contumeliae fanum et Inpudentiae; virtutes enim, *non vitia* consecrare decet. araque vetusta in Palatio Febris et altera Esquiliis Malae Fortunae detestataque omnia eius modi repudianda sunt. quodsi fingenda nomina, Vicae Potae potius vicendi atque potiundi, Statae standi cognominaque Statoris et Invicti Iovis rerumque expetendarum nomina, Salutis, Honoris, Opis, Victoriae. quoniamque expectatione rerum bonarum erigitur animus, recte etiam Spes a Calatino consecrata est. Fortunaque sit vel Huiusce Diei (nam valet in omnes dies) vel Respiciens ad opem ferendam vel Fors, in quo incerti casus significantur magis, vel Primigenia, a gignendo comes.

---

[1] For the "crime of Cylon," see Thucyd. I, 126. For Epimenides' purification, see Diogenes Laertius, I, 10, 110; Plutarch, *Solon* 12; Aristotle, *Const. of Athens* 1.

[2] Φησὶ Θεόφραστος ἐν τῷ περὶ νόμων Ὕβρεως καὶ Ἀναιδείας παρὰ τοῖς Ἀθηναίοις εἶναι βωμούς, Zenobius, IV, 36 (Paroemiographi Graeci).

[3] Aulus Atilius Calatinus consecrated a temple to Hope (*Spes*) during the First Punic War (Tacitus, *Annales* II, 49)

[4] With this section compare Cicero, *De Nat. Deor.* II, 61.

Now the law which prescribes *the worship of those of the human race who have been deified, such as Hercules and the rest,* makes it clear that while the souls of all men are immortal, those of good and brave men are divine. It is a good thing also that *Intellect, Piety, Virtue, and Good Faith should be arbitrarily deified ;* and in Rome temples have been dedicated by the State to all these qualities, the purpose being that those who possess them (and all good men do) should believe that the gods themselves are established within their own souls. For that was a bad thing which was done at Athens on the advice of Epimenides[1] the Cretan, when, after the crime of Cylon had been expiated, they established a temple to Disgrace and Insolence ;[2] for it is proper to deify the virtues *but not the vices.* The ancient altar to Fever on the Palatine and the one to Bad Fortune on the Esquiline as well as all other abominations of that character must be done away with. But if we must invent names for gods, we ought rather to choose such titles as Vica Pota, derived from Victory and Power, and Stata, from the idea of standing firm, and such epithets as those of the Strengthener and the Invincible, which are given to Jupiter ; also the names of things which we should desire, such as Safety, Honour, Wealth, and Victory. And since the mind is encouraged by the anticipation of good things, Calatinus[3] was right in deifying Hope also. We may also have as gods Fortune, or the Fortune of This Day, for that applies to every day, or Fortune the Provident, that she may help us, or Chance Fortune, which refers particularly to the uncertainty of future events, or First-born Fortune, our companion from birth.[4]

29 XII. Tum *feriarum* festorumque dierum ratio in liberis *requietem litium habet et iurgiorum, in servis operum et laborum;* quas compositor[1] anni conferre debet ad perfectionem operum rusticorum. quod ad[2] tempus, ut sacrificiorum *libamenta* serventur *fetusque pecorum*, quae dicta in lege sunt, diligenter habenda ratio intercalandi est ; quod institutum perite a Numa posteriorum pontificum neglegentia dissolutum est. iam illud ex institutis pontificum et aruspicum non mutandum est, *quibus hostiis* immolandum *cuique deo*, cui maioribus, cui lactentibus, cui maribus, cui feminis. *plures autem deorum omnium, singuli singulorum sacerdotes* et respondendi iuris et confitendarum[3] religionum facultatem adferunt. cumque Vesta quasi focum urbis, ut Graeco nomine est appellata, quod nos prope idem Graecum, non[4] interpretatum nomen tenemus, conplexa sit, ei colendae *virgines* praesint, ut advigiletur facilius ad *custodiam ignis* et sentiant mulieres in illis[5] naturam feminarum omnem castitatem pati.

30 Quod sequitur vero, non solum ad religionem pertinet, sed etiam ad civitatis statum, ut sine eis, *qui sacris publice praesint,* religioni privatae satis facere non possint ; continet enim rem publicam

---

[1] *compositor* dett. ; *conpositior* A ; *compositior* B ; *compositio* H.
[2] *ad* supplied by R. Klotz ; omitted in MSS.
[3] *confitendarum* ABH ; *confiriendarum* dett.
[4] *non* dett. ; omitted in ABH.
[5] *illis* supplied by Vahlen ; omitted in MSS.

---

[1] Compare Livy I, 19, where Numa is also given credit for dividing the year into twelve months.
[2] *i.e.* Vesta = Ἑστία. Compare Cicero, *De Nat. Deor.* II, 67. The two names have a common root, but *Vesta* is probably not borrowed from the Greek.

XII. Next, our provision for *holidays* and festivals ordains *rest from lawsuits and controversies for free men, and from labour and toil for slaves.* Whoever plans the official year ought to arrange that these festivals shall come at the completion of the various labours of the farm. So far as the dates are concerned, in order that *the offerings of firstfruits and offspring of the flocks,* which are mentioned in the law, may be maintained, care must be taken in arranging for the insertion of intercalary months, a custom which was wisely instituted by Numa,[1] but has now become obsolete through the neglect of the pontiffs of later periods. Now, no change should be made in the prescriptions of the pontiffs and soothsayers as to *the offerings appropriate for each of the gods,* as to which should receive full-grown victims, which sucklings, which males, and which females. The custom of having *a number of priests for the worship of all the gods, and also one particular priest for every god,* is conducive both to the interpretation of the law and the confession of offences against religion. And since Vesta, who gets her name from the Greek [2] (for we preserve the Greek word almost exactly, instead of translating it), has taken the city hearth under her protection, *virgins should have charge of her worship, so that the care and guardianship of the fire* may be more easily maintained, and other women may perceive by their example that their sex is capable by nature of complete chastity.

The provision which follows really has to do with the condition of the State as well as with religion, its object being that private worship may not be satisfactorily performed without the assistance of *those in charge of the public rites;* for the people's

consilio et auctoritate optimatium semper populum
indigere.

Descriptioque sacerdotum nullum iustae religionis
genus praetermittit. nam sunt ad placandos deos
alii constituti, qui *sacris praesint sollemnibus,* ad
interpretanda, alii *praedicta vatium* neque multorum,
ne esset infinitum, neque ut ea ipsa, quae *suscepta
publice* essent, quisquam extra conlegium nosset.

31 maximum autem et praestantissimum in re publica
ius est *augurum* cum auctoritate coniunctum. neque vero hoc, quia sum ipse augur, ita sentio, sed
quia sic existimare nos est necesse. quid enim
maius est, si de iure quaerimus, quam posse a
summis imperiis et summis potestatibus comitiatus
et concilia vel instituta dimittere vel habita rescin-
dere? quid gravius quam rem susceptam dirimi,
si unus augur "alio die"[1] dixerit? quid magni-
ficentius quam posse decernere, ut magistratu se
abdicent consules? quid religiosius quam cum
populo, cum plebe agendi ius aut dare aut non
dare? quid leges non iure rogatas tollere, ut
Titiam decreto conlegii, ut Livias consilio Philippi
consulis et auguris? nihil domi, nihil militiae per
magistratus gestum sine eorum auctoritate posse
cuiquam probari?

32 XIII. *A.* Age, iam ista video fateorque esse

---

[1] *die* supplied by Turnebus; omitted in MSS.

[1] Compare Book III, 9.
[2] Compare § 14.

constant need for the advice and authority of the aristocracy helps to hold the State together.

My provisions for priests omit no legitimate type of worship. For some are appointed to win the favour of the gods *by presiding over the regular sacrifices ;* others to *interpret prophecies of the soothsayers*—though not of too many of them, for that would be an endless task—and in such a way that no one outside the college of priests shall have knowledge even of those prophecies *which are recognized by the State.* But the highest and most important authority in the State is that of the *augurs,* to whom is accorded great influence. But it is not because I myself am an augur that I have this opinion, but because the facts compel us to think so. For if we consider their legal rights, what power is greater than that of adjourning assemblies and meetings convened by the highest officials, with or without *imperium,*[1] or that of declaring null and void the acts of assemblies presided over by such officials? What is of graver import than the abandonment of any business already begun, if a single augur says, "On another day"? What power is more impressive than that of forcing the consuls to resign their offices? What right is more sacred than that of giving or refusing permission to hold an assembly of the people or of the plebeians, or that of abrogating laws illegally passed? Thus the Titian Law was annulled by a decree of the college of augurs, and the Livian Laws by the wise direction of Philippus, a consul and augur.[2] Indeed, no act of any magistrate at home or in the field can have any validity for any person without their authority.

XIII. *A.* One moment, please; I am already

magna; sed est in conlegio vestro inter Marcellum
et Appium, optimos augures, magna dissensio (nam
eorum ego in libros incidi), cum alteri placeat
auspicia ista ad utilitatem esse rèi publicae composita, alteri disciplina vestra quasi divinare[1] videatur posse. hac tu de re quaero quid sentias.

M. Egone? divinationem, quam Graeci μαντικήν
appellant, esse sentio, et huius hanc ipsam partem,
quae est in avibus ceterisque signis, quod disciplinae
nostrae. si enim deos esse concedimus, eorumque
mente mundum regi, et eosdem hominum consulere
generi et posse nobis signa rerum futurarum osten-
33 dere, non video cur esse divinationem negem. sunt
autem ea, quae posui; ex quibus id, quod volumus,
efficitur et cogitur. iam vero permultorum exem-
plorum et nostra est plena res publica et omnia
regna omnesque populi cunctaeque gentes augurum
praedictis multa incredibiliter vera cecidisse; neque
enim Polyidi neque Melampodis neque Mopsi neque
Amphiarai neque Calchantis neque Heleni tantum
nomen fuisset, neque tot nationes id ad hoc tempus retinuissent, ut Phrygum, Lycaonum, Cilicum
maximeque Pisidarum, nisi vetustas ea certa esse
docuisset. nec vero Romulus noster auspicato

---

[1] *divinare* Mueller; *divinari* AB; *divinari* or *divinare* H.

---

[1] Compare Cicero, *Ep. ad Fam.* III, 4, 1.

familiar with these powers and admit they are great; but there is a great disagreement in your college between Marcellus and Appius,[1] both excellent augurs. For I have consulted their books and find that the one thinks that those auspices were invented to be of practical use to the State, while the other believes that your art is really capable of divination in some degree. I should like to have your opinion on this matter.

M. My opinion? I think that an art of divination, called μαντική by the Greeks, really exists, and that a branch of it is that particular art which deals with the observation of birds and other signs—this branch belonging to our Roman science of augury. For if we admit that gods exist, and that the universe is ruled by their will, that they are mindful of the human race, and that they have the power to give us indications of future events, then I do not see any reason for denying the existence of divination. But these premises are in fact true, so that the conclusion which I desire to draw from them follows as a necessary consequence. Furthermore, the records of our Republic, as well as those of all kingdoms, nations, and races, are full of a multitude of instances of the marvellous confirmation of the predictions of augurs by subsequent events. For Polyidus and Melampus and Mopsus and Amphiaraus and Calchas and Helenus could never have attained such fame, nor could so many nations, such as the Phrygians, Lycaonians, Cilicians and, most of all, the Pisidians have retained their reputation in this art up to the present day, had not antiquity demonstrated its trustworthiness. Nor indeed would our own Romulus have taken the auspices before founding Rome, nor

urbem condidisset, neque Atti Navii nomen memoria
floreret tam diu, nisi omnes hi multa ad veritatem
admirabilia dixissent. sed dubium non est, quin
haec disciplina et ars augurum evanuerit iam et
vetustate et neglegentia. ita neque illi adsentior,
qui hanc scientiam negat umquam in nostro collegio
fuisse, neque illi, qui esse etiam nunc putat; quae
mihi videtur apud maiores fuisse duplex, ut ad rei
publicae tempus non numquam, ad agendi consilium
saepissime pertineret.

34 *A.* Credo hercle ita esse istique rationi potissimum
adsentior. Sed redde cetera.

XIV. *M.* Reddam vero, et id, si potero, brevi.
sequitur enim de iure *belli;* in quo et suscipiendo
et gerendo et deponendo ius ut plurimum valeret
et fides, eorumque ut *publici interpretes* essent, lege
sanximus. iam de *haruspicum* religione, de *expia-
tionibus* et *procurationibus* sat esse plane in ipsa lege
dictum puto.

A. Adsentior, quoniam omnis haec in religione
versatur oratio.

M. At vero quod sequitur quo modo aut tu
adsentiare aut[1] ego reprehendam sane quaero, Tite.

35 *A.* Quid tandem id est?

M. De *nocturnis sacrificiis mulierum.*

A. Ego vero adsentior, excepto praesertim in
ipsa lege *sollemni sacrificio ac publico.*

---

[1] *aut* supplied in the editions ; omitted in MSS.

---

[1] Here we find the Stoic doctrine, which is combated by
Cicero in *De Divin.*, where he maintains the impossibility of
divination, following the scepticism of the New Academy.

would the name of Attius Navius have been remembered all these years, had not all these people made many prophecies which were in remarkable agreement with the truth. But there is no doubt that this art and science of the augurs has by now faded out of existence on account of the passage of time and men's neglect. Therefore I cannot agree with Marcellus, who denies that this art was ever possessed by our college, nor do I subscribe to Appius' opinion that we still possess it. What I believe is that among our ancestors it had a double use, being occasionally employed in political crises, but most often in deciding on a course of action.[1]

A. I believe that you are absolutely right, and concur in the view you have expressed, in preference to any other. But pray go on with the law.

XIV. *M.* I will do so, and, if possible, briefly. We come next to the law of war. My law provides that in undertaking, carrying on, and ending a *war*, justice and good faith shall be supreme, and that the State shall have its *official interpreters* of this provision. Also in regard to the *rites performed by the soothsayers,* to *expiations* and *purifications,* I think the law itself is clear enough.

A. I agree with you, since these are all matters of religious ceremonial.

M. But in regard to what follows, I am wondering, Titus, how you can agree with me or how I can attack your position.

A. To what do you refer?

M. To *the performance of sacrifices by women at night.*

A. But I am in agreement with you, especially as the law itself makes an exception of *the customary public sacrifice.*

M. Quid ergo aget Iacchus Eumolpidaeque nostri [1]
et augusta illa mysteria, siquidem sacra nocturna
tollimus? non enim populo Romano, sed omnibus
bonis firmisque populis leges damus.

36   *A.* Excipis, credo, illa, quibus ipsi initiati sumus.

M. Ego vero excipiam; nam mihi cum multa
eximia divinaque videntur Athenae tuae peperisse
atque in vitam hominum attulisse, tum nihil melius
illis mysteriis, quibus ex agresti immanique vita
exculti ad humanitatem et mitigati sumus, initiaque
ut appellantur, ita re vera principia vitae cogno-
vimus; neque solum cum laetitia vivendi rationem
accepimus, sed etiam cum spe meliore moriendi.
Quid autem mihi displiceat in nocturnis, poëtae
indicant comici. qua licentia Romae data quidnam
egisset ille, qui in sacrificium cogitatam libidinem
intulit, quo ne inprudentiam quidem oculorum adici
fas fuit?

A. Tu vero istam Romae legem rogato; nobis
nostras ne ademeris.

37   XV. *M.* Ad nostra igitur revertor; quibus profecto
diligentissime sanciendum est, ut mulierum famam
multorum oculis lux clara custodiat *initienturque eo*

---

[1] *nostri* ABH; *vostri* is the common reading.

---

[1] Iacchus=Dionysus. The *Eumolpidae* were an Attic
family which held continuously a priesthood at Eleusis.
The whole reference is to the Eleusinian mysteries.

[2] Compare Isocrates, *Panegyricus* 28.

[3] Irregularities at nocturnal religious celebrations are
commonly used in Greek New Comedy to account for
illegitimacy. See, for example, Menander, *Arbitrants* 234
ff., and Plautus, *Aulularia* 36.

[4] Clodius, who entered the house of Julius Caesar disguised
as a woman on the occasion of the nocturnal rites of Bona Dea
(see § 27 and note) in December 62 B.C. This was the cause of

M. Then what will become of our Iacchus and Eumolpidae[1] and their impressive mysteries, if we abolish nocturnal rites? For we are composing laws not for the Roman people in particular, but for all virtuous and stable nations.

A. I take it for granted that you make an exception of those rites into which we ourselves have been initiated.

M. I will do so indeed. For among the many excellent and indeed divine institutions which your Athens has brought forth and contributed to human life, none, in my opinion, is better than those mysteries. For by their means we have been brought out of our barbarous and savage mode of life and educated and refined to a state of civilization; and as the rites are called "initiations," so in very truth we have learned from them the beginnings of life, and have gained the power not only to live happily, but also to die with a better hope.[2] But the ground of my general objection to nocturnal rites is indicated by the comic poets.[3] For if such licence had been granted at Rome, what would that man[4] have done, who, as it was, intruded his lustful designs into a ceremony so sacred that even an unintentional glance at it was a sin?

A. Very well then; propose such a law for Rome, but do not deprive us of our customs.

XV. *M.* I will, then, return to our own enactments. Assuredly we must make most careful provision that the reputation of our women be guarded by the clear light of day, when they are observed by many eyes, and that *initiations into the*

Caesar's divorcing his wife Pompeia (see Plutarch, *Caesar* 9–10; *Cicero* 28–29).

MARCUS TULLIUS CICERO

ritu Cereri, quo Romae initiantur. quo in genere
severitatem maiorum senatus vetus auctoritas de
Bacchanalibus et consulum exercitu adhibito quaestio
animadversioque[1] declarat. atque omnia nocturna,
ne nos duriores forte videamur, in media Graecia
Diagondas Thebanus lege perpetua sustulit; novos
vero deos et in his colendis nocturnas pervigilationes
sic Aristophanes, facetissumus poëta veteris comoediae, vexat, ut apud eum Sabazius et quidam alii
dei peregrini iudicati e civitate eiciantur.

Publicus autem *sacerdos inprudentiam consilio
expiatam* metu liberet, *audaciam* in et inmittendas
religionibus foedas[2] damnet atque *impiam iudicet.*

38 Iam *ludi publici* quoniam sunt cavea circoque
divisi, sint *corporum certationes* cursu et pugillatu
et luctatione *curriculaque* equorum usque ad certam
victoriam circo constituta;[3] cavea *cantu* vigeat[4]
fidibus et tibiis, dum modo ea *moderata sint,* ut
lege praescribitur. adsentior enim Platoni nihil

---

[1] *que* supplied in editions; omitted in MSS.
[2] Corrupt: *audaciam in et inmitendas religionibus foedas*
A : *audaciam in et inmittendis religionibus foedas* B ; *audaciam
meti mitendas religionibus foedas* H ; *audaciam ad libidines
inmittendas religionibus foedas* suggested by Vahlen.
[3] *curriculaque . . . constituta* C.W.K. ; *curriculisque . . .
constitutis* ABH.
[4] *vigeat* H[2]; *vice ad* B[1]; *vice ac* AB[2]; *viceat* H[1].

---

[1] The excesses committed at these nocturnal assemblies
were so serious that in 186 B C. the Senate passed a decree
for their suppression, the text of which has come down to
us (see *Corpus Inscriptionum Latinarum* I, 196 ; Livy
XXXIX, 8-20).
[2] Probably in the lost comedy *Horae* (compare Schol. to
Aristophanes' *Birds* 874 and *Wasps* 9).

*mysteries of Ceres be performed only with those rites
which are in use in Rome.* The strictness of our
ancestors in matters of this character is shown by
the ancient decree of the Senate with respect to the
Bacchanalia,[1] and the investigation and punishment
conducted by the consuls with the assistance of a
specially-enrolled military force. And, that we may
not perchance seem too severe, I may cite the fact
that in the very centre of Greece, by a law enacted
by Diagondas of Thebes, all nocturnal rites were
abolished for ever; and furthermore that Aristophanes,[2] the wittiest poet of the Old Comedy, attacks
strange gods and the nightly vigils which were part
of their worship by representing Sabazius and certain
other alien gods as brought to trial and banished
from the State.

To proceed: *unintentional offences are carefully
to be expiated by the official priest* and the offender
relieved from fear; but *effrontery* in introducing
[disgraceful lust into the midst of religious rites] he
must condemn and *adjudge impious.*[3]

Next, since *the public games* are divided between
theatre and circus, in the circus there shall be *contest of body with body,* consisting of running, boxing,
and wrestling; and also *horse-races,* which shall last
until a decisive victory is won; on the other hand,
the theatre shall be filled with *song to the music of
harp and flute,* the only limitation being that of
moderation, as the law prescribes. For I agree with

---

[3] This translation follows Vahlen's suggestion as to the
text. If he is right, Cicero is referring again to the event
which he mentions in § 37. The meaning of the law seems
to be that slight offences may be ritually expiated, while
heinous ones can only be atoned for by the punishment of the
offender.

tam facile in animos teneros atque molles influere
quam varios canendi sonos, quorum dici vix potest
quanta sit vis in utramque partem; namque et
incitat languentes et languefacit excitatos et tum
remittit animos, tum contrahit, civitatiumque hoc
multarum in Graecia interfuit, antiquum vocum
conservare modum; quarum mores lapsi ad mollitiam[1] mollitis pariter sunt inmutati cum cantibus,
aut hac dulcedine corruptelaque depravati, ut quidam putant, aut, cum severitas eorum ob alia vitia
cecidisset, tum fuit in auribus animisque mutatis
39 etiam huic mutationi locus. quam ob rem ille
quidem sapientissimus Graeciae vir longeque doctissimus valde hanc labem veretur; negat enim
mutari posse musicas leges sine mutatione legum
publicarum. ego autem nec tam valde id timendum
nec plane contemnendum puto; illud quidem video,[2]
quae solebant quondam conpleri severitate iucunda
Livianis et Naevianis modis, nunc ut eadem exul-
tent et cervices oculosque pariter cum modorum
flexionibus torqueant. graviter olim ista vindicabat
vetus illa Graecia, longe providens quam sensim
pernicies inlapsa in[3] civium animos malis studiis
malisque doctrinis repente totas civitates everteret,
siquidem illa severa Lacedaemo nervos iussit, quos

---

[1] *mollitiam* supplied by Vahlen; omitted in MSS.
[2] *video* supplied by Vahlen; omitted in MSS.
[3] *in* supplied by Lambinus; omitted in MSS.

---

[1] *Republic* IV, 424 D.
[2] Plato, *Republic* IV, 424 C.

Plato[1] that nothing gains an influence so easily over youthful and impressionable minds as the various notes of song, the greatness of whose power both for good and evil can hardly be set forth in words. For it arouses the languid, and calms the excited; now it restrains our desires, now gives them free rein. Many Greek States considered it important to retain their old tunes; but when their songs became less manly, their characters turned to effeminacy at the same time, perhaps because they were corrupted by the sweetness and debilitating seductiveness of the new music, as some believe, or perhaps when other vices had first caused a relaxation of the strictness of their lives, and their ears and their hearts had already undergone a change, room was offered for this change in their music as well. For this reason the man who was by far the wisest and by far the most learned whom Greece has produced was very much afraid of such a degeneration. For he says there can be no change in the laws of music without a resulting change in the laws of the State.[2] My opinion, however, is that such a change is neither so greatly to be feared, nor, on the other hand, to be considered of no importance at all; and yet I do observe that audiences which used to be deeply affected by the inspiring sternness of the music of Livius and Naevius, now leap up and twist their necks and turn their eyes in time with our modern tunes. Ancient Greece used to punish such offences severely, perceiving long before the event that corruption gradually creeps into the hearts of citizens, and, by infecting them with evil desires and evil ideas, works the swift and total destruction of States—if indeed it be true that the

plures quam septem haberet, in Timothei fidibus
incidi.

40 XVI. Deinceps in lege est, ut *de ritibus patrius colantur optumi;* de quo cum consulerent Athenienses
Apollinem Pythium, quas potissimum religiones
tenerent, oraclum editum est: "eas, quae essent
in more maiorum." quo cum iterum venissent
maiorumque morem dixissent saepe esse mutatum
quaesissentque, quem morem potissimum seque-
rentur e variis, respondit: "optumum." et profecto ita est, ut id habendum sit antiquissimum
et deo proximum, quod sit optumum.

Stipem sustulimus nisi eam, quam ad paucos dies
propriam *Idaeae Matris* excepimus; implet enim
superstitione animos et exhaurit domus.

Sacrilego poena est, neque ei soli, *qui sacrum abs-*
41 *tulerit,* sed etiam *ei, qui sacro commendatum;* quod
et nunc multis fit in fanis, et[1] Alexander in Cilicia
deposuisse apud Solensis in delubro pecuniam dicitur
et Atheniensis Clisthenes Iunoni Samiae, civis egre-
gius, cum rebus timeret suis, filiarum dotis credidisse.

Iam de *periuriis,* de *incesto* nihil sane hoc quidem
loco disputandum est.

Donis impii ne placare audeant deos, Platonem
audiant, qui vetat dubitare, qua sit mente futurus

---

[1] *et* supplied by Madvig; omitted in MSS.

---

[1] Timotheus is recorded to have added four strings to
the usual seven (compare Pausanias, III, 12, 10; Athenaeus,
XIV, 9, 636 E).
[2] The particular occasion is unknown, but compare
Xenophon, *Memor.* IV. 3, 16; I, 3, 1.
[3] *Laws* IV, 716 E.

strict Sparta of tradition ordered all the strings above seven to be removed from Timotheus' harp.[1]

XVI. The next provision of the law ·is that *the best of the ancestral rites shall be preserved.* For when the Athenians consulted the Pythian Apollo on this point, as to what religious rites they should by preference retain, the oracle answered: "Those which were among the customs of your ancestors."[2] And when they came a second time, and, saying that their ancestors' customs had undergone many changes, asked which custom they should follow by preference out of the many, the answer was, "The best." And it is assuredly true that that is to be considered most ancient and nearest to God which is the best.

I have forbidden *the collection of contributions, with the exception of that collection for the Idaean Mother* which occupies only a few days; for such customs fill men's minds with superstition and empty their homes.

There is a penalty for sacrilege, and this word is to be applied to the theft not merely of *what is sacred, but also of anything entrusted to what is sacred.* The custom of making such deposits still exists at many temples, and it is said that Alexander deposited a sum of money in a temple at Soli in Cilicia, and that Clisthenes, an eminent citizen of Athens, entrusted the dowry of his daughters to Juno of Samos, since he was fearful of his own fortunes.

In regard to *perjury* and *incest,* surely no discussion is necessary here.

The wicked shall not dare to attempt to appease the gods with gifts. Let them hear the words of Plato,[3] who says that there can be no doubt how God would

deus, cum vir nemo bonus ab inprobo se donari
velit.

Diligentiam votorum satis in lege dictum est . . . .[1]
ac votis sponsio, qua obligamur deo. *poena* vero
violatae religionis iustam recusationem non habet.
quid ego hic sceleratorum utar exemplis, quorum
plenae tragoediae ? quae ante oculos sunt, ea potius
adtingam. etsi haec commemoratio vereor ne supra
hominis fortunam esse videatur, tamen, quoniam
sermo mihi est apud vos, nihil reticebo volamque
hoc, quod loquar, diis inmortalibus gratum potius
42 videri quam grave. XVII. omnia tum perditorum
civium scelere discessu meo religionum iura polluta
sunt, vexati nostri Lares familiares, in eorum sedibus
exaedificatum templum Licentiae, pulsus a delubris
is, qui illa servarat. circumspicite celeriter animo
(nihil enim attinet quemquam nominari), qui sint
rerum exitus consecuti. nos, qui illam custodem
urbis omnibus ereptis nostris rebus ac perditis violari
ab impiis passi non sumus eamque ex nostra domo
in ipsius patris domum detulimus, iudicia senatus,
Italiae, gentium denique omnium conservatae patriae
consecuti sumus ; quo quid accidere potuit homini
praeclarius ? quorum scelere religiones tum pro-

---

[1] *dictum est ac votis sponsio* ABH; *dictum est (servari
oportere si quidem est) haec voti vis, sponsio* is suggested by
Vahlen.

---

[1] Cicero was in exile 58–57 B.C., the law of banishment
being proposed by Clodius.
[2] Cicero scornfully calls the goddess to whom a temple
was erected on the site of his house *Licentia* instead of
Libertas.
[3] A small statue of Minerva which Cicero kept in his
house. Before going into exile he carried it to the temple

feel about such a thing, since no good man would be willing to receive gifts from the wicked.

As for *the scrupulous performance of vows,* the words of the law suffice, [if a vow is really a] contract, by which we are bound to God. Surely *punishment for the violation of obligations sanctioned by religion* is open to no just criticism. Why should I give here those examples of the fate of such criminals of which the tragedies are full? I prefer to touch on deeds which are present before our eyes. Though I fear this instance may seem beyond human fortune, yet, since I am speaking to you, I shall keep nothing back, in the hope that what I am about to say will be pleasing rather than offensive to the immortal gods. XVII. In the matter of my exile,[1] all the laws of religion were violated by the crimes of depraved citizens; the Lares of our family were mistreated, on the site of their home a temple to Licence[2] was erected, and the man who had saved our shrines was driven from them. Think for a few moments (for there is no reason for us to mention the name of any particular person) what consequences followed these acts. I, who would not allow that guardian of the city to be violated by the wicked, even when all my property was snatched from me and destroyed, but conveyed her from my house to her father's[3]—I have been vindicated by the judgment of the Senate, of Italy, and indeed of all nations, as the saviour of the fatherland. And what more glorious honour could come to a man? But those by whose crimes

of Jupiter Capitolinus, designating the goddess in an inscription as guardian of the city (compare Plutarch, *Cicero* 31; Dio Cassius, XXXVIII, 17).

stratae adflictaeque sunt, partim ex illis distracti ac
dissipati iacent, qui vero ex iis et horum scelerum
principes fuerant et praeter ceteros in omni religione
inpii, non solum vita ignominia[1] cruciati atque de-
decore, verum etiam sepultura et iustis exsequiarum
caruerunt.

43   *Q.* Equidem ista agnosco, frater, et meritas dis
gratias ago ; sed nimis saepe secus aliquanto videmus
evadere.

M. Non enim, Quinte, recte existimamus, quae
poena divina sit, sed opinionibus vulgi rapimur in
errorem nec vera cernimus ; morte aut dolore corporis aut luctu animi aut offensione iudicii hominum
miserias ponderamus ; quae fateor humana esse et
multis bonis viris accidisse.   sceleris est poena tristis
et praeter eos eventus, qui sequuntur, per se ipsa
maxima est.   vidimus eos, qui nisi odissent patriam,
numquam inimici nobis fuissent, ardentis tum cupiditate, tum metu, tum conscientia, quidquid[2] age-
rent, modo timentis, vicissim contemnentis religiones,
iudicia, perrupta ab isdem corruptela hominum, non
deorum.

44   Reprimam iam et non insequar longius, eoque
minus, quo plus poenarum habeo quam petivi ; tantum ponam brevi, duplicem poenam esse divinam,
quod constet ex vexandis vivorum animis et ea fama

---

[1] *ignominia* conjecturally supplied by Vahlen ; omitted
in MSS.
[2] *quidquid* Lambinus ; *quid* ABH.

---

[1] See Introduction, p. 289, note 2 ; Cicero, *Pro Milone* 86.

religion was trampled down and violated are partly scattered and dispersed; and those who were the leaders in those crimes and guilty beyond the rest of the violation of everything sacred have not only been tortured during their lives by [disgrace] and dishonour, but have even been deprived of a grave and of the proper rites of burial.[1]

Q. I am aware of these facts, my dear brother, and I render due thanks to the gods, but only too frequently we see things happen somewhat differently.

M. That, Quintus, is because we have a mistaken view of the nature of divine punishment; we are led into error by popular opinions, and do not perceive the truth. We estimate the unhappiness of men on the basis of death, physical pain, mental anguish, or condemnation in the courts; things which are common in human life, I admit, and happen to many good men. But crime carries with it a terrible vengeance, and, in addition to its results, from its very nature it is its own worst punishment. We have seen those men, who would never have been my personal enemies unless they had hated the fatherland, on fire now with greed, now with fear, and now with remorse, and, whatever the business on which they were engaged, filled now with fear of the gods, now with scorn of religion and the courts, whose authority they had overthrown by bribing not gods but men.

But I will stop there, and speak of them no more, especially as I have been more terribly avenged than I ever desired. One fact only I will state briefly: the punishment of the gods is a double one, consisting of mental tortures during life, and of such ignominy after death that the living not only approve

mortuorum, ut eorum exitium et iudicio vivorum et gaudio conprobetur.

45 XVIII. *Agri autem ne consecrentur,* Platoni prorsus adsentior, qui, si modo interpretari potuero, his fere verbis utitur : "Terra igitur, ut focus domiciliorum, sacra deorum omnium est ; quocirca ne quis iterum idem consecrato. *aurum* autem et *argentum* in urbibus et privatim et in fanis invidiosa res est. tum *ebur* ex inani corpore extractum haud satis castum donum deo. iam aes atque ferrum duelli instrumenta, non fani. ligneum autem, quod quisque[1] voluerit, uno e ligno dicato itemque lapideum in delubris communibus, textile ne operosius quam mulieris opus menstruum. color autem albus praecipue decorus deo est cum in cetero, tum maxime in textili ; tincta vero absint nisi a bellicis insignibus. divinissima autem dona aves et formae ab uno pictore uno absolutae die ; itemque cetera huius exempli dona sunto." haec illi placent ; sed ego cetera non tam restricte praefinio vel hominum vitiis vel subsidiis temporum victus ; terrae cultum segniorem suspicor fore, si ad eam utendam ferroque subigendam superstitionis aliquid accesserit.

A. Habeo ista ; nunc *de sacris perpetuis* et *de Manium iure* restat.

---

[1] *quod quisque* Mueller ; *quodque* ABH.

---

[1] *Laws* XII, 955 E–956 B.

of the destruction of the guilty but even rejoice thereat.

XVIII. In my prohibition of *the consecration of land* I am in complete agreement with Plato, who expresses his opinion in about the following words, if I can translate the passage :[1] "The earth, therefore, like the hearth in a dwelling, is sacred to all the gods ; wherefore no one should consecrate it a second time. *Gold* and *silver* in cities, whether in private possession or in temples, are things which cause covetousness. *Ivory* also, which is taken from an animal's dead body, is not sufficiently pure to be given to a god. Bronze and iron are suitable for war, not for a temple. Any wooden object, however, if made out of a single piece of wood, or anything of stone, one may dedicate at public shrines, and woven work, too, provided its production has not been more than a month's task for a woman. White is the colour most suitable for a god, especially in woven work ; no dyes should be used except for military standards. But the gifts best suited of all to the gods are birds, and pictures produced by a single painter in a single day ; other gifts should be of this same character." These are his provisions : as for mine, in other respects I have not laid down such strict rules as his, out of consideration for the faults of men and the resources of human life in our time ; but regarding the land, I am afraid its cultivation will decline if any superstitions should grow up about its use or subjection to the plough.[2]

A. You have given me a clear idea of these subjects ; now *the perpetual rites* and *the privileges of the gods of the lower world* await your treatment.

[2] Compare § 67.

M. O miram memoriam, Pomponi, tuam ! at mihi ista exciderant.

46 A. Ita credo, sed tamen hoc magis eas res et memini et expecto, quod et ad pontificium ius et ad civile pertinent.

M. Vero, et a peritissimis sunt istis de rebus et responsa et scripta multa, et ego in hoc omni sermone nostro, quod ad cumque legis genus me disputatio nostra deduxerit, tractabo, quoad potero, eius ipsius generis ius civile nostrum, sed ita, locus ut ipse notus sit, ex quo ducatur quaeque pars iuris, ut non difficile sit, qui modo ingenio possit moveri, quaecumque nova causa consultatiove acciderit, eius tenere ius, cum scias a quo sit capite repetendum.

47 XIX. Sed iuris consulti sive erroris obiciundi causa, quo plura et difficiliora scire videantur, sive, quod similius veri est, ignoratione docendi (nam non solum scire aliquid artis est, sed quaedam ars [1] etiam docendi) saepe, quod positum est in una cognitione, id in infinitam [2] dispertiuntur, velut in hoc ipso genere quam magnum illud Scaevolae faciunt, pontifices ambo et eidem iuris peritissimi ! "Saepe," inquit Publii filius, "ex patre audivi pontificem bonum neminem esse, nisi qui ius civile cognosset."

---

[1] *ars etiam* ABH ; *ars est etiam* Lambinus.
[2] *id in infinitam* Halm ; *id infinita* AH ; *infinita (id* omitted) B.

---

[1] Publius Mucius Scaevola and his son Quintus Mucius Scaevola.

428

M. What a remarkable memory is yours, Pomponius! I had forgotten those subjects.

A. No doubt; but my chief reason for remembering them and looking forward to your discussion of them was the fact that they are concerned both with the rules of the pontiffs and with the civil law.

M. True; and a great deal has been said and written on these subjects by men of great learning. And it is my intention, during the whole of our conversation, to take up, as far as I can, in connection with every branch of law to which our discussion leads us, the corresponding division of our own civil law; but my treatment will extend only far enough to make clear the source of every one of these divisions. For thus it will not be difficult for anyone who is capable of following a line of thought to know the law with respect to any strange case or knotty problem which may come up, when the basic principle underlying it is once understood.

XIX. But the consultants often divide up into an infinite number of parts what is really based on a single principle, either for the purpose of deception, so that their knowledge may seem greater in amount and more difficult to acquire, or else, as is more likely, through lack of skill in teaching; for an art consists not merely in the possession of knowledge, but also in skill in imparting it to others. To take an example from this very branch of the law, how extensive do the Scaevolae [1] (both of them pontiffs and also most learned in the law) make that very subject of which we have just been speaking! Scaevola, the son of Publius, says: "How often have I heard my father say that no one could be a good pontiff without a knowledge of the civil law!" A

Totumne? quid ita? quid enim ad pontificem de
iure parietum aut aquarum aut ullo omnino nisi eo,
quod cum religione coniunctum est? id autem
quantulum est! de sacris, credo, de votis, de feriis
et de sepulchris, et si quid eius modi est. cur igitur
haec tanta facimus, cum cetera perparva sint, de
sacris autem, qui locus patet latius, haec sit una
sententia, ut conserventur semper et deinceps familiis
prodantur et, ut in lege posui, *perpetua sint sacra?*

48 Exposite[1] haec iura pontificum auctoritate consecuta sunt, ut, ne morte patris familias sacrorum memoria occideret, iis essent ea adiuncta, ad quos
eiusdem morte pecunia venerit. hoc uno posito,
quod est ad cognitionem disciplinae satis, innumera-
bilia nascuntur, quibus implentur iuris consultorum
libri. quaeruntur enim, qui astringantur sacris.
heredum causa iustissima est; nulla est enim persona, quae ad vicem eius, qui e vita emigrarit,
propius accedat. deinde, qui morte testamentove
eius tantundem capiat, quantum omnes heredes. id
quoque ordine; est enim ad id, quod propositum
est, adcommodatum. tertio loco, si nemo sit heres,

---

[1] *exposite* Baiter; *haec posite* AH; omitted in B.

---

[1] *i.e.* as a legacy.
[2] *i.e.* half of the estate.

knowledge of the whole of it? Why so? For of what use to a pontiff is the law of house-walls or aqueducts, or, in fact, any part of the civil law at all except that which is connected with religion? And that is a very small part of the whole, including only the provisions in regard to sacrifices, vows, holidays, graves, and things of like nature, I believe. Why, then, do we make so much of these matters, when all the rest except this one problem of the rites amount to very little? Indeed, even this subject, which is of somewhat wider importance, can be reduced to one basic principle; namely, that these rites shall ever be preserved and continuously handed down in families, and, as I said in my law, that *they must be continued for ever.*

Clearly our present laws on the subject have been laid down by the authority of the pontiffs, in order that the performance of the rites may be imposed upon those to whom the property passes, so that the memory of them may not die out at the death of the father of the family. After this single rule was laid down—a rule which is quite sufficient for the understanding of the proper procedure—innumerable others have come into existence, and filled the books of the consultants. For they attempt to fix with exactness the persons who are bound to perform the rites. With respect to the heirs the requirement is altogether just; for no one else can more truly be said to take the place of the dead. Next comes the person who, either by a death-bed gift or a will, receives [1] as much of the estate as all the heirs put together.[2] It is quite proper that he too should be bound, for this is in accordance with the principle just stated. In the third place, if there is no heir,

is, qui de bonis, quae eius fuerint, cum moritur, usu
ceperit plurimum possidendo. Quarto, qui, si nemo
sit, qui ullam rem ceperit, de creditoribus eius
49 plurimum servet. extrema illa persona est, ut is, si
qui ei, qui mortuus sit, pecuniam debuerit neminique
eam solverit, proinde habeatur, quasi eam pecuniam
ceperit.

XX. Haec nos a Scaevola didicimus, non ita
descripta [1] ab antiquis. nam illi quidem his verbis
docebant : tribus modis sacris adstringi, aut here
ditate, aut si maiorem partem pecuniae capiat, aut,
si maior pars pecuniae legata est, si inde quippiam
ceperit.

50 Sed pontificem sequamur. videtis igitur omnia
pendere ex uno illo, quod pontifices cum pecunia
sacra coniungi volunt isdemque ferias [2] et caerimonias adscribendas putant. atque etiam dant hoc
Scaevolae, cum est partitio, ut, si in testamento
deducta scripta non sit ipsique minus ceperint, quam
omnibus heredibus relinquatur, sacris ne alligentur.

---

[1] *descripta ab* Ed. Ascensiana; *descripta sunt ab* AB[2];
descriptas ab H ; *descriptis ab* B[1].
[2] *ferias* ABH ; *hereditates* suggested by Mommsen ; see
explanatory note.

---

[1] See Book I, 55.
[2] This appears to refer to the private or family holydays
on which the rites were performed. Mommsen's emendation
(see textual note) is therefore unnecessary. However, Cicero
may possibly be using *feriae* to mean "the ease (holidays)
made possible by the inheritance."
[3] It seems to have been customary for the author of a will

the man who acquires by possession [1] the ownership of the greater part of the property of which the deceased died possessed is bound by the obligation. In the fourth place, if nobody acquires any of the property of the deceased, then the obligation falls upon that one of the creditors who retains most of the estate. In the last place of all stands any person who owed money to the deceased and never paid it to anyone, for his position is considered the same as if he had received that money from the estate.

XX. This is what we learn from Scaevola, but the doctrine of the older authorities is differently stated. For their rule was expressed in the following terms: that men are bound to perform the rites in three different ways, either by being heirs, or by receiving the greater part of the property, or, in case the greater part of the property was bequeathed in legacies, by receiving anything whatever by that means.

But let us follow the pontiff. Now you see that all his rules depend on one principle, namely, the decision of the pontiffs that the rites are to go with the property, and that the holydays [2] and the ceremonies are to be assigned to the same persons. And the Scaevolae add that, when the will provides for a partition of the estate, but not for any deduction from legacies,[3] in case the legatees voluntarily take less than what is left to all the heirs together, these legatees shall not be bound to the performance of

who wished to leave half of his estate in legacies to make a deduction of a nominal amount from this half, in order to relieve the legatees from the burden of the rites. Here Cicero evidently means that when this is not done in the will, the legatees can escape the burden by accepting slightly less than half of the estate.

in donatione hoc idem secus interpretantur, et, quod
pater familias in eius donatione, qui in ipsius potestate est, adprobavit, ratum est; quod eo insciente
factum est, si id is non adprobat, ratum non est.

51　　His propositis quaestiunculae multae nascuntur,
quas quis qui intellegat[1] non, si ad caput referat,
per se ipse facile perspiciat? veluti, si minus quis
cepisset, ne sacris alligaretur, et post de eius heredibus aliquis exegisset pro sua parte id, quod ab eo,
cui ipse heres esset, praetermissum fuisset, eaque
pecunia non minor esset facta cum superiore exac-
tione, quam heredibus omnibus esset relicta, qui eam
pecuniam exegisset, solum sine coheredibus sacris alligari. quin etiam cavent, ut, cui plus legatum sit,
quam sine religione capere liceat, is per aes et libram
heredes testamenti solvat, propterea quod eo loco
res est ita soluta hereditate, quasi ea pecunia legata
non esset.

52　　XXI. Hoc ego loco multisque aliis quaero a vobis,
Scaevolae, pontifices maximi et homines meo quidem
iudicio acutissimi, quid sit quod ad ius pontificium
civile appetatis; civilis enim iuris scientia ponti-

---

[1] *quas quis qui intellegat* suggested by Vahlen; *quas qui*
nascuntur intellegat ABH.

---

[1] This decision seems to be thought of as inconsistent with
the former because the scheme made use of by the legatees is
really a gift of part of the estate, made without the approval
of the testator.

[2] For example, suppose A leaves to B a legacy of 10,000
sesterces. A's heir, C, is bound to pay this legacy out of the
estate. But B makes a contract with C by which he re-
linquishes all his rights to the legacy in consideration of the
payment to him of 10,000 sesterces by C personally. Then
B has "sold" his right to the legacy, and, as he receives

the rites. In the case of a gift they give a different sort of interpretation : if the head of a family approves a gift made by a person under his authority, then the gift is valid ; but if such a gift is made without his knowledge, it is invalid unless he gives his approval later.[1]

From these principles many minor problems have arisen, but any intelligent person could easily solve them without assistance, simply by referring them to the basic principle. For example, suppose some-one accepted less than all the heirs, in order not to be bound to the rites, and later one of this person's heirs collected on his own account the amount which had been refused by the person from whom he had inherited ; and suppose that the whole sum, including what had been collected before, amounted to not less than had been left to all the heirs ; then it would be easy to conclude that the man who had collected this amount was alone bound to the rites, to the exclusion of his co-heirs. In fact the authorities even provide that, if a greater legacy is left to any-one than he can accept without the religious obliga-tion, this person may release the heirs under the will from the payment of the legacy by going through the form of a sale, because in that way the property is freed from its character as a legacy, just as fully as if it had not been bequeathed at all.[2]

XXI. Now with reference to this and many other matters, I wish to ask the Scaevolae, supreme pontiffs, and the cleverest of men in my opinion, a question : Why do you wish to add an acquaintance with the civil law to your familiarity with the rules

nothing whatever from A's estate, is freed from the obligation of the rites without pecuniary loss. Compare § 53.

435

ficium quodam modo tollitis. nam sacra cum pecunia
pontificum auctoritate, nulla lege coniuncta sunt.
itaque si vos tantum modo pontifices essetis, pontificalis maneret auctoritas, sed quod idem iuris civilis
estis peritissimi, hac scientia illam eluditis. placuit
P. Scaevolae et Ti. Coruncanio, pontificibus maximis,
itemque ceteris, eos, qui tantundem caperent, quan-
53 tum omnes heredes, sacris alligari. habeo ius pontificium; quid huc accessit ex iure civili? partitionis
caput scriptum caute, ut centum nummi deduceren-
tur; inventa est ratio cur pecunia sacrorum molestia
liberaretur. quasi[1] hoc, qui testamentum faciebat,
cavere noluisset, admonet iuris consultus hic quidem
ipse Mucius, pontifex idem, ut minus capiat, quam
omnibus heredibus relinquatur; super dicebant
quicquid cepisset, adstringi; rursus sacris liberantur.
hoc vero nihil ad pontificium ius et e medio est iure
civili, ut per aes et libram heredem testamenti sol-
vant et eodem loco res sit, quasi ea pecunia legata
non esset, si is, cui legatum est, stipulatus est id
ipsum, quod legatum est, ut ea pecunia ex stipula-
tione debeatur, sitque ea non . . .[2]

---

[1] *quasi* Vahlen; *quid si* AH; *quisi* B; *quodsi* Stephanus.
[2] To complete the sentence, Turnebus suggests *legata* or
sacris non astricta.

---

[1] *i.e.* from half the estate, in order to avoid the rites.
(The amount is about £4.)

of the pontiffs? For by your knowledge of the civil law you have to some extent nullified the rules of the pontiffs. For the rites are connected with the property by the authority of the pontiffs, not by any law. Hence, if you were pontiffs and nothing more, then the authority of the pontifical college would be maintained ; but as you are also learned in the civil law, you use your learning to evade your own pontifical rules. Publius Scaevola, Tiberius Coruncanius, and other supreme pontiffs have decided that those who received as much as all the heirs together were bound to the rites. There we have the rule of the pontiffs. What addition has been made to it out of the civil law? The directions for the division of the estate are cleverly written, to the effect that a hundred nummi should be deducted ;[1] thus a method was found by which the property might be freed from the burden of the rites. Just as if the author of the will had not wished to guard against such an act, the legal consultant, this very Mucius himself, who is also a pontiff, advises the legatee to accept less than is left to all the heirs. Previously the pontiffs had said that he was bound, whatever amount he accepted ; but now they free him from the rites. This other device of theirs, however, is taken directly from the civil law, and has nothing to do with the pontiffs' rules—the scheme, I mean, by which the heir under the will is freed from his obligation to pay the legacy by a sale. This makes the situation the same as if the money had not been left as a legacy at all, provided only that the legatee makes a formal contract in regard to the legacy, so that the money is owed to him under the contract, and not [under the legacy]. . .

54 . . . doctum hominem sane, cuius fuit Accius per-
familiaris, sed mensem, credo, extremum anni, ut
veteres Februarium, sic hic Decembrem sequebatur.
hostia autem maxima parentare pietatis esse adiunc-
tum putabat.

55 XXII. Iam tanta religio est sepulchrorum, ut
extra sacra et gentem inferri fas negent esse, idque
apud maiores nostros A. Torquatus in gente Popillia
iudicavit. nec vero tam denicales, quae a nece
appellatae sunt, quia residentur mortuis, quam
ceterorum caelestium quieti dies feriae nominarentur, nisi maiores eos, qui ex hac vita migrassent, *in
deorum numero esse* voluissent. eas in eos dies
conferre ius, ut nec ipsius neque publicae feriae
sint; totaque huius iuris conpositio pontificalis magnam religionem caerimoniamque declarat. neque
necesse est edisseri a nobis, quae finis funestae
familiae, quod genus sacrificii Lari vervecibus fiat,
quem ad modum os resectum terra obtegatur, quaeque in porca contracta iura sint, quo tempore
incipiat sepulchrum esse et religione teneatur.

---

[1] This is evidently a gap of considerable length : in the
lost passage Cicero concluded his discussion of the *sacra
privata* and began that of the *deorum Manium iura* (compare
§ 22). At the point where our manuscripts resume, the subject is the offering of sacrifices in honour of dead relatives
(*parentare*). Plutarch (*Quaest. Rom.* 34) states that, according to Cicero, these offerings were regularly made by the
Romans in February (originally the last month of the year),
while Decimus Junius Brutus (consul 138 B.C.) made them in
December. Therefore he is evidently the person referred to
here, and Cicero is explaining why he made this change.

[2] Cicero derives *denicales*, the technical term for these
days, from *de* and *nex*, death.

[3] For the purification of the family.

. . . [Decimus Brutus],[1] surely a learned man, and a great friend of Accius; but I believe he used December as the last month of the year, as the ancients had used February. Moreover, he considered it the part of piety to use the largest victims in offerings in honour of the dead.

XXII. Now graves are the objects of so much religious veneration that it is considered sinful to bury in them corpses not belonging to the clan or participating in its rites; in the time of our ancestors this was the decision of Aulus Torquatus in the case of the Popilian clan. Nor would the days of purification, which derive their name from death because they are celebrated for the dead,[2] be referred to as holidays in common with the days of rest in honour of the celestial gods, unless our ancestors had desired that those who depart this life should *be included among the gods.* It is the law that those holidays are to be placed at such times that they shall not coincide with other public or private holidays. This whole body of pontifical law shows deep religious feeling and a respect for the solemnity of religious ceremony. It is unnecessary for me to explain when the period of family mourning is ended, what sort of a sacrifice of wethers is offered to the Lar,[3] in what manner the severed bone is buried in the earth,[4] what are the rules in regard to the obligation to sacrifice a sow,[5] or when the grave first takes on the character of a grave and comes under the protection of religion.[6]

---

[4] When the body was burned a finger was cut off and buried in the earth in deference to the older custom of burial.

[5] For the consecration of the grave.

[6] See § 57.

56   At mihi quidem antiquissimum sepulturae genus
illud fuisse videtur, quo apud Xenophontem Cyrus
utitur; redditur enim terrae corpus et ita locatum
ac situm quasi operimento matris obducitur. eodemque ritu in eo sepulchro, quod haud[1] procul a Fontis
ara est, regem nostrum Numam conditum accepimus
gentemque Corneliam usque ad memoriam nostram
hac sepultura scimus esse usam.   C. Marii sitas
reliquias apud Anienem dissipari iussit Sulla victor
acerbiore odio incitatus, quam si tam[2] sapiens fuisset,
57 quam fuit vehemens.   quod haud scio an timens ne[3]
suo corpori possit accidere primus e patriciis Corneliis
igni voluit cremari.   declarat enim Ennius de
Africano: "Hic est ille situs." vere; nam siti
dicuntur ii, qui conditi sunt.   nec tamen eorum ante
sepulchrum est, quam iusta facta et porcus caesus
est.   et quod nunc communiter in omnibus sepultis
venit usu, ut[4] humati dicantur, id erat proprium tum
in iis, quos humus iniecta contexerat, eumque morem
ius pontificale confirmat.   nam prius quam in os
iniecta gleba est, locus ille, ubi crematum est corpus,
nihil habet religionis; iniecta gleba tum et illis

---

[1] *haud* supplied by H. Grotius; omitted in MSS.
[2] *si tam* dett.; omitted in ABH.
[3] *ne* supplied by Lambinus; omitted in MSS.
[4] *venit usu ut* Moser; *penitus* AB; *penit* H; *ponitur ut*
Turnebus.

---

[1] *i.e.* the burial of the uncovered body in the earth.   Compare Xenophon, *Cyropaedia* VIII, 7, 25.

But in my opinion the most ancient mode of burial was that which, according to Xenophon, was used in the case of Cyrus. For the body is restored to earth, and placed and laid to rest as if its mother's covering were drawn over it.[1] The tradition is that our own King Numa was buried with these very rites in that tomb which is not far from the altar of Fons, and we know that this method is used by the Cornelian clan even up to our own day. Sulla, when victorious, ordered the remains of Marius, which had been buried, to be scattered abroad in the river Anio,[2] for he was actuated by a hatred more cruel than he could have entertained if he had been as wise as he was bitter. Perhaps it was through fear that the same fate might befall himself that Sulla, for the first time in the history of the patrician Cornelii, ordered his own body to be cremated. For Ennius says of Africanus, "Here is he laid";[3] and rightly, for "laid" is used of those whose bodies are buried. Yet their places of burial do not really become graves until the proper rites are performed and the pig is slain. And the expression which has now come to be used in regard to all who are buried, namely, that they are "laid in the earth," was then confined to those cases where earth was cast upon the bodies and covered them. The existence of this custom is confirmed by the rules of the pontiffs. For until turf is cast upon the bones, the place where a body is cremated does not have a sacred character; but after the turf is cast, [the burial is

---

[2] Compare Valerius Maximus IX, 2, 1.

[3] These are generally believed to have been the first words of an epigram (see *De Re Pub.*, Unplaced Fragments, No. 4 and note).

humatus est, et gleba[1] vocatur, ac tum denique
multa religiosa iura conplectitur. itaque in eo, qui
in nave necatus, deinde in mari proiectus esset,
decrevit P. Mucius familiam puram, quod os supra
terram non extaret; porcam heredi esse contractam,
et habendas triduum ferias, et porco femina piaculum pati,[2] si in mari mortuus esset, eadem praeter
piaculum et ferias.

58   XXIII. *A.* Video, quae sint in pontificio iure, sed
quaero ecquidnam sit in legibus.

M. Pauca sane, Tite, et, uti arbitror, non ignota
vobis; sed ea non tam ad religionem spectant quam
ad ius sepulchrorum. "Hominem mortuum," inquit
lex in duodecim, "in urbe ne sepelito neve urito,"
credo vel propter ignis periculum. quod autem
addit: "neve urito," indicat, non qui uratur, sepeliri,
sed qui humetur.

A. Quid, qui post duodecim in urbe sepulti sunt
clari viri?

M. Credo, Tite, fuisse aut eos, quibus hoc ante
hanc legem virtutis causa tributum est, ut Poplicolae,
ut Tuberto, quod eorum posteri iure tenuerunt, aut
eos, si qui hoc, ut C. Fabricius, virtutis causa soluti

---

[1] Corrupt: *tum et illis humatis est et gleba* H; *tumulus et
humatus et gleba* AB; *tum mortuus humatus est, et sepulchrum
vocatur* suggested by Vahlen.
[2] Corrupt: *piaculum pati* ABH; *piandum atqui* Davies.

---

[1] The text is corrupt and the passage obscure.
[2] The text is corrupt and the passage obscure.

considered accomplished, and the spot is called a grave]; [1] then, but not before, it has the protection of many laws of sanctity. Thus in the case of a man who died on shipboard and whose body was thrown into the sea, Publius Mucius declared the family free from defilement, because none of the bones lay above the earth; yet the sow was required of his heir; a holiday of three days had to be kept, [and expiation made by sacrificing the sow]; [2] if he had met death in the sea, the same rule would have held with the exception of the expiatory offering and the holidays.

XXIII. *A.* I understand the provisions of the pontiffs, but should like to inquire if there is anything on the subject in the laws.

M. Really very little, Titus, and I believe you are not ignorant of what there is; but those provisions are not concerned so much with religion as with the legal status of graves. "A dead man," says a law of the Twelve Tables, "shall not be buried or burned inside the city." I suppose the latter is on account of danger of fire. But this addition of the words " or burned " proves that a body which is cremated is not considered as buried, but only one which is laid in the earth.

A. What about the burial of famous men inside the city since the time of the Twelve Tables?

M. I suppose, Titus, that there were men to whom this privilege had been granted on account of their merit before this law was enacted, such as Poplicola and Tubertus, and that this privilege was legally retained by their descendants, or else that there were those who, like Gaius Fabricius, were made exempt from the operation of the law on

443

legibus consecuti sunt. sed ut[1] in urbe sepeliri lex
vetat, sic decretum a pontificum collegio non esse
ius in loco publico fieri sepulchrum. nostis extra
portam Collinam aedem Honoris; aram in eo loco
fuisse memoriae proditum est; ad eam cum lamina
esset inventa et in ea scriptum lamina, " Honoris,"
ea causa fuit, cur aedes haec dedicaretur.[2] sed cum
multa in eo loco sepulchra fuissent, exarata sunt;
statuit enim collegium locum publicum non potuisse
privata religione obligari.

59   Iam cetera in duodecim minuendi sumptus sunt
lamentationisque funebris, translata de Solonis fere
legibus. " Hoc plus," inquit, "ne facito : rogum
ascea ne polito." nostis, quae sequuntur ; discebamus
enim pueri duodecim ut carmen necessarium ; quas
iam nemo discit. extenuato igitur sumptu " tribus riciniis et tunicla purpurea et decem tibicinibus" tollit
etiam lamentationem : " Mulieres genas ne radunto
neve lessum funeris ergo habento." hoc veteres
interpretes Sex. Aelius, L. Acilius non satis se in-
tellegere dixerunt, sed suspicari vestimenti aliquod
genus funebris, L. Aelius lessum quasi lugubrem
eiulationem, ut vox ipsa significat ; quod eo magis
iudico verum esse, quia lex Solonis id ipsum vetat.

---

[1] *ut* supplied by Madvig ; omitted in MSS.
[2] *cur aedis haec dedicaretur* suggested by Vahlen ; *aedis haec
dedicare* ABH ; *ut aedis haec dedicaretur* Huschke.

---

[1] Compare Plutarch, *Quaest. Rom.* 79.
[2] See Plutarch, *Solon* 21.

account of their merit.[1]   But just as the law forbids
burial within the city, so it has been decreed by
the college of pontiffs that it is unlawful for a grave
to be made in a public place.   You are acquainted
with the Temple of Honour outside the Colline
Gate; there is a tradition that an altar once
stood on that spot, and, when a metal plate was
found near it with the inscription "To Honour,"
this caused the dedication of the present temple.
But, as there were many graves in that place, they
were dug up; for the college decided that a place
which was public property could not receive a sacred
character through rites performed by private
citizens.

There are other rules, too, in the Twelve Tables,
which provide for the limitation of the expense and
the mourning at funerals, which were borrowed for
the most part from the laws of Solon.[2]   The law
says, "Do no more than this: do not smooth the
pyre with an axe."   You know what follows, for
we learned the Law of the Twelve Tables in our
boyhood as a required formula; though no one
learns it nowadays.   The expense, then, is limited
to "three veils, a purple tunic, and ten flute-
players"; the mourning is also limited: "Women
shall not tear their cheeks, nor have a *lessum* at
a funeral."   The older interpreters, Sextus Aelius
and Lucius Acilius, admitted that they did not
fully understand this, but suspected that it referred
to some kind of a mourning garment.   Lucius Aelius
thought a *lessum* was a sort of sorrowful wailing,
for that is what the word would seem to signify.
I incline to the latter interpretation, since this is
the very thing which is forbidden in Solon's law.

haec laudabilia et locupletibus fere cum plebe communia; quod quidem maxime e natura est, tolli fortunae discrimen in morte.

60 XXIV. Cetera item funebria, quibus luctus augetur, duodecim sustulerunt. "Homini," inquit, "mortuo ne ossa legito, quoi pos funus faciat." excipit bellicam peregrinamque mortem. haec praeterea sunt in legibus de unctura . . .[1] que; servilis unctura tollitur omnisque circumpotatio; quae et recte tolluntur neque tollerentur, nisi fuissent. "Ne sumptuosa respersio, ne longae coronae, ne acerrae" praetereantur. illa iam significatio est laudis ornamenta ad mortuos pertinere, quod coronam virtute partam et ei, qui peperisset, et eius parenti sine fraude esse lex inpositam iubet. credoque, quod erat factitatum, ut uni plura funera[2] fierent lectique plures sternerentur, id quoque[3] ne fieret, lege sanctum est. qua in lege cum esset: "Neve aurum addito," videte[4] quam humane excipiat altera lex: "At[5] cui auro dentes iuncti[6] escunt, ast im cum illo sepeliet uretve, se fraude esto." et simul illud videtote, aliud habitum esse sepelire et urere.

[1] Vahlen suggests *de unctura (cena)que.*
[2] *funera* is commonly supplied; omitted in MSS.
[3] *id quoque* B[2]; *id quodque* AB[1]H; *id quod* R. Schoell.
[4] *videte* supplied by Vahlen; omitted in MSS.
[5] *altera lex: at* Mueller; *altera lex praecipit altera lege at* A[2]BH; *altera lex praecepit altera lege at* A[1].
[6] *iuncti* H; *iuncti* or *vincti* AB.

[1] Compare Pliny, *Nat. Hist.* XXI, 3, 7.

These provisions are praiseworthy and applicable in general both to the rich and the common people; for it is quite in accordance with nature that differences in wealth should cease with death.

XXIV. Other funeral customs likewise, which tend to increase grief, are forbidden by the Twelve Tables. One of these laws runs: "A dead man's bones shall not be gathered up so that a funeral may be held later." Here an exception is made in case of death in war or on foreign soil. These laws also contain the following provisions about anointing and [a dinner]; anointing by slaves is prohibited, and also any sort of drinking-bout. It is quite proper that these things should have been abolished, and the law would not have forbidden them unless they had actually occurred. Let us pass over the prohibition: "No costly sprinkling, or long garlands, or censers." Obviously the principle on which these provisions are based is that only the rewards which have been bestowed as a mark of honour belong to the dead, for the law provides that a garland earned by bravery may be worn with impunity both by the man who earned it and also by his father.[1] And I suppose that it was because the custom had grown up of making more than one funeral and preparing more than one bier for a single person, that these things were also forbidden by law. And whereas the same law forbids the use of gold, note what a considerate exception is made by another: "If a man's teeth are joined with gold, it shall be no violation of the law to bury or burn his body along with that gold." Note that in this case also burial and cremation are treated as different things.

61　　Duae sunt praeterea leges de sepulchris, quarum altera privatorum aedificiis, altera ipsis sepulchris cavet. nam quod "rogum bustumve novum" vetat "propius sexaginta pedes adigi aedes alienas invito domino," incendium veretur acerbum ; quod[1] autem "forum," id est vestibulum sepulchri, "bustumve usu capi" vetat, tuetur ius sepulchrorum.

　　Haec habemus in duodecim sane secundum naturam, quae norma legis est; reliqua sunt in more : funus ut indicatur, si quid ludorum, dominus-
62 que funeris utatur accenso atque lictoribus, honoratorum virorum laudes in contione memorentur easque etiam cantus ad tibicinem prosequatur, cui nomen neniae, quo vocabulo etiam apud[2] Graecos cantus lugubres nominantur.

　　XXV. *A.* Gaudeo nostra iura ad naturam accommodari maiorumque sapientia admodum delector ; sed requiro, ut ceteri sumptus, sic etiam sepulchrorum modum.

　　M. Recte requiris ; quos enim ad sumptus progressa iam ista res sit, in C. Figuli sepulchro vidisse te[3] credo. minimam olim istius rei fuisse cupiditatem

---

[1] *acerbum [vetat]* ; *quod* Vahlen ; *acerbum vetat quod* ABH.
[2] *apud* supplied by Wesenberg ; omitted in MSS.
[3] *te* supplied by Madvig ; omitted in MSS.

---

[1] If Cicero is right, the Greek word is unknown to us.

In addition there are two laws about graves, one of which protects buildings which are private property, and the other the graves themselves. For the provision: "No new pyre or mound may be erected nearer than sixty feet to another person's building without the consent of its owner," is made through fear of dangerous fires. But the rule that ownership of the "forum" (that is, the entrance court of a tomb), or of the mound may not be acquired by possession protects the special privileges of graves.

These are the rules which we find in the Twelve Tables, and they are certainly in agreement with Nature, which is the standard of law. Our other rules are based on custom; namely, that a funeral is to be announced, if any games are to take place; that the person who conducts it may be provided with an attendant and lictors; that in the case of men who have been honoured by the State a laudatory oration is to be pronounced before an assembly of the people, and that this oration is to be followed by a song to the music of the flute. To this song the name "nenia" is given, a word which signifies a song of mourning in Greek also.[1]

XXV. *A.* I am pleased to hear that our laws are in accord with Nature, and the wisdom of our ancestors delights me exceedingly. But I look in vain for any limitation of the cost of monuments, such as is provided in the case of the other expenditures.

M. You are right in looking for such a provision; for I suppose that you have seen in the monument of Gaius Figulus an example of how far extravagance has gone in that respect. Many proofs have come to us that in the time of our ancestors there was

multa extant exempla maiorum. nostrae quidem legis
interpretes, quo capite iubentur sumptum et luctum
removere a deorum Manium iure, hoc intellegant
in primis, sepulchrorum magnificentiam esse minu-
63 endam. nec haec a sapientissimis legum scriptoribus
neglecta sunt; nam et Athenis iam ab illo primo
rege[1] Cecrope, ut aiunt, permansit hoc ius terra
humandi; quam[2] cum proxumi fecerant obductaque
terra erat, frugibus obserebatur, ut sinus et gremium
quasi matris mortuo tribueretur, solum autem frugibus expiatum ut vivis redderetur. sequebantur
epulae, quas inibant propinqui coronati, apud quos
de mortui laude cum, si quid[3] veri, erat praedicatum
(nam mentiri nefas habebatur), . . . ac[4] iusta con-
64 fecta erant. posteaquam, ut scribit Phalereus,
sumptuosa fieri funera et lamentabilia coepissent,
Solonis lege sublata sunt; quam legem eisdem
prope verbis nostri decemviri in decimam tabulam
coniecerunt; nam de tribus riciniis et pleraque illa
Solonis sunt; de lamentis vero expressa verbis sunt:
"Mulieres genas ne radunto neve lessum funeris
ergo habento."

XXVI. De sepulchris autem nihil est apud
Solonem amplius quam "ne quis ea deleat neve

---

[1] *ab illo primo rege* Mueller; *illo mores a* ABH.
[2] If the text is not to be considered corrupt, *humationem,*
supplied from *humandi,* must be taken as the antecedent of
quam, as Vahlen suggests.
[3] *si quid* Turnebus; *ni quid* AB; *vi quid* H.
[4] *ac* Turnebus; *ad* ABH. Vahlen marks a gap in the
text before *ac.*

---

[1] The tomb of Cecrops was on the Acropolis at Athens
(*Frag. Hist. Graec.,* Antiochus, 15).
[2] Demetrius of Phalerum.

very little desire for such luxury. Those who interpret our law, indeed, understand the command that extravagance in expenditure and in mourning is to be considered as no part of the rights of the gods of the lower world, to mean primarily that lavishness in the erection of monuments is to be limited. Nor has this subject been neglected by the wisest of the lawgivers; for at Athens, it is said, the present law providing for burial in the earth comes down from their first king Cecrops;[1] and when the nearest relatives had performed this rite, and the body was covered with earth, then the spot was sown with grain, that the breast and bosom of his mother, as it were, might be granted to the dead, but that the soil, purified by grain, might be restored to the use of the living. A feast followed, at which the near relatives were crowned with garlands; and on this occasion, after the praiseworthy deeds of the deceased had been commemorated, if this could be done with truthfulness (for it was considered wicked to give false praise), . . . and the proper rites were performed. Later, according to the man of Phalerum,[2] when extravagance in expenditure and mourning grew up, it was abolished by the law of Solon—a law which our decemvirs took over almost word for word and placed in the tenth Table. For what it contained about the three veils, and most of the rest, comes from Solon, and in regard to mourning they have followed his wording exactly: "Women shall not tear their cheeks or have a *lessum* at a funeral."

XXVI. But Solon has no other rules about graves except one to the effect that no one is to destroy them or place the body of a stranger in them. And

alienum inferat," poenaque est, " si quis bustum "
(nam id puto appellari τύμβον) " aut monimentum,"
inquit, " aut columnam violarit, laeserit, fregerit."
sed post aliquanto propter has amplitudines sepulchrorum, quas in Ceramico videmus, lege sanctum
est, " ne quis sepulchrum faceret operosius quam
65 quod decem homines effecerint triduo "; neque id
opere tectorio exornari nec hermas, quos vocant,
licebat inponi, nec de mortui laude nisi in publicis
sepulturis nec ab alio, nisi qui publice ad eam rem
constitutus esset, dici licebat. sublata etiam erat
celebritas virorum ac mulierum, quo lamentatio
minueretur ; auget enim luctum concursus hominum.
66 quocirca Pittacus omnino accedere quemquam vetat
in funus aliorum. sed ait rursus idem Demetrius
increbruisse eam funerum sepulchrorumque magnificentiam, quae nunc fere Romae est ; quam consuetudinem lege minuit ipse ; fuit enim hic vir, ut
scitis, non solum eruditissimus, sed etiam civis e re
publica maxime tuendaeque civitatis peritissimus.
is igitur sumptum minuit non solum poena, sed
etiam tempore ; ante lucem enim iussit efferri.
sepulchris autem novis finivit modum ; nam super
terrae tumulum noluit quicquam[1] statui nisi colu-

---

[1] *quicquam* Lambinus ; *quod* ABH.

---

[1] A " Hermes-pillar " consisted of a head carved on the top
of a square pedestal.

a penalty is fixed in case anyone violates, throws
down, or breaks a burial mound (for that, I think,
is what he means by τύμβος), or monument, or
column. But somewhat later, on account of the
enormous size of the tombs which we now see in the
Ceramicus, it was provided by law that no one
should build one which required more than three
days' work for ten men. Nor was it permitted to
adorn a tomb with stucco-work nor to place upon it
the Hermes-pillars,[1] as they are called. Speeches
in praise of the deceased were also forbidden except
at public funerals, and then allowed to be made
only by orators officially appointed for the purpose.
The gathering of large numbers of men and women
was also forbidden, in order to limit the cries of
mourning; for a crowd increases grief. It was for
this reason that Pittacus forbade anyone at all who
did not belong to the family to attend a funeral.
But Demetrius also tells us that pomp at funerals
and extravagance in monuments increased again to
about the degree which obtains in Rome at present.
Demetrius himself limited these practices by law.
For this man, as you know, was not only eminent in
learning, but also a very able citizen in the practical
administration and maintenance of the government.
He, then, lessened extravagance not only by the
provision of a penalty for it, but also by a rule
in regard to the time of funerals; for he ordered
that corpses should be buried before daybreak.[2]
But he also placed a limit upon newly erected
monuments, providing that nothing should be built
above the mound of earth except a small column no

[2] Compare the provisions of the Emperor Julian (Julian,
Ep. 77).

mellam tribus cubitis ne altiorem aut mensam aut labellum et huic procurationi certum magistratum praefecerat.

67   XXVII. Haec igitur Athenienses tui.   sed videamus Platonem, qui iusta funerum reicit ad interpretes religionum; quem nos morem tenemus. de sepulchris autem dicit haec : vetat ex agro culto eove, qui coli possit, ullam partem sumi sepulchro; sed quae natura agri tantum modo efficere possit, ut mortuorum corpora sine detrimento vivorum recipiat, ea potissimum ut conpleatur; quae autem terra fruges ferre et ut mater cibos suppeditare possit, eam ne quis nobis minuat neve vivus neve

68 mortuus.   extrui autem vetat sepulchrum altius, quam quod quinque homines [1] quinque diebus absolverint, nec e lapide excitari plus nec inponi, quam quod capiat laudem mortui, incisam ne plus quattuor herois versibus, quos "longos" appellat Ennius.   habemus igitur huius quoque auctoritatem de sepulchris summi viri, a quo item funerum sumptus praefinitur ex censibus a minis quinque usque ad minam.   deinceps dicit eadem illa de inmortalitate animorum et reliqua post mortem tranquillitate bonorum, poenis impiorum.

69   Habetis igitur explicatum omnem, ut arbitror, religionum locum.

----

[1] *quinque homines* supplied by Turnebus (from Plato); omitted in MSS.

----

[1] *Laws* XII, 958 D–E.
[2] Compare Isidore, *Orig.* I, 38, 6 : hexametros Latinos primum fecisse Ennius traditur eosque longos vocat.

more than three cubits in height, or else a table or small basin; and he put a special official in charge of the enforcement of these laws.

XXVII. These, then, are the laws of your beloved Athenians. But let us turn to Plato, who referred the proper rites for funerals to the counsellors on religious matters; a custom which still holds among us. But he does state the following rules about graves:[1] he forbids any piece of land which is in cultivation or capable of cultivation to be used for a grave, but provides that the greatest possible use shall be made of the sort of land which can receive the bodies of the dead without injury to the living. But land which is capable of producing crops and of supplying us with food like a mother should not be decreased in extent by anyone, living or dead. He forbids the erection of any loftier monument than could be completed by five men in five days. He also prohibits the setting up or placing upon the grave of a larger block of stone than is sufficient to contain the praise of the deceased, inscribed upon it in not more than four heroic verses—those which Ennius calls "long verses."[2] Thus we have also the authoritative opinion of this eminent man on the subject of graves. He also fixes the expenditure for the funeral at from one mina[3] to five, in accordance with a man's wealth. After this follows the famous passage on the immortality of the soul, the tranquil rest which awaits the good after death, and the punishments in store for the wicked.

This completes, I believe, my consideration of this whole subject of religion.

[3] Plato, *Laws* XII, 959 D. 1 mina = about £3 10*s.*

Q. Nos vero, frater, et copiose quidem ; sed perge cetera.

M. Pergam equidem et, quoniam libitum est vobis me ad haec inpellere, hodierno sermone conficiam, spero, hoc praesertim die ; video enim Platonem idem fecisse, omnemque orationem eius de legibus peroratam esse uno aestivo die.   sic igitur faciam et dicam de magistratibus ; id enim est profecto, quod constituta religione rem publicam contineat maxime.

A. Tu vero dic et istam rationem quam coepisti tene.

---

[1] Plato, *Laws* III, 683 C.

Q. It is complete, my dear brother, and nothing is lacking. Now continue with what remains.

M. I will continue, indeed, and since you have been pleased to urge me on to this discussion, I will finish it in to-day's conversation, I hope—especially since it is a day like this. Indeed, I remember that Plato did the same thing, completing his whole discussion of the laws in one summer day.[1] Therefore I will do so too, and will take up the magistrates next. For, next to the establishment of religion, they are surely the most important in the formation of a commonwealth.

A. Continue then, and carry out the plan you have begun.

DE LEGIBUS

LIBER TERTIUS

1   I. *M.* Sequar igitur, ut institui, divinum illum virum, quem quadam admiratione commotus saepius fortasse laudo, quam necesse est.

A. Platonem videlicet dicis.[1]

M. Istum ipsum, Attice.

A. Tu vero eum nec nimis valde umquam nec nimis saepe laudaveris ; nam hoc mihi etiam nostri illi, qui neminem nisi suum laudari volunt, concedunt, ut eum arbitratu meo diligam.

M. Bene hercle faciunt. quid enim est elegantia tua dignius, cuius et vita et oratio consecuta mihi videtur difficillimam illam societatem gravitatis cum humanitate ?

A. Sane gaudeo, quod te interpellavi, quoniam quidem tam praeclarum mihi dedisti iudicii tui testimonium. sed perge, ut coeperas.

2   *M.* Laudemus igitur prius legem ipsam veris et propriis generis sui laudibus.

A. Sane quidem, sicut de religionum lege fecisti.

M. Videtis igitur magistratus hanc esse vim, ut praesit praescribatque recta et utilia et coniuncta

---

[1] *dicis* dett. ; *diligis* ABH.

---

[1] The Epicureans.

LAWS

BOOK III

I. *M.* I will follow again, then, as I did before, the example of that divine personage, whom I praise oftener, perhaps, than I should, such is the admiration I feel for him.

A. Of course you mean Plato.

M. None other, Atticus.

A. Surely you can never praise him too highly or too often; for even those friends of ours [1] who object to the praise of anyone outside their own company allow me to be as fond of him as I like.

M. And they are certainly right in that. For what could be more appropriate to the good taste of a man like yourself, who in both his life and his language has achieved, in my opinion, that most difficult combination of dignity and refinement?

A. I am very glad indeed that I interrupted you, since you have given me so fine a proof of your good opinion. But go on as you have begun.

M. First, then, let us commend the law itself with words of praise which are both merited and appropriate to its character.

A. By all means, just as you did in the case of the law of religion.

M. You understand, then, that the function of a magistrate is to govern, and to give commands which are just and beneficial and in conformity with the law.

459

cum legibus. ut enim magistratibus leges, ita
populo praesunt magistratus, vereque dici potest
magistratum legem esse loquentem, legem autem
3 mutum magistratum. nihil porro tam aptum est
ad ius condicionemque naturae (quod cum dico,
legem a me dici intellegi volo) quam imperium;
sine quo nec domus ulla nec civitas nec gens nec
hominum universum genus stare nec rerum natura
omnis nec ipse mundus potest; nam et hic deo
paret, et huic oboediunt maria terraeque, et
hominum vita iussis supremae legis obtemperat.
4   II. Atque ut ad haec citeriora veniam et notiora
nobis, omnes antiquae gentes regibus quondam
paruerunt. quod genus imperii primum ad homines
iustissimos et sapientissimos deferebatur (idque
in[1] re publica nostra maxime valuit, quoad ei regalis potestas praefuit), deinde etiam deinceps
posteris prodebatur, quod et in[2] iis etiam, qui
nunc regnant, manet. quibus autem regia potestas
non placuit, non ii nemini, sed non semper uni parere
voluerunt. nos autem, quoniam leges damus liberis
populis, quaeque de optima re publica sentiremus,
in sex libris ante diximus, accommodabimus hoc
tempore leges ad illum, quem probamus, civitatis
5 statum. magistratibus igitur opus est, sine quorum
prudentia ac diligentia esse civitas non potest,
quorumque descriptione omnis rei publicae moderatio continetur. neque solum iis praescribendus
est imperandi, sed etiam civibus obtemperandi

---

[1] *idque in* A; *idque ut in* BH; *idque et in* Davies.
[2] *quod et in* ABH; *quod in* Baiter.

For as the laws govern the magistrate, so the magistrate governs the people, and it can truly be said that the magistrate is a speaking law, and the law a silent magistrate. Nothing, moreover, is so completely in accordance with the principles of justice and the demands of Nature (and when I use these expressions, I wish it understood that I mean Law) as is government, without which existence is impossible for a household, a city, a nation, the human race, physical nature, and the universe itself. For the universe obeys God; seas and lands obey the universe, and human life is subject to the decrees of supreme Law.

II. But to return to matters which are closer to us and better known : all ancient nations were at one time ruled by kings. This kind of authority was entrusted at first to those who excelled in justice and wisdom, as was notably the case in our own State while the monarchy lasted. Later the kingship was handed down to the king's descendants, which is still the custom in present-day kingdoms. Now those who objected to monarchy desired, not to have no one to obey, but not always to obey the same man. But we, since we are providing a system of law for free nations, and have presented our conception of the ideal State in our six earlier books,[1] shall now propose laws appropriate to the kind of State there described, which we consider the best. Accordingly we must have magistrates, for without their prudence and watchful care a State cannot exist. In fact the whole character of a republic is determined by its arrangements in regard to magistrates. Not only must we inform them of the limits of their administrative authority ; we must also instruct the citizens as to the extent of their obligation to obey them.

modus; nam et qui bene imperat, paruerit aliquando necesse est, et qui modeste paret, videtur,
qui aliquando imperet, dignus esse. itaque oportet
et eum, qui paret, sperare se aliquo tempore im-
peraturum et illum, qui imperat, cogitare brevi
tempore sibi esse parendum. nec vero solum ut
obtemperent oboediantque magistratibus, sed etiam
ut eos colant diligantque, praescribimus, ut Charondas
in suis facit legibus; noster vero Plato Titanum e
genere statuit eos, qui, ut illi caelestibus, sic hi
adversentur magistratibus.

Quae cum ita sint, ad ipsas ıam leges veniamus,
si placet.

A. Mihi vero et istud et ordo iste rerum placet.

6 III. *M. Iusta imperia sunto, ısque civis modeste ac
sine recusatione parento ; magistratus nec oboedientem
et noxium*[1] *civem multa vinculis verberibusve coherceto,
ni par maiorve potestas populusve prohibessit, ad quos
provocatio esto. quom magistratus iudicassit inrogassitve,*[2]
*per populum multae poenae certatio esto. militiae ab eo,
qui imperabit, provocatio nec esto, quodque is, qui bellum
geret, imperassit, ius ratumque esto.*

---

[1] *noxium* Victorius; *innoxium* ABH, Mommsen (see
Strafrecht p. 38, n. 1).
[2] *inrogassitve* H ; *inrogasitve* AB.

---

[1] See Stobaeus, *Florilegium* 44, 40.
[2] *Laws* III, 701 C.
[3] Cicero's commentary on the fiıst part of these "laws" is
lost ; see §§ 9, 17, and 18.

For the man who rules efficiently must have obeyed
others in the past, and the man who obeys dutifully
appears fit at some later time to be a ruler. Thus he
who obeys ought to expect to be a ruler in the future,
and he who rules should remember that in a short
time he will have to obey. And we must provide,
as Charondas[1] does in his laws, not only that the
citizens be obedient and dutiful toward the magistrates, but also that they love and honour them.
Indeed my beloved Plato[2] thought that those who
rebel against their magistrates, as the Titans did
against the gods, are to be classed as of the Titans'
brood.

Having established these facts, we shall now
proceed to the statement of the laws themselves, if
that plan meets with your approval.

A. Indeed I approve not merely of that, but of
your whole order of treatment.

III. *M.*[3] *Commands shall be just,*[4] *and the citizens
shall obey them dutifully and without protest. Upon the
disobedient or guilty citizen the magistrate shall use
compulsion by means of fines, imprisonment, or stripes,
unless an equal or higher authority, or the people, forbid
it ; the citizen shall have the right of appeal to them.
After the magistrate has pronounced sentence, either of
death or fine,*[5] *there shall be a trial before the people for
the final determination of the fine or other penalty.
There shall be no appeal from orders given by a
commander in the field ; while a magistrate is waging war
his commands shall be valid and binding.*

---

[4] *i.e.* in accordance with law ; compare §§ 2–3.

[5] For the rendering of *indicassit inrogassitve* see Strachan-
Davidson, *Problems of the Roman Criminal Law*, Oxford, 1912,
pp. 173–8.

MARCUS TULLIUS CICERO

Minoris magistratus partiti iuris ploeres[1] *im ploera
sunto. militiae, quibus iussi erunt, imperanto eorumque
tribuni sunto, domi pecuniam publicam custodiunto,
vincula sontium servanto, capitalia vindicanto, aes, argentum aurumve publice signanto, litis contractas iudicanto,
quodcumque senatus creverit, agunto.*

7 *Suntoque aediles curatores urbis, annonae ludorumque
sollemnium, ollisque ad honoris amplioris gradum is
primus ascensus esto.*

*Censoris populi aevitates, suboles, familias pecuniasque
censento, urbista*[2] *templa, vias, aquas, aerarium, vectigalia
tuento populique partis in tribus discribunto, exin pecunias,
aevitatis, ordinis partiunto, equitum peditumque prolem
describunto, caelibes esse prohibento, mores populi regunto,
probrum in senatu ne relinquonto; bini sunto, magistratum
quinquennium habento; reliqui magistratus annui sunto;
eaque potestas semper esto.*

8 *Iuris disceptator, qui privata iudicet iudicarive iubeat,
praetor esto; is iuris civilis custos esto; huic potestate
pari, quotcumque senatus creverit populusve iusserit, tot
sunto.*

Regio imperio duo sunto, iique praeeundo, iudicando,

[1] *ploeres* Mueller; *plures* ABH.
[2] *urbista templa* (corrupt) ABH; *urbis tecta templa* Bake.

---

[1] The *quaestores.*
[2] The *triumviri capitales.*
[3] The *triumviri aere argento auro flando feriundo.*

There shall be minor magistrates with partial authority, who shall be assigned to special functions. In the army they shall command those over whom they are placed, and be their tribunes ; in the city they shall be custodians of public moneys ;[1] they shall have charge of the confinement of criminals ; they shall inflict capital punishment ;[2] they shall coin bronze, silver, and gold money ;[3] they shall decide lawsuits ;[4] they shall do whatsoever the Senate shall decree.

There shall be aediles, who shall be curators of the city, of the markets, and of the customary games. This magistracy shall be their first step in the advancement to higher office.

Censors shall make a list of the citizens, recording their ages, families, and slaves and other property. They shall have charge of the temples, streets, and aqueducts within the city, and of the public treasury and the revenues. They shall make a division of the citizens into tribes, and other divisions according to wealth, age, and rank. They shall enrol the recruits for the cavalry and infantry ; they shall prohibit celibacy ; they shall regulate the morals of the people ; they shall allow no one guilty of dishonourable conduct to remain in the Senate. They shall be two in number, and shall hold office for five years. The other magistrates shall hold office for one year. The office of censor shall never be vacant.

The administrator of justice, who shall decide or direct the decision of civil cases, shall be called praetor ; he shall be the guardian of the civil law. There shall be as many praetors, with equal powers, as the Senate shall decree, or the people command.

There shall be two magistrates with royal powers. Since they lead, judge, and confer, from these functions

---

[4] The *decemviri litibus iudicandis.*

MARCUS TULLIUS CICERO

consulendo praetores, iudices, consules appellamino ; [1]
militiae summum ius habento, nemini parento ; ollis salus
populi suprema lex esto.

9 Eumdem magistratum, ni interfuerint decem anni, ne
quis capito ; aevitatem annali lege servanto.

Ast quando duellum gravius, discordiae civium escunt,
oenus ne amplius sex menses, si senatus creverit, idem
iuris quod duo consules teneto, isque ave sinistra dictus
populi magister esto ; equitatumque qui regat habeto pari
iure cum eo, quicumque erit iuris disceptator.

Ast quando consulis magisterve populi nec escunt,[2]
reliqui magistratus ne sunto ;[3] auspicia patrum sunto,
ollique ec se produnto, qui comitiatu creare consules rite
possit.[4]

Imperia, potestates, legationes, quom senatus creverit
populusve iusserit, ex urbe exeunto, duella iusta iuste
gerunto, sociis parcunto, se et suos[5] continento, populi
sui gloriam augento, domum cum laude redeunto.

---

[1] appellamino B ; apellamino H[1] ; appellanto AH[2] (impera-
tives in -mino occur in early Latin. but, with this exception,
only in the passive second and third persons singular).

[2] escunt is the common reading ; т̄ AB ; runt H ; erunt Halm.

[3] reliqui magistratus ne sunto is transposed by Huschke
to the end of the preceding paragraph (after disceptator).

[4] possit Turnebus ; possim A[1]BH[1] ; possint A[2]H[2] ; possit
Buecheler.

[5] suos Turnebus ; servos AH ; servus B.

---

[1] In the early days of the Republic the consul appears to
have been called praetor (prae-itor) and iudex, names which
evidently refer to his military and civil powers respectively.
According to tradition these titles are older than that of
consul, which the ancients derived from consulere ; Mommsen
thinks it to have been formed from cum and salire, and to be
equivalent in meaning to collega.

[2] Leges annales fixed the earliest ages at which the various
public offices could be held.

they shall be called praetors, judges, and consuls.ᵃ In *the field they shall hold the supreme military power ; they shall be subject to no one ; the safety of the people shall be their highest law.*

No one shall hold the same office a second time except after an interval of ten years. They shall observe the age limits fixed by a law defining the year.[2]

But when a serious war or civil dissensions arise, one man shall hold, for not longer than six months, the power which ordinarily belongs to the two consuls, if the Senate shall so decree. And after being appointed under favourable auspices, he shall be master of the people.[3] He shall have an assistant to command the cavalry,[4] whose rank shall be equal to that of the administrator of justice.[5]

But when there are neither consuls nor a master of the people, there shall be no other magistrates, and the auspices shall be in the hands of the Senate, which shall appoint one of its number [6] to conduct the election of consuls in the customary manner.

Officials with and without *imperium* [7] and ambassadors shall leave the city when the Senate shall so decree or the people so command ; they shall wage just wars justly ; they shall spare the allies ; they shall hold themselves and their subordinates in check ; they shall increase the national renown ; they shall return home with honour.[8]

---

[3] The *dictator.*

[5] The *praetor.*

[4] The *magister equitum.*

[6] The *interrex.*

[7] *Imperium* was the full power of the State, originally held by the king, and exercised by the higher republican magistrates. *Potestas* was a general word for the ordinary power of the magistrate ; it is here used in reference to magistrates without *imperium*, such as the quaestors. *Legati* are ambassadors and also assistants to magistrates with *imperium* acting as commanders of armies or as provincial governors.

[8] From this point on, Cicero's commentary on his laws is preserved : see §§ 18 ff.

Rei suae ergo ne quis legatus esto.

Plebes quos pro se contra vim auxilii ergo decem creassit, ei tribuni eius sunto, quodque i prohibessint quodque plebem rogassint, ratum esto ; sanctique sunto neve plebem orbam tribunis relinquunto.

10 *Omnes magistratus auspicium iudiciumque habento, exque is senatus esto ; eius decreta rata sunto ; ast potestas par maiorve prohibessit, perscripta servanto.*

Is ordo vitio vacato, ceteris specimen esto.

Creatio magistratuum, iudicia populi, iussa vetita quom suffragio cosciscentur, optumatibus nota, plebi libera sunto.

IV. Ast quid erit, quod extra magistratus coerari oesus sit, qui coeret populus creato eique ius coerandi dato.

Cum populo patribusque agendi ius esto consuli, praetori, magistro populi equitumque eique quem patres produnt[1] *consulum rogandorum ergo ; tribunisque, quos sibi plebes creassit,*[2] *ius esto cum patribus agendi ; idem ad plebem quod oesus erit ferunto.*

Quae cum populo quaeque in patribus agentur, modica sunto.

[1] *produnt* ABH ; *prodent* Moser.
[2] *creassit* Bake ; *rogassit* ABH.

No one shall be made an ambassador for the purpose of attending to his own personal affairs.

The ten officials whom the plebeians shall elect to protect them from violence shall be their tribunes. Their prohibitions and resolutions passed by the plebeians under their presidency shall be binding. Their persons shall be inviolable. They shall not leave the plebeians without tribunes.

All magistrates shall possess the right of taking the auspices, and the judicial power. The Senate shall consist of those who have held magistracies. Its decrees shall be binding. But in case an equal or higher authority than the presiding officer shall veto a decree of the Senate, it shall nevertheless be written out and preserved.

The senatorial order shall be free from dishonour, and shall be a model for the rest of the citizens.

When elective, judicial, and legislative acts of the people are performed by vote, the voting shall not be concealed from citizens of high rank, and shall be free to the common people.

IV. But if any acts of administration shall be necessary in addition to those done by the regular magistrates, the people shall elect officials to perform them, and give them the authority to do so.

Consuls, praetors, masters of the people, masters of the horse, and those officials whom the Senate shall appoint to conduct the election of consuls shall have the right to preside over meetings of the people and the Senate. The tribunes chosen by the plebeians shall have the right to preside over the Senate, and shall also refer whatever is necessary to the plebeians.

Moderation shall be preserved in meetings of the people and the Senate.

11   *Senatori, qui nec aderit, aut causa aut culpa esto ; loco senator et modo orato ; causas populi teneto.*

Vis in populo abesto. par maiorve potestas plus valeto.. ast quid turbassitur in agendo, fraus actoris esto. intercessor rei malae salutaris civis esto.

Qui agent, auspicia servanto, auguri publico parento, promulgata proposita in aerario cognita agunto, nec plus quam de singulis rebus semel consulunto, rem populum docento, doceri a magistratibus privatisque patiunto.

Privilegia ne inroganto ; de capite civis nisi per maximum comitiatum ollosque, quos censores in partibus populi locasint,[1] *ne ferunto.*

Donum ne capiunto neve danto neve petenda neve gerenda neve gestu potestate.

Quod quis earum rerum migrassit noxiae poena par esto.

Censoris[2] *fidem legum custodiunto ; privati ad eos acta referunto nec eo magis lege liberi sunto.*

Lex recitata est.   discedere et tabellam iubebo dari.

12   V. Q. Quam brevi,[3] frater, in conspectu posita

---

[1] *locasint* A[1] ; *locarint* A[2] ; *locassint* BH.
[2] *censoris* H[2] (cf. § 7) ; *caesoris* AB ; *caesaris* H[1].
[3] *quam brevi* is commonly read ; *quam com brevi* A ; *quam con brevi* H ; *quam cum brevi* B.

---

[1] *i.e.* a magistrate with equal or higher legal authority than the presiding officer shall have the right to veto acts done in a popular assembly.

A senator's absence from a meeting of the Senate shall be either for cause or culpable. A senator shall speak in his turn and at moderate length. He shall be conversant with public affairs.

No violence shall be used at meetings of the people. An equal or higher authority shall have the greater power.[1] But the presiding officer shall be responsible for any disorder which may occur. He who vetoes a bad measure shall be deemed a citizen of distinguished service.

Presiding officers shall observe the auspices and obey the State augur. They shall see that bills, after being read, are filed among the archives in the State treasury. They shall not take the people's vote on more than one question at a time. They shall instruct the people in regard to the matter in hand, and allow them to be instructed by other magistrates and by private citizens.

No law of personal exception shall be proposed. Cases in which the penalty is death or loss of citizenship shall be tried only before the greatest assembly and by those whom the censors have enrolled among the citizens.

No one shall give or receive a present, either during a candidacy or during or after a term of office.

The punishment for violation of any of these laws shall fit the offence.

The censors shall have charge of the official text of the laws. When officials go out of office, they shall refer their official acts to the censors, but shall not receive exemption from prosecution thereby.

The law has been read: "disperse, and I will order the ballots to be distributed."[2]

V. Q. In what brief form, my dear brother, you have placed before us your provisions in regard to

---

[2] A quotation from the formal proclamation of a magistrate presiding over a popular assembly.

est a te omnium magistratuum descriptio, sed ea paene nostrae civitatis, etsi a te paulum adlatum est novi.

M. Rectissime, Quinte, animadvertis; haec est enim, quam Scipio laudat in illis[1] libris et quam maxime probat temperationem rei publicae, quae effici non potuisset nisi tali descriptione magistratuum. nam sic habetote, magistratibus iisque, qui praesint, contineri rem publicam, et ex eorum conpositione, quod cuiusque rei publicae genus sit, intellegi. quae res cum sapientissime moderatissimeque constituta esset a maioribus nostris, nihil[2] habui, sane non multum,[3] quod putarem novandum in legibus.

13   *A.* Reddes igitur nobis, ut in religionis lege fecisti admonitu et rogatu meo, sic de magistratibus, ut disputes, quibus de causis maxime **placeat** ista descriptio.

M. Faciam, Attice, ut vis, et locum istum totum, ut a doctissimis Graeciae quaesitum et disputatum est, explicabo, et, ut institui, nostra iura attingam.

A. Istud maxime expecto disserendi genus.

• *M.* Atqui pleraque sunt dicta in illis libris, quod faciendum fuit, cum de optuma re publica quaereretur; sed huius loci de magistratibus sunt propria

---

[1] *illis* supplied by Turnebus ; omitted in MSS.
[2] H ends with the word *nihil.*
[3] *sane non multum* AB ; *sane non modo multum* dett.

the whole body of magistrates! Yet they are practically the same as those of our own State, though you have proposed a few innovations.

M. You are quite right, Quintus. For this is the balanced type of State which Scipio praises and most highly approves in the treatise to which I have referred, and such a State could not have been constituted without such provisions as these in regard to its magistrates. For you must understand that a government consists of its magistrates and those who direct its affairs, and that different types of States are recognized by their constitution of these magistracies. And since the wisest and most evenly balanced system has been devised by our own ancestors, I had no innovations, or at least only a few, which I thought ought to be introduced into the constitution.

A. And will you now be kind enough to present your reasons for considering these provisions in regard to the magistrates to be the best, as you did, at my suggestion and request, in your treatment of the laws of religion?

M. I will do as you ask, Atticus, treating the whole subject in accordance with the investigations and discussions of the most learned of the Greek writers. I shall also touch on our laws, as I did before.

A. That is exactly the method of treatment to which I am looking forward.

M. However, I included a great deal of general matter on this subject in my former work, as was necessary in an inquiry into the nature of the ideal State; but on this topic of the magistrates there are certain special points which have been investigated

473

quaedam a Theophrasto primum, deinde a Diogene[1]
Stoico quaesita subtilius.

14 VI. *A.* Ain tandem? etiam a Stoicis ista tractata
sunt?

M. Non sane nisi ab eo, quem modo nominavi,
et postea a magno homine et in primis erudito,
Panaetio. nam veteres verbo tenus acute illi quidem, sed non ad hunc usum popularem atque civilem
de re publica disserebant. ab hac familia magis
ista manarunt Platone principe; post Aristoteles
inlustravit omnem hunc civilem in disputando locum
Heraclidesque Ponticus profectus ab eodem Platone;
Theophrastus vero institutus ab Aristotele habitavit,
ut scitis, in eo genere rerum, ab eodemque Aristotele
doctus Dicaearchus huic rationi studioque non defuit;
post a Theophrasto Phalereus ille Demetrius, de quo
feci supra mentionem, mirabiliter doctrinam ex umbraculis eruditorum otioque non modo in solem
atque in pulverem, sed in ipsum discrimen aciemque
produxit. nam et mediocriter doctos magnos in re
publica viros, et doctissimos homines non nimis in
re publica versatos, multos commemorare possumus;
qui vero utraque re excelleret, ut et doctrinae

---

[1] *Diogene* Turnebus; *Dione* AB.

---

[1] We have record of treatises on law by both Theophrastus
(Περὶ Νόμων) and Diogenes (Νόμοι).
[2] See *De Re Pub.* I, 34, and Introduction to the *De Re Pub.*
p. 5.
[3] Here Academics and Peripatetics are classed together.
[4] Fragments remain of his work (or works), Περὶ Πολιτειῶν.

first by Theophrastus, and then with greater
accuracy by Diogenes the Stoic.[1]

VI. *A.* Do you really mean to say that even the
Stoics have treated these problems ?

M. None of them except the philosopher I have
just mentioned, and, after his time, the eminent and
very learned Panaetius.[2] For though the older
Stoics also discussed the State, and with keen
insight, their discussions were purely theoretical and
not intended, as mine is, to be useful to nations and
citizens. The other school[3] led by Plato provides
most of our present material. After him Aristotle
and Heraclides of Pontus,[4] another of Plato's pupils,
illuminated this whole subject of the constitution of
the State by their discussions. And, as you know,
Aristotle's pupil Theophrastus specialized in such
topics. Dicaearchus,[5] another of Aristotle's disciples, did not neglect this field of thought and
investigation. Later a follower of Theophrastus,
Demetrius of Phalerum,[6] whom I mentioned before,
had remarkable success in bringing learning out of
its shady bowers and scholarly seclusion, not merely
into the sunlight and the dust, but even into the
very battle-line and the centre of the conflict. For
we can mention the names of many great practical
statesmen who have been moderately learned, and
also of many very learned men who have had some
little experience in practical politics ; but who can
readily be found, except this man, that excelled in

[5] His work (Τριπολιτικός) on the mixed constitution of
Sparta is lost. For a controversy between Dicaearchus and
Theophrastus, see Cicero, *Ep. ad At* . II, 16, 3.

[6] A complete list of his political works, which include a
treatise on Laws (Περὶ Νόμων), is found in Diogenes Laertius,
V, 5, 80.

studiis et regenda civitate princeps esset, quis facile praeter hunc inveniri potest?

A. Puto posse, et quidem aliquem de tribus nobis; sed perge, ut coeperas.

15 VII. *M.* Quaesitum igitur ab illis est, placeretne [1] unum in civitate esse magistratum, cui reliqui parerent, quod exactis regibus intellego placuisse nostris maioribus. sed quoniam regale civitatis genus probatum quondam postea non tam regni quam regis vitiis repudiatum est, nomen tantum videbitur regis repudiatum, res manebit, si unus omnibus reliquis 16 magistratibus imperabit. quare nec ephori Lacedaemone sine causa a Theopompo oppositi regibus nec apud nos consulibus tribuni. nam illud quidem ipsum, quod in iure positum est, habet consul, ut ei reliqui magistratus omnes pareant excepto tribuno, qui post extitit, ne id, quod fuerat,[2] esset. hoc enim primum minuit consulare ius, quod exstitit ipse qui eo non teneretur, deinde quod attulit auxilium reliquis non modo magistratibus, sed etiam privatis consuli non parentibus.

17 *Q.* Magnum dicis malum; nam ista potestate nata gravitas optimatium cecidit convaluitque vis multitudinis.

---

[1] *-ne* is commonly supplied; omitted in MSS.
[2] *fuerat* Turnebus; *fuerit* AB.

both careers, so as to be foremost both in the pursuit of learning and in the actual government of a State?

A. Such a man can be found, I believe; in fact I think he would be one of us three! But continue with what you were saying.

VII. *M.* Well, then, these philosophers have considered whether it is best for the State to have one magistrate who shall be obeyed by everyone else. I understand that this was considered the best plan by our ancestors after the expulsion of the kings. But since the monarchy, which had formerly been approved, was later rejected, not so much through the fault of the kingship as that of the king, if one magistrate is to rule over all the others, it will seem that it was merely the name of king that was abolished, the institution remaining. Thus it was not without good reason that ephors were set up in opposition to the Spartan kings by Theopompus, and tribunes in opposition to the consuls among us. For the consul has the legal right to enforce obedience from all other officials except the tribunes, whose office was instituted later than that of the consul for the purpose of preventing what had taken place from ever happening again. For the existence of an official who was not subject to his orders was the first step in the diminution of the consul's power, the second being the fact that this same official upheld others also, private citizens as well as magistrates, in disobedience to the consul.

Q. What you have just mentioned was a great misfortune. For it was the institution of this office that brought about the decline in the influence of the aristocracy and the growth of the power of the multitude.

M. Non est, Quinte, ita. non ius enim illud solum superbius populo et violentius videri necesse erat? quo posteaquam modica et sapiens temperatio accessit. . .[1]

. . . Qui poterit *socios tueri*, si dilectum rerum utilium et inutilium non habebit? . . . (Macrob., *De Differ. et Societ. Gr. Lat. Verbi* 17, 6.)

. . . converte,[2] lex in omnis est.

18   VIII. *Domum cum laude redeunto.* nihil enim praeter laudem bonis atque innocentibus neque ex hostibus neque a sociis reportandum.

Iam illud apertum est profecto, nihil esse turpius quam est quemquam *legari nisi rei publicae causa.* omitto quem ad modum isti se gerant atque gesserint, qui legatione hereditatis aut syngraphas suas persequuntur; in hominibus est hoc fortasse vitium; sed quaero, quid reapse sit turpius quam sine procuratione senator legatus, sine mandatis, sine ullo rei publicae munere. quod quidem genus legationis ego consul, quamquam ad commodum senatus pertinere videbatur, tamen adprobante senatu frequentissimo, nisi mihi levis tribunus plebis tum intercessisset, sustulissem. minui tamen tempus et, quod erat infinitum, annuum feci. ita turpitudo manet diuturnitate sublata.

Sed iam, si placet, de provinciis decedatur in urbemque redeatur.

----

[1] See explanatory note.
[2] *converte* Vahlen; *convertem* AB.

----

[1] There is a great gap in our text at this point, at the end of which we find ourselves in the midst of Cicero's commentary on his laws. The following fragment, and the words with which the manuscript resumes, appear to be parts of his remarks on *sociis parcunto* and *populi sui gloriam augento* (§ 9).

M. You are mistaken, Quintus. For was it not inevitable that the consul's authority, when it stood alone, should seem too arrogant and tyrannical to the people? But a moderate and wise limitation of that power has occurred since then[1] . . . .

. . . Who will be able to *protect allies,* if he cannot distinguish between the useful and the useless? . . .

. . . apply [this to the rest]; the law refers to all.

VIII. *They shall return home with honour.* For nothing but honour from enemy or ally should be brought home by good and upright officials.

Also, it is obvious at once that nothing can be more disgraceful than *the appointment of an ambassador for any other than a public purpose.* I will say nothing of the behaviour, either at present or in the past, of those who go out as ambassadors to claim legacies or enforce contracts, for perhaps that is due to a weakness of human nature. But I ask only this: what could be more disgraceful than the mere fact of a senator's holding an appointment as ambassador without official duties, without instructions, without any public business whatever to attend to? In fact, when I was consul I should have been able to abolish embassies of this kind with the approbation of a full meeting of the Senate, in spite of the fact that the custom gave the Senate valuable privileges, if it had not been for the intercession of an irresponsible plebeian tribune; but I did limit the duration of such appointments, which had previously been unrestricted, to one year. And so the disgrace still persists, but with the allowance of time limited.

But now, if you please, let us leave the provinces and return to the city.

A. Nobis vero placet, sed iis, qui in provinciis sunt, minime placet.

19 *M.* At vero, Tite, si parebunt his legibus, nihil erit iis urbe, nihil domo sua dulcius nec laboriosius molestiusque provincia.

Sed sequitur lex, quae sancit eam *tribunorum plebis* potestatem, quae est[1] in re publica nostra; de qua disseri nihil necesse est.

Q. At mehercule ego, frater, quaero, de ista potestate quid sentias. nam mihi quidem pestifera videtur, quippe quae in seditione et ad seditionem nata sit; cuius primum ortum si recordari volumus, inter arma civium et occupatis et obsessis urbis locis procreatum videmus. deinde cum esset cito necatus tamquam ex duodecim tabulis insignis ad deformitatem puer, brevi tempore nescio quo pacto recreatus multoque taetrior et foedior renatus[2] est. IX. quae[3] enim ille non edidit? qui primum, ut impio dignum fuit, patribus omnem honorem eripuit, omnia infima summis paria fecit, turbavit, miscuit; cum adflixisset principum gravitatem, numquam tamen conquievit. namque ut C. Flaminium atque ea, quae iam prisca videntur propter vetustatem, relinquam, quid iuris bonis viris Ti. Gracchi tribunatus reliquit? etsi quinquennio ante Decimum[4] Brutum

---

[1] *est* supplied by Turnebus ; omitted in MSS.
[2] *renatus* Lambinus ; *natus* AB.
[3] *quae* dett. ; *quem* AB ; *quid* Madvig.
[4] *Decimum* Victorius ; *dum* A¹B ; *decium* A².

---

[1] At the time of the Decemvirs (see *De Re Pub.* II, 61–63), when there were neither consuls nor tribunes.

[2] The limitation of the exposure of male children to those who were deformed is traditionally ascribed to Romulus (Dionys. Halic. II, 15 ; Seneca, *Dial.* III, 15, 2).

A. We are glad to do so indeed, but those who are in the provinces are not glad at all!

M. And yet, Titus, if they will obey these laws, nothing will be dearer to them than the city and their own homes, and nothing will seem more laborious and irksome than a province.

But the following law, which establishes the power of the *tribunes of the plebeians* just as it exists in our State, needs no discussion.

Q. But, my dear brother, I certainly want to ask your opinion of this power. For it seems to me a mischievous thing, born in civil strife and tending to civil strife. For if we take the trouble to recall its origin, we shall see that it was begotten in the midst of dissension among our citizens, after parts of the city had been occupied and besieged by armed forces. Then, after it had been quickly killed,[1] as the Twelve Tables direct that terribly deformed infants shall be killed,[2] it was soon revived again, somehow or other, and at its second birth was even more hideous and abominable than before. IX. Of what crimes has it not been guilty! Its first acts—deeds worthy of its impious nature—were to deprive the senators of all their privileges, to make the lowest equal to the highest everywhere, and to produce utter confusion and disorder. But even after destroying the authority of the aristocracy, it never rested. For, to omit the cases of Gaius Flaminius[3] and others, which occurred so long ago as to seem out of date, what rights did the tribunate of Tiberius Gracchus leave to the best citizens? Yet it was even five years before Gracchus that the

---

[3] See Cicero, *Brutus* 57 ; *De Senec.* 11.

et P. Scipionem consules (quos et quantos viros!)
homo omnium infimus et sordidissimus, tribunus
plebis C. Curiatius, in vincula coniecit, quod ante
factum non erat. C. vero Gracchi ruinis et iis sicis,
quas ipse se proiecisse in forum dixit, quibus digla-
diarentur inter se cives, nonne omnem rei publicae
statum permutavit? quid iam de Saturnino, Sul-
picio, reliquis dicam, quos ne depellere quidem a
21 se sine ferro potuit res publica? cur autem aut
vetera aut aliena proferam potius quam et nostra et
recentia? quis umquam tam audax, tam nobis
inimicus fuisset, ut cogitaret umquam de statu
nostro labefactando, nisi mucronem aliquem tri-
bunicium exacuisset in nos? quem cum homines
scelerati ac perditi non modo ulla in domo, sed
nulla in gente reperirent, gentes sibi in tenebris rei
publicae perturbandas putaverunt. quod nobis
quidem egregium et ad inmortalitatem memoriae
gloriosum, neminem in nos mercede ulla tribunum
potuisse reperiri, nisi cui ne esse quidem licuisset
22 tribuno. sed ille quas strages edidit, eas videlicet,
quas sine ratione ac sine ulla spe bona furor edere
potuit inpurae beluae multorum inflammatus furo-
ribus! quam ob rem in ista quidem re vehementer
Sullam probo, qui tribunis plebis sua lege iniuriae
faciendae potestatem ademerit, auxilii ferendi reli-

---

[1] In 138 B.C.
[2] Gracchus' revolutionary proposals, which excited bitter
party strife, appear to be meant.
[3] A reference to Clodius, a patrician, who induced a
plebeian to adopt him, that he might become eligible for the
plebeian tribunate, in order to attack Cicero

plebeian tribune Gaius Curiatius,[1] the meanest and
vilest of mankind, committed an act that was
absolutely without precedent, casting into prison the
consuls Decimus Brutus and Publius Scipio—and
what men they were! Furthermore, was it not the
overthrow of Gaius Gracchus and the casting of
daggers into the forum, that citizens might use
them to stab one another[2] (this is Gracchus' own
description of what he did), that brought about,
through the tribunate, a complete revolution in the
State? Why should I go on to mention Saturninus,
Sulpicius, and all the other tribunes from whom the
republic could not protect herself without resorting
to the sword? But why should I cite ancient
examples which affected others rather than recent
instances from our own experience? Who has ever
been so bold or so personally hostile to us as to plot
the undermining of our position, that he has not
sharpened some tribune's dagger against us? And
when wicked and depraved men could find no such
instrument in any family, or even in any clan, they
actually thought it necessary, in those dark days
of the republic, to throw the clans into confusion.[3]
And to us indeed it is a proud distinction which
will bring us an immortality of fame that no
tribune could be induced for any reward to act
against us, except one who had no right ever to be
a tribune. But he, what ruin did he create—ruin
assuredly such as could only have been created by
the unreasoning and hopeless frenzy of a foul
beast inflamed by the frenzy of a mob! Wherefore
I heartily approve of Sulla's laws on this subject,
which took from the plebeian tribunes the power
of doing mischief, and left them only the right to

querit, Pompeiumque nostrum ceteris rebus omnibus
semper amplissimis summisque ecfero laudibus, de
tribunicia potestate taceo ; nec enim reprehendere
libet nec laudare possum.

23   X. *M.* Vitia quidem tribunatus praeclare, Quinte,
perspicis, sed est iniqua in omni re accusanda praetermissis bonis malorum enumeratio vitiorumque
selectio ; nam isto quidem modo vel consulatus
vituperari potest, si consulum, quos enumerare nolo,
peccata collegeris. ego enim fateor in ista ipsa
potestate inesse quiddam mali ; sed bonum, quod
est quaesitum in ea, sine isto malo non haberemus.
"nimia potestas est tribunorum plebis." quis negat ?
sed vis populi multo saevior multoque vehementior,
quae, ducem quod habet, interdum lenior est, quam
si nullum haberet. dux enim suo se [1] periculo progredi cogitat, populi impetus periculi rationem sui
24 non habet. "at aliquando incenditur." et quidem
saepe sedatur. quod enim est tam desperatum
collegium, in quo nemo e decem sana mente sit ?
quin ipsum Ti. Gracchum non solum neglectus,[2] sed
etiam sublatus intercessor evertit,[3] quid enim illum

---

[1] *se* dett. ; omitted in AB.
[2] *neglectus* Manutius ; *nectus* AB.
[3] *evertit* Vahlen ; *fuerat* AB.

---

[1] Sulla's laws, passed in 81 B.C., forbade the tribunes to propose laws before the plebeian assembly, and shut them off
from advancement to the higher offices of the State. The
repeal of these laws and the restoration of the full powers
of the tribunes, which had been begun in 75 B.C., was completed in Pompey's consulship (70 B C.).
[2] Marcus Octavius, Tiberius' colleague and political
opponent, was illegally deposed from the tribunate by the
people at Tiberius' request in 133 B.C.

give relief; and as for our friend Pompey, though in all other matters I always give him generous and, indeed, the highest praise, yet as regards his attitude toward the power of the tribunes I have nothing to say, for I do not wish to criticize him, and I cannot praise him.[1]

X. *M.* You see the faults of the tribunate very clearly, Quintus, but in an attack on any institution it is unfair to omit all mention of its advantages, and enumerate only its disadvantages, picking out its special shortcomings. Even the consulship can be condemned by the use of such a method, if you collect the bad deeds of certain consuls whom I do not care to name. And indeed I acknowledge that there is an element of evil in the very power of the tribunate; but we could not have the good aimed at when the office was established without the evil you refer to. "The tribunes of the plebs have too much power," you say. Who can deny it? But the power of the people themselves is much more cruel, much more violent; and yet this power is sometimes milder in practice because there is a leader to control it than if there were none. For a leader is conscious that he is acting at his own risk, whereas the impulse of the people has no consciousness of any risk to itself. "But," you object, "the tribunes sometimes excite the people." Yes, and they often calm them too. For what college of tribunes could be of so desperate a character that not a single one of the ten retained his sanity? Why, it was the fact that Tiberius Gracchus not only disregarded another tribune's veto, but even deprived him of his powers,[2] that caused his own downfall. For what else overthrew him but his act of

485

aliud perculit, nisi quod potestatem intercedenti [1]
collegae abrogavit ?

Sed tu sapientiam maiorum in illo vide : concessa
plebei ista a patribus potestate [2] arma ceciderunt,
restincta seditio est ; inventum est temperamentum,
quo tenuiores cum principibus aequari se putarent ;
in quo uno fuit civitatis salus. "at duo Gracchi
fuerunt." et praeter eos quamvis enumeres multos
licet, cum deni creentur, non [3] nullos in omni
memoria reperies perniciosos tribunos, leves etiam,
non bonos, fortasse plures ; invidia quidem summus
ordo caret, plebes de suo iure periculosas conten-
25 tiones nullas facit. quam ob rem aut exigendi reges
non fuerunt aut plebi re, non verbo danda libertas ;
quae tamen sic data est, ut multis institutis [4] praeclarissimis adduceretur, ut auctoritati principum
cederet.

XI. Nostra autem causa, quae, optume et dulcissume
frater, incidit in tribuniciam potestatem, nihil habuit
contentionis cum tribunatu ; non enim plebes incitata nostris rebus invidit, sed vincula soluta sunt et
servitia concitata, adiuncto terrore etiam militari.
neque nobis cum illa tum peste certamen fuit, sed
cum gravissimo rei publicae tempore, cui ni [5] cessis-

---

[1] *intercedenti* Madvig ; *intercedendi* AB.

[2] *concessa plebei ista a patribus potestate* Vahlen ; *concessa plebe ista patribus ista potestas* A ; *concesse plebe ista potestas* B.

[3] *non* supplied by Turnebus ; omitted in MSS.

[4] *institutis* supplied by Vahlen ; omitted in MSS.

[5] *ni* supplied by Goerenz ; omitted in MSS.

---

[1] According to tradition the plebeian tribunate was
instituted in 494 after the first secession of the plebeians to
the Sacred Mount (Livy, II, 33 ; *De Re Pvb.* II 58).

[2] Clodius.

expelling his colleague from office when he exercised the right of veto against him?

But consider the wisdom of our ancestors in this matter. When the Senate had granted this power to the plebeians,[1] conflict ceased, rebellion was at an end, and a measure of compromise was discovered which made the more humble believe that they were accorded equality with the nobility; and such a compromise was the only salvation of the State. "But we have had the two Gracchi," you say. Yes, and you could mention many more besides; for when a college of ten is elected, you will find some tribunes in every period whose activities are harmful, and perhaps more who **are** irresponsible and without influence for good; but in the meantime the senatorial order is not subject to envy, and the common people make no desperate struggles for their rights. Thus it is clear that either the monarchy ought never to have been abolished, or else that real liberty, not a pretence of it, had to be given to the common people; but this liberty has been granted in such a manner that the people were induced by many excellent provisions to yield to the authority of the nobles.

XI. But, my dear and excellent brother, to speak of my own case, which had to do with the power of the tribunes, it gave me no cause of complaint against the tribunate itself. For it was not the common people who were excited to envy of my position; on the contrary, the prisons were opened, the slaves were enlisted against me, and the threat of military force was employed. What I really had to contend with was not that villain,[2] but a most serious crisis in the life of the State; and if I had

sem, non diuturnum beneficii mei patria fructum
tulisset. atque haec rerum exitus indicavit; quis
enim non modo liber, sed servus [1] libertate dignus
26 fuit, cui nostra salus cara non esset? quodsi is casus
fuisset rerum, quas pro salute rei publicae gessimus,
ut non omnibus gratus esset, et si nos multitudinis
furentis inflammata invidia pepulisset tribuniciaque
vis in me populum, sicut Gracchus in Laenatem,
Saturninus in Metellum, incitasset, ferremus, o
Quinte frater, consolarenturque nos non tam philosophi, qui Athenis fuerunt, qui hoc facere debent,
quam clarissimi viri, qui illa urbe pulsi carere ingrata
civitate quam manere inprobam [2] maluerunt.

Pompeium vero quod una ista in re non ita valde
probas, vix satis mihi illud videris attendere, non
solum ei, quid esset optimum, videndum fuisse, sed
etiam quid necessarium. sensit enim deberi non
posse huic civitati illam potestatem; quippe quam
tanto opere populus noster ignotam expetisset, qui
posset carere cognita? sapientis autem civis fuit
causam nec perniciosam et ita popularem, ut non
posset obsisti, perniciose populari civi non relinquere.

---

[1] *liber sed servus* Goerenz; *liber servus* AB; *liber sed etiam
servus* dett.
[2] *improbam* AB; *in improba* is the common reading.

---

[1] The tribune Gaius Gracchus had Publius Popilius Laenas
banished in 123 B.C.
[2] Quintus Caecilius Metellus Numidicus refused to take
the oath required of senators to observe the Agrarian law of
Lucius Apuleius Saturninus, and went into exile (in 100 B.C.).
[3] Cicero is evidently thinking of the ostracism of such
leaders as Aristides, Themistocles, and Cimon (compare *De
Re Pub.* I, 5).

not yielded to it my country would not have had
the benefit of my services very long. And the
result proved that I was right; for who was there,
not merely among the free citizens, but even among
the slaves who were worthy of freedom, who was
not devoted to my safety? But if the outcome of
the services which I performed for the safety of the
republic had not met with universal approval; if the
hatred of a raging mob had been aroused against me
and had brought about my exile; if the tribunician
power had excited the people against me, as it was
excited against Laenas by Gracchus,[1] and against
Metellus by Saturninus,[2] nevertheless I could have
endured it, my dear brother, and I should have
been consoled not so much by the Athenian philosophers, whose business it is to supply such comfort,
as by those illustrious citizens of Athens who, when
driven into exile, preferred to give up an ungrateful
city rather than allow it to continue in its wrong-
doing.[3]

You say that you cannot fully approve of Pompey
in this one matter; but it seems to me that you
have hardly given sufficient consideration to this
point—that he had to determine, not merely what
was ideally best, but also what was practically
necessary. For he realized that this office was indispensable in our republic; for when our people
had so eagerly sought it before having had any
experience of it, how could they dispense with it now
that they had learned what it was? It was the duty
of a wise citizen, in dealing with an institution not
evil in itself and so dear to the people that it could
not be combated, not to leave its defence to a popular
leader, which would have had evil consequences.

Scis solere, frater, in huius modi sermone, ut transiri alio possit, dici "admodum" aut "prorsus ita est."

Q. Haud equidem adsentior, tu tamen ad reliqua pergas velim.

M. Perseveras tu quidem et in tua vetere sententia permanes?

A. Nec mehercule ego sane a Quinto nostro dissentio, sed ea, quae restant, audiamus.

27 XII. M. Deinceps igitur *omnibus magistratibus auspicia et iudicia* dantur, iudicia, ut esset populi potestas, ad quam provocaretur, auspicia, ut multos inutiles comitiatus probabiles inpedirent morae; saepe enim populi impetum iniustum auspiciis di immortales represserunt.

Ex iis autem, qui magistratum ceperunt, quod *senatus efficitur,* populare sane neminem in summum locum nisi per populum venire sublata cooptatione censoria. sed praesto est huius viti temperatio, quod senatus lege nostra confirmatur auctoritas;

28 sequitur enim: *Eius decreta rata sunto.* nam ita se res habet, ut, si senatus dominus sit publici consilii, quodque is creverit, defendant omnes, et si ordines reliqui principis ordinis consilio rem publicam guber-

490

You are aware, my dear brother, that it is customary in dialogues of this kind, to say " Quite right," or " That is certainly true," in order to introduce a transition to a new subject.

Q. As a matter of fact I do not agree with you, but for all that I should like you to go on to the next topic.

M. You are persistent then, and hold to your previous opinion ?

A. Neither am I at variance with Quintus, I assure you ; but let us hear what remains to be said.

XII. *M.* In the next law, then, *the right of taking the auspices and the judicial power* are granted *to all magistrates.* The grant of the judicial power is made to establish the people's right of judgment on appeal : that of taking the auspices is intended to bring about the adjournment of many unprofitable meetings of the assembly through plausible excuses for delay ; for the immortal gods have often put down unjust assertions of the people's will by means of the auspices.

The law which provides that *the Senate is to consist exclusively of ex-magistrates* is certainly a popular measure, as it ensures that no one shall enter that exalted order except by popular election, the censors being deprived of the right of free choice. But we have provided for a mitigation of this disadvantage, since the authority of the Senate is legally established by our next provision, which is : *Its decrees shall be binding.* For the fact is that if the Senate is recognized as the leader of public policy, and all the other orders defend its decrees, and are willing to allow the highest order to conduct the government by its wisdom, then this com-

nari velint, possit ex temperatione iuris, cum potestas in populo, auctoritas in senatu sit, teneri ille moderatus et concors civitatis status, praesertim si proximae legi parebitur. nam proximum est: *Is ordo vitio careto, ceteris specimen esto.*

Q. Praeclara vero, frater, ista lex, sed et late patet, ut vitio careat ordo, et censorem quaerit[1] interpretem.

29   *A.* Ille vero etsi tuus est totus ordo gratissimamque memoriam retinet consulatus tui, pace tua dixerim, non modo censores, sed etiam iudices omnes potest defatigare.

XIII. *M.* Omitte ista, Attice; non enim de hoc senatu nec his de hominibus, qui nunc sunt, sed de futuris, si qui forte his legibus parere voluerint, haec habetur oratio. nam cum omni vitio carere lex iubeat, ne veniet quidem in eum ordinem quisquam vitii particeps. id autem difficile factu est nisi educatione quadam et disciplina; de qua dicemus aliquid fortasse, si quid fuerit loci aut temporis.

30   *A.* Locus certe non deerit, quoniam tenes ordinem legum, tempus vero largitur longitudo diei. ego autem, etiamsi praeterieris, repetam a te istum de educatione et de disciplina locum.

---

[1] *quaerit* Turnebus; *quaerat* AB.

---

[1] Compare Book II, 69.

promise, by which supreme power is granted to the people and actual authority to the Senate, will make possible the maintenance of that balanced and harmonious constitution which I have described, especially if our next law is obeyed. It is as follows: *That order shall be free from dishonour, and shall be a model for the rest of the citizens.*

Q. That is certainly an excellent law, brother; but the provision that the order shall be free from dishonour is a very general one, and needs a censor to interpret it.

A. Although that order is thoroughly loyal to you and retains the most grateful recollection of your consulship, with your permission I may say that the task of punishing its misdeeds would wear out all the judges as well as the censors!

XIII. *M.* We need not enter into that, Atticus. For we are not talking about the present Senate or the men of our own day, but about those of the future; that is, in case any of them ever are willing to obey these laws of mine. For as our law requires that senators be free from all dishonour, no one who is guilty of anything dishonourable will so much as enter that order. Of course this is difficult of accomplishment except through education and training; and on this point I may perhaps have something to say, if I can find the place for it and we have the time.

A. You will certainly have no difficulty in finding a place for it, since you are taking up the whole system of law in regular order, and as for time, the long day gives us that in abundance.[1] But if you do omit this discussion of education and training, I shall insist on your returning to it.

M. Tu vero et istum, Attice, et si quem alium praeteriero.

Ceteris specimen esto. quod si tenemus,[1] tenemus omnia. ut enim cupiditatibus principum et vitiis infici solet tota civitas, sic emendari et corrigi continentia. vir magnus et nobis omnibus amicus, L. Lucullus, ferebatur, quasi commodissime respondisset, cum esset obiecta magnificentia villae Tusculanae, duo se habere vicinos, superiorem equitem Romanum, inferiorem libertinum; quorum cum essent magnificae villae, concedi sibi oportere, quod iis, qui inferioris ordinis essent, liceret. non vides, Luculle, a te id ipsum natum, ut illi cuperent? 31 quibus id, si tu non faceres, non liceret. quis enim ferret istos, cum videret eorum villas signis et tabulis refertas, partim publicis, partim etiam sacris et religiosis? quis non frangeret eorum libidines, nisi illi ipsi, qui eas frangere deberent, cupiditatis eiusdem[2] tenerentur? XIV. nec enim tantum mali est peccare principes, quamquam est magnum hoc per se ipsum malum, quantum illud, quod permulti imitatores principum existunt. nam licet videre, si velis replicare memoriam temporum, qualescumque summi civitatis viri fuerint, talem civitatem fuisse; quaecumque mutatio morum in principibus extiterit, 32 eandem in populo secutam. idque haud paulo est

---

[1] *tenemus* supplied by Bake; omitted in MSS.
[2] *cupiditatis eiusdem* AB; *cupiditatibus eisdem* dett.

M. Yes, Atticus, call my attention to that or to anything else I may omit.

It shall be a model for the rest of the citizens. If we secure this, we shall have secured everything. For just as the whole State is habitually corrupted by the evil desires and the vices of its prominent men, so is it improved and reformed by self-restraint on their part. The reply made by our common friend, the eminent Lucius Lucullus, to a criticism of the luxury of his villa at Tusculum was considered a very neat one. He said that he had two neighbours, a Roman knight living above him, and a freedman below; as their villas also were most luxurious, he thought that he ought to have the same privilege as members of a lower order. But, Lucullus, do you not see that even their desire for luxury is your own fault? If you had not indulged in it, it would not have been permissible for them to do so. For who could have endured seeing these men's villas crowded with statues and paintings which were partly public property and partly sacred objects belonging to the gods? Who would not put an end to their inordinate desires, if those very men whose duty it was to put an end to them were not guilty of the same passions? XIV. For it is not so mischievous that men of high position do evil—though that is bad enough in itself—as it is that these men have so many imitators. For, if you will turn your thoughts back to our early history, you will see that the character of our most prominent men has been reproduced in the whole State; whatever change took place in the lives of the prominent men has also taken place in the whole people. And we can be much more confident of the soundness of

verius, quam quod Platoni nostro placet, qui musicorum cantibus ait mutatis mutari civitatum status.
ego autem nobilium vita victuque mutato mores
mutari civitatum puto. quo perniciosius de re
publica merentur vitiosi principes, quod non solum
vitia concipiunt ipsi, sed ea infundunt in civitatem,
neque solum obsunt, quod ipsi corrumpuntur, sed
etiam quod corrumpunt, plusque exemplo quam
peccato nocent. atque haec lex dilatata in ordinem
cunctum coangustari etiam potest; pauci enim atque
admodum pauci honore et gloria amplificati vel corrumpere mores civitatis vel corrigere possunt.

Sed haec et nunc satis et in illis libris tractata
sunt diligentius. quare ad reliqua veniamus.

33   XV. Proximum autem est de suffragiis, quae iubeo
nota esse optimatibus, populo libera.

A. Ita mehercule attendi nec satis intellexi, quid
sibi lex aut quid verba ista vellent.

M. Dicam, Tite, et versabor in re difficili ac
multum et saepe quaesita, suffragia in magistratu
mandando ac de reo iudicando sciscendaque[1] in
lege aut rogatione clam an palam ferri melius esset.

---

[1] *sciscenda* supplied by Vahlen ; omitted in MSS.

---

[1] Compare Book II, 39.
[2] The passage of the *De Re Pub.* referred to is lost.

this theory than of that of our beloved Plato's. For he thought that the characteristics of a nation could be changed by changing the character of its music.[1] But I believe that a transformation takes place in a nation's character when the habits and mode of living of its aristocracy are changed. For that reason men of the upper class who do wrong are especially dangerous to the State, because they not only indulge in vicious practices themselves, but also infect the whole commonwealth with their vices ; and not only because they are corrupt, but also because they corrupt others, and do more harm by their bad examples than by their sins. But this law, which applies to the whole senatorial order, could be made even narrower in its application. For a few men—very few, in fact—on account of their high official position and great reputation, have the power either to corrupt the morals of the nation or to reform them.

But I have said enough on this subject, which is treated even more completely in my former work ;[2] therefore let us proceed to what follows.

XV. The next law takes up the subject of votes, which, according to my decree, *shall not be concealed from citizens of high rank, and shall be free to the common people.*

A. I certainly paid careful attention, but I could get no clear idea of the meaning of this law or of the terms in which you have stated it.

M. I will explain it, Titus. The subject is a difficult one, which has frequently been investigated. The problem is this : in electing magistrates, judging criminal cases, and voting on proposed laws, is it better for votes to be recorded openly or secretly ?

497

Q. An etiam id dubium est? vereor ne a te rursus dissentiam.

M. Non facies, Quinte. nam ego in ista sum sententia, qua te fuisse semper scio, nihil ut fuerit in suffragiis voce melius; sed obtineri an possit[1] videndum est.

34 *Q.* Atqui, frater, bona tua venia dixerim, ista sententia maxime et fallit imperitos et obest saepissime rei publicae, cum aliquid verum et rectum esse dicitur, sed obtineri, id est obsisti posse populo, negatur. primum enim obsistitur, cum agitur severe, deinde vi opprimi in bona causa est melius quam malae cedere. quis autem non sentit omnem auctoritatem optimatium tabellariam legem abstulisse? quam populus liber numquam desideravit, idem oppressus dominatu ac potentia principum flagitavit. itaque graviora iudicia de potentissimis hominibus extant vocis quam tabellae. quam ob rem suffragandi nimia libido in non bonis causis eripienda fuit potentibus, non latebra danda populo, in qua bonis ignorantibus, quid quisque sentiret, tabella vitiosum occultaret suffragium. itaque isti rationi[2] neque

---

[1] *obtineri an possit* is the common reading; *optineri an possunt* A B; *obtineri ne ea non possint* Mueller.

[2] *rationi* A; *ratione* B; *rogationi* Lambinus.

498

Q. Can there be any question about that? I am afraid I am going to disagree with you again.

M. I am sure you will not, Quintus. For my opinion is the one I know you have always held, namely, that no method of voting could be better than that of open declaration. But we must consider whether or not this method is a practicable one.

Q. But, my dear brother, allow me to say with your permission that this is a view which, more than any other, both leads the inexperienced astray, and is very frequently a hindrance in public affairs; the belief, I mean, that certain measures are wise and good, but are impracticable; that is, that the people cannot be opposed. For, in the first place, the people can be opposed if things are carried with a high hand by the presiding officer; and, secondly, it is better even to be overpowered in the defence of a good cause than to surrender to a bad one. But everyone knows that laws which provide a secret ballot have deprived the aristocracy of all its influence. And such a law was never desired by the people when they were free, but was demanded only when they were tyrannized over by the powerful men in the State. (For this very reason we have records of severer condemnations of powerful men under the oral method of voting than when the ballot was used.) Therefore means should have been found to deprive powerful leaders of the people's undue eagerness to support them with their votes even in the case of bad measures, but the people should not have been provided with a hiding-place, where they could conceal a mischievous vote by means of the ballot, and keep the aristocracy in ignorance of their real opinions. For these reasons

lator quisquam est inventus nec auctor umquam
35 bonus. XVI. sunt enim quattuor leges tabellariae,
quarum prima de magistratibus mandandis. ea est
Gabinia, lata ab homine ignoto et sordido. secuta
biennio post Cassia est de populi iudiciis a nobili
homine lata, L. Cassio, sed, pace familiae dixerim,
dissidente a bonis atque omnis rumusculos populari
ratione aucupante. Carbonis est tertia de iubendis
legibus ac vetandis, seditiosi atque inprobi civis, cui
ne reditus quidem ad bonos salutem a bonis potuit
36 adferre. uno in genere relinqui videbatur vocis
suffragium, quod ipse Cassius exceperat, perduellio-
nis. dedit huic quoque iudicio C. Coelius tabellam
doluitque, quoad vixit, se, ut opprimeret C. Popilium,
nocuisse rei publicae. et avus quidem noster singulari virtute in hoc municipio, quoad vixit, restitit
M. Gratidio, cuius in matrimonio sororem, aviam
nostram, habebat, ferenti legem tabellariam; exci-
tabat enim fluctus in simpulo, ut dicitur, Gratidius,
quos post filius eius Marius in Aegaeo excitavit mari.

---

[1] Proposed by Aulus Gabinius, tribune 139 B.C. Compare
the newly discovered Livy epitome (Book LIV, *Papyri Oxyr.*
IV, 101, lines 193 ff.) : A. Gabinius verna[e nepos rogationem
tulit] suffragium per ta[bellam ferri].

[2] Proposed by Lucius Cassius Longinus Ravilla, tribune
137 B.C. (compare Cicero, *Brutus*, 97 and 106).

[3] The *Lex Papiria*, proposed by Gaius Papirius Carbo,
tribune 131 B.C.

[4] The *Lex Coelia*, proposed by Gaius Coelius Caldus,
tribune 107 B.C.

[5] Arpinum.

[6] This Marius Gratidianus was adopted by one of the
Marii ; the reference is probably to the excitement about the

no man of high character has ever proposed or supported a measure like yours.   XVI. There are indeed four such balloting laws in existence.   The first is concerned with the election of magistrates; this is the Gabinian Law,[1] proposed by a man who was unknown and of low degree.   That was followed two years later by the Cassian Law,[2] which referred to trials before the people; it was proposed by Lucius Cassius, who was a nobleman, but—I say it without prejudice to his family—stood apart from the aristocracy, and, by favouring popular measures, was always seeking the fickle applause of the mob.   The third law is that of Carbo,[3] which applies to the adoption or rejection of proposed laws; this Carbo was a factious and mischievous citizen, who could not gain his personal safety from the aristocracy even by returning to his allegiance to their party.   The method of oral voting, then, appeared to have gone out of existence except in trials for treason, which even Cassius had omitted from his balloting law. But Gaius Coelius[4] provided the ballot even for such trials; however, he regretted to the end of his days that he had done an injury to the republic in order to destroy Gaius Popilius.   And in fact our grandfather, during his whole life, opposed with the greatest energy the passage of a balloting law in this town,[5] although his wife (our grandmother) was the sister of Marcus Gratidius, the man who was proposing such a law.   For Gratidius raised a storm in a wine-ladle, as the popular saying goes, just as his son Marius[6] did later in the Aegean Sea.

coinage during his praetorship in 86 B.C. (Cicero, *De Officiis* III, 80), the wine-ladle and the Aegean Sea signifying respectively Arpinum and Rome.

ac nostro quidem . . . cui cum res esset ad se delata,
M. Scaurus consul : " Utinam," inquit, " M. Cicero,
isto animo atque virtute in summa re publica nobiscum versari quam in municipali maluisses ! "

37   Quam ob rem, quoniam non recognoscimus nunc
leges populi Romani, sed aut repetimus ereptas aut
novas scribimus, non quid hoc populo obtineri possit,
sed quid optimum sit, tibi dicendum puto. nam
Cassiae legis culpam Scipio tuus sustinet, quo
auctore lata esse dicitur. tu si tabellariam tuleris,
ipse praestabis ; nec enim mihi placet nec Attico
nostro, quantum e vultu eius intellego.

   XVII. *A.* Mihi vero nihil umquam populare placuit, eamque optimam rem publicam esse dico, quam
hic consul constituerat, quae sit in potestate optimorum.

38   *M.* Vos quidem, ut video, legem antiquastis sine
tabella. sed ego, etsi satis dixit pro se in illis libris
Scipio, tamen ita libertatem istam largior [1] populo,
ut auctoritate et valeant et utantur boni. sic enim
a me recitata lex est de suffragiis : *optimatibus nota,
plebi libera sunto.* quae lex hanc sententiam con-

---

[1] *tamen ita libertatem istam largior* Klotz ; *tamen ista
libertatem istam largior* A B ; *tamen istam libertatem largior*
Vahlen.

---

[1] Something, probably only a few words, has been lost at
this point.

Indeed [1] . . . . to our [grandfather] . . . . when the matter was reported to him, Marcus Scaurus the consul said to him : " Marcus Cicero, I wish you had chosen to dedicate your efforts to the welfare of the great republic with the same spirit and energy which you have shown in the affairs of a small town."

Wherefore, since we are not now simply rehearsing the actual laws of Rome, but restoring old laws which have been lost, or else originating new ones, I think you ought to propose, not what can be secured from the Roman people such as it is at present, but what is actually the best. Your beloved Scipio received the blame for the Cassian Law, since his support is said to have made its enactment possible, and if you propose a balloting law, you must take the responsibility for it alone. For it will not receive my approval, nor that of Atticus, so far as I can judge from his expression.

XVII. *A.* Certainly no popular measure has ever pleased me, and I think the best government is that which was put in force by Marcus here during his consulship—one that gives the power to the aristocracy.

M. Well, I see that you have rejected my law without the use of the ballot ! But let me explain —though Scipio has given a sufficient defence of these ideas in my former work—that I am granting this freedom to the people in such a way as to ensure that the aristocracy shall have great influence and the opportunity to use it. For the text of my law in regard to votes is as follows: *they shall not be concealed from citizens of high rank, and shall be free to the people.* This law implies the

503

tinet, ut omnes leges tollat, quae postea latae sunt,
quae tegunt omni ratione suffragium, ne quis inspi-
ciat tabellam, ne roget, ne appellet; pontes etiam
39 lex Maria fecit angustos. quae si opposita sunt
ambitiosis, ut sunt fere, non reprehendo; sin non[1]
valuerint tamen leges ut ne sit ambitus, habeat sane
populus tabellam quasi vindicem libertatis, dum
modo haec optimo cuique et gravissimo civi ostenda-
tur ultroque offeratur, ut in eo sit ipso libertas, in
quo populo potestas honeste bonis gratificandi datur.
eoque nunc fit illud, quod a te modo, Quinte, dictum
est, ut minus multos tabella condemnet, quam
solebat vox, quia populo licere satis est. hoc re-
tento reliqua voluntas auctoritati aut gratiae traditur.
itaque, ut omittam largitione corrupta suffragia, non
vides, si quando ambitus sileat, quaeri in suffragiis
quid optimi viri sentiant? quam ob rem lege nostra
libertatis species datur, auctoritas bonorum retinetur,
contentionis causa tollitur.

40   XVIII. Deinde sequitur, quibus *ius sit cum populo
agendi aut cum senatu.* tum[2] gravis et, ut arbitror,
praeclara lex: *quae cum populo*[3] *quaeque in patribus*

---

[1] *non* supplied by Vahlen ; omitted in MSS.
[2] *tum* supplied by Vahlen ; omitted in MSS.
[3] *quae cum populo* supplied in dett. and by Turnebus;
omitted in A B.

---

[1] The citizens deposited their ballots from "bridges" or
"passages," which were evidently made narrow in order to
keep spectators at a distance.

repeal of all the recent laws which ensure the
secrecy of the ballot in every possible way, providing as they do that no one shall look at a ballot,
and that no one shall question or accost the voters.
The Marian Law even made the passages narrow.[1]
If such provisions as these are made to interfere
with the buying of votes, as they usually are, I do
not criticize them ; but if laws have never actually
prevented bribery, then let the people have their
ballots as a safeguard of their liberty, but with the
provision that these ballots are to be shown and
voluntarily exhibited to any of our best and most
eminent citizens, so that the people may enjoy
liberty also in this very privilege of honourably
winning the favour of the aristocracy.   By this
means the result which you just mentioned, Quintus,
is already accomplished—that the ballot condemns
a smaller number than were condemned by the
oral vote, because the people are satisfied with
possessing the power ; let them but keep that,
and in everything else they are governed by
influence and favour.   And so, to leave out of
account the corrupting effect of general donations
upon the people's votes, do you not see that if
bribery can ever be got rid of, the people, before
they vote, will ask the opinion of the aristocracy?
Hence our law grants the appearance of liberty,
preserves the influence of the aristocracy, and
removes the causes of dispute between the classes.

XVIII. The next law designates *those who have
the right to preside over meetings of the people and
the Senate.*   This is followed by an important and,
in my opinion, an excellent provision : *Moderation
shall be preserved in meetings of the people and the*

agentur, modica sunto, id est modesta atque sedata;
actor enim moderatur et fingit non modo mentem
ac voluntates, sed paene vultus eorum, apud quos
agit. quod si in . . . senatu[1] non difficile, est
enim ipse senator is, cuius non ad auctorem re-
feratur animus, sed qui per se ipse spectari velit.
huic iussa tria sunt : *ut adsit;* nam gravitatem res
habet, cum frequens ordo est; *ut loco dicat,* id est
rogatus ; *ut modo,* ne sit infinitus; nam brevitas
non modo senatoris, sed etiam oratoris magna laus
est in sententia. nec est umquam longa oratione
utendum, nisi aut peccante senatu (quod fit ambi-
tione saepissime) nullo magistratu adiuvante tolli
diem utile est, aut cum tanta causa est, ut opus
sit oratoris copia vel ad hortandum vel ad do-
cendum; quorum generum in utroque magnus noster
41 Cato est. quodque addit : *causas populi teneto,* est
senatori necessarium nosse rem publicam (idque late
patet : quid habeat militum, quid valeat aerario,
quos socios res publica habeat, quos amicos, quos
stipendiarios, qua quisque sit lege, condicione,

---

[1] *quod si in . . . senatu* Vahlen, who conjectures *quod si
in* (*populo arduum est, in*) *senatu.* *quod si in senatu* A B ;
quod est in senatu Stephanus.

---

[1] *i.e.* in order to prevent the passage of a decree.

Senate. By moderation I mean calm and quiet behaviour, for the presiding officer regulates and determines not only the spirit and desires, but almost the facial expressions, of those over whom he is presiding. But though [it is hard to preserve such moderation in popular assemblies], in the Senate it is not difficult, for a senator is not the kind of person to form his opinion on the basis of another's authority; rather, he wishes to be respected for himself. To him we give three injunctions: first, *to be present*, for a full attendance adds dignity to the Senate's deliberations; second, *to speak in his turn*, that is when called upon; third, *to be brief* and not run on indefinitely. For brevity in the expression of an opinion is a great virtue on the part of a speaker in the Senate as well as everywhere else. A long speech should never be indulged in unless, in the first place, the Senate is taking some mischievous action—which most usually comes about through some illegitimate influence—and no magistrate is taking any steps to prevent it, in which case it is a good thing to use up the whole day;[1] or else, in the second place, when the matter under consideration is so important that copiousness is necessary either to win the Senate to a wise policy or to furnish it with information. Our friend Cato, by the way, is very skilful in the use of both these types of oration. I have also added the injunction: *He shall be conversant with public affairs.* It is obviously necessary for a senator to be familiar with the condition of the republic. And this rule has a wide application; he must know the number of troops available, the condition of the treasury, who our allies, friends, and tributaries are, and what laws, agreements, and

foedere), tenere consuetudinem decernendi, nosse exempla maiorum. videtis iam genus hoc omne scientiae, diligentiae, memoriae, sine quo paratus esse senator nullo pacto potest.

42 Deinceps sunt cum populo actiones, in quibus primum et maximum : *vis abesto.* nihil est enim exitiosius civitatibus, nihil tam contrarium iuri ac legibus, nihil minus et civile est et humanum [1] quam composita et constituta re publica quicquam agi per vim. *parere* iubet *intercessori,* quo nihil praestantius ; inpediri enim bonam rem melius quam concedi malae.

XIX. Quod vero *actoris* iubeo esse *fraudem,* id totum dixi ex Crassi, sapientissimi hominis, sententia ; quem est senatus secutus, cum decrevisset C. Claudio consule de Cn. Carbonis seditione referente, invito eo, qui cum populo ageret, seditionem non posse fieri, quippe cui liceat concilium, simul atque intercessum turbarique coeptum sit, dimittere. quod qui permovet, cum agi nihil potest, vim quaerit, cuius

---

[1] *est et humanum* A[2] ; *est humanum* A[1] B.

---

[1] Probably a reference to Gaius Claudius Pulcher (consul 92 B.C.) and Gnaeus Papirius Carbo (tribune 96 B.C., aedile 93 B.C.).

treaties apply to each. He must also understand the customary procedure in the passage of a decree, and know the precedents which our ancestors have handed down to us. Thus you can form a conception of the wide knowledge, the great industry, and the excellent memory which are absolutely indispensable for a senator who is prepared for the performance of his duties.

Our next topic is the assemblies of the people, and our first and most important provision in regard to them is: *No violence shall be used.* Nothing is more destructive to governments, nothing is in such complete opposition to justice and law, nothing is less suitable for civilized men, than the use of violence in a State which has a fixed and definite constitution. Another provision orders *a veto to be respected.* Nothing is more advantageous than the observance of this custom, for it is better that a good measure should fail than that a bad one should be allowed to pass.

XIX. My provision in regard to *the responsibility of the presiding officer* is derived entirely from the opinion of that supremely wise man, Crassus. And the Senate adopted his view in its decree when the disorder instigated by Gnaeus Carbo was brought to its attention by Gaius Claudius the consul.[1] For it voted that disorder could not occur during an assembly of the people against the will of the presiding officer, since he has the right to adjourn the meeting as soon as a measure had been vetoed and confusion started. But one who encourages such confusion when business can no longer be done is inviting violence, and by this law he loses his immunity from punishment

inpunitatem amittit hac lege.   sequitur illud : *in-*
43 *tercessor rei malae salutaris civis esto.*   quis non
studiose rei publicae subvenerit hac tam praeclara
legis voce laudatus ?

Sunt deinde posita deinceps, quae habemus etiam
in publicis institutis atque legibus : *auspicia ser-*
vanto, auguri parento.   est autem boni auguris
meminisse se[1] maximis rei publicae temporibus
praesto esse debere, Iovique optimo maximo se
consiliarium atque administrum datum, ut sibi eos,
quos in auspicio esse iusserit, caelique partes sibi
definitas esse traditas, e quibus saepe opem rei
publicae ferre possit.

Deinde de *promulgatione,* de *singulis rebus agendis,*
de *privatis magistratibusve audiendis.*

44   Tum leges praeclarissimae de duodecim tabulis
tralatae[2] duae, quarum altera *privilegia tollit,* altera
de capite civis rogari nisi maximo comitiatu vetat.
et nondum inventis seditiosis tribunis plebis, ne
cogitatis quidem, admirandum tantum maiores in
posterum providisse.   in privatos homines leges ferri
noluerunt; id est enim privilegium ; quo quid est

---

[1] *se* supplied by Lambinus ; omitted in MSS.
[2] *tralatae* A ; *traslatae* B.

---

[1] Compare Cicero, *Pro Sest.* 65 ; *De Domo* 43 : *De Re Pub.*
II, 61.

for doing so. The next law is: *He who vetoes a bad measure shall be deemed a citizen of distinguished service.* Who would not be eager to come to the rescue of the republic in the hope that his praise might be heralded forth by the clear voice of this law?

This is followed by provisions which are already to be found in the customs and laws of our State: *Presiding officers shall observe the auspices and obey the State augur.* But it is the duty of a good augur to remember that he should come to the rescue of the State in great emergencies. He must also bear in mind that he has been appointed the interpreter and assistant of Jupiter the Best and Greatest, exactly as those men are his assistants whom he commands to observe the auspices; and also that those carefully designated parts of the sky have been assigned to him in order that he may obtain from them frequent assistance for the republic.

After that come the provisions which deal with *the promulgation of laws,* with *action on only one question at a time,* and with *the opportunity to speak which is to be given to private citizens and magistrates.*

Then come two excellent laws taken over from the Twelve Tables,[1] one *prohibiting laws of personal exception,* and the other *forbidding cases in which the penalty is death or loss of citizenship from being tried elsewhere than before the greatest assembly.* For before the tribunes of the plebeians had begun their troublesome existence or had ever been thought of, what admirable measures our ancestors provided for the protection of future generations! They desired that no laws should be proposed which penalized particular individuals, for that is what a law of personal exception is. For nothing could be more unjust

511

iniustius, cum legis haec vis sit, scitum et iussum
in omnis? ferri de singulis nisi centuriatis comitiis
noluerunt; descriptus enim populus censu, ordinibus,
aetatibus plus adhibet ad suffragium consilii quam
45 fuse in tribus convocatus. quo verius in causa nostra
vir magni ingenii summaque prudentia, L. Cotta,
dicebat nihil omnino actum esse de nobis; praeter
enim quam quod comitia illa essent armis gesta
servilibus, praeterea neque tributa capitis comitia
rata esse posse neque ulla privilegii; quocirca nihil
nobis opus esse lege, de quibus nihil omnino actum
esset legibus. sed visum est et vobis et clarissimis
viris melius, de quo servi et latrones scivisse se [1]
aliquid dicerent, de hoc eodem cunctam Italiam,
quid sentiret ostendere.

46   XX. Sequitur de *captis pecuniis* et de *ambitu*.
legesque cum magis iudiciis quam verbis sanciendae
sint, adiungitur: *noxiae poena par esto*, ut in suo
vitio quisque plectatur, vis capite, avaritia multa,
honoris cupiditas ignominia sanciatur.

Extremae leges sunt nobis non usitatae, rei

---

[1] *se* supplied by Turnebus; omitted in MSS.

---

[1] The laws banishing Cicero (spring of 58 B.C.) are referred
to; compare Velleius Paterc., II, 45; Cicero, *De Domo* 47.
[2] The law recalling Cicero from banishment (August 4, 57
B.C.) is referred to; compare Cicero, *Ep. ad Att.* IV, 1, 4.

than such a law, when the very word "law" implies a decree or command which is binding upon all. They also desired that decisions affecting the fate of individuals should be made only in the Comitia Centuriata ; for when the people are divided according to wealth, rank, and age, their decisions are wiser than when they meet without classification in the assembly of the tribes. For this reason Lucius Cotta, a man of great talent and the highest wisdom, was all the more surely correct in his opinion with reference to my own case—that no legal action at all had really been taken against me.[1] For he said that, in addition to the fact that armed slaves were employed at the assembly, no sentence of death or loss of citizenship by the Comitia Tributa could be valid, and that the passage of a law of personal exception by any assembly was invalid. From this he concluded that I needed no law to repeal what had never been legally enacted against me. But you and other eminent men thought it better that all Italy should declare its opinion of a man against whom slaves and brigands claimed to have enacted a law.[2]

XX. The next law is concerned with *the reception of money* and with *bribery*. And as our provisions cannot be made effective merely by being embodied in legal form, but must also be enforced by the courts, I have added : *The punishment shall fit the offence*, so that everyone may be paid in his own coin, violence being punished by death or loss of citizenship, greed by a fine, and too great eagerness for the honour of public office by disgrace.

The last of my laws have never been in use among us, but are necessary for the public interest.

publicae necessariae. legum custodiam nullam habemus ; itaque eae leges sunt, quas apparitores nostri volunt ; a librariis petimus, publicis litteris consignatam memoriam publicam nullam habemus. Graeci hoc diligentius, apud quos νομοφύλακες creabantur, nec ei solum litteras (nam id quidem etiam apud maiores nostros erat), sed etiam facta hominum observabant ad legesque revocabant. 47 haec detur cura censoribus, quandoquidem eos in re publica semper volumus esse. apud eosdem, *qui magistratu abierint, edant et exponant, quid in magistratu gesserint,* deque iis censores praeiudicent. hoc in Graecia fit publice constitutis accusatoribus ; qui quidem graves esse non possunt, nisi sunt voluntarii. quocirca melius rationes referri, causamque exponi censoribus, *integram tamen legi, accusatori iudicioque servari.*

Sed satis iam disputatum est de magistratibus, nisi forte quid desideratis.

A. Quid ? si nos tacemus, locus ipse te non admonet, quid tibi sit deinde dicendum ?

M. Mihine ? de iudiciis arbitror, Pomponi ; id est enim iunctum magistratibus.

48   *A.* Quid ? de iure populi Romani, quem ad modum instituisti, dicendum nihil putas ?

---

[1] These guardians of the law (νομοφύλακες) appear to have been given special powers by Demetrius of Phalerum.

[2] This is an adaptation to Rome of the Athenian provisions according to which officials, upon going out of office, underwent an examination (εὔθυνα) upon their official acts, and opportunity was given to register complaints against their administration (see Aristotle, *Const. of Athens* 48, 4).

We have no guardianship of the laws, and therefore they are whatever our clerks want them to be; we get them from the State copyists, but have no official records. The Greeks were more careful about this, for they elected " guardians of the law," who not merely kept watch over the text of the laws, as was formerly done at Rome also, but in addition they observed men's acts and recalled them to obedience to the laws.[1] According to my law this duty would be assigned to the censors, for I decree that the censorship shall never be vacant. And *magistrates, after completing their terms, are to report and explain their official acts to these same censors,* who are to render a preliminary decision in regard to them. In Greece this is attended to by publicly appointed prosecutors, but as a matter of fact it is unreasonable to expect real severity from accusers unless they act voluntarily. For that reason it seems preferable for official acts to be explained and defended before the censors, but for *officials to remain liable to the law, and to prosecution before a regular court.*[2]

Now our discussion of the magistrates is at an end, unless you have other questions in connection with them to propose.

A. But even if we are silent, does not the subject itself bring to your mind the point which still remains to be discussed?

M. A point which remains? I suppose you mean the courts, Pomponius; that subject is related to that of the magistrates.

A. But do you not think you ought to say anything about the law of the Roman people, as you planned to do?

MARCUS TULLIUS CICERO

M. Quid tandem hoc loco est quod requiras?

A. Egone? quod ignorari ab iis, qui in re publica versantur, turpissimum puto. nam ut modo a te dictum est leges a librariis peti,[1] sic animadverto plerosque in magistratibus ignoratione iuris sui tantum sapere, quantum apparitores velint. quam ob rem, si de sacrorum alienatione dicendum putasti, cum[2] de religione leges proposueras, faciendum tibi est, ut magistratibus lege constitutis de potestatum iure disputes.

49   *M.* Faciam breviter, si consequi potuero; nam pluribus verbis scripsit ad patrem tuum M. Iunius sodalis perite meo quidem iudicio et diligenter; nos autem de iure naturae cogitare per nos atque dicere debemus, de iure populi Romani quae relicta sunt et tradita.

A. Sic prorsum censeo et id ipsum, quod dicis, expecto . . .

---

[1] *peti* Manutius : *lego* A B.
[2] *cum* or *quom* dett. ; *quoniam* AB.

M. What do you think I have neglected in that connection?

A. Something of which it is most disgraceful for those concerned with public affairs to be ignorant. For you just mentioned the fact that we get the text of our laws from the State copyists; and, in the same way, I notice that many of those who hold magistracies, being in ignorance of the official powers granted to them by the law, know only so much as their clerks wish them to know. Therefore, if you thought the transference of the obligation to perform religious rites a topic worthy of special discussion after you had presented your laws on the subject of religion, surely you must discuss the legal powers of officials, now that your magistrates have been established by law.

M. I will do so briefly, if I can. For Marcus Junius, your father's friend, dedicated to him a long treatise on the subject,[1] which was written with learning and care, in my opinion. Now we ought to investigate and discuss the law of Nature independently, but in regard to the Roman law we must follow precedent and tradition.

A. I agree with you, and that is exactly the kind of treatment I am expecting.[2]

---

[1] Marcus Junius Gracchanus' lost work *De Potestatibus* is referred to.

[2] The remainder of this book, and of the work, with the exception of the fragments which follow, is lost. See Introduction, pp. 290-291.

FRAGMENTA

LIBRORUM DE LEGIBUS

1. Gratulemurque nobis, quoniam mors aut meliorem, quam qui est in vita, aut certe non deteriorem adlatura est statum; nam sine corpore animo vigente divina vita est, sensu carente nihil profecto est mali. (*Lactant., Inst. Div. III*, 19.)

2. Sicut una eademque natura mundus omnibus partibus inter se congruentibus cohaeret ac nititur, sic omnes homines inter se natura confusi pravitate dissentiunt nec se intellegunt esse consanguineos et subiectos sub unam eandemque tutelam; quod si teneretur, deorum profecto vitam homines viverent. (*Lactant., Inst. Div. V*, 8.)

3. Visne igitur, quoniam sol paululum a meridie iam devexus videtur nequedum satis ab his novellis arboribus omnis hic locus opacatur, descendamus ad Lirim eaque, quae restant, in illis alnorum umbraculis persequamur? (*Macrob., Saturn. VI*, 4, 8: *Cicero in quinto De Legibus.*)

FRAGMENTS

OF

THE LAWS

1. Let us deem ourselves happy that death will grant us either a better existence than our life on earth, or at least a condition that is no worse. For a life in which the mind is free from the body and yet retains its own powers is god-like; on the other hand, if we have no consciousness, at any rate no evil can befall us.

2. As one and the same Nature holds together and supports the universe, all of whose parts are in harmony with one another, so men are united by Nature; but by reason of their depravity they quarrel, not realizing that they are of one blood and subject to one and the same protecting power. If this fact were understood, surely man would live the life of the gods!

3. Shall we then, since the sun has now gone a little way beyond noon and this whole place is not sufficiently shaded by these young trees, go down to the Liris, and finish our conversation under the shade of the alders there?[1]

---

[1] From the fifth book; see Introduction, p. 291.

INDEX OF PROPER NAMES

R = *De Re Publica.* L = *De Legibus.* References are to book and section. All dates are B.C.

INDEX OF PROPER NAMES

INDEX OF PROPER NAMES

INDEX OF PROPER NAMES

INDEX OF PROPER NAMES

INDEX OF PROPER NAMES

INDEX OF PROPER NAMES

INDEX OF PROPER NAMES

INDEX OF PROPER NAMES

INDEX OF PROPER NAMES

INDEX OF PROPER NAMES

INDEX OF PROPER NAMES